MW01698287

Presented to Professor
Thomas E. Patterson
for his love of learning
and friendship and for
an Introductory Foreward.
by Meshack M. Sagini
Author

On
December 21st, 2015

# GLOBALIZATION

*The Paradox of Organizational Behavior:*
*Terrorism, Foreign Policy, and Governance*

**Meshack M. Sagini**

**Foreword by Dr. Thomas E. Patterson**

**University Press of America,® Inc.**
**Lanham · Boulder · New York · Toronto · Plymouth, UK**

**University Press of America,® Inc.**
4501 Forbes Boulevard
Suite 200
Lanham, Maryland 20706
UPA Acquisitions Department (301) 459-3366

Unit A, Whitacre Mews, 26-34 Stannary Street,
London SE11 4AB, United Kingdom


Printed in the United States of America
British Library Cataloging in Publication Information Available

Library of Congress Control Number: 2013937437
ISBN: 978-0-7618-5952-9 (clothbound : alk. paper)
eISBN: 978-0-7618-5953-6

∞™ The paper used in this publication meets the minimum requirements of American National Standard for Information Sciences—Permanence of Paper for Printed Library Materials, ANSI Z39.48-1992

# Contents

# Figure List

# Table List

# Foreword

Professor Sagini has uniquely and marvelously employed the disciplines of political economy, political science, history, international relations, religious studies and security studies to construct *Globalization: The paradox of organizational behavior-terrorism, foreign policy and governance (2014).*

First, to write this great work, professor Sagini used rich and rigorous interdisciplinary scholarly analysis to historically and comparatively reflect on the origin, nature, character, and challenges of contemporary globalization. He also employed historical inference as examples to compare contemporary globalization with classical, medieval, and modern globalizations. The historical approach revealed breath, understanding and wisdom prevalent in analyzing culturally different forms of globalization. The comparative approach provided us with intellectual insight and predictive normative criteria for estimating the strengths, weaknesses, and probable longevity of contemporary, paradoxical and exploitative globalization.

Second, professor Sagini went an extra mile to define the meaning and origin of domestic, transnational, and global terrorism by focusing on the cultural, economic, political and historical forces that produce and habituate it, the kind of foreign policy and historical texture that informs it, the ideologically oriented politicoeconomic culture that animates it, and the personal and legal ideas and interests that motivate its driving dynamics. The analysis on terrorism does not only tell us about cause and effect, but it also logically prescribes comprehensive policy oriented global solutions and strategies for its containment.

Third, this book is not only unique in scope and thematic structure and texture, but its comparative analysis of the 21st century (U.S., EU and China led East Asia) provides insight on the challengers of Western security in a potentially powerful and Asianist dominated hegemonic multipolarity, within an increasingly declining U.S. Western unipolarity. The implications of this new notion for U.S. technological, administrative, and geostrategic interests are mind-boggling. This kind of challenge is not without historical parallels particularly in the realm of ancient imperial governance. In this struggle for global dominance and governance, which is the anarchical struggle for survival, those who read history well and do something for "self edification" particularly the control and management of the bottlenecks survive the potential side effects of the global and culturally based, geostrategically rationalized, political, economic, and military tsunami.

Dr. Thomas E. Patterson
Bradlee Professor of Government and the Press
JFK School of Government at Harvard University

orderly than the old one that ended at the close of the 20th century. Therefore, it is the purpose of this book to argue that while a bipolar or unipolar system of globalization was logically and teleologically possible in the past, the 21st century is more likely to be deglobalized by the evolving, intercontinental, triadic and competitive elements of Americentric, Eurocentric and Sinocentric regionalism. Asia, Europe and America will vigorously compete for global domination and governance. The 21st century will be shaped by the human values, visions and destiny yet to be known through a variety of possible and competing scenarios embedded in contemporary and global paradigmatic regionalism.

The book is about 400 pages long. Several simple tables have been used for illustrative clarity. Chapter one is an introductory part for the whole text. Each of the chapters 2 through 15 contains contents, conclusions and references. The last chapter, which is 16, is a referenced, deconstructive, comparative and conclusive paradigm for the new century. The detailed contents for each chapter are illustrative of the organizational structure, and morphology of the text. The book is comparable to *Globalization: The transformation of social worlds* by D. Stanley EIszen and Maxine Baca Zinn (2009), Published by Wadsworth: Cengage Learning. Marketwise, the book is an excellent resource for competitive undergraduate and graduate programs in political science, public policy, international relations and global political economy. In addition, policy makers, professors and the broader intelligentsia will greatly benefit from reading the text.

In a globalized, multiparadigm, economically and geostrategically challenging environment, where resources for addressing the problems of healthcare, HIV/AIDs, education, war, energy, and transnational terrorism are scarce, the role of government in addressing these concerns matters. Worldwide, countries are jockeying more fiercely than at any other time for markets, technologies, kills, foreign investment, and distribution channels that are necessary for the rowth of their economies and the advancement of their standards of living. In is competitive and globalized world, the specific strategies that will be employed by each government will either cause it to decline or become the base d synergistic dynamic that will drive and sustain growth, reduce conflict and verty, accommodate urbanization, and create opportunity and employment.

In other words, the way in which countries will continue to compete, strate-, restructure, and reengineer their economic and political systems will deine the direction, creativity, and productivity of their economic systems which millions of people depend. In the current hypercompetitive and l environment, each nation's government tries to provide many tested adges that firms, corporations and business enterprises need in order to comith their rivals. The advantages include but are not limited to high savings, terest rates, foreign investments, sound property rights, good governance, ologically motivated and committed workforce, a low rate of inflation, idly expanding domestic and international markets. Specifically, differial, economic, cultural, technological, climatic and historical forces tend nce each country's or each region's competitive edge in the light of its

# Preface

*Globalization: The paradox of organizational behavior – Terrorism, for policy and governance(2014)* has 16 chapters categorized into four sec Section one has five chapters that address terrorism in the new millenniur tion two has four chapters that comparatively analyze the divergent forei cies of the great powers of the 21st century. Section three consists of fi ters that highlight the effects of globalization. Finally, section four, wh conclusion, is a deconstructive critique and newly proposed paradigm ing new global directions.

Specifically, chapter one is an analysis of the five paradigms o tion. Chapter two explains why the United States was attacked o Chapter three is about the seven-year war between the United St Chapter four is about the challenges of Iraq reconstruction. Cha cerns Western and Islamic interpretations of transnational terro six, seven, eight, and nine compare and contrast the respective of the U.S., China and the EU. Chapter ten discusses the role global political economy. Chapter eleven describes the chall world order. Chapter twelve highlights the political econo Chapter thirteen is a synopsis on terrorism and its risks. Ch centrates on the effects of terrorism in the United States fifteen analyzes the challenges of global energy security wh a deconstructive critique that also serves as the new paradi ry and beyond.

The thesis of this document asserts that globalizat structed historical, materialistic and supranational mov political, technological, cultural and social forces cor transformation of human civilization (world system). al processes, structures and solutions could inherentl cal to the needs of larger human interests. After the history by Western civilization, the emergent, v model of global regionalism seems to rival its We ing and inconclusive implications. The New Wor geopolitical and geoglobal trajectory. In the wake of economic and political turbulence the world has experienced under George Bush II's global political regime, the economically, politically and environmentally negative effects of its aftermath require the creation of a new global paradigm that will enhance the productive, creative and peaceful co-existence of human civilization during the 21st century and beyond. As alluded to earlier,that sixth paradigm will be intercontinentally triadic, politically moderated by the G20 as opposed to the G8 and regionally and comparatively competitive, supranational, and hyberglobal.

This book has been written by using interdisciplinary sources in the fields of history, political science, religion, international relations, political economy, security studies, and organizational behavior. It is an excellent resource for students and scholars, and a reference document for policy makers and the intelligentsia worldwide.

Globalization is humanity's classical, medieval and contemporary imagination. The Globalization regime is a cyclical way through which humanity (man) can make himself/herself by using strategies that are controlled by historical circumstances. The same circumstances tend to cut his/her quest for perpetual illumination and cosmological immortality. Globalization is the process of human imagination through which humans creatively use to perceive and practically translate into reality by making themselves in an historically, materialistically and philosophically circular or zigzag fashion. In its contemporary manifestations, the globalization process cyclically regulates itself through social interaction and integration of different people, corporations, governments and cultural diffusion. This form of diffusionary manifestations may be displayed in terms of international trade and investment, information technology, demographic and environmental complexity and political systems designed for human physical well-being, economic development, and prosperity in all societies throughout the world. This form of globalizing, amidst its dialectical nature, produces civilizations whose character helps to define their behavior. Behavioristically, contemporary globalization defines itself in many ways, of which the democratization index and commercial and technocultural diffusion are classic.

Meshack Mairura Sagini, Ph.D.
Professor of History, Political and Social Science, Langston University
Edmond, Oklahoma
January 2014

# Acknowledgements

These are interesting times to study and analyze the scope, content, and role of globalization in contemporary civilizations. In this analysis, a work of this caliber could not have been concluded without a lot of personal indebtedness to people who sacrificed their time, effort, and talents to see it come to fruition. Dr. Edward Manyibe, Assistant professor at Langston University's graduate school proof-read the entire manuscript and made suggestions for improvement. Dr. D. Chongo Mundende, Associate Professor and Director of the Center for Outreach Programs at Langston University formatted the document for publication. Professor Bob England of Oklahoma State University, Dr. Thomas E. Patterson, Bradlee Professor of Government and the Press at the John F. Kennedy School of Government, Harvard University, and Professor Maxwell Owusu of the University of Michigan read segments of the book and provided constructive scholarly critique. Kathy Sagini of the University of Central Oklahoma, and Paul Anunda of the University of Texas at Austin, helped with electronic logistics. Finally, Professors Maxwell Owusu, Thomas E. Patterson and Professor Toyin Falola of the University of Texas at Austin reviewed the document.

# Abbreviations

APEC Asian Pacific Economic Cooperation
ASEAN Association of South East Asian Nations
AU African Union
AD Anno Domini
BC Before Christ
BCE Before the Christian Era
CCPPCC Common Program of the Chinese People's Political Consultative Conference
CFSP Common Foreign and Security Policy
CAP Common Agricultural Policy
CAFTA Central America Free Trade Agreement
CEO Chief Executive Officer
CDC Center for Disease Control and Prevention
CCP Communist Party of China
DNA Deoxyribonucleic Acid
DOD Department of Defense
EU European Union
EEC European Economic Community
EC European Commission
CEU Council of European Union
ECJ European Court of Justice
ECB European Central bank
PJCC Police and Judicial Cooperation in Criminal Matter
FDA Food and Drug Administration
FTA Free Trade Area
GOS Government of Sudan
GAO Government Accountability Office
GATT General Agreement on Tariffs and Trade
GDP Gross Domestic Product
GNP Gross National Product

| | |
|---|---|
| GPCR | Great Proletarian Cultural Revolution |
| IOCs | International Oil Companies |
| IMF | International Monetary Fund |
| INC | International Concepts |
| JEM | Justice and Equality Movement |
| JCS | Joint Chiefs of Staff |
| KMT | Kuomintang |
| LNG | Liquefied National Gas |
| MNC | Multinational Corporations |
| MLG | Multilevel Governance |
| NATO | North Atlantic Treaty Organization |
| NOCs | National Oil Companies |
| NEPAD | New Partnership for Africa's Development |
| NAFTA | North American Free Trade Agreement |
| NGOs | Non-Governmental Organizations |
| NIDA | National Institute on Drug Abuse |
| NSC | National Security Council |
| OECD | Organizational for European Cooperation and Development |
| OPEC | Organization of Petroleum Exporting Countries |
| OAPEC | Organization of Arab Petroleum Exporting Countries |
| OCA | Optimal Currency Area |
| PRC | Peoples Republic of China |
| RTAs | Regional Trading Agreements |
| R and D | Research and Development |
| SPLA | Sudan People's Liberation Army |
| SPLM | Sudan People's Liberation Movement |
| SAPs | Structural Adjustment Policies |
| STD | Sexually Transmitted Diseases |
| TCC | Transnational Capitalist Class |
| TNS | Transnational State |
| UNSC | United Nations Security Council |
| U.K. | United Kingdom |
| U.S. | United States of America |
| UNO | United Nations Organization |
| USSR | Union of the Soviet Socialist Republics |
| USAFB | United States of America Foundations and Businessman |
| WMD | Weapons of Mass Destruction |
| WTO | World Trade Organization |
| WEG | Western European Governments |
| WBCSD | World Business Community for Sustainable Development |
| WEU | Western European Union |

# Section One
# Terrorism in the New Millennium

Section one covers the first five chapters. These chapters describe how the U.S. domestic, economic, and strategic interests make it necessary to come into contact with Middle Eastern Countries that have different local, regional, and national cultures, values and interests. What happens in this natural and diffusionist experiment is the evolution of profound cultural assimilation of Western modernization whose influence continues to spasmodically provoke irrational, orientalist, and fundamentalist emotions that clash individual political systems with other world civilizations. The clash between the Western and Eastern minds has not only historically been observed to have taken place for over 5,000 years, but it has become the major dialectic in contemporary civilizations that also remained to be the logical motor for social and synergistic change.

# Chapter I
# Introduction: Competing Paradigms of Globalization

*Globalization: The paradox of organizational behavior - terrorism, foreign policy and governance(2014)* is an interdisciplinary and comparative analysis of the foreign policy menu of the three major regions of the world (U.S., E.U., and China led East Asia) and how their comparative competitive advantage or disadvantage contributes to the resultant foreign policy decisions they make and the implications of those decisions on their domestic and global agenda. This theoretical analysis' elasticity and eclecticism is rooted in the disciplines of history, religion, political science, international relations, economics and a variety of sub disciplines in the social sciences. The "scale, extent, variety, speed, and magnitude of the cross-border social, economic, military, political and cultural interactions" (Krieger 2006, 3) of globalization produces differential gains and losses. Those who gain from the benefits of globalization are in the core areas of globalization while those who experience losses are exclusively marginalized at the periphery of world civilizations (Sagini 2001). The construction of this book has been carried out in the light of the three major international relations theories of realism, liberalism, constructivism and their relevant extensions: The manner in which the theories in question influence elite policy makers to formulate domestic and foreign policy decisions concerning current issues on war, multilateral corporations, terrorism, HIV/AIDS, energy security, drugs, and a variety of other timely, dramatic, or compelling natural or manmade issues, determines the character, behavior and personality of individuals, organizations or nations that make them or respond to them in one way or the other. Five major paradigms through which culturally, politically, institutionally and feministically oriented globalization is rationalized have been digested and offered by prominent scholars of international relations theory and its relevance to the globalization process. In other words, globalization is not a humanistic, Christian, Marxist, socialist, or communist movement. Instead, it is materialistic in spirit, imperialistically hegemonic in domestic and foreign policy, neocolonial in human motivation and control, and it is a perpetually reconstructive and deconstructive process of instability, change, chaos, misery, and the exploitation of "small fish by big ones". The globalization process has drastically contributed to the decline of state authority and power in terms of "one size fits all styles of the liberal politics" (Krieger 2006, 7) that is associated with welfare retrenchment, free trade and less state involvement in national economic planning. Such minimalist state of involvement in economic planning is a form of laissez-faire post-mercantilist economic philosophy whose absence of regulatory or Keynesian measures contributes to economic stagnation, instability, recession, Great Depression, and perpetual misery, particularly at the periphery.

The first paradigm which rationalizes the globalization system was advanced by Thomas L. Friedman (journalist). In his work the *Lexus and the olive tree*, Friedman metaphorically argues that the globalization era is a great challenge to individuals at the local communities (Olive Tree) because the pressures, strains, and stresses produced by imperious free market capitalism (Lexus) are overwhelming. In order to triangulate in the globalized system; states that are interested in the welfare of their citizens need to formulate public and economic policies that enhance "market confidence in any government or national economy. ... Such as balanced budgets, privatization, relatively low taxes, and minimal government regulation of markets" (p. 8). These are the Keys to success in the globalization era. Scholars also assert that any national or regional economic system which does not understand this form of logical behavior of the global market remains risking or getting trampled upon by the more powerful high-tech forces through which electronic interconnectivity and suzerainty controls the global market. In addition, Friedman's recent book on the flatness of the world indicates that in the post Cold War era, there is no single nation or politico-economic system that can dominate the world because we now live in a multipolar world in which each nation or region interdependently struggles to survive rather than dominate. That form of struggle for interdependent survival will be enhanced by the availability of intellectual capital whose imagination, ingenuity, creativity, and innovation will enable states and regions to become competitive in the global marketplace. The implications of articulating the "Survival instinct" in terms of the employment of the strategic machinery for rationalizing the brain-drain could have far-reaching consequences. Already, largely due to the brain drain syndrome, a variety of negative consequences have been evidently displayed at the periphery.

Globalization, whether it is/was in the form of historical Sinification in East Asia, or the Hellenization and Romanization of classical European traditions and values of antiquity; or the Arab or Ottoman influence of central Asia, Northern and Western Africa, Europe and the Middle East; or the Russification of Eastern and Central Europe and some areas of Eurasia; the current Americanization of the world, tends to harmonically integrate, homogenize, and universalize the demographic content of its population. Each global regime used relevant technology to globalize. The fundamental technologies of contemporary globalization are "computerization, miniaturization digitization, satellite communications, fiber optics and the internet" (p. 14). While the cold war was defined by the

"Way" of bipolarization and the arms race, globalization is defined by multiplicity; "speed of commerce, travel, communication and innovation" (p. 14). The Cold War was also defined by Einstein's theory of relativity in which the formula of mass is equal to energy and energy is equal to mass ($e = mc^2$).

The two fathers of modern globalization (Americanization) are Joseph Schumpeter (Former Austrian Minister of Finance and Harvard Business School Professor) and Andy Grove, Chairman of Intel. In his *Capitalism, socialism and democracy*, Schumpeter argues that "the essence of capitalism is the process of 'creative destruction' "the perpetual cycle of destroying the old and less efficient product or service and replacing it with new and more efficient ones." Andy Grove complemented Schumpeter's notion of destructive creativity and reconstruction by adding that 'only the paranoid survive' (p. 15). He popularized the speed with which new innovations dramatically change industrial productivity. The speed with which the paranoid destructively complete will not only keep them a head, but it will enable them to survive. Both globalization gurus reinforce the idea that in the essence of globalization economics, "innovation replaces tradition" and the present. ... Future replaces tradition" and the present ... future replaces the past" (p. 15) only when what exists is overturned does something new come to replace it. The friends and enemies of the Cold War era have become global competitors. The manner in which the global system overlappingly equilibrates itself happens in three ways: first, the traditional balance of nation- states in which U.S. Versus the rest of the world is rationalized. Second, the relationship between the nation-states and global markets is a global political economy in which countries at the core regulate and control the supermarkets while those at the periphery negotiatively try to triangulate the global system in order to penetrate the supermarkets at the core countries that use the modern and mouse to set global standards for investment and gains and losses. The third way of maintaining equilibrium in the global market place is one in which the rise of the "super-empowered individuals" take advantage of the opportunities provided by nation states in order to influence markets and nation states. The interplay of forces in this global phenomenon of triangular parity is magnetically motivated by competition for the maximization of profits, as opposed to losses, that the market avails.

The second paradigm of the globalization process has been advanced by Professor Samuel P. Huntington of Harvard University's John M. Olin Institute for Strategic Studies and Center for International Affairs. In his book *The clash of civilizations and the remaking of the world order* (1996), constructed after the Cold-War, Huntington assertively argues that in the wake of the collapse of the Soviet empire, the principle of bipolarity vanished with its replacement by a univocal, democratic and free enterprise system dominated by the United States. Historian Francis Fukuyama called this new and bipolarless paradigm of international relations "the end of history." By that he meant that the world's most powerful, aggressive, and destructive ideological systems of the twentieth century had experienced natural extinction by being replaced with universally accepted democratic and liberal political systems and values. Though his conclusion was logical, it may have been over interpreted for distortion. However, what is true is that a new paradigm, according to Huntington, has replaced the old one. That new paradigm clings around the idea that global politics, which is associated with conflicts that arise from "cultural faultiness," "has been reconfigured along these cultural lines" largely due to "deep seated cultural differences" that are the fundamental cause of economic and political problems. The post 9/11 sensitivity with which this hypothesis has been interpreted leaves much to be desired and more to explain. In its controversial nature, the hypothesis, which is an analytic and reflective product of nine civilizations, contends that "Muslim culture largely determines the failure of democracy in much of the Islamic world, where the West represents the culture of modernization, industrialization, innovation, and the American Creed" (Krieger 2006, 20) in terms of the promotion of individualism, liberty, diversity, rule of law, equality, self-government and unity (Patterson 2008). In other words, the most important controversial differences in human civilization are not their ideologies, economic and political systems on their strategic, chaotic, or orientalist and Occidentalist paradigms that were historically and anthropologically constructed in the nineteenth century, and that were rooted in dialectical, structural, functionalist mythological paradigms, but rather, the cultural identities that make these civilizations to cohere, disintegrate and cause conflict are reminiscent of the post-Communist Soviet era and the dawn of the twenty-first century Middle East. Huntington's hypothesis (paradigm) asserts that

> For the first time in history, global politics is both multipolar and multicivilizational; modernization is distinct from Westernization and is producing neither a universal civilization in any meaningful sense nor the westernization of non-Western societies. ... The balance of power among civilizations is shifting: the West is declining in relative influence; Asian civilizations are expanding their economic, military, and political strength; Islam is exploding demographically with destabilizing consequences for Muslim countries and their neighbors; and non Western civilizations generally are reaffirming the value of their own cultures. ... A civilization based world order is emerging: societies sharing cultural affinities cooperate with each other; efforts to shift societies from one civilization to another are unsuccessful; and countries group themselves around the lead or core states of their civilization. ... The West's universalistic pretenses increasingly bring it into conflict with other civilizations, most seriously with Islam and China; at the local level faultline wars, largely between Muslims and nonMuslims, generate kin-country rallying the threat of broader escalation, and hence efforts by core states to halt these ways. ... The survival of the West depends on Americans reaffirming their Western identity and Westerners accepting their civilization as unique not universal and uniting to renew and preserve it against challenges from non-Western societies. Avoidance of a global war of civilization depends on world leaders accepting and cooperating to maintain the multicivilizational character of global politics (Krieger 2006, 21-22; Huntington 1996, 20-21).

What is obvious is that both the unipolar and the bipolar worlds are being extinguished by multipolar elements of regionalism that are also politically, demographically, religiously, linguistically, and semantically multicivilizational in character. On the global scale, the dynamics of these forms of regionalism are the ones that drive the global agenda whose pragmatism is systematically associated with various structures of multilevel and multidimensional governance at the local, regional, national, and supranational levels. For instance, the regions of North America (NAFTA), Europe which has formed the E.U., Russia and its sister commonwealth states, the Middle East and its globally inspired Islamic fundamentalism, the Sino-Japanese entente and the evolving EAFTA, the African Union, Mercouser and the Hindi are the cultural elements of multicivilizational regionalism that compete for the global agenda. During the last five hundred years, countries in the Western civilization have successively colonized other people in the Americas (Spain, England and France); in Asia (England, Holland, Spain, France, Russia, Japan, Portugal and America); in Africa (England, Holland, France, Spain, Portugal, German, Italy and Belgium). Except for the period of the Crusades, The Dark Ages of Europe, Muslims or Chinese civilizations have been involved in a strategically organized globalization comparable to the historically organized one in the West.

Huntington's thesis is intellectually elaborate but also biased as an irresponsible form of scientific scholarship that is highly generalized and lacking in specificity, empathy and human brotherhood. The danger with it is that it might inspire, in a climate of myopic political leadership, forms of twenty-first century elements of Hitlerism and Hitlerization of the global civilization.

The third paradigm that explains how globalization works has been advanced by Joseph E Stiglitz, former chairman of the Council of Economic Advisers and former economics professor at Stanford and chief economist of the World Bank. Stiglitz has advanced a theory of exploitation of the Third World by the Bretton Woods institutions that managerially govern the processes of globalization. In particular, he has negatively provided a sharp and radical, but also convincing critique of the role the World Bank, the World Trade Organization (WTO), and International Monetary Fund (IMF) play in a variety of Third World and Second World Nations. Stiglitz argues by asserting that "the most powerful states- the key industrial countries and, in particular, the United States, have hijacked the IMF and steered it towards 'one-size-fits' all policies that fail to address the specific problems faced by developing states … concludes that policies intended to reduce expenditures on education, health care, and infrastructure and increase interest rates lead only to a contraction in the economy, and increased misery and insecurity" (Stiglitz 2006, 36). In other words, commenting on Stiglitz's assertion, Quinn and Toyoda (2007) have also argued that both domestic and global forces encourage the employment of ideology, as reflected in electoral preferences in public opinion assessments, to determine the diffusionist nature of financial globalization by both open and closed systems of the international and global economy. Changes in "both global and domestic ideology robustly influence liberalization and closure- the capital account policies of neighboring countries (positively) and of leading economies (negatively) also influence a country's capital account liberalization" (p. 344). The aim of the two scholars is to "unrest, establish whether, where, and by how much worldwide anticapitalist and procapitalist ideology influenced international financial liberalization" (p. 359). The results strongly suggested that "for a society-centered views of diffusion in general and for the proposition that changes in global preferences directly affected national capital account policies, in particular, and in relation to the influence of IMF, when leading economies were liberalizing, many emerging market economies were closing largely due to the side effects of structural dependency that cause democracy to be inflated at the periphery and influence investment, revolutions, and coup d'êtres either way. There is also negative influence on growth and income (Quinn and Toyoda 2007).

Joseph Stiglitz's analysis of the three Bretton Woods systems and the role they play to permanently and economically exploit, marginalize and underdevelop the nations of the Third World is grimly revealing. In contrasting the missions of the World Bank and IMF, he says that

> often confused in the public mind, present marked contrasts that underline the differences in their cultures, styles and missions: one is devoted to eradicating poverty, one to maintaining global stability. While both have teams of economists flying into developing countries for three-week missions, the World Bank has worked hard to make sure that a substantial fraction of its staff live permanently in the country they are trying to assist; the IMF generally has only a single "resident representative whose powers are limited. IMF programs are typically dictated from Washington and shaped by the short missions during which its staff members pore over numbers in the finance ministries and control banks and make themselves comfortable in five-star hotels in the capitals. ...The unemployed are people, with families whose lives are affected-sometimes devastated by the economic policies that outsiders recommend, and in the case of the IMF, effectively impose (Stiglitz 2006, 37).

Stiglitz convincingly argues that the major obstacle developing countries face are man made, unnecessary, and rooted in the colonial mentality of the "white man's burden" (p. 38). The obstacles have contributed to global poverty in which 1.2 billion people live on the dollar a day and 2.8 billion, on two dollars a day. Created in 1944, the IMF's main goal is to promote international monetary and financial systems. Its role is to "help governments manage or resolve economic and financial crises" in developing countries. Also, in times of difficulty, developing countries seek financial assistance from the IMF for "paying its imports or servicing its foreign debt" (Oatley 2008, 321).

Oatley shows that the IMF loans are conditional. In terms of conditionality, each loan has detailed and specific conditions for repayment attached to it. The conditions make the loan offer "a policy tool" (Stiglitz 2006, 46). "There is little evidence that it leads to improved economic policy, but it does have adverse political effects because countries resent having conditions imposed on them ... conditionality imposed by the IMF and the World Bank ... reduced the likelihood of repayment" (p. 46). These loans are given without eliminating" (p. 46) for the repatriation of capital. Though the morality and legality of issuing the loans may be justified, a plethora of internal and external economic, natural, political, cultural and institutional problems may make it impossible for each country to use the loans to address the main problems for which the loans were given. If these countries' central banks do not manage inflation, unemployment, and economic growth – all of them major macroeconomic issues, the IMF imposes austerity measures which sometimes are intolerable. "While Conditionality did not engender resentment, it did not succeed in engendering development. Studies at the World Bank and elsewhere show not just that conditionality did not ensure that money was well spent and that countries would grow faster but that there was little evidence it worked at all" (pp. 47-48). Sometimes it does not work because government failed to eliminate "macroeconomic imbalances by cutting government budget deficits and reducing the rate of growth and the money supply" (Oatley 2008, 321). Since 1980s, the measures used to stabilize the global economy "have been accompanied by far reaching structural reforms, including trade liberalization, privatization of state owned industries, and the liberalization of foreign investment" (p. 321). The white man, rather than the Latin's, Africans, Asians and West Indians, may have created the burden that is so heavy to lift with equanimity and instrumentality. The IMF confuses means with enduring order to benefit global capital markets of the core countries rather than those of peripheral states. Its policies contribute to inflation, recessions, and depressions (Oatley 2008).

What is the meaning of conditionality? Conditionality is a term that refers to the International Monetary Fund, the World Bank, and some other international financial institutions or agencies of "attaching conditions to their loans and grants" (Butler 2003, 211). These conditions made the countries that receive them to devalue their currencies, to lift controls on prices, to cut their budgets, and to reduce barriers to trade, investment, and capital flows. Though such conditions are always politically unpopular for their short or long term economic pains, and though they are viewed as a form of external interference in domestic national socioeconomic realms, they are too difficult but not impossible to eliminate. That is why they cause a vicious circles in developing countries.

The fourth paradigm of globalization has been advanced by Siskin Sassen who has given a powerful, radical and feminist critique of the globalization debate which challenges the dominant narrative' of "high-technology and high-flyers" (Sassen 2008, 60). She "examines globalization from the perspective of poor women who are compelled to become the agents of globalization as they cross borders, moving from poorer to richer countries to seek employment as domestics, sex workers, secretaries, and janitors" (p. 60). In their plight and exploitation, they play their roles in the global cities of New York, London, Berlin, Paris, Tokyo, Madrid, Beijing, Chicago, Los Angels and others which "operate increasingly as key nodes in a global network, and become increasingly reliant on migrant and immigrant women to provide essential services.... The incorporation of low-paid women service workers into strategic economic sectors describes an important and far reaching alternative narrative about globalization" (p. 61).

The women work in global cities in which they have creatively devised their own survival circuits in the world economy. This economy makes the cities its home. In this home, global financial flows are structured within urban systems; city networks and physically articulate national and international markets. Historically, cities have been built around markets too. Founded on trade routes, "they formed growing economies in themselves; they gave rise to and nurtured the dynasties and institutions that manage the decisions that guide national economies. Cities are settings of political command, and centers of culture. Here, society's leading images and messages are produced and packaged, shaping social reality and articulating aspirations. The great urban centers of civilization were the main stages of their respective political settings. Democracy was developed by urban societies, and it was shaped and supported in the public spaces and institutions of major cities" (Droege 2007, 55).

Today, half of the world population lives in cities whose form, economies, and growth contains changing dynamics that provide systematic energy for dominating their eras and environments. As centers of civilization and interaction, they define the security profile of a particular age, nation or region and help the balance of global relations. "Global trade, sprawling cities, or periods of large scale city formation" are not a new phenomenon in the history of urbanization and urbanism. However, the "speed and sheer mass of current urbanization wave, and the formation of super and mega-sized cities as widespread, simultaneous, indeed, global phenomenon is unprecedented" (p. 55). These Urban centers have been described as "world cities, global cities, mega cities," or have been referred to broadly as the global urban system. Regardless of the label used, "this conception connotes primacy of global markets, corporate control, seats of national power, homes to regional security apparatuses and, above all, the agency and relevance of technological innovation in surface, air and sea transport, defense, and the advent of advanced communications" (p. 56).

In the global age, the "information economy, instant communication and electronic markets are managed and operationalized by highly educated professionals who command the language of material infrastructure and business communications for which their skills, training and expertise are marketable. As such, the dominant narrative of globalization is about "the upper circuits of global capital" rather than the "lower ones" and "with the hyper mobility of capital rather than with capital that is bound to take place" (Sassen 2006, 61) regardless of its (capital) liquidity, sociality or promissory nature. In the light of such conditions, "Third World laborers ... maids, nannies, nurses, sex workers, and contract brides" (p. 61) are women who have migrated to perform the domestic roles of "First World" women whom they have replaced. Globalization, regardless of its more than 6,000 year history, has globalized what used to be domestically localized in specific regional or national i.e. colonial enclaves. For instance, a "comparative world view of the treatment of imperial subjects and the Mulatto population reveals how state policies of rule were elements of exclusionary power, race, sex, class and gender domination. Such a form of colonial and post colonial characterization of ... is consistent with neo-Marxist feminist, Freudian and humanistic interpretations of history" (Sagini 2004, 61) within the mercantilist and capitalist world formations.

Within the global economy itself ... Third World economies on the periphery of the global system struggle against debt and poverty, they increasingly built survival circuits on the backs of women- whether these are trafficked low-wage workers and prostitutes or migrant workers sending remittances back home. Through their work and remittances, these women contribute to the revenue of deeply indebted countries. Entreprepreneur's who have seen other opportunities vanish as global firms entered their countries see profit-making potential in the trafficking of women; so, too, do long-term criminals who have seized the opportunity to operate their illegal trade globally. These survival circuits are often complex; multiple locations with sets of actors that constitute increasingly far-reaching chains of traders and 'workers' (Sassen 2006, 62).

Though women were culturally suppressed and viewed to be economically valueless in the past, now they use their skills, both the formerly and informally acquired, to circuit or navigate their global environments for their survival. In doing that, they contribute to building new economics on the foundations of the old ones. In this regard, globalization plays a double role: "helping to forge links between sending and receiving countries and enabling local and regional practices to assume a global scale. ... The dynamics that converge in the global city produce a strong demand for low-wage workers, while the dynamics that mobilize women into survival circuits produce an expanding supply of migrants who can be pushed-or sold- into such jobs" (p. 62). Alternatively ... the very technological infrastructure and transnationalism that characterize global industries tend to influence other agents or actors to globally spread out as money launderers, drug traffickers, terrorists, and human traffickers.

The major factors which have caused people to migrate to industrialized Western democracies for employment are three. First, the most advanced service professions have corporately been consolidated in global cities of the core economic centers of the world that attract low-wage and relatively unskilled workers. Second, the decline of the industrial economy and its dynamic replacement with the high-tech post-industrialism has made competition for cheap labor and cheap imports to produce profits that attract "manufacturing ... telecommunications, finance ... corporate services" (p. 66). Third, the sweatshop that is informally produced in domestic industrial environments and business centers has created an effective local demand for their products, goods and services that cannot compete with high profit firms of the advanced services and high-tech economic sector that is managed by highly trained professional computer engineers, scientists and corporate bureaucrats whose ideological landscape places emphasis on success, wealth and careerism. These high wage workers' responsibilities are incompatible with those of the low-wage earners who perform clerical, repair, cleaning (household maids and nannies) or who provide labor- intensive services in expensive restaurants, luxury houses and hotels, laundries, boutiques and gourmet shops. Some are blue-collar workers who work in the trucking industry. This new "serving class" (p. 67), has replaced the historical female servant or mother and wife of the colonial and postcolonial society. They work in global cities in whose niches they have cultivated survival circuits. Their duties and responsibilities are in the process of being standardized. In some cases, both the professional and serving classes are immigrants. The former is technically trained, well paid and middle class in lifestyle. The latter is poorly trained, lower class and poorly paid. Both have labor markets that have been internationally or transnationally globalized by their suppliers. However, one class is highly exploited while the other is relatively privileged and civilizationally deterministic.

Though the serving class is linguistically, religiously and philosophically diverse, these lumpen proletariats who have not been fully encultured and assimilated into the culture of the global metropoles are politically and economically powerless to initiate any major organizational or institutional changes in their new environments. Generally speaking, though poor economic conditions are the push/pull factors responsible for their transmigration, agencies such as drug and human traffickers, smugglers and some governments capitalize on the plight of these women. In this case, traders may have contributed to the plight of these women who earn less to maintain the lifestyles of the professional class and its organizational life. Overall, "Globalization allows links to be forged between countries that send migrants and countries that receive them; it also enables local and regional practices to go global. The dynamics that come together in the global city produce a strong demand for migrant workers, while the dynamics that mobilize women into survival circuits produce an expanding supply of workers who can be pushed or sold into those types of jobs" (p. 69). Schumpeter's theory of destructive and innovative creativity has indeed been economically and institutionally life controlling to many societies, organizations and individuals.

The fifth paradigm of globalization is anarchy-the struggle for power in international relations of world politics. Professor John J. Mearsheimer of the University of Chicago argues that "states inhibit a zero-sum world of competition over power, which is intense, dangerous, and unforgiving" (Mearsheimer 2006, 49). As a realist who strongly advocates globalization, he advances his theory of globalization through which states "Pursue hegemony and compete for power"...in terms of " offensive realism-suggest that states want more power than they possess, to protect themselves and to advance their interests" (Mearsheimer 2006, 49) in order to survive in a turbulent and competitive social, economic and political environment. To attain the goal of survival, they have to behave aggressively in order to assert their power and influence.

This hegemonic power is "America's global role that has implications for its grand strategy: for what policies will maintain, enhance, or erode its security. Scholars and policy makers operate with an assumption that, either implicit or explicit, the United States is an empire, the preeminent power in a unipolar-system, or the leader of a hegemonic order shaping the basic dynamics of international politics. With a few notable exceptions, however, scholarly and popular assessments of the implications of American empire revolve around concerns associated with unipolar and hegemonic orders" (Nixon and Wright 2007, 253). Even as Niall Ferguson (2003, 6) has concluded, "the very concept of 'hegemony' is really just a way to avoid talking about empire, 'empire' being a word to which most Americans remain averse" (p. 6)

According to Gilpin (1981) and Ikenberry (2001), the hegemonic order theory of the American empire comprises of several strands that include "hegemonic-stability theory, power- transition theory, and constitutional order theory (a distinctive subtype of hegemonic order)" (Neon and Wright 2007, 8). In essence, the eventuality of the hegemonic systems depends on the "ability of the hegemony to sustain its economic, military and technological leadership; the degree to which potential challengers perceive themselves as benefiting from the existing hegemonic orders; and the propensity for hegemonic overextension. The hegemonic order theorists tend to treat states as unitary actors, although their vision of hegemonic systems involves elements of both anarchy and hierarchy" (Gilpin 1981, 26-27).

The five paradigms of globalization through which American hegemony (dominance) has influenced states to make policies that are controlled by the dominant power or its subsidiary agents such as the WTO, U.N., NGOS, the IMF, and the World Bank are forces of globalization that explain how it works. Such a form of multilevel institutional governance of the world has made heads of states and their governments' ineffective administrators because they have lost the capacity to control policy decisions and their outcomes. In this context, the dominant and hegemonic international system rather than the domestic state and its institutional agents, has acquired power and authority to influence domestic politics, restructure institutional arrangements, rationalize ideological choices, reconfigure partisan arrangements and finalize policy outcomes. Through these kinds of processes, national (state) interests are made to converge rather than diverge from those of the global, geopolitical, geo-economic and geostrategic agenda. Through this way, globalization helps to shape the exercise of state power and in turn "shapes the contours, defines goals, and determines the agendas of key institutions of global economic and political governance" (Krieger 2006, 110). Stiglitz's previous analysis of the role these institutions play in the development of underdevelopment cannot be understated.

American hegemony is a form of "reluctant, penetrated and highly institutionalized" (p. 126) liberalism that also assumes the messianic import of biblical semantics. This form of U.S. hegemonic uniqueness has cultural, ideological, political and economic imperatives that inherently contribute to its stability, durability and expansiveness. The imperatives are tenets that closest global allies have democratically, politically and constitutionally ratified in order to accept American hegemony and in return for America to protect their security with principles" of openness, reciprocity and multilateralism" (p. 127). And as professor Joseph P. Nye of Harvard University has concluded, the durability and effectiveness of the alliance must recognize and adhere to the following global public goods: "maintain the balance of power in important regions, promote an open international economy, preserve international commons, maintain international rules and institutions, assist economic development, and act as convener of coalitions and mediator of disputes" (p. 140). This is a form of global leadership and governance that contributes to U.S. stability and durability.

American hegemonic dominance is a globally interdependent as opposed to a globally autonomous, economic, political, intellectual and labor system. Economically, governments and business employ ideas, ideals and philosophical ideologies of their nations to manage and control or regulate the global economy inspite of the risks involved in doing it. Such risks or potential risks have generated debates in academia and in bureaucratic and nonbureaucratic policy-making arenas. The debates have been articulated in the light of three main categories whose dynamism involves the global economy. First, the categories have been articulated in the light of the following questions: How has globalization progressed? Has the world entered an unprecedented era of global markets, or is the current world economy still less deeply integrated than it was in the late nineteenth century.... (What is the First wave of globalization)? What are the consequences of globalization for individuals, groups, governments and nations? Has the life of a typical person ... improved or worsened by globalization? Are governments losing the capacity to govern in the face of global markets, or do they retain the capacity to use national policies to a achieve most of their desired domestic objectives? Are global markets undermining the nation state, and is political authority therefore gradually being transferred to international economic organizations like The World Trade Organization (WTO), the International Monetary Fund (IMF), and the European Union (E.U.)? (Oatley 2008, 4). Each of these debates concerns controversial issues about which the depth and outcomes of globalization is the subject. Interestingly enough, more people at the periphery are likely to answer all the questions affirmatively or negatively while those at the core of globalization might either say no or they may say that they are not sure because it depends on many other forces.

The second category of hegemonic debates includes debates about foreign economic ideas (polices) that governments employ to regulate the relationship between their national economies and the global economy. These controversial debates concern the extent to which each country should participate in globalization and under what terms it can do so. For instance, Should a government pursue additional trade liberalization or should it take steps to protect certain domestic industries from trade? If more liberalization is desired, is it best to achieve it through the World Trade Organization's multilateral processes or is it better to precede through regional free trade agreements? Should governments, particularly in developing countries, liberalize capital flows as well as trade, or should they continue to control and regulate capital flows? Should governments attempt to maintain fixed exchange rates, or should they allow their currency to float: should they strive to maintain a strong national currency, or is it better to keep the currency a bit undervalued" (p. 5). Sometimes these are difficult questions to answer.

The third set of questions or debates concern global issues of governance and its multilevel, multidimensional, and multifaceted contradictions at the local, state (provincial or regional), national and supranational levels. Both the political institutions that set the rules for governance and regulation of the global economy and the manner in which economic institutions and business leaders use the rules to gravitate the complex terrain and economic tapestry of the global North and global South, in open or closed social climates, in democratic or non-democratic political environments, in the Eastern or Western geopolitical and strategic markets, and in white, brown or black sociocultural and politico economic regions requires more analysis and reflection than cheap talk and culturally biased and a scientific conclusions. The questions or debates that may arise in this area include but are not limited to: Should the WTO decision-making process be reformed, perhaps by opening participation to nongovernmental Organizations? Should the WTO and regional trade arrangements like the .... NAFTA incorporate explicit rules concerning labor and the environment? Should government establish a set of international rules that would govern the activities of MNCs? (p. 5). How should the various aspects of the global economy be governed? Has globalization widened or narrowed economic inequality? Have peoples' lives become better because of globalization? Is globalization necessary for the edification and positive reconstruction of global and world civilizations? Has globalization contributed to the destruction and enslavement of certain civilizations for its own survival? Is the survival of one civilization more necessary than that of another? How do globalization regimes, structures and Organizations strengthen the economically weak among us? The hungry among us? The destitute among us? The dying innocents among us? The poor in spirit among us? The millions of orphans among us? The homeless among us? The lawful and hardworking foreigners among us? And our families among us?

Globalization shows prospects and challenges that affect all people and that need humongous social cooperation to solve the problems associated with ozone depletion, global warning, terrorist fundamentalism, drug trafficking, disease control and constructive engagement and regionalization of the globe as opposed to current mercantilist globalization. Although globalization as perceived by reactionary movements tries to strengthen parochial distinctiveness, it's universalist and cosmopolitan outlook promotes radical but beneficial diffusionist influences while technologically lessening geographic and social distances among the human organizations, civilizations and our universe.

According to Antony Black of the University of Dundee (2008), the global and historical relationship between the West, Islam and Byzantium has been interesting when examining their religious and political ideas and thought patterns in World History. Having viewed the thought patterns during antiquity, medieval, and contemporary periods, he concluded that the ideas and thought processes of these three civilizations were largely interrelated and interpreted as issues of church and state relationships. Although Professor Black argues that ancient and medieval thought patterns did and didn't contribute to modern developments, these thought patterns and processes about sacred monarchy and justice that were either revealed or natural were legitimized by the state whose people's culture assimilated them. The professor examined the period from the rise of Islam during the sixth century AD to the end of the European Middle Ages, although the period is interpreted comprehensively and holistically to include modern contemporary periods. The three civilizations had more in common than it is believed. However, what made the West more different was the papal revolution of the eleventh century. Western European's twelfth century Renaissance, and the gradual secularization and dereligionization of political thought witnessed the decline of ecclesiastical influence on state institutions. On the other hand, this was the time when Islam blossomed, dominated the West and Byzantine empires particularly when ideas of Ibn Rushd and Ibn Khaldun became dominant and commonplace. After 1150 AD, Islamic political and religious philosophy and power started to decline. Western political, economic and philosophical ascendance evolved gradually and continuously. Its ideas informed and influenced the West and both Muslims and Byzantium although Islamists were not and never have been. It is interesting to observe how the past inspired contemporary Islamic and Islamist movements, reactionaries and fundamentalists.

Though the Bretton Woods institutions and the NGO'S have contributed to the erosion of legitimacy of democratic processes through which globalization of markets attains their legitimacy, the global and systematic reinforcement of regionalization of the major centers of globalism, which have found it painfully more difficult to craft a coordinated solution to financial problems related to the regulation and supervision of the banking industry, have started to settle for regionalism instead of globalization. Even though these regions and nations tend to choose supranational coordination and cooperation, and in spite of the fact that their national institutional configurations still function as filters within the globalization process, its wishes are far from the reality of contemporary Sino-American global dialects. For example, in the context the 5th paradigm of globalization, transitional capital is one of the most important driving forces of economic globalization; yet, we know little about what determines cross – border portfolio investments. In addition to recent economic literature's focus on information asymmetries as one key determinant of cross – border investment, this study brings in a political aspect to the field of international trade in assets. The "race to the bottom" thesis connects domestic institutions, and levels of transparency to attract portfolio investments that are only sensitive to some fiscal policy indictors and only within the OECD countries. Therefore, for non–OECD countries, there is still 'room to move' in maneuvering different aspects of fiscal policies. Finally, it is clear why investors care about the nature of political institutions as democratic institutions tend to be associated with higher levels of democratization. In addition to democratization for peace, increased foreign capital further incentivizes a progression towards democratization (Cao 2009, 1). This "behavior is rationalized through imperial, organizational and institutionalist ideology and practices" (p. 1).

## REFERENCES

Butler, Michael J., and Rourke, John T. 2003. *International politics on the world stage.* Boston: The McGraw-Hill Companies.

Cooley, Alexander. 2005. *Logics of hierarchy: The organization of empires, states, and military occupation.* Ithaca, N.Y: Cornell University Press.

Droege, Peter. 2007. Energy, Cities and security: Tackling climate change and fossil fuel risk. *The Whitehead, Journal of Diplomacy and International Relations* VIII, 2:55-64.

Ferguson, Niall. 2003. Hegemony or empire? *Foreign Affairs* 82:5.

Friedman, Thomas. 2006. Globalization and state power. In Joel Krieger, ed. *Globalization and state power: A reader.* New York: Pearson Longman: 7-19.

Fukuyama, Francis. 2006. *America at the cross roads: Democracy, power and the neo-conservative legacy.* New Haven, Ct: Yale University Press.

Gilpin, Robert. 1981. *War and change in world politics.* New York: Cambridge University Press.

Huntington, Samuel P. 2006. The new era in world politics. In Joel Krieger, ed. *Globalization and state power: A reader.* New York: Pearson Longman: 20-36.

__________. 1996. *The clash of civilizations and the remaking of the world order.* New York: Simon and Schuster.

Ikenberry, G. John. 2001. *After victory: Institutions, strategic restraints, and the rebuilding of order after major war.* Princeton, NJ.

Krieger, Joel. 2006. ed. *Globalization and state power: A Reader.* New York: Pearson Longman.

Nexon, Daniel H., and Thomas Write. 2007. What's at stake in the American empire debate? *American Political Science Review* 101, 2: 253-271.

Oatley, Thomas. 2008. *The global economy: Contemporary debates.* New York: Pearson Longman.

Patterson, Thomas. 2008. *We the people: A concise introduction to American politics.* New York: McGraw-Hill.

Quinn, Dennis P., and A. Maria Toyoda. 2007. Ideology and voter preferences as determinants of financial globalization. *American Journal of Political Science* 51, 2: 344-63.

Sagini, Meshack M. 2004. The African diaspora and the challenges of adaptation. *Journal of Scholarly and Scientific Perspectives* 1:61-72.

__________. 2001. *Organizational behavior: The challenges of the new millennium.* Lanham, MD: University Press of America, Inc.

Sassen, Saskio. 2006. Global cities and survival circuits. In Joel Krieger, ed. *Globalization and state power: A reader.* New York: Pearson Longman: 60-69.

Stiglitz, Joseph. 2008. What I learned at the world economic crisis. In Thomas Oatley, ed. *The global economy: Contemporary debates.* New York: Pearson Longman: 323-329.

__________. 2006. Broken promises. In Krieager, Joel, ed. *Globalization and state power: A reader*, New York: Pearson Longman: 36-48.

Waylaid, Kurt. 2004. *The politics of market reform in fragile democracies.* Princeton, NJ: Princeton University Press.

# Chapter II
## Why the United States Was Attacked: Meaningful Reflections

The current crisis in which Osama Bin Laden is viewed as a ring leader may theoretically be explained in the light of social science and humanities disciplines from which ancient, Medieval, and modern historical parallels which animate it are rooted. Specifically, Mr. Bin Laden who superficially appears to be simple, is, I think, a complex political, militaristic, and religious reactionary who is driven by four or five inextricably intertwined factors. First, it is difficult to understand what drives Mr. Bin Laden to do what he does. Is it alienation from his family, group, and country (which Columbine and Durkheimian models help to explain)? Second, "Is it the old, endless, psycho-politically, historicized anti-Semitic dialectic?" Third, "Is it the East/West competitive and cultural clash of values?" Fourth, "Is Bin Laden a radical, violent, and religious reactionary who also is a truncated opportunist trying to capitalize on the fragile Afghanistan and Israel-Palestinian quest for an equilibrating dialectic?" Fifth, "Is Osama Bin Laden a manifestation of *Kikuumacho Kinguoni Mwako*, in other words, is he the enemy who knows you better?" If the answer to these questions is "yes", then this discussion about which we are the victims does not exonerate us.

### What Is Terrorism?

Terrorism is as old as the evolution of ancient, medieval, and modern civilizations. Its domestic, national, international, and transnational nature has made it more difficult to define contextually, semantically, and historically. Its capacity to be ruthlessly potent, destructive, and lethal is determined by the nature and sophistication of used technology and the degree of hatred or intent and purpose of the attack. The F.B.I. has defined it as "The unlawful use of force or violence against persons or property to intimidate or coerce a government, the civilian population, or any segment thereof in furtherance of political or social objectives" (Muraskin and Roberts 1996: 23). The U.S. Department of State calls it "premeditated, politically motivated, violence perpetrated against non-combatant targets by sub-national or clandestine agents usually intended to influence an audience." Examples of terrorist activity include but are not limited to kidnapping, murder, school shootings, gangs, mobs, drug trafficking, bombing, arson, hijacking and the use of chemical and biological agents as weapons of mass destruction.

Terrorism is effective because it disrupts or destroys a society's physical, industrial, economic, and technological infrastructure. In the age of democracy, unipolarity, technology, multinational corporations and globalism, terrorism has become an effective voice of the weak and disenfranchised. The goals of these dispossessed groups may include "redress for specific grievances, ...extraction of specific concessions ..., the coercion, destruction or overthrow of a government, ... the dissemination by print or electronic media of the group's demands or message" (p. 25). Essentially, this attack may have been directed at extracting specific concessions. If this is true, the terrorists have partially won. Terrorism is highly cost effective because it can not be fought with the use of conventional warfare strategies. New ways of fighting it need to be discovered or invented. In addition, most nations do not have the resources to fight it. In the New World Order, terrorism will remain to be a painful thorn in the flesh whose constricted muscles will be challenged by it.

## THEORETICAL UNDERPININGS

What has happened may be explained in the light of reflections of historians, political theorists, and philosophers. Of these, three eminent scholars (Khaldun, Euben, and Qutb) have tried to theorize, theologize, and philosophize about the historicity of the current crisis. Khaldun is a Medieval thinker while Euben and Qutb are post-modern radical intellectuals. The crisis originated with the terrorist attack on the United States on September 11, 2001. On that day, four American transcontinental planes were hijacked by 19 Middle Eastern men. Each plane except the one which crashed outside Pittsburgh, PA had five hijackers. Each of the first two hijacked planes was crashed into either of the two 110 story World Trade Center skyscrapers in New York City. The third plane crashed into the Pentagon in Washington, D.C. The total number of casualties was more than 2,830. These dead people were citizens of 86 countries including the U.S. The short-term implications of this attack have been tactically shocking, psychologically alarming, intellectually paralyzing, emotionally humiliating, and humanistically dehumanizing. The long-term implications are politically strategic, spiritually nationalistic and religious, economically destructive and disruptive, militarily aggressive and retaliatory, and diplomatically and domestically alert but seismic. Three-quarters of the victims were men. The average age of those killed was 40. Most were in their 30s and 40s, prime parenting age.

Some were new fathers; others, like Deanna Galente, who was eight months pregnant, were expecting children. A total of 230 were vice presidents at major financial institutions. At least 130 victims were brokers of one sort or another. Three hundred forty-three of the missing and dead were firefighters. There were also salesmen, housekeepers, engineers and janitors, as well as dozens of cooks, military accountants, electricians, secretaries and travel agents. Eight children died. The youngest was 2 years old. Forty-one were over 65. The oldest was retiree Robert Norton, 82, of Lubec, Maine. Almost 800 cities and towns scattered across 43 states and the District of Columbia lost people in the attacks (*The Daily Oklahoman, October, 2001*). It is difficult to understand why America was attacked. The experience may be likened that of a robbed bank in this way:

> Metaphorically, this is a situation in which Bankers experienced a business boom, felt very good and went to bed to sleep but forgot to lock the entrance and security locks of the bank and its premises. When thieves who were not prepared to break in found that the bank's entrance doors and security locks were not locked despite the fact that the doors were closed and loosely guarded, the thieves negotiated their entry using minimal force and took away our national fortune leaving us dumbfounded, frustrated, confused, injured, dead and coldly calculating but boldly irresolute.

The causes of the attack are complex but triangulatively explicable in terms of perceptions associated with the absence of superpower leadership in Asia in the wake of the collapse of the USSR which created a power vacuum in central and southwestern Asia. In the absence of a magnetic and equilibrating supranational political authority, small states that lack a stabilizing role model tend to advocate for the laws of the jungle in order to average what they see as Western economic, political and psychological exploitation of the poor. Second, since these Western states have cumulatively and historically used colonial, postcolonial, and post-modern tenets to hegemonically perpetuate and advance their dominance at the expense of the poor and ignorant (ajahili), the poor who suffer from unequal access to goods and services, and who are locally dominated by traditional bureaucratic elite, theocratic autocratic dictators, orthodox monarchs, and conservative political regimes, have galvanized forces that challenge these petty bourgeoisie and anachronistic regimes which America and the West usably penetrate and control in order to dominate the masses at the expense of the latter. Third, ideologically, Cold-War superpower politics and extreme elements of World War II anti-Semitism in Western Europe contributed to the evolution of Zionism and the creation of the state of Israel in the Middle East in 1948 (Holton 2000; Hecht, 2000). The new state of Israel is a product of Lapougian-Nazist nihilism, scientific racism, and materialistic amorality of the twentieth century (Hecht, 2000). Since its creation, Israel's existence has never been accepted in the Holy Land largely because the Jews are viewed as "outsiders" who bought or forcibly acquired the holy land of Muslims, Allah, and Muhamed the Prophet. As a U.S. buffer state that is also a regional power that uses an aggressive and

Zionistic hegemonic ideology for its survival, its parochial paraphernalia enables it to complicate both the U.S. foreign policy objectives and significantly contributes to Israel's own contextual exceptionalism (Aronoff 2001).

Ibn Khaldum (1332-1406) concentrated on understanding the meaning of the history through which he had lived, focusing on the rise and fall of dynasties or states. This Medieval Tunisian historian, sociologist and philosopher was an eclectic scholar (McLean 1996). He authored *The book of exemplaries and the collection of origins and information respecting the history of Arabs, foreigners, and Barbers and others who possess great power.* His scholarly learning enabled him to conclude that the progress of history, the emergence of communities, and the creation and decline of the dynastic states—depended on group solidarity, culture, and power. In his view, the social nature of humankind impels him/her to form co-operative communities for survival. The form that the community takes is conditioned by the specific circumstances of its material existence particularly, the climate and material environment. Because his studies were based on his analysis of a desert civilization, he concluded that nomadic society, based on kinship, possessed the strongest characteristic of solidarity. By its nature nomadic life is "non-territorial, frequently marginal, distinctly egalitarian, and precarious" (p. 232). The coming together of tribal solidarity and the reinforcement of that solidarity with the vitality of the prophetic impulse of Islam transformed nomadic solidarity into an inspired and powerful historic movement. The expansion of Arab tribal power led to a dynastically ruled complex community pursuing both nomadic and sedentary lifestyles throughout North Africa, Southern Europe, and the Middle East. A dynastically ruled state, however, contained the seeds of its decay and destruction because the security of existence in settled communities, the comparative luxury, the segmented character of labor, and the conspicuous consumption of the elite leads to a decline in resolute boldness and integrity, and rising corruption. Such a situation produces populations debilitated by desire and moral decline, and, most importantly to a loss of a sense of solidarity (McLean 1996). It is self-evident that Osama bin Laden, who is a Saudi exiled national, is antiestablishment, anti-democracy, anti-Western and anti-civilization although he banks and profits from there, understood this pristine theoretical essay which Ibn Khaldun advanced. Osama bin Laden has tried to advance it by becoming a reactionary. If he can attack or overthrow the United States, Israel and the U.S. supported conservative, autocratic, and monarchial regimes in the Middle East, al Qaeda movement, which is fundamentalist, evasive and extremely revolutionary, could restore the image of Islam which the West has debased due to ignorance, chaos, crisis, and impurity within the Islamic community. Osama bin Laden believes that those who exploit the poor and debase Islam should be attacked using the Jihad (holy war). The war is to be waged by a movement called (al-Qaeda) which means the base.

The "base" is a new product of disgruntled and diverse factions in Islam. Its fundamentalist philosophy is inspired by the Islamic ways of life in antiquity. The base enables the community to transcended divisions of class, clan, tribe, race and country. This statement does not underscore the process Osama Bin

Laden has utilized to recruit disciples from many countries across the globe. He is like an ascetic who "practices the principles of self-denial and austerity. Asceticism is a doctrine whose teachings and practices releases the soul from bondage to the body and allows it to unite with the divine" (*Webster's II: New Collegiate Dictionary* 1986: 65). If using the Jihad to fight infidels (unbelievers) causes one to die, one's soul will not only be released from bondage, but by uniting with the divine it attains paradise which is one of the highest forms of calling and self-actualization.

In comparative perspective, it is instructive to briefly compare Bin Laden with Luther. Martin Luther was a son of working class parents, a monk, a humanistic scholar, and a superstitious philosophical thinker. He wrote the 95 statements (theses) and severely challenged the papacy and Christian theology for its reliance on the canonicity of indulgences for salvation instead of reliance on biblical faith. His final stand at the Diet of Worms and his genuine and authentic mysticism (speculative, intelligent, and spiritual communion with God) enabled him to gain followers both at home and abroad. His subjective and impassioned attitude led him to use theology to reform the Roman Catholic Church and to advocate the use of Pauline doctrine of faith rather than the works of the law for salvation. He did not use his followers to physically attack medieval civilization. He used his learning, knowledge and profession of faith to critique his church's beliefs and practices which spiritually and economically impoverished rural and urban communities in Western Christendom. To make a long story short, Luther's stand among other things, produced the Protestant Reformation, made it possible for scientific rationality to be accepted and used in the age of scholasticism, influenced the Roman Catholic Church, for its survival, to reform its theology and all social and religious institutions. Although Luther's attack on the church caused War, his stand improved human civilization by empowering the human spirit with a superior vision which liberated them from the darkness of Medieval antiquity. Osama bin Laden is an ascetic and Sunni follower. Asceticism in (Greek-askeo') is a philosophy which advocates how to train or exercise both the body and mind. The philosophy emphasizes the employment of physical and psychological desires in order to attain the spiritual ideal noted in the development of the whole person, human creativity, his/her elevating the self by using ideas, skills demanding technical proficiency.

In athletics, "Greek- askesis" is training involving the ideal bodily fitness and excellence to produce the highest degree of physical fitness for warfare. Other ascetic ideals that are developed include mental facility, moral vitality, and spiritual ability which bring wisdom and mental prowess, develops training in intellectual faculties— similar to that which produced Greek teachers and philosophers of the fourth and fifth century BC. Such training of the intellect led to the pedagogical system of the Sophists—itinerant teachers, writers, and lecturers of the fourth and fifth century BC who instructed in return for fees. Another change in the concept of *askesis* occurred in ancient Greece when the notion of such training was applied to the realm of ethics in the ideal of the sage who was able to act freely to choose or refuse a desired object or an act of physical pleasure. This kind of *askesis*, involving training the will against a life of sensual pleasure, was exemplified by the Stoics (ancient Greek philosophers who advocated the control of the emotions by reason).

The view that one ought to deny one's lower desires—understood as sensuous, or bodily—in contrast with one's spiritual desires and virtuous aspirations, became a central principle in ethical thought. Plato believed that it is necessary to suppress bodily desires so that the soul can be free to search for knowledge. This view was also propounded by Plotinus, a Greek philosopher of the third century AD and one of the founders of Neoplatonism, a philosophy concerned with hierarchical levels of reality. The Stoics, among whom asceticism was primarily a discipline to achieve control over the promptings of the emotions, upheld the dignity of human nature and the wise man's necessary imperturbability, which they believed would become possible through the suppression of the affective and appetitive part of human nature.

In a similar manner, the value of asceticism in strengthening an individual's will and his deeper spiritual powers has been a part of many religious and philosophical systems throughout history. The nineteenth-century German philosopher Arthur Schopenhauer, for example, advocated a type of asceticism that annihilates the will to live; his fellow countryman and earlier contemporary, the philosopher Immanuel Kant, held to a moral asceticism for the cultivation of virtue according to the teachings of the Stoics. Many factors were operative in the rise and cultivation of religious asceticism: the fear of hostile influences from the demons; the view that one must be in a state of ritual purity as a necessary condition for entering into communion with the supernatural; the desire to invite the attention of divine or sacred beings to the self-denial being practiced by their suppliants; the idea of earning pity, compassion, and salvation by merit because of self-inflicted acts of ascetical practices; the sense of guilt and sin that prompts the need for atonement; the view that asceticism is means to gain access to supernatural powers; and the power of dualistic concepts that have been at the source of efforts to free the spiritual part of humanity from the defilement of the body and physically oriented living.

Among the higher religions such as Hinduism, Buddhism, and Christianity, other factors became significant in the rise and cultivation of asceticism. These factors included the realization of the transitory nature of earthly life, which prompts a desire to anchor one's hope in otherworldliness, and the reaction against secularization that is often coupled with a belief that spirituality can best be preserved by simplifying one's mode of life.

## Forms of Religious Ascetism

In all strictly ascetic movements, celibacy has been regarded as the first commandment. Virgins and celibates emerged among the earliest Christian communities and came to occupy prominent status. Among the earliest Mesopotamian Christian communities, only the celibates were accepted as full members of the church, and in some religions only celibates have been permitted to be priests (particularly in Aztec religion and Roman Catholicism). Abdication of worldly goods is another fundamental principle. In monastic communities there has been a strong tendency toward this ideal. In Christian monasticism this ideal was enacted in its most radical form by Alexander Akoimetos, a founder of monasteries in Mesopotamia. He died in 430. Centuries before the activities of the medieval Western Christian monk St. Francis of Assisi, Alexander betrothed himself to poverty, and through his disciples, he expanded his influence in Eastern Christian monasteries. These monks lived from the alms they begged but did not allow the gifts to accumulate and create a housekeeping problem, as occurred among some Western monastic orders, such as the Franciscans. In the East, wandering Hindu ascetics and Buddhist monks also live according to regulations that prescribe a denial of worldly goods.

Abstinence and fasting are by far the most common of all ascetic practices. Among the primitive peoples, it originated, in part, because of a belief that taking food is dangerous, for demonic forces may enter the body while one is eating. Further, some foods regarded as especially dangerous were to be avoided. Fasting connected with religious festivals has very ancient roots. In ancient Greek religion, rejection of meat appeared particularly among the Orphics, a mystical, vegetarian cult; in the cult of Dionysus, the orgiastic god of wine; and among the Pythagoreans, a mystical, numerological cult. Among the number of churches the most important period of fasting in the liturgical year is the 40 days before Easter while among Muslims the most important period of fasting is the month of Ramadan. The ordinary fasting cycles, however, did not satisfy the needs of ascetics, who therefore created their own traditions. Among Jewish-Christian circles and Gnostic movements, various regulations regarding the use of vegetarian food were established, and Manichaean monks won general admiration for the intensity of their fasting achievements. Christian authors write of their ruthless and unrelenting fasting, and, between their own monks and the Manichaeans, only the Syrian ascetical virtuosos could offer competition in the practice of asceticism. Everything that could reduce sleep and make the resultant short period of rest as less troublesome as possible was tried by Syrian ascetics. In their monasteries, Syrian monks tied ropes around their abdomens and were then hung in an awkward position, and some were tied to standing posts.

Personal hygiene also fell under condemnation among ascetics. In the dust of the deserts—where many ascetics made their abodes—and in the blaze of the Oriental sunshine, the abdication of washing was equated with a form of asceticism that was painful to the body. With respect to the prohibition against washing, the Persian prophet Mani seems to have been influenced by those ascetic figures who had been seen since ancient times in India, walking around with their long hair hanging in wild abandonment and dressed in filthy rags, never cutting their fingernails and allowing dirt and dust to accumulate on their bodies. Another ascetic practice, the reduction of movement, was especially popular among the Syrian monks, who were found of complete seclusion in a cell. The practice of restriction in regard to contact with human beings culminated in solitary confinement in wilderness, cliffs, frontier areas of the desert, and mountains. In general, any settled dwelling place has been unacceptable to the ascetic mentality, as noted in ascetical movements in many religions.

Psychological forms of asceticism have also been developed. A technique of pain-causing introspection was used by Buddhist ascetics in connection with their practices for meditation. The Syrian Christian theologian S. Ephraem Syrus counseled the monks that meditation on guilt, sin, death, and punishment—i.e., the pre-enactment of the moment before the Eternal Judge—must be carried out with such ardor that the inner life becomes a burning lava that produces an upheaval of the soul and torment of the heart. Syrian monks striving for higher goals created a psychological atmosphere in which continued fear and dread, methodically cultivated, were expected to produce continual tears. Nothing less than extreme self-mortification satisfied the ascetic virtuosos (skillful and refined artists).

Pain-producing asceticism has appeared in many forms. A popular custom was to undergo certain physically exhausting or painful exercises. The phenomena of cold and heat provided opportunities for such experiences. The Hindu fakirs (ascetics) of India provide painful forms of asceticism. In the earliest examples of such radical forms of self-mortification that appeared in India, the ascetic stared at the sun until he went blind or held up his arms above the head until they withered. Syrian Christian monasticism was also inventive in regard to forms of self-torture. A highly regarded custom involved the use of iron devices, such as girdles or chains, placed around the loins, neck, hands, and feet and often hidden under garments. Pain-producing forms of asceticism include self-laceration, particularly castration, and flagellation (whipping), which emerged as a mass movement in Italy and Germany during the Middle Ages and is still practiced in parts of Mexico and the southwestern United States.

## Variations of Asceticism in World Religions

In the primitive religions, asceticism in the form of seclusion, physical discipline, and the quality and quantity of food prescribed has played an important role in connection with the puberty rites and rituals of admission to the adult tribal community. Isolation for shorter or longer periods of time and other acts of asceticism have been imposed on medicine men, since severe self-discipline is regarded as the chief way leading to the control of occult powers. Isolation was and is practiced by young men about to achieve the status of manhood in the Blackfoot and other Indian tribes of the northwestern United States. In connection with important occasions, such as funerals and war, taboos (negative restrictive injunctions) involving abstinence from certain food and cohabitation were imposed. For the priests and chiefs these were much stricter. In Hellenistic culture (c. 300 BC - AD 300), asceticism in the form of fasting and refraining from sexual intercourse was practiced by communities of a religiomystical character, including the Orphics and Pythagoreans. A new impetus and fresh approach to ascetic practices (including emasculation) came with the expansion of the Oriental mystery religions (such as the cult of the Great Mother) in the Mediterranean area.

In India, in the late Vedic period (c. 1500 BC - c. 200 BC), the ascetic use of *tapas* ("heat", or austerity) became associated with meditation and *yoga*, inspired by the idea that *tapas* kills sin. These practices were embedded in the Brahmanic (ritualistic Hindu) religion in the *Upanisads* (philosophical treatises), and this view of *tapas* gained in importance among the Yogas and the Jainas, adherents of a religion of austerity that broke away from Brahmanic Hinduism. According to Jainism, liberation becomes possible only when all passions have been exterminated. Under the influences of such ascetic views and practices in India, Siddhartha Gautama himself underwent the experiences of bodily self-mortification in order to obtain spiritual benefits; but since his expectations were not fulfilled, he abandoned them. But his basic tenet, which held that suffering lies in causal relation with desires, promoted asceticism in Buddhism. The portrait of the Buddhist monk as depicted in the Vinaya (a collection of monastic regulations) is one of who avoids extreme asceticism in his self-discipline. The kind of monasticism that developed in Hinduism during the medieval period also was moderate. Asceticism generally has no significant place in the indigenous religions of China and Japan (Confucianism and Taoism were dominant respectively). Only the priests in Confucianism practiced discipline and abstinence from certain foods during certain periods, and some movements with Taoism observed similar marginally ascetic practices.

Judaism, because of its view that God created the world and that the world (including man) is good, is non-ascetic in character and includes only certain ascetic features, such as fasting for strengthening the efficacy of prayer and for gaining merit. Though some saw a proof of the holiness of life in some ascetic practices, a fully developed ascetical system of life has remained foreign to Jewish thought, and ascetic trends could, therefore, appear only on the periphery of Judaism. Such undercurrents rose to surface among the Essenes, a monastic sect associated with the Dead Sea Scrolls, who represented a kind of religious order practicing celibacy, poverty, and obedience. The archaeological discovery (1940s) of their community at Qumran (near the Dead Sea in an area that was a part of Jordan) has thrown new light on such movements in Judaism.

In Zoroastrianism (founded by the Persian prophet Zoroaster, 7$^{th}$ Centrury BC), there is officially no place for asceticism. In the Avesta, the sacred scriptures of Zoroastrianism, fasting and mortification are forbidden, but ascetics were not entirely absent even in Persia.

In Christianity, all of types of asceticism have found realization. In the Gospels, asceticism is never mentioned, but the theme of following the historical Christ gave asceticism a point of departure. An ascetic view of the Christian life is found in the First Letter of Paul to the Corinthians in his use of the image of the spiritual athlete who must constantly discipline and train himself in order to win the race. Abstinence, fasts, and vigils in general characterized the lives of the early Christians, but some ramifications of developing Christianity became radically ascetic. Some of these movements, such as the Encratites (an early ascetic sect), a primitive form of Syrian Christianity, and the followers of Maroon, played important roles in the history of early Christianity. During the first centuries, ascetics stayed in their communities, assumed their role in the life of the church, and centered their views of asceticism on martyrdom and celibacy. Toward the end of the third century, monasticism originated in Mesopotamia and Egypt and secured its permanent form in cenobitism (communal monasticism). After the establishment of Christianity as the official religion of the Roman Empire (after AD 313), monasticism was given a new impetus and spread all over the Western world. In Roman Catholicism, new orders were founded on a large scale. Though asceticism was rejected by the leaders of the Protestant Reformation, certain forms of asceticism did emerge in Calvinism, Puritanism, Pietism, early Methodism, and the Oxford Movement (an Anglican movement of the nineteenth century espousing earlier ecclesiastical ideals). Related to asceticism is the Protestant work ethic, which consists of a radical requirement of accomplishment symbolized in achievement in one's profession and, at the same time, demanding strict renunciation of the enjoyment of material gains acquired legitimately.

The adherents of Islam in its beginnings knew only fasting, which was obligatory in the month of Ramadan. Monasticism is rejected in the Qur'an (the Islamic sacred scripture). Yet ascetic forces among Christians in Syria and Mesopotamia, vigorous and conspicuous, were able to exercise their influence and were assimilated by Islam in the ascetic movement known as *zuhd* (self-denial) and later in that of Sufism, a mystical movement that arose in the eighth century and incorporated ascetic ideals and methods (*The New Encyclopedia Britannica* (1988).

Two scholars, Gilles Kepel who authored *The war of Muslim minds: Islam and the West*, (2004) and Oliver Roy the author of *Globalized Islam: The search for a need ummah* (2004), have extended this culturalist model of Islamic activist rationality from generalist and descriptive semantics to particularist and doctrine-based religious, cultural and interpretivist explanatory argument. For instance, while Kepel looks at the problem from an intellectual and historical perspective, Roy's analysis focuses on sociological conditions which influence Muslims to think, internalize, and act violently. The following quotation explains this phenomenon in a more detailed fashion.

"Kepel tracks two radically different strands of Islamic thought: the ultrastrict, quietist Salafist, or Wahhaabi school, and the more political thinking to the Muslim Brotherhood. These two schools later merged, producing the more hybrid ideology now identified with Osama bin Laden.

Kepel traces the origins of Salafism to Saudi Arabia and the ides of the radical theologian Muhammad ibn Abd al-Wahhab. In the opening decade of the nineteenth century, the Wahhabis and the House of Saud Formed and alliance, commencing a state-building project that was completed a century later. Wahhab agreed to glorify the Saudi tribal raids on neighboring oases by treating them as jihads, in return for King Muhammad bin Saud's promise to elevate Wahhabism to a state ideology. The project did not survive the Ottoman invasion in 1818, however, and had to be renewed with a series and 1920s. By that time, the jihad was no longer a stand-alone affair: Wahhabi blessings for the Ikhwan, the religious militia of King Saud, were doled out along with bombs dropped by the British, who by then were occupying the Arabian Peninsula. After World War II, the Americans replaced the British as the kingdom's main patrons. And under the presidency of Ronald Reagan, who was eager to use the Saudis as foils for the Soviet Union, "Wahhabism was elevated to the status of a liberation theology-one that would free the region of communism."

According to Kepel, a second, more autonomous and activists strand a political Islam originated in Egypt in the 1920s when the Muslim Brotherhood resolved to go beyond observing sharia (Islamic law) to establish a full-fledged Islamic state. Their slogan was "The Quran is our constitution." The Brothers joined Gamal Abdel Nasser in the Free Officers' Revolution that toppled King Farouk in 1952, but the alliance soon dissolved. Repression, at first in Egypt and then in Baathist Iraq and Syria, forced them to decamp to Saudi Arabia in the 1970s, where they joined forces with religious Palestinians who were uncomfortable with the Palestine Liberation Organization's secular nationalism. Gradually, the brotherhood tool control of Saudi intellectual life, positioning itself to shape the country's religious and political awakening after the Iranian revolution of 1979. Its power grew with the attack on the Great Mosque in Mecca on November 20 of that year, which brought the Wahhabists under official suspicion. The religious "awakening" of "a plethora of young radicals" followed; like the Iranian revolutionaries who combined traditional Shiite rhetoric with Third World anti-imperialism (portraying Saudi officials as American lackeys, for example), they mixed the activism of the brotherhood with quietist Salafism creating "an explosive blend that would detonate throughout the region and the whole world" (Mamdani 2005, 148-150).

Kepel uses the approach of an intellectual historian to study political Islam while Roy depends on the Islamist discourse to deconstruct the Koran which he discovers to be made of many forces of which the religious, political, cultural and doctrinal are paramount. He observes that the most strikingly important force is not what the Koran says but how Muslims interpret it.

"In *Globalized Islam*, Roy tries to explain why jihadist Islam resonates in the communities in which it does. He sees the spread of jihadist Islam today as "a consequence of and [a] reaction to sociological changes," rather than "evidence of the permanence of unchanging values" (the culturalist view) or as a direct historical consequence of the Saudis' and Reagan's support for the Wahhabi project (Kepel view). Roy distinguishes contemporarily neofundamentalists from traditional fundamentalists, such as Wahhabis who have tried "to delink Islam from ethnic cultures" for centuries and have everywhere "fought against local Islams"- "Sufism in South Asia, marabouts in North Africa, specific music and rituals everywhere," and even Shafism, Hanafism, and other historical schools of sharia.

For Roy, neofundamentalist Islam is "born-again Islam" and strictly a product of the diaspora. Islamic religious debate is no longer monopolized by the learned *ulema* (teachers) as they have turned to the Internet, the neofundamentalists have also become *tulaab* (students). As a result, "religion has been secularized, not in the sense that it is under the scrutiny of modern sciences, but to the extent that it is debated outside any specific institutions or corporations." With the traditional ethnic community left behind, "the disappearance of traditional values... [has lain] the groundwork for re-Islamisation," which has largely become an individual project. "Islamic revivalism goes hand in hand" with a modern trend: the "culture of the self."

The growing individualization of religious practices has prompted believers to create new community that transcends strict geography. The consequences of those who have succeeded in reconciling the self with religion has tended to embrace a "liberal" or "ethical" version of Islam; those who have not been prone to embrace "neo fundamentalist Salafism." Meanwhile, the quest "to build a universal religious identity, de-linked from any specific culture," has come at a price, because such and Islam is "by definition an Islam obvious to its own history." As a result, "the quest for a pure Islam [has] entail[ed] also an impoverishment of its content," Roy writes, and the ironic consequence of this quest is secularization, but in the name of fundamentalism.

This transformation has had particularly radical consequence for the Muslims of Europe, setting them apart form their cousins in the Middle East. According to Roy, political Islam is bifurcated between Islamist parties in Muslim-majority countries in the Middle East and Islamists in the diaspora. Because in the Middle East, Islamist parties have mobilized in response to particular state policies, by the end of the 1900s, most Islamist movements have become "more nationalist than Islamist." As a consequence of their political integration, "violence related to Islam has been decreasing in the Middle East since 1996." Islamist violence has increased outside the Middle East, however. The question is why, and why specifically in the West? The answer, Roy ventures, is that the violence of al Qaeda is politically, but religiously, inspired. After all, al Qaeda did not target St. Peter's Basilica in Rome, but the World Trade Center and the Pentagon. It targets modern imperialism, as the ultra-leftists of the late1960s and 1970s did with less success" (Mamdani 2005, 152-153).

## Rationalism in the Islamic Organizational Tradition

Roxanne L. Euben (1997) has argued that rationalism is not necessarily the monopoly of the Western intellectual and analytical tradition. Euben refutes the affirmative of the assertion by arguing that an Islamist and fundamentalist (original, biblical) critique of rationalism can be used to critique Western rationalism to demonstrate that rationality is not a monopoly of a specific racial or ethnic group. This anti-enlightenment position is a form of anti-foundationalist political discourse whose deconstructive tone may be viewed to be an element of post-modern and extreme radicalism whose norms denigrate Western and monocentric imperialism and colonialism (Euben 1997). In the post modern world, national or regional ethnocentrism is viewed to be irrelevant, myopic, and unscientific.

## Fundamentalist Theory of Political Islam

This critique is an analysis of the political theory of an "influential Islamic fundamentalist theorist" (p. 28). The critique shows that in spite of divine influence on Muslim socioeconomic and intellectual sphere of life, it is irrelevant and immaterial to assume that Islamic ideas are "irrational or purely epiphenomenal" (p. 28). Actually, these fundamentalist political ideas contain and need to be understood "as an apparently compelling ... ethicopolitical vision for the future, one that, furthermore, is part of a broader critique of rationalism and modernity that we in the West not only recognize, but in which we often participate" (p. 28). In other words, Islamic fundamentalism should not only be viewed as "reactive, defensive," (Fischer 1982; Ibrahim 1980; Tussler 1993; Euben 1997, 30), but it should be seen as genuine and rational system similar to Western rationalism. According to Sunni and Shiite Islamic fundamentalist thought, the challenge of modern political and economic sovereignty in the Middle East is also the same challenge for the Western countries. Such challenge is a form of crisis that is attributed to the failure of Western Marxism, liberalism, and socialism. The failure of these Western socioeconomic and political systems also portrays the failure of Western "rationalist discourse" (p. 31) which is the incubator of reason from which "truth, knowledge and authority" emanate (p. 31). Hence, "the rationalist rejection of transcendent foundations is the source of modern malaise in general, and the impoverishment of community, authority and morality" (p. 31).

The failure of fundamentalist political practice will continue to challenge liberal and democratic ideas of all political communities. This form of thinking is a system of comparative political theory that shows how human and Western systems challenge each other on the ladder of social progress and how they are challenged due to their own ignorance. Ignorance is a condition that is characterized by "crisis, decay and malaise" (p. 33) in Western Society.

According to Qutb (1991), the problem of modern civilization is *jahiliyya*—ignorance. This type of ignorance has made society to descend by deviating from the Islamic path of progress. The *jahili* (ignorant) society has refused to submit to the will of Allah—God. As a result, "Allah's sovereignty in the realm of belief, worship, and law, through a denial of his existence, restriction of his authority or dilution of His sovereignty with false 'gods'" (Euben 1997, 35) has been undermined. In addition, the Muslim community has decayed like some eras of early Islam. In other words, contemporary jahiliyya in terms of "people's ideas, their beliefs, habits, traditions, culture, art, literature, rules and laws...Islamic sources, philosophy and thought are jahili constructs" (p. 32; and Qutb 1991, 17). Universally, according to Islamic world view (*tasawwur*), the values of Islam have corrupted the souls of the entire Islamic society.

Qutb argues that the Islamic community has morally, spiritually, and socially degenerated because it is inspired by Western material, scientific, and technological achievements rather than by morality, real freedom, and authentic Islamic justice. To gain moral, spiritual, and social ascendance, the Islamic society must perceptively realize a new vision and redefinition of its true "progress, true civilization, true justice and genuine freedom" (p. 35). The same society should challenge Western cultural hegemony, valuelessness and inhumanity with values that will enable it to regenerate, become humane and built a strong civilization. In other words, Muslims should not "struggle to imitate alien models" which make them to "replicate the ills of Western society in the Islamic world" (p. 36). This usurpation of divine authority by man-made authority unites communist, liberal, socialist and nationalist systems" (p. 36). Legislative and political authority of these systems is secular rather than divine. Such authority supplants the divine sovereignty of humanity by alienating its moral discernment that makes him/her beastly. People in the West have become beastly because they are morally bankrupt. Moral bankruptcy is characterized by family alienation, disintegration, disorganization, disunity, and social dislocation rather than family, love, unity, nurturance, family values, social integration, and tolerance. The family is the smallest social unit in civilized and backward society. It fortifies the young through social conventions and transmission of cultural heritage. The abuse, rejection, and destruction of the family in liberal Christian systems is equivalent to the rejection of heaven, denial of the sovereignty of God on earth and the cultivation of an abysmal civilization.

Sovereignty belongs to God alone. It needs to be expressed in the context of Islamic law (*Shariah)* which includes the thoughts and practices of Mohammed the Prophet. Every believer knows and utters the *Shahadah* (confession of faith) by pronouncing that "There is no God but Allah, and Muhammed is His Prophet" (p. 38). The prophet is the teacher of God's will (Qutb 1991). Contemporary authority has lost his Islamic path for progress because he has become more political and less spiritual instead of vice versa. In doing that, the authority has become an unbeliever.

Islamic path is a form of Islamic law. The "law provides guidelines for everything from ritual washing to dispensation of property to political treaties. Since it dictates the principles of administration, justice, morality and social and domestic norms, it governs as a totality" comparable to contemporary Western political theory (rationality) which separates 'public' from 'private' sovereignty (*hakimiyya)* (p. 38).

## Islam as Freedom and Equality

According to Qutb, real Islamic civilization is based on freedom and equality for everyone in society. Freedom is positive and negative liberty (Berlin 1986) for the *Umma* (all Muslims). Freedom for the Umma (in a supranational sense—without political or geographical boundaries) "is freedom from obedience to tyrannical rule, the essence of which is an absence of (Sovereign's) restraint, and evil..." that is also "freedom to submit to membership in God's community, to repudiate the dominance of passion and license that has passed as freedom" for full humanhood (p. 39; Qutb 1991, 125).

The Islamic traditions of equality under the divine sovereign are grounded on the idea that "each member is equal by virtue of common submission to God, as opposed to a society in which one man rules another or where certain races or nationalities claim supremacy" (Euben 1997, 39). The Islamic doctrine of equality is different from "Locken idea of equality" in which "all persons are free and equal in that each has natural rights to life, liberty and property" (p. 39). In this case, Lockeanism is not only natural law derived from thirteenth century Christian thinkers such as Aquinas (McKenna 1994), but that natural law and legal right is not indiscriminately applied in capitalistic, competitive, and racist environments in which the weak, poor, and minority are, through no fault of their own, less competitive. In other words, in individualistic, competitive, and liberal environments, equality is de facto and relatively materialistically determined in terms of the collectivity within each class stratum of the socioeconomic structures. Natural rights are human civil rights. These rights are also individual rights for the "rights of man" though they are not the only rights for individuals and their respective social collectivities. However, in the Islamic tradition, all Muslims are equal and subject to the Call of Allah. They have equal citizenship. This citizenship is citizenship of belief through which all "are equal under the banner of Allah" (p.39; Qutb 1991, 25). Those who submit to the will of God are free and equal because of their membership in the Islamic and Godly community. This freedom and equality brought about their membership in a theocratic community transforms the believers' status that becomes "both the precondition to and fulfillment of the" collective "actualization of the Umma" (Euben 1991, 39). Though righteous servitude is far more preferable rather than unjust slavery, police coercion, and constitutional rationality (regulation of social behavior), faith and conscience (God's wrath and pleasure and reward of paradise), which are carried out in the context of the jihad (holy war) are the constraints that can appropriately control social behavior and the character or "condition of the Soul" (p. 39). Jihad is pious martyrdom that liberates people by bringing God's kingdom on earth. It makes the world a better place by eradicating the jahili society replacing it with a Godly one. Analogically, as the communist state withers in a state of distributive "perfection," the Islamic state would also wither if Islamic law were to be applied strictly and blindly.

## The State in Islam

Symbolically, Qutb (1991) has likened the Islamic state to a far-reaching, deep rooted and extremely valuable and productive tree. To illustrate his empirical symbolism, he asserts that "Islam is just like a strong, towering tree which casts a long shadow, its intertwined branches striking the sky. By nature, its roots penetrate deep into the earth, extending to its farthest recesses, in proportion to its splendor or greatness" (p. 31; Euben 1997, 46). Qutb has used metaphorical symbolism of the state. This tree is "organic and dynamic" (p. 46) because it is comprised of a variety of live organs whose growth is singly patterned and whose universal and immutable outlook is comprehensive enough to accommodate prevailing circumstances and needs. In other words, there are no theoretical specificities for its applicable empirical explanation due to the fact that Islam is more of a practice than a scientific or speculative theory. An actualized Islamic community has only one God, Allah and no other. Given the fact that such a belief has been canonized for hundreds of years, it is self-evident that all Islamic political, bureaucratic, economic and philosophical organizational structures, values, and norms derive their essence and vitality from this type of belief system that tends to be mythologically rationalizable. In other words, Islam is "a model or universally recognized religious or scientific accomplishments that provide problems and solutions to a community of scholars, believers, and practitioners" (Sagini 1996, 93; Kuhn 1962).

Though Qutb does not, for obvious reasons, specify the political institutions of the Islamic state, for this would be viewed as a form of theorizing that is "a jahili tactic designed both to distract believers and to nneurtralize the essential practicality of the Islamic worldview" (Euben 1997, 46) and was destructive and sophisticated gamesmanship and sophistry, he conceived it as a dynamic and continuous program whose active and transforming capacity is beyond theoretical intellectualization in its practice. Theorizing is against the authority of Islamic legal philosophy. In other words, the statehood of Islam is oriented to its "religious doctrine ... oriented praxis" (p. 47). Government must practice social justice in Islam (Al-Adala al-Ijtima 'iyya fi-l-Islam) and the principle of consultation (*Shura)*. The Qu'ran indicates that Allah expects believers to 'settle their affairs' "by" 'mutal consultation' (p. 47). Sura "42:38" admonishes believers to 'seek counsel' from their brethren in all affairs (Sura 3, 159)" (p. 47). In other words, all human activity is regulated by divine law. Government does not legislate but administers the given religio-politically inspired Islamic law that keeps the theocracy afloat. It is clear that the system resembles "Plato's philosopher kings ... selfless instruments of timeless truths" (p. 47) that are deeper than "human legislators" (p. 47; Wolin, 1960, 53-55).

Though the Islamic theocracy is an extended and tyrannical function of the state, its extreme and monolithic element resembles its Marxian counterpart whose bankruptcy in democratic theory does not invalidate the superiority of democratic rationality. The "responsibility of the ruler is thus mediated by the

Shar'iah: justice flows from adherence to Islamic law alone, not from adherence, for example, to the terms of a political contract. Because the ruler's authority is entirely derivative, he has no claims to hereditary succession, special privileges, or elevated status" (Euben 1997, 47-48). Even when a political leader uses his own discretion, he does so in consonant with Islamic Shariah. If Reform and innovation are justifiable in "reference to Islamic principles and can facilitate the reality of the ethico-political worldview implicit in Islamic Law" (p. 48) it will be carried forward through legally and officially recognized channels of authority.

Economically, Islamic law regulates property ownership. Ownership of common property is viewed as a form of stewardship. Islamic government redistributes the property as it sees fit. This theocratic and socialistic tendency does not only reject the ideal concept of free market competition, but, it also rejects the laws of self-interest through which individuals, groups, and corporations can accumulate wealth and exchange it for cash or for goods and services.

Qutb and other scholars believe that the Islamic state's fundamental political purpose is the provision of social justice. Its community has the moral responsibility to maintain and protect weaker members. This is a collective legal and moral obligation. In essence "Islamic social justice is the natural expression of an organic worldview. It is one practical corollary of the universalistic ethic of unity, mercy, love and mutual responsibility" (p. 48). The way in which wealth is redistributed expresses responsibility. In Qutbian analysis, Marxist economic equality is philosophically reductionist in the context of Islamic understanding of justice, for in Islam, "equality must be manifested simultaneously in the social, political, and spiritual realm. Therefore, when justice is abundantly available in all life's facets," attentiveness to social justice is the path to Allah's pleasure and avoidance of his vengeance for both the individual and ... the community" (p. 48). Though justice is viewed as an "expression of and catalyst for the solidarity" (p. 48) of human beings, it is mitigated through the distribution of property to the community. Much like John Locke's philosophy, ... the right of ownership of property, i.e. acquisition is gained through labor. However, acquisition is not only attained through "hunting, irrigation, mining, and wage-labor" (p. 48), but, it is also the "appropriation of the possessions of unbelievers killed by a Muslim" (p. 48 and Qutb 1953, 110). In a sense, both Islam and Christianity can kill or enslave in order to acquire property and redistributive justice. This form of aggressive behavior in inherently characteristic in human nature irrespective of man's cultural endowments.

The Marxist tradition of historical materialism or dialectical materialism has some moral affinity with the Qur'anic revelation of the economic principles of the Islamic community. The principles assert that each Muslim should be able to earn a living. "One of the five Pillars of Islam is an obligatory poor-tax (*Zakat,* literally meaning purification, but also charity), a property tax that functions to provide a kind of safety net for the poor" (Euben 1997:9). According to (Sura 24:56) of the Qu'ran, when believers observe their devotional obligations by paying the Zakat and obeying the Apostle, they will be shown mercy. In this sense, they generously practice piety because they minimally care for the poor. Such generosity, piety, and caring spirit tends to militate against the love of selfish personal gain. In a Western sense, personal or selfish gain is self-interestedness that is characteristic of basic elements of human nature. In Islamic traditional religious and political culture, both the individual and the community, group, or collectivity need to resist the selfish instincts of human nature for the successful construction of a just society. Even ancient Greeks and Medieval Europeans agree with what Averroes has affirmed, that the autocratic *Wazir* (prime minister) managed their resources in terms of wealth and prosperity of the empire in order to support the military and the commercial population. The peasantry and merchant classes were not heavily taxed for this would affect commerce and productivity. Municipal market managers (*muhtasib*), according to hisba literature, supervised business activity in line with the business principles of Roman Sensors (*aediles*) and Greek market regulators (*agoranomai* and *metronamai*). When the demand was low (*talaqqi)* merchandise was sold cheaply. Sometimes, this state of affairs encouraged hoarding activities that encouraged the sale of goods to intermediaries to take place. In spite of the extended family agriculture and stock-raising activities, particularly commercial credit, use of checks and bookkeeping are originally Arabic rather than European. Additionally, old terms like storehouse, warehouse, and magazine are Arabic rather than European. In other words, both economic theory and intellectual historical legacy seem to have evolved in Muslim or Arabic lands rather than Caucasian ones (Essid 1995).

As an eminent critic, Qutb condemns monopolies and usury. His vilification of capitalism has been observed in the *book Marikat al-Islam wa al-ra 'smaliya (The battle of Islam and capitalism* (1952). This form of economic and political rationality is not only shared by Islamic and Western peoples, but, it was also immensely exercised by the magnetic bureaucratic Egyptian empire of antiquity whose spirit of intellectual and mythical rationalism has been inherited in the West (Redford 1992, 48-55; Sagini 1996, 1-37).

## CONCLUSION

It is possible that Mr. Bin Laden was an extremely intelligent and complex man who is also a violent ascetic. Asceticism advocates abstinence, fasting, celibacy, and poverty. Classical, Eastern, Protestant, and Catholic societies which practiced asceticism displayed it in thorough physical and intellectual activity. It encouraged the cultivation of Stoic mentality, strengthening of the individual's meditation and willpower. Some cherished life in the dusty desert which made them to abdicate their washing habits, walking around with long hair, and in filthy rags, dirt and dust accumulated on their bodies, possessed long finger nails, reduced movement and lived in cells that cherished solitary confinement in the wilderness and caves. Some aspects of asceticism are physically painful, psychologically debilitating, and selflessly advocate self-torture and austerity. Asceticism is predominately priestly and less relatively practiced by others in temporal and secular environments. In the Christian tradition, abstinence, fasting, prayer, and vigils are elements of asceticism. Ascetic life is by nature holy, peaceful and spiritually elevating. Once it is accompanied by acts of violence, the results are far reaching. For instance, Osama Bin Laden, who controlled the Taliban government, used it to attack the U.S., discriminates against women by veiling them, denying them education, professionalism, and property ownership. He advocates destruction of historical Buddhist monuments—civilization itself.

Euben argues that it is rational to use Islamic fundamentalist (original premodernism) beliefs to critique Western rationalism and to deconstruct contemporary and ignorant Islamic Arabism. The West thinks that Islamic ideas are not irrational and epiphenomenal. Epiphenomenalism is a doctrine which asserts that mental activities are epiphenomena of the neural processes of the brain. Therefore, Islamic fundamentalism is reactive or defensive. Muslims think that there is a crisis because Western Marxism, liberalism, and socialism have failed. This failure contributes to the failure of Western rationalist discourse too from which truth, knowledge, and authority spring. Rationalist rejection of transcendent foundations produces malaise by impoverishing the community, authority, and morality. Muslims believe that Western society and thought promotes inequality but the Islamic transcendent tradition promotes equality based on the call of Allah.

Qutb argues that the problem of contemporary civilization is ignorance (jahiliyya). People are ignorant because they have deviated from the transcendent Islamic path of progress. They have deviated because they are ignorant, have refused to submit to the will of Allah. Allah's sovereignty in the area of belief, worship, law has been undermined. His existence has been denied and has been replaced with false materialistic and idealistic gods. This ignorance from which Islamic civilization suffers is in the realm of people's ideas, beliefs, habits, traditions, culture, art, literature, rules, laws, Islamic sources, and philosophy and thought. These constructs are pregnant with ignorance. Contemporary Islamic values have corrupted the souls of the people (pp. 18-21).

Western science, philosophy, rationality and freedom have been used to deflect people's attention from Allah. This has caused people to become victims of transgression. The transgression has caused corrosive and contradictory understanding in Muslim reason, interpretation, and definition of the world. This confusion or chaotic state has made humanity to abandon its stewardship of God's World which is constantly mismanaged. Man who was God's deputy has become a beast rather than a saint. As a beast, man uses modern technology, the mass media, and sophisticated weapons to propagate fundamentalist ideology, assassinations, and control of the masses. The ignorant society should be eradicated if man has to regain his originally God given status.

In terms of freedom, the Qur'an condemns oppression more than killing. In other words, Islam views killing to be better because oppression conducted through ignorance has multiple power to oppress morally, educationally, technologically, and coercively. Islam is seen as freedom from ignorance, freedom from slavery, and freedom of choice. Islam is not only a way of life (din) in belief and faith, but it is also a way of life that attacks institutions and traditions in order to liberate humanity. Islamic belief is the locus of sovereignty. It is more of a practice rather than a speculative or scientific theory. Its community has one God, Allah. Islam is a model that universally provides problems and solutions to a community of scholars, believers, and practitioners (Sagini 1996; Kuhn 1962).

In terms of morality and politics, Islamic moral philosophy is a divine program for institutionalizing authority which radiates from God and which is universally and legally rationalized and theologically and freely practiced in the theocracy. Morality and political power are integratively inextricable forces that enable the individual and the community to attain redemption. Concerning the state in Islam, both Qutb and Euben assert that it towers into the heavens and casts a long shadow. Its interwoven branches reach the sky. Its roots penetrate deep into the earth in splendor and greatness. This image of the state is organic and dynamic because many living organisms are universally protected and nurtured by it. Although they do not specify the political institutions of the Islamic state, for this will be viewed as a firm of theorizing that is destructively sophisticated sophistry and gamesmanship, these radical scholars see the state to be a dynamic and continuous program whose active and transforming power is beyond theoretical and creative intellectualization. Theorizing is against the authority of the malikite Islamic legal philosophy. In other words, the Islamic statehood is derived from its religious doctrine that is oriental to its praxis rather than scientific theorizing. To make the state real, government must practice social justice and the principle of consultation (shura). The Qu'ran empowers believers to settle problems by consultation because human activity is regulated by divine law. The state is a theocracy. The ruler's (leader's) responsibility is mediated by law (shariah). Justice is rooted in Islamic law and political contract. The ruler's authority is derivative rather than hereditary and privileged. Economically, property ownership, which is common stewardship, is regulated by Islamic law. The concept of free market is rejected. The Islamic state rejected socialism because it provided economic rather than social, political, and spiritual equality. Socialism lucked mercy, love, and mutual responsibility. The poor-tax (zakat) is a form of purification, piety, and charity. The action militates against intense individualism and enhances social justice. Such post-modern and radical thinking is what animates Osama Bin Laden. No wonder he is a terrorist.

Terrorism is rooted in individual, group, and organizational behavior that springs from human interaction, rationality, and irrationalism. Terrorist behavior can be adopted by anyone for nationalistic, patriotic, religious or environmental causes. Because terrorists have strong beliefs in a cause, and since these intense and extreme beliefs can lead to destruction and murder, they influence decision makers, their future opinions, and actions. Terrorist actors influence policy makers in an unimaginable ways.

## REFERENCES

Aronoff, Myron J. 2001. Radical change in Israel: A review essay. *Political Science Quarterly* 116, 3: 447-453.

Dillenberger, J. and C. Welch. 1954. *Protestant Christianity: Interpreted through its development.* New York: Charles Scribner's Sons.

Euben, Roxanne L. 1997. Comparative political theory: An Islamic fundamentalist critique of rationalism . *The Journal of Politics* 59, 1:28-55.

Hecht, J.M. 2000. Vacher de Lapouge and the rise of Nazi science. *Journal of the History of Ideas*, 285-304.

Holton, G. 2000. The rise of postmodernisms and the end of science. *Journal of the History of Ideas*, 327-341.

Kelly, J. 2001. *World Trade Center toll: Mostly men, mostly young. Sunday Oklahoman*: 13-A.

Kissinger, H. 1994. *Diplomacy*. New York: Simon and Schuster.

Kuhn. 1962. *The Structure of scientific revolutions.* Chicago: The University of Chicago Press.

McLean, I. 1960. *The concise Oxford dictionary of politics.* New York: Oxford University Press.

Muraskin, R., and A.R. Roberts. 1996. *Visions for change: Crime and justice in the twenty-first century.* Upper Saddle River, N.J.: Simon and Schuster Company.

Qutb, S. 1991. *Ma' alim fi- Tariq* [*Signposts along the road*]. Beirut: Dar al- Shuruq [Originally published in 1961].

__________. 1953. *Social justice in Islam.* Translated by John B. Hardie. Washington, D.C.: American Council of Learned Societies.

Redford, D.B. 1992. *Egypt, Canaan, and Israel in ancient times.* Princeton, N.J.: Princeton University Press.

Sagini, M.M. 1996. *The African and the African-American university: A historical and sociological analysis.* Lanham, MD: The University Press of America, Inc.

# Chapter III
# International Diplomacy and the U.S. vs. Iraq War

After 9/11/2001, Republicans became dominant in national politics (House, Senate, Presidency, Judiciary). They used foreign policy issues to strengthen their base by articulating universal ideals of the empire: trade, war on global terrorism and universal democracy. It was a referendum which was a means of ensuring that politicians do not lose touch with the preferences of the electorate. The referendum is a mechanism which allows voters to make a choice between alternative courses of action on a particular issue (such as war on terrorism vs. the economy). The referendum on terrorism was supported by Congress and popular with the electorate, and it caused popular disaffection with domestic issues which traditionally resonate well with a liberal and democratic public, particularly the Democratic Party. Having been the victim of a brutal transnational terrorist attack, the U.S. responded by attacking Afghanistan, Osama bin Laden, and Saddam Hussein without clear objectives. Such a response has seismically shaken up the power balance of international relations which became the driving dynamic in the search for diplomatic solutions in order to avert war between the U.S. and Iraq. It was breathtaking to watch the flurry of the interplay of diplomatic styles and activities used to cool tempers, produce reason, unite allies, and solve the problem either way in the sea of global indignation and theoretical "inexactitude." Such behavior of misplaced hostility is not only consistent with the realist position of nations which display super power to resolve conflicts, but such display of power is the essence of globalization and its attendant hegemonic regionalization, both of which tend to supplant dependent elements of sustainability in the name of freedom and democratization.

Diplomacy is as old as the evolution of ancient civilizations. It is the science of international relations through which strategic, trade, diplomatic, and tactical negotiations between nations are conducted. The Greek city states of antiquity conducted diplomatic relations between and among themselves. This method of tactical and strategic thinking and action was revived by Italian city states during the Renaissance and was reinforced on the European diplomatic landscape after the Reformation. Likewise, Eastern, Confucian, Arabic, and Hindic civilizations carried out their diplomacy in various and different ways. In other words, antiquity, Medievalism and Modernity, European and Eastern geopolitical and social conflicts appear to have been resolved, other things being equal, through well orchestrated diplomatic overtures. Whenever leadership was weak, lack of intellectual, philosophical, and diplomatic rationality promoted war as a substitute. In this crisis, it was interesting to observe how the search for solutions through diplomacy and inexact theoretical legitimation failed to produce the universally desired effect.

## STYLES OF INTERNATIONAL DIPLOMACY

The development of modern diplomacy as a scientific study and practice of international relations evolved with the state system of the Congress of Vienna. In 1815, diplomacy became a

> ...regularized system of permanent diplomacy as a necessary and important aspect of relations between states. The great powers exchanged embassies and ambassadors, while relations involving smaller powers were conducted through legations and ministers. A recognized diplomatic profession developed, characterized by the aristocracy of its members and the secrecy of its methods. After the First World War more open or 'democratic' diplomacy flourished for a short while. At the end of the Second World War the distinction between embassies and legations were abandoned, and ambassadors proliferated, especially when new states were formed from the European Colonies (McLean 1996, 141).

Currently, there are three major styles of diplomacy that are interlinked. First, the European style views diplomacy as an "instrument" (p. 141) for providing diplomatic solutions to international problems through the processes of negotiation, bargaining, compromise, détente, and ostpolitik (Kissinger 1994; Duffield 1995). Second, the American style, which is revolutionary in nature, is rooted in realist and neorealist schools of thought. The schools' beliefs converge on the national interest which is rationalized in twentieth century Wilsonian ideals of "peace, stability, progress, and freedom for mankind" (Kissinger 1984, 836). To some extent, these ideals have not been deflected from the central focus on enlightenment ideas of life, liberty, and the pursuit of happiness which are enshrined in the American Constitution and Declaration of Independence and canonized in the Constitution (Patterson 2002). Based on the revolutionary style of American diplomacy,

> bureaucracy is for the most part staffed by individuals who have dedicated themselves to what is, in American society, a rather unorthodox career so that they may promulgate and implement their views of a better world. Their opinions, moreover, are honed by a system in which policy emerges from bureaucratic struggles which...are never finally settled. Segmented into services of individual, and at times isolated, initiatives geared to highly specific problems, American foreign policy is rarely approached from the point of view of an overall concept. Ad hoc departmental approaches have more – and more passionate – spokesmen than does an overall strategy, which often has no spokesman at all. It takes an unusually strong and determined president, skilled in the ways of Washington, to break this pattern (Kissinger 1984, 718).

The third style of international diplomacy originates from a variety of Third World nations that represent a plethora of diverse interests that are different from the two previously discussed cases above. These Third World styles of diplomacy place emphasis on the morality of recognizing and dealing with other states. Generally speaking, these Third World diplomatic styles are profoundly influenced by European diplomatic traditions which treat diplomacy as an instrumental function. In these traditions, diplomats negotiate disputes by considering both sides of the "coin," which Third World nations capitalize on to alienate the U.S. at the United Nations. Such marginalization of the United States would make it to use force to solve diplomatic problems in order to assert its power. What happened in Iraq has become a classic case study.

## THEORIES OF DIPLOMACY

The three major theories of international relations are realism, liberalism, and constructivism and their extensions (Lake and Ochmanek 2001). Theoretically, Hobbes (1588-1679) was a brilliant political philosopher who used Euclidian geometrical theory to argue that when the regime abandons high ideals, it declines due to incompetence and indifference to real-politic. Using geometrical axioms such as the square of two sides of a right-angled triangle is equivalent to the square of its hypotenuse, which is a form of rationality, he argued that humans are rational because they want to protect their own preservation. That is why they go to war – to protect their interests essential for self-preservation.

His work the *Leviathan*, which is about game theory, was used to strategically rationalize the national interest of states, particularly England. Unlike Locke's and Rousseau's real state of nature in which life is "solitary, poor, nasty, brutish and short" rather than one where "life, liberty and property" are protected, Hobbes' state of nature is an intellectually and scientifically reconstructed logical argument of what could happen if sovereignty were divided; it would lead to civil war because of the failure of diplomacy. Failure of diplomacy is failure of leadership.

Realist intellectuals of antiquity and Medievalism were giants such as Locke, Thucydides, Machiavelli, Hobbes, and Rousseau and modern scholars like E. H. Carr, Hans Morgenthau and John Herz. These academics are or were proponents of neorealism, which evolved in the 1970s by being championed by Kenneth M. Waltz. Realism emphasizes the continuities of the human condition at all levels, especially the international level. To escape life in a cruel state of nature, the social contract between the people and the sovereign (King) was provided. Through the social contract, protection is promised the citizens in return for their loyalty to the sovereign. Loyalty is demonstrated by citizens who serve in the military and pay taxes to the government. Though Hobbes, the author of *Leviathan* was an absolutist, he was a promoter of parliamentary sovereignty. The central tenet in his realism was the belief that world politics is, in essence and in practice, a struggle among self-interested states that seek power and position in an anarchical and competitive environment in which each state pursues its own national interests (Kegley 2002).

In his book *The prince*, Machiavelli advocated that leaders and regimes need to use deception in order to succeed politically. Rousseau condemned both deception and corruption as forms of hypocrisy because these forms did not promote regime honesty, goodness, innocence, and virtue, values that are moral and ethical principles of republican princes and other bureaucratic and aristocratic elite (Grant 1997). Machiavelli's ideas are more than 500 years old. The art of contemporary political practice, particularly in a liberal–democratic republic, may not be devoid of hypocritical, deceptive, and corrupt practices, as Machiavelli shows, which are or may be by-products of socio-psychological dependence and cooperative ventures that at times became victims of antagonistic elements of alliance irreconcilability. Such cooperation, regardless of its structure and content, may be a product of choice rather than necessity for achieving group goals irrespective of their lofty or baseless nature. However, to secure mutually beneficial cooperation,

> People naturally must try to disguise or play down their self-interested motives and the instrumental quality of their ties to allies and potential allies; they exaggerate the coincidence of their personal preferences and the common goal; they compromise their principles in order to achieve the best feasible outcome, and they conceal the strategies that aim at maximizing their self interest (*The Journal of Politics* 60, 4:235).

Therefore, liberating Iraq to make it democratic by removing Saddam Hussein, who was a tyrant, was not the same thing as liberating it in order to steal its natural resource particularly oil.

Machiavelli's deceptive and manipulatory assertion is a realist political tradition in historical statecraft and political craftsmanship of regimes whose moralism and integrity are negative elements of constructive political engagement similar to the U.S.'s relations with South Africa, due to strategic minerals, during the Cold War Era. Generally, deceptive and manipulative political practice is conducted in an "open, honest, rational" (p. 1236) manner. Those who use manipulative, realist or neorealist approaches in political practice may be "complacent hypocrites, hypocritical anti-hypocrites, or self-righteous fanatics" (p .1236) whose ethical morality is psycho-politically questionable overall, though deception occasionally creates a climate for righteous political practice in which "virtuous citizens pursue the common good defined by the general will" (p. 1237). This frees them from depending on each other. In this case, deceptive political self-interest looks to be uniquely different from the one in which there is permanent tension between collective alliances and strategic planners and actors. Klemons von Metternich and Otto von Bismarck exemplified realist theory during Napoleonic and German unification war eras (Kegley and Raymond 2002). All realists believe that conflicts of interest among nations are inevitable and that the purpose of statecraft is to ensure national survival by acquiring power. The following beliefs comprise the central tenets of realism:

1. History teaches that people are by nature sinful and wicked.
2. Of all people's evil ways, no sins are more prevalent or dangerous than the lust for power and the desire to dominate others.
3. The possibility of eradicating the instinct for power is a utopian aspiration.
4. Under such conditions, international politics is a struggle for power, "a war of all against all," as the sixteenth-century English philosopher Thomas Hobbes put it.
5. The primary obligation of every state in this environment – the goal to which all other national objectives and moral considerations should be subordinated – is to promote the "national interest," defined in terms of survival and national security through power.
6. The anarchical nature of the international system necessitates the acquisition of military capabilities sufficient to deter or subdue any potential rival.
7. Economics is less relevant to national security than military might and is important primarily as a means to acquire national power and prestige.
8. Allies might increase the ability of a state to defend itself, but their loyalty and reliability should not be assumed.
9. International law and international organizations cannot be trusted to preserve peace.
10. International stability results from maintaining a balance of power (Kegley and Raymond 2002, 10-11).

Both instrumentalism and realism are important theories in the realm of international relations. International relations is governed by international law that is different from municipal (national) law (McLean 1996). *International law* is a code of etiquette that sanctions the behavior of relations between states. International law takes a positivist or a naturalist view. Positivistically, international law is the command or authority of the sovereign (rulers, state, reinforced by force). This is the position the U.S. takes in its dealings with Iraq. The U.S. takes this position because the international system is an anarchy which has no supreme or absolute authority. This lack, of necessity, makes international law and international relations to be deficiently lacking. If President Bush realized the existence of this lack, he may have tried to use "any means necessary" in order to assert that authority and control Saddam's influence. As events have proved, it is not easy to break international laws in order to assert absolute or imperial authority.

Naturalistically, international law is different from its positivist counterpart. The naturalist view of international law is based on historical custom and traditional principles rooted in the medieval natural law tradition of Thomas Aquinas. Thomistic natural legal philosophy, which is Christian, Roman Catholic, and European, argues that God created an orderly and law-governed world. An orderly and law-governed world can be rationalized mathematically, deductively, and theoretically by using logical reasoning. Quasi-deductive reasoning approaches such as "Do unto others as you would be done by" are elements of national law. Even the works and thoughts of Shakespeare, Henry V of England, and statutory elements of municipal law have become the sources of conventional international law.

Further still, naturalistic international law is created by treaties to which only certain nations are signatories. Treaties that have a large number of signatories are called a *convention* because of their multilateralism. Conventions have become international law. Examples of conventions which are regarded as naturalistic international law include but are not limited to

> territory, the sea, the responsibility of states, human rights, treaties, dispute settlement, and the use of force....law relating to shipping, coastlines, territorial waters, exclusive economic zones, and the rights to resources on and under the deep sea bed. Law relating to the responsibilities of states to each other's citizens covers both the care of refugees and asylum seekers, and the expropriation and compensation of multinational corporations (p. 246).

When nations observe and respect these multilateral conventions to which the nations are signatories, international diplomacy is enhanced and the peace and security of states are promoted. Both states and individuals have rights recognized by the international system. For instance, the transition from customary law to conventional international law has made slavery a punishable act which existed as customary international law before 1815. In other words, freedom from slavery became conventional international law during the twentieth century when all nations abolished it. In addition, since 1945 the European Convention on Human Rights and the United Nations Universal Declaration on Human Rights (which is not a convention) have reinforced the need for states to protect human rights. The U.N. Charter, which is not legally enforceable, suggests rights that are suitable without attaching them to individuals. The final act of the 1975 Helsinki Conference on Security and Corporation in Europe, though specified, does not have legal enforcement either. This act liberalized Soviet behavior in terms of human rights to the extent that the system became ideologically, economically and militarily uncompetitive and unintentionally gave way to its own dissolution (Thomas 2001; Sagini 2001).

The ways in which states "accede to, abrogate, and interpret" (p. 246) international treaties is governed by the 1969 Vienna convention which concerns the Law of Treaties. These treaties came into force in 1980. Legal "procedures for the settlements of disputes between states range from the exercise of good offices by third party, through mediation and conciliation, to formal arbitration" (pp. 246-247). Under the 1899 Convention on the Pacific Settlement of International Disputes and subsequent conventions, states have been able to submit disputes for settlement, but the process depends on the consent of both parties. However, since the creation of the Permanent Court of International Justice in 1922 and its successor, the International Court of Justice, in 1946, there has been a court to which a state could unilaterally bring a complaint against another state. In 1928, the Kellogg-Briand Pact was ratified to outlaw war in states that used it as an instrument of national policy (Kegley 2000). Both institutions inform American leaders about the current national interest and its relation to them.

Under international and municipal law, a state can use force against another in self defense. Specifically, under the "United Nations Charter of 1945, the use of force by states against one another is illegal except in self-defense." Though the U.S. has attacked Iraq on such grounds, the majority of world public opinion, as expressed in the conclusion, views the attack to be immoral, pre-emptive, and unwarranted. Other international conventions govern the kinds of weapons which states may use. For instance, the treatment of noncombatants and prisoners of war and the conduct of U.N. peace-keeping forces are governed by international conventions. Though the United States is trying to link Osama bin Laden with Saddam for their complicity in 9/11/2001, evidence provided to the U.N. by Colin Powell, former U.S. Secretary of State, as observed by the "Court of World Opinion" including the majority of the UN Secretariat and the Security Council, appears to be circumstantial and therefore refutable. Perhaps more convincing evidence which proves Iraq to be in "material breach" may have been given by International Atomic Energy Agency IAEA representatives (inspectors) who left Iraq on March 18, 2003, because hostilities broke out. In any case, great powers can manipulate small ones by moving from "low politics" of foreign economic policy to "high politics" of using military strategy to control the oil economy (Skalnes 2000). In doing that, the foreign policy elite can further strengthen national diplomacy by coopting allies and securing their Strategic Objectives. Such commercial policy enables great powers to control the trade of adversaries for the benefit of allies who control the trade with less to pay on tariffs. This is grand strategy. Examples of this realist manipulative behavior can historically be found in German-Austro-Hungarian relations or Franco-Russian ties during the time preceding World War I, Britain's relations with its colonies, United States' relations with France and Germany during the interwar period, and U.S. relations with Japan and Europe between 1945 and 1967 (Skalnes

2000). Adversaries can be pacified through trade, aid, investment and technology transfer. The same adversaries can be lured with ostpolitik, détente, and U.S. policy toward other nations such as China in terms of World Trade Organization (TWO) accession.

In the Nuclear Age, realism as a traditional theory of international relations has been viewed with consternation and pessimism in policy-making centers and academic institutions. The psychopolitical and geostrategic climates of World War II, the Cold War, Cold War East-West controversy, the arms race, global violence resulting from competition rather than cooperation, and the selfishness and incorrigibility of power-seeking states have become important limitations of the realist school of thought. This threatening international environment necessitated the precedence of foreign policy over its domestic counterpart. Threats of war and the rationale for realpolitik reinvigorated the thinking that military security was essential to the practice of world politics. To overcome realism's inherent limitations, neorealism and neoclassical realism emerged to meet contemporary theoretical needs wherein the limitations of realism's relevance made it difficult and wanting. *Neorealism* places emphasis on the "anarchic nature of global society without governance rather than the traditional realist emphasis on the unceasing lust for power inherent in human nature" (Kegley 2002:39). It allows states to display behavior in terms of their differential status in power rather than differential status in values, type of government, and domestic considerations. For this reason, neorealism is also called *structural realism*. It emphasizes the influence of global power structure on the states' behavior within it.

The anarchism of neorealism is characterized by the absence of central institutions. States rather than leaders are the primary actors. They act in accordance with the principles of self-help and self-preservation. The neorealist ideology argues that "states do not differ in the tasks they face, only in their capabilities" (p. 41). The capabilities "define the position of states in the system, and the distribution of capabilities defines the structure of the system and shapes the ways the units interact with one another" (p. 41). Power is the essence of neorealism although its quest is not an end in itself as realism is. The same power is not derived from human nature. Individual states pursue power as a means of survival in the "global jungle." According to Waltz (1979), states use internal creativity and effort to maximize economic capability, military strength, and clever strategies.

Likewise, the same states use external efforts to strengthen and enlarge alliances and weaken or eliminate opposition. Since states are driven by the survival instinct, the balance of power for these states forms naturally, regardless of whether some states want to establish and sustain the balance or whether or not they aim for universal domination (Waltz 1979). "Once the global system is formed, its structure becomes a force that the units may not be able to control; it constrains their behavior and interposes itself between their intentions and the outcomes of their actions" (Kegley 2002, 41).

The current policy of American hegemony toward Iraq was constructed by Paul Wolfowitz, Assistant Secretary of Defense under George H. Bush twelve years ago. President George W. Bush, who is a realist like Colin Powell, Brent Scowcroft, Condoleesa Rice, and General Myers, rejected the policy of containment of Iraq for its aggressiveness on grounds of international law and morality. Between 1992 and 2000, Wolfowitz and Rumsfeld persuaded President Clinton to contain Iraq preemptively because Iraq had almost developed a bomb in 1990 by using enriched uranium from France and because it possessed anthrax, VX, and sarin. These radiological, biological, and chemical agents are weapons of mass destruction whose possession by a tyrannical regime threatens neighbors and their allies in the Middle East and elsewhere. Clinton was convinced. The U.N. and U.S. allies, however, did not support the idea.

Consistent with neorealist conceptions of the use of power to dominate the structure of the international system irrespective of domestic and multilateral concerns, neorealists, whose neo-Reaganite ideology has become a model for decision-making, have embraced an evangelical and fundamentalist religious ideology for pursuing global domination. Among these rightist extremists are Paul Perle, an ideologue and former chairperson of policy in the Pentagon, who was forced to resign in March 2003; Paul Wolfowitz, the original architect of the policy of containment of Iraq and former Assistant Secretary of Defense; Henry Kissinger, the father of contemporary neorealism; Rumsfeld, the Secretary of Defense, and Dick Cheney, the Vice President. These are the hawks who "will not distinguish the terrorists from those who harbor them" because everyone else is "either with us or with the terrorists" whose ring leaders are the "axis of evil" – Iraq, Iran, and North Korea (President Bush). The "hawks" wanted to use force preemptively to attack Third World dictatorial and armed regimes in order to transform and democratize them. This policy may be self-defeating for its antiglobalization, for its anti-international law, and for its immorality, and injustice.

## International Diplomacy and Alliance Division: Theoretical Challenges

The interplay of international diplomacy within the global, regional, and military alliances that have been divided over the conflict between Iraq and the United States is also likely to have far reaching consequences. If *globalization* is "the process by which markets and production in different countries are becoming increasingly interdependent due to the dynamics of trade in goods and services and flows of capital and technology" (European Commission 1997, 45), then the divisions within the political, regional, and military alliances of NATO and U.N. are an inevitable wake-up call for potential self-destruction of the United Nations and the Western alliance. Such divisions tend to undermine issues of "technological developments, criminal activity, international relations theory, modernization, and development strategies" (Thompson 1999, 39) through which the globalization development debate is brought to bear. For instance,

> To explain these questions, we analyze longitudinal data on international commodity trade using the social network approach. Data analysis shows that the world became increasingly globalized between 1959 and 1996 in the sense that each country studied traded with more countries in 1996 than in 1959. As a result, the world trade of this process has been the development of countries in the middle strategy. We also find that the structure of the world trade network became decentralized over time, a change that provides greater support for neoclassical economic theory than for World-system/dependency theory. Regarding regionalization, we find that intraregional density is greater than interregional density and that intraregional ties are stronger than interregional ones. Moreover, both intraregional and interregional density increased significantly between 1959 and 1996, indicating, first, that the flow of world trade became regionalized and, second, that globalization and regionalization are not contradictory processes but rather complementarily concomitant ones (Kim and Shin 2002, 445).

In a deeper sense, globalization is not only the regionalization and internationalization of markets, goods and services, but this process of economic, political, and cultural recolonization of the periphery by the core countries is also a renewed structure that possesses mechanisms, institutions, organizations, conventions and regulations for both global and regional governance of the international system/world system. The governance system has players or states that are more "internally globalized" regionally than they are internationally. This requires policy makers of major globalizers like the United States to learn and be informed as to how to manage the "devolved evolution" of the newly forged global and world system. Exposure to learning requires leaders to be sensitive about the extent to which the international economy can be integrated to alleviate poverty, hopelessness, and misery at the periphery while facing challenging regulatory measures within the regional and global frame-works (Thompson 1999). If peripheral economic problems translate their agents to become terrorists and if terrorist behavior is causing divisions within the global and regional governance systems, then managers of the global system (world system) need to respond with understanding, investment opportunities, development plans and projects, and educational, scientific, and cultural exchanges that promote progress and international understanding rather than responding in kind with weapons of mass destruction and other punitive measures which could widen the cleavage between East and West. In other words, in order to succeed, globalization, which is the process of hegemonization, has to rely on post structuralism, postmodernism, technology, democratization, and neocolonization of the most sophisticated nature (*Michigan Today* 2002).

The center of globalization is geopolitically triadic. Its triadism (triadicism) is rooted in the triangular economic, military and political relationships of the U.S., E.U. and Japan. This triadic alliance is not only a brilliant experiment in intraregional and interregional alliance, but this experiment is the essence of multilateralism which provides the security system for the protection markets, trade, and investment both in the stable politico-economic climates and even within the areas that are viewed as the "theatre of cruelty" (Valaskakis 1999). While the use of transnational information and communication structures for sharing knowledge and experience helps to transform international transactions, these processes, particularly those of nongovernmental organizations (NGOS), multilateral institutions (World Bank & International Monetary Fund), and global regionalism tend to negatively undermine national policies on sustainable development at the periphery (Petil and Soete 1999; Sagini 2001). The policies tend to deflate and devalue currencies (Boer-Ashworth 2000). Therefore, in essence, national policies of sustainable development may be sustainable in a triadic sense rather than in a peripheral one. As long as complex and severe economic, health, political, and technological problems exist at the periphery, these problems' logics will continue to question their relationship with the triadic center in terms of cause and effect nexus.

## THEORETICAL CHALLENGES

*Liberalism* is a theoretical paradigm grounded on the understanding that the use of rational reason and universal ethics to solve problems, concerns, and conflicts of structures in international relations "can lead to a more orderly, just, and cooperative world, and that international anarchy and war can be policed by institutional reforms that empower international organizations and laws" (Kegley 2002, 33). The eighteenth century pioneers of the liberal theory were David Hume of Scotland, Jean-Jacques Rousseau of France, and Immanuel Kant of Germany. Richard Cobden has argued that the liberal theoretical experiment would be suitable for the global and borderless environment, "communication among people could expand through free trade, so too would international friendship and peace, secured by prosperity that would create interdependence and eliminate the need for military forces to pursue rivalries" (p. 33). Although twentieth century political realities suggested the opposite, Wilsonian pragmatic idealism (Eisendrath, Marsh, and Goodman 2001) significantly contributed to the advancement of the liberal theoretical project which became a model for the construction and implementation of public policy at home and abroad.

Liberal thinkers are pragmatic idealists who embrace collective security (League of Nations) and self-determination as positive approaches for influencing constructive global and international behavior. The behavior enhances international relations when emphasis is placed on the principles of equality, dignity, and liberty of individuals and the necessity to protect individuals from unnecessary state control and manipulation. These forms of idealistic thinking are rooted in ancient and medieval political traditions which have been transmogrified by modern and post-modern thinkers, of whom Alfred Zimmerman, Norman Angell, Woodrow Wilson, Thomas Jefferson, James Madison, John Stuart Mill, John Locke, and Adam Smith are luminary examples.

Politically, the liberal world view advocates the search for agreement concerning shared values that are essential for global cooperation. The principle of collective security enables the powers that set the rules of the game (peacekeeping) to enforce them collectively when an aggressor has violated the principles of international law. *International law* is a governance system of legal jurisprudence (mediation and arbitration) that influences the behavior of states and the actions of their leaders. To control and regulate the behavior of nations and their leaders, post-World War I liberal idealists constructed the following principles for managing international relations:

1. Human nature is essentially "good" or altruistic, and people are therefore capable of mutual aid and collaboration through reason and ethically inspired education.
2. The fundamental human concern for others' welfare makes progress possible.
3. Sinful or wicked human behavior, such as violence, is the product not of flawed people but of evil institutions that encourage people to act selfishly and to harm others.
4. War and international anarchy are not inevitable and wars frequently can be reduced by strengthening the institutional arrangements that encourage their disappearance.
5. War is a global problem requiring collective or multilateral, rather than national, efforts to control it.
6. Reforms must be inspired by a compassionate ethical concern for the welfare and security of all people, and this humanitarian motive requires the inclusion of morality in statecraft.
7. International society must reorganize itself in order to eliminate the institutions that make war likely, and states must reform their political systems so that democratic governance and civil liberties within states can protect human rights and help pacify relations among states (Kegley 2002, 4).

Many liberal idealistic thinkers did not accept these seven principles despite their relative interpretations. These thinkers admired with conviction the morality, optimism, and glorious universality with which the principles are enriched. The liberal political and theoretical tradition of international relations further reformed itself by advocating the belief that states can follow the biblical mandate to fight and disarm the aggressor in order to end war. This orientation, though ideological in nature, tends to place emphasis on fostering global cooperation via the use of international institutions, law, and disarmament. The ideas with which this project is characterized include but are not limited to:

1. The need to substitute attitudes that stressed the unity of humankind for those that stressed parochial national loyalties to independent sovereign states.
2. The importance of individuals – their essential dignity and fundamental equality throughout the course of history, and the corollary need to protect and promote human rights and civil liberties.
3. The use of the power of ideas through education to arouse world public opinion against warfare.
4. The promotion of free international trade in place of states' economic competition.
5. The replacement of secret diplomacy by a system of "open covenants, openly arrived at."
6. The termination of interlocking bilateral alliances and the power balances they sought to achieve (p. 35).

Neoliberalism is postmodern liberalism which describes the way international institutions and regimes try to promote global change, cooperation, peace, and prosperity by using collective reforms.

One of the ways of organizing theoretical inquiry about international relations in order to explain world politics apart from realism/neorealism and liberalism/neoliberalism is by using the constructivist paradigm. *Constructivism* is the conceptual and scholarly approach to inquiry which emphasizes the importance of agents, such as people and groups, "who construct shared meanings to define their identities, interests, and institutions" (p. 31). The construction of the meanings enables them to understand and influence or be influenced by the norms and values of international behavior. Since international complexity defies descriptive, explanatory, and predictive theories, people's understanding of global realities is relative because the realities are fickle. In other words, the validity and objectivity of principles depend on how they are continuously and deconstructively interpreted. Based on its French intellectual roots, the postmodern theory of deconstruction argues that world complexity makes its description impossible. The only way scholarship can be advanced in order to understand the intentions and motives of actors is through the deconstruction of their textual statements. Constructivism can be advanced with the use of a deconstructive paradigm.

## European Perceptions of Theoretical Reality

The previous subsection highlighted how transnational issues in the periphery can cause divisions in the triadic center that is the core of global alliance. This subsection demonstrates that the current and historic U.S.-Iraq crisis was not solely and directly responsible for the observed radical divisions in the triadic alliance but rather that the mismanagement of the center itself may be to blame. Within the triadic center, cultural and linguistic diversity may cause these regional and world powers to see the reality of the war differently. For instance, the U.S. is viewed domestically as a moral exemplar, an active crusader, and benevolent superpower (Matarese 2001). The problems which resonate with utopianism are imbedded in the leadership of the triadic center. In the light of this assertion, Participation rates in elections to the European Parliament ... are low and declining. Turnout has fallen from 66% in 1977 to 59% in 1994 – 20–40% below levels in national elections. This is a critical issue, and the authors insist, because low turnout confirms pervasive doubts that the European Union...is "democratically legitimate." Behind this lies the central question of this era in modern European History, namely, whether a transnational policy with a common discourse and shared institutions can form (Blondel, Sinnott, and Svensson 1998, 512), given the territorialization of politics and economics and significant antiunion forces that emanate from elements of the region's cultural and linguistic diversity (Anderson and Bort 2000).

If public attitudes are a barometric measure/yardsticks for sensitizing major issues such as European integration, international cooperation, and the current politics of globalization, then understanding the causes of low voter turnout is inherently nationalistic, regionalistic, and Eurocentric. Though European citizens view their political participation legitimately, the manner in which they interpret domestic versus foreign policies varies considerably. For instance many people abstain from participation partly due to institutional conditions such as "the legacy of compulsory voting, the timing of elections and the generally higher level of participation in proportional representation systems" (p. 512). In addition, low levels of information and knowledge, as they also are found in the U.S., tend to influence low voter turnout. Based on public opinion attitudes toward European integration, low voter turnout encourages political apathy except in Belgium, Greece, Italy, and Luxembourg, where voter turnout rates are high. Paradoxically, voter turnout rates are low in Britain, the Netherlands, and Portugal because most voters in these countries do not support European integration. Suggestions to increase turnout include holding elections on Sunday, making registration simpler, and holding concurrent elections for the individual nations and the European parliament. The low voter turnout rates are also influenced by polyethnicity or the "new demographic form of Medievalism" (Koslowski 2000). The new pan-European culture concerned with pensions, job security, health care, regulations of labor relations, exclusionary immigration policies and the new right cannot find a unified voice in foreign policy (*Michigan Today* 2002). Demographic shifts that are influenced by migrant populations from Asia, the Middle East, and Africa tend to determine how people's attitudes in participation rates toward domestic and foreign policy issues of individual nation states and the E.U. in general should be. In recent times, these epistemic communities have become a force to reckon with. The Middle East population alone has 20 million Muslims in Europe. In this endeavor,

> Recent demographic changes have heralded a shift back to polyethnicity and have thus created a 'mismatch' between resident populations and political insti-

> tutions....The presence of durable immigrant-origin communities, the emergence of an neur labor mobility regime, the negative effects of unilateral national actions, the domestically driven proliferation of individual rights and their acquisition by noncitizens...most notable in the spread of dual nationality... the challenges to nation-state sovereignty in Europe have been relentless. They have also tended to act at cross-purposes, as migration has stirred up a titanic clash among democracy, citizenship, based on bloodline (jus sanguinis), and federalism (Koslowski 2000, 33-134).

Evidently, European polyethnicity, which has been exacerbated by push-pull factors, tends to make European voters react toward political participation, regionalism, and the international system in newly reconfigured ways. Some of the ways include, but are not limited to, how they react to domestic and foreign policy issues. These polycentric voters display less support concerning how the E.U. handles trade policy, monetary policy, constitutional adjudication, human rights, and environmental policies and peacekeeping, especially in the Middle East (Blondel, Sinnott, and Svensson 1998). However, domestic issues for the nation-states tend to be received well as public opinion and the policy debates show. Issues such as social welfare provisions, public procurement, small business regulation, cultural policy, education and immigration issues are major domestic political concerns for Europeans. Overall, voters are more apathetic to federation-related issues that are of a regional nature than those of the individual nation states. Since public attitudes concerning U.S. conflict with Iraq are federal, regional and global foreign policy issues rather than domestic concerns, European voter turnout on these issues is extremely unpopular as recent polling trends have shown. The percentages of those who opposed the U.S. potential for war with Iraq were 84% in France, 81% in Germany, and 74-80% in Britain. France, Germany, Belgium, Russia and China were opposed to a U.S. attack on Iraq because they saw that the linkage between Osama bin Laden and Iraq's Saddam Hussein was irreconcilable and contradictory. Still, there is no clear evidence linking the two tyrants whatsoever. Only 28% of Americans polled in March 2003 supported the U.S.'s unilateral action against Iraq, while 62-67% of the citizens favored a multilateral American engagement. In spite of such obvious antiwar sentiments, the U.S. opted for a unilateral and preemptive action.

A majority of the members of the U.N. and the Security Council favored Iraq's position while rejecting an American unilateral attack. In other words, 11 out of 15 members of the Security Council members, 3 out of 5 permanent members of the Security Council, 51 members of the African nations, and all Arab nations except Qatar, Kuwait, and Bahrain were opposed to an American attack. The three oil-rich nations allowed American military arsenals to be stationed on their soil in preparation for the incalculable consequences of the March 19, 2003, Armageddon which partially led to the defeat of Hussein. The policy of linking Osama bin Laden with Saddam was used by Americans to attack Iraq. British Prime Minister Tony Blair, who is the strongest supporter of President Bush, experienced a revolt in his coalition government because 122 legislators in his party joined the conservative party to vote down a motion supporting the war. His foreign minister, Mr. Cook, resigned on those grounds. Even Schroder, the Chancellor of Germany, was re-elected with the help of former East Germans and the U.S. threat to attack Iraq. Table 1 illustrates the four major theories of international diplomacy of which the neo-realist paradigm has become dominant in this conflict.

Table III.1. The Quest for Theory: Four Major Perspectives

| *Feature Realism* | | *Neorealism* | *Liberalism* | *Neo-liberalism* | *Constructivism* |
|---|---|---|---|---|---|
| Key Units | Independent states | The international systems structure | Institutions transcending states | Individuals, "penetrated" states and nonstate transnational actors | Social groups, their socially constructed images of international conditions |
| Core Concern | War and security | Struggle for position and power under anarchy | Institutionalizing peace | Fostering interstate cooperation on the globe's shared economic, social, and ecological problems | Social collectivities shared meanings and images of contemporary international life; the theoretical implication of these visions |
| Major Approach | Balance of Power | Balance of terror; military preparedness and deterrence | International law; international organization; democratization | Complex interdependence and regimes | Advocacy of normative innovation through construction of new images; tracing assumptions within various theoretical traditions; discovering how and why they color mental maps of world affairs |
| Outlook on Global Prospects | Pessimistic/ stability | Pessimistic | Optimistic/ progress | Expectation of cooperation and creation of a global community | Neither optimist nor pessimistic; depending on the most popular or socially accepted visions about the potential for humanity to engineer changes that either improve or harm future global conditions |
| Motives of Actors | National interests; zero-sum competition; security; power | Power, prestige, and advantage (relative gains) over other states | Collaboration; mutual aid; meeting human needs | Global interests (absolute gains); justice; peace and prosperity; liberty; morality | Contingent upon the socially constructed explanations about the basic drives of international actors, in various epochs |
| Central Concepts | Structural anarchy; power; national interests; balance of power; polarity | Structural anarchy; rational choice; arms races | Collective security world order; law; integration; international organization | Transnational relations; law; free markets; interdependence; integration; liberal republican rule; human rights; gender | Ideas; identities; ideals; images; all as socially constructed by various groups |

| | | | | | |
|---|---|---|---|---|---|
| Prescriptions | Increase national power; resist reduction of national autonomy | Preserve nuclear deterrence; avoid disarmament and supernational organizations | Institutional reform | Develop regimes and promote democracy and international institutions to coordinate collective responses to global problems | Broader understanding of the ways international actors construct their images of international relations to clarify the limitations of rival theoretical interpretations and the policies on which they are based |

*Source:* Kegley, C.W. 2002. *World politics: Trends and transformation.* Manuscript 50-51.

## THE CHALLENGES TO INTERNATIONAL DIPLOMACY

Since 9/11/ 2001, a flurry of intense diplomatic activity has been carried out by high-level international political executives, bureaucratic statesmen, diplomatic experts and specialized U.N. agencies. That activity has been carried out largely in the three regions of the triadic center including the U.N., Middle East, South Korea, China, Russia, and the Indian sub-continent. Diplomatic flights across the Atlantic, Indian, and Pacific oceans sensitized the global community about the need for dialogue, détente, solutions and peaceful coexistence between Palestinians and Israelis, for the continuation of Indo-Pakistan historical rapprochement, for the struggle to disarm Iraq peacefully or by force for its probable possession of biological, chemical, radiological, and "nuclear weapons" with which she threatened the interests of neighbors, including those of the United States, and for the purpose of influencing Russia, China, Japan and South Korea to collectively persuade North Korea to disarm through peaceful denuclearization of its two ballistic and plutonium-enriched missiles, which, if war breaks out, would reach its enemy territory.

Though the U.S. president continued to influence the heads of states to support America by cooperating to disarm or fight the "axis of evil" (Iraq, Iran, and North Korea) in order to eliminate their belligerent behavior, most of the communication was analyzed by experts, structured by bureaucrats, and formally delivered by or through normal diplomatic channels - the office of the Secretary of State. That is why Colin Powell has become the roving ambassador who constantly and effectively shuttled U.S. "ping-pong" diplomacy. Powell's diplomatic trips to South Korea, Japan, Russia, and China were aimed at influencing them individually and collectively to persuade North Korea to de-escalate the potential to use its ballistic missiles against the U.S. or Japan or South Korea. Initially, Powell's diplomatic initiative, which was a U.S. initiative, did not materialize in the light of the U.S. objectives. Instead, these nations asked Powell to inform Washington to iron out its differences with Pyongyang. China emphasized that the U.S. should negotiate a peaceful settlement with North Korea on a nation-to-nation equality basis. President Bush, who provoked the North Koreans by nullifying President Clinton's treaty of appeasement which was an effective diplomatic strategy, found it difficult to face a formidable opponent (Kim

Jong) whom he cautiously tried to negotiate a deal with. The latest U.S./N.K. meeting in China has demonstrated that Kim Jong does not blink, although he has encouraged all the six countries to pursue peaceful dialogue.

The U.S.'s belligerent rhetoric, President Bush's coercive diplomacy toward the Middle East, his unilateralist foreign policy, and his rejection of the creation of the European Court of Justice have been interpreted negatively by Europeans, particularly the Germans. His nullification of Kyoto complicates the issues further. The ideas have produced a policy that has become a hindrance to alliance and world support of the U.S. position in the Middle East and North Korea. This policy has caused divisions in the Korean Peninsula, in Asia, in Britain, in NATO, in the Security Council, in the United Nations, in America, and in the world.

Why was President Bush II's foreign policy be a source of world disunity rather than unity in the global age? The problem of American foreign policy during the Bush administration was rooted in inability to cognitively digest, connect and holistically integrate complex ideas rapidly and arrive at acceptable resolutions.

*Cognition* is intellectual capability to demonstrate prudent awareness, decisiveness, rational thought, and objectivity. Absence of cognitive and decisive intellectual capability at the highest level of statesmanship weakens the machinery for digesting voluminous information emanating from complex and contradictory foreign and domestic policy spheres of the American empire. Such doubts compel the regime to delegate decision making to a competent but divisively "belligerent" foreign policy team of four (Vice President Cheney, Secretary Powell, National Security Advisor Condy Rice and Secretary of Defense Don Rumsfeld). In this division, Powell is the "lone ranger" behind the United Nations. The source of belligerency is influenced by the President's enforcement of the unilateralist policy on the global agenda. Unilateralism is a form of myopic vision which causes isolationism and alienates U.S. from the rest of the world, especially the United Nations and NATO both of which America created to become its successful twentieth century foreign policy instruments.

Apparently President Bush used military power to attack Iraq on the Ides of March. After Saddam Hussein was deposed, American occupation with General Garner's and Paul Bremer's leadership instituted a Marshal-like plan for the reconstruction of the Middle East; Garner and Paul Bremer would not only dictate the terms of the new democratic constitutions of the "conquered and liberated" territories, but the conquest will expand the globalization project, confine Chinese global ambitions within East Asia, use the containment strategy to strengthen the empire and together, with cooperative allies, reap the fruits of the struggle – oil and gas, from Central and Southwestern Asia. As the Old World Order vanished with the evolution of the New one, so have the roles, norms, expectations, and practices of diplomacy and challenges to international relations. Perhaps it is time for the world to produce a new cadre of leaders who will be challenged to manage the world with a sense of progressive optimism rather than with the pessimism of neorealist and neoReaganite extremism.

## CONCLUSION AND DISCUSSION

The processes of understanding the U.S.'s role in world affairs are a complex interplay of forces such as the regionalized styles of diplomacy, theories of international relations and world politics, and the functional and structural but belligerent role played by the national bureaucratic elite, particularly those who dominate the foreign policy decision-making in the United States government. In other words, understanding the U.S. role in the world requires thorough knowledge of American foreign policy, how the foreign policy is constructed, historical and cultural texture that informs it, the ideologically oriented political and economic culture that animates it, the political texture that sustains it, and the legal ideas and interests that are inherent dynamics that drive it. Some of the agencies which, collectively, are instrumental to being the eventual variants in the construction of American foreign policy include, but are not limited to, leading scholars and experts from government, think tanks, interest groups, international organizations, non-profit organizations, the media, and foreign embassies. The main institutions that shape the U.S. foreign policy, however, are the President, U.S. Department of State, Department of Commerce, foreign embassies, the World Bank, International Monetary Fund, think tanks, and media outlets and interest groups. The driving dynamics of American foreign policy agenda are the ones that frame and shape it for application and its ipso facto consequences. At one point in time, whatever group or person(s) dominate such policy construction tend to surprise others, including the whole world if the policy fails. The rest of this conclusive discussion will paraphrase Sam Makinda's keen observations (aobie@mercury.oktax.state.ok.us).

There have been claims and counter-claims about the legality of the American-led war against Iraq. The United States, Britain, and Australian governments claimed they were on strong legal grounds, but their critics believe they are occupation powers trampling on international law. U.S. President George Bush, British Prime Minister Tony Blair, and Australian Prime Minister John Howard have told their citizens that this war was "legal" on the basis of 17 U.N. Security Council resolutions passed between 1990 and 2002. They cited three U.N. Security Council resolutions to support their claims, namely 678 of 29 October 1990, 687 of 3 April 1991, and 1441 of 8 November 2002. However, critics argue that the war was illegal and that none of the three resolutions could be invoked to support it. Only Resolution 678 of 29 October 1990 authorized force against Iraq to evict its troops from Kuwait, but it stated specifically that this was to be done only if Iraq had not left Kuwait by 15 January 1991. This resolution could not be invoked in any way because Iraqi forces were expelled from Kuwait in early 1991.

Resolution 678 was overridden by the cease-fire contained in Resolution 687 of 3 April 1991. It is this resolution that demanded the disarmament of Iraq. The U.S., Britain and Australia claimed that by failing to comply fully with Resolution 687, Iraq had violated the terms of the cease-fire and that the countries that expelled it from Kuwait in 1991 were free to use force against it. This would have not been the case if Resolution 687 had stated so. However, the resolution stated that a formal cease-fire would be effective once Iraq had notified the U.N. Secretary-General and the Security Council of its acceptance of the terms of the resolution. Moreover, Resolution 687 stated that any non-compliance by Iraq would have to be reported to the Council and that it was the Security Council that would "take such further steps as may be required for the implementation" of the resolution and "to secure peace and security in the region." With such terms, Resolution 687 could not be invoked to go to war with Iraq. This led to the third resolution that Washington, London, and Canberra had used as their legal basis for waging war, namely Resolution 1441 of November 2002. Resolution 1441 was detailed and gave Iraq one final chance to disarm. It also warned of severe consequences should Iraq fail to cooperate and comply fully and immediately with the terms of the resolution. Whether Iraq had cooperated and complied fully with the resolution is a matter of debate. The U.S. and Britain argued that it had not, but other members of the Security Council believed that there had been sufficient cooperation. Whatever the differing interpretations of Iraq's behavior, Resolution 1441 did not give any country authority to wage war outside the U.N. framework. Resolution 1441 said that the Security Council would "convene immediately upon receipt of a report" on weapons inspections "in order to consider the situation and the need for full compliance with all of the relevant Council resolutions in order to secure international peace and security." In the debate on resolution 1441, British ambassador to the U.N. Sir Jeremy Greenstock said, "We heard loud and clear during the negotiations the concerns about automaticity and hidden triggers" (Makinda 2003).

As co-sponsor of the resolution with the U.S., Greenstock said: "There is no automaticity in this resolution. If there is further Iraqi breach of its disarmament obligations, the matter will return to the Council for discussion as required." Given the terms of resolutions 678, 687 and 1441, the war against Iraq had no legal basis. The point is that the U.S., Britain, and Australia are occupation powers, and their position in Iraq is similar to that of Israeli in Gaza and the West Bank. In other words, Anglo-American political, military and commercial interests rather than the legal principles of the U.N. were instrumental to the current crisis which was caused by a preemptive strike. Iraq's decision to favor the Euro rather than the dollar (Sino and Ndichu 2003) for its oil for food programs made the U.S. ignore the principles and values of international morality and law and opt for the "law of the jungle." By going this route, the Anglo-American world has not only contributed to the diminution of global boundaries for sustainable development, but the globalization project has more firmly reinforced and fortified an avalanche of geo-political and racial boundaries. The U.S. and its allies will win the war but lose the peace largely due to the fact that the new Iraq leadership will emerge from the same security structure as Saddam Hussein's. If that happens, as it normally does in the Middle East, the unfortunate misperceptions would have been enlightened by the reality of war.

The illegality of the war has dealt a severe blow and deepened new cleavages in the trans-Atlantic alliance and East-West geostrategic road map. The Germans, French, and Russians who had heavily invested in Iraq felt that their own partners in the Alliance were intentionally, illegally, and unusually fighting against them. They totally abstained from fighting with the U.S. Had Iraq been a white nation, this war would have become the Third World War, whose nuclear winter would have created mushroom clouds around the globe. Such should not be allowed to happen.

Even now, nobody knows how it will end. However, further consequences of this war appear to be evolving in terms of the division and gradual destruction of NATO as a major instrument of Western Security, trans-Atlantic alliance, and Western civilization. Further still, the war undermined the legitimacy of the U.N. and its charter. The theoretical sources of European dissension with American-led action against Iraq are rooted in European moral jurisprudence and legal supranationalism. Morally, European leaders, including the papacy (Holy See), condemned the war action for its injustice. Legally, the European Court of Justice (ECJ), in constituting the European Community (EC), innovatively created a transnational and federated system that has internationally become the constitutional court for Europe that has power to "practice the judicial review of European law and national law" (Alter 2001, 225). This European legal system is international rule of law in Europe because it is transnationally supranational. This law, which is international, was interpretively empowered by the Treaty of Rome (1992) i.e., European-level law that bases finality for democratic accountability on the process of negotiation. Conclusively negotiated conflicts or settlements are universally multilateral as opposed to unilateral actions. Parenthetically, such were the political, moral, and legal imperatives that influenced European opposition to American Unilateralism over Iraq.

## References


Abernethly, D.B. 2001. *The dynamics of global dominance: European overseas empires 1415-1980.* New Haven, CT: Yale University Press.

Acharya, A. 2001. *Constructing a security community in southeast Asia: ASEAN and the problem regional order.* New York: Routledge.

Alter, K.J. 2001. *Establishing the supremacy of European law: The making of international rule of law in Europe.* Oxford: Oxford University Press.

Anderson, M. and Bort, E. 2000. *The frontiers of the European Union.* New York: Palgrave.

Appadurai, A. 1999. Globalization and the research imagination. *International Social Science Journal*: 229-38.

Bailey, J. and R. Godson. eds. 2000. Pittsburgh: University of Pittsburgh Press.

Barnett, M.N. 1997. Bringing in the new world order: Liberalism, legitimacy, and the United Nations. World Politics, 49: 526-51.

Betts, R.K. 1997. Should strategic studies survive? *World Politics* 50: 7-33.

Blonondel, J.; R. Sinnott, and P. Svensson. 1998. People and parliament in the European Union: Parliament, democracy, legitimacy. Oxford: Clarendon.

Boer-Ashworth, E. 2000. *The global political economy and post 1989 change: The place of the central European transition.* New York: St. Martin's Press.

Braunschwig, G. V. 1992. Order into chaos? How scientific knowledge shapes our world view. *Universities: An Interdisciplinary Journal for the Social Sciences and Humanities* 34.

Chernoff, F. 1996. *After bipolarity: The vanishing threat, theories of cooperation, and the future of the Atlantic Alliance.* Ann Arbor: University of Michigan Press.

Clark, A.M. 2001. *Diplomacy of conscience: Amnesty International and changing human rights norms.* Princeton, NJ: Princeton University Press.

Cohen, B.J. 1998. *The geography of money.* Ithaca, NY: Cornell University Press.

Duffield, J.S. 1995. *Power rules: The evolution of NATO's conventional force posture.* Stanford: Stanford University Press.

Dunn, K.C., and T.M. Show 2001. *Africa's challenges to international relations theory.*

Eisendrath, C., M.A. Goddman, and G.E. Marsh .2001. *The phantom defense: America's pursuit of the star wars illusion.* Westport, CT: Praeger.

Eribo, F. 2001. *In search of greatness: Russia's communication with Africa and the world.* Westport, CT: Abex.

Esman, M.J. and S. Telhami. 1995. *International organizations and ethnic conflict.* Ithaca. Cornell University Press.

Franke, M.F.N. 2001. *Global limits: Immanuel Kant; international relations and a critique of world politics.* Albany: State University of New York Press.

Garver, J.W. 2001. *Protracted contest: Sino-Indian rivalry in the twentieth century.* Seattle: University of Washington Press.

Ghanem, A. 2001. *The Palestinian-Arab minority in Israel, 1948-2000 A political study.* Albany: State University of Washington Press.

Ginsberg, R.H. 2001. *The European Union in International Politics: Politics by Fire.* Lanham, MD: Rowman and Littlefield.

Grant, R.W. 1997. *Hypocrisy and integrity: Machiavelli, Rousseau, and the ethics of politics.* Chicago: University of Chicago Press.

Handberg, R. (2001). *Ballistic Missile Defense and the Future of American Security: Agendas, Perceptions, Technology, and Policy.* New York: Praeger.

Howard, R.D., and R.L. Sawyer .2003. *Terrorism and Counterterrorism: Understanding the New Security Environment.* New York: The McGraw-Hill Companies.

Ikenberry, G.J. 2000. *After victory: Institutions, strategic restraint, and the rebuilding of order after major wars.* Princeton, NJ: Princeton University Press.

Jackson, R. 2000. *The global covenant: Human conduct in a world of states.* Oxford: Oxford University Press.

Kaelberer, M. 2001. *Money and power in Europe: The political economy of European monetary cooperation.* Albany: State University of New York Press.

Kappen, T. R. 1995. *Cooperation among democracies:* The European Influence on U.S. Foreign Policy. Princeton: Princeton University Press.

Kaufman, S.J. 2001. *Modern hatreds: The symbolic politics of ethnic war.* Ithaca, N.Y.: Cornell University Press.

Kegley, C.W. 2002. *World politics: Trends and transformation.* Manuscript.

Kegley, C.W. Jr., and G.A. Raymond. 2002. *From war to peace: Fateful decisions in international politics.* Boston: St. Martins Press.

Kegley, C.W., and E.R. Wittkopf. 2003. *World politics: Trends and transformation.* Thomson Wadsworth.

Kim, S. and E. Shin. 2002. A longitudinal analysis of globalization and regionalization in international trade: A social network approach. *Social Forces* 81, 21: 445-68.

Kolodziej, E.A., and R.R. Kanet. 1996. *Coping with conflict after the cold war.* Baltimore, MD: Johns Hopkins University Press.

Koslowski, R. 2000. *Migrants and citizens: Demographic change in the European state system.* Ithaca, NY: Cornell University Press.

Lake, A., and D. Ochmanek. eds. 2001. *The real and the honor of Richard H. Ullman.* Lanham, MD: Rowman and Littlefield.

Lang, A.F. 2001. *Agency and ethics: The politics of military intervention.* Albany: State University of New York Press.

Lubbe, H. 1992. European unification is irreversible: Adelbert Reif in conversation with Herman Lubbe. *Universities: An Interdisciplinary Journal for the Social Science and Humanities 34.*

Makinda, S. 2003. *Comment: Gulf attack has no legal backing.* aobie@mercury.oktax.state.ok.us.

Martin, P., and M.R. Bramley. eds. 2001. *Alliance politics, Kosovo, and NATO's war: Allied force or forced allies.* New York: Palgrave.

Matarese, S.M. 2001. *Foreign policy and the utopian imagination.* Amherst: University of Massachusetts Press.

McLean, I. 1996. *The Concise Oxford Dictionary of Politics.* Oxford, UK: Oxford University Press.

McMahon, R.J. 2001. The cultures of empire. *Journal of American History* 88, 3: 888-92.

*Michigan Today.* 2002. 34, 3: 1-24.

Mlyn, E. 1995. *The state, society and limited nuclear war.* Albany: State University of New York Press.

*New Webster's Dictionary and Thesaurus of the English Language.* 1992. Danbury, CT: Lexicon Publications, Inc.

Nincic, M., and J. Lepgold. 2000. *Being useful: Policy relevancy and international relations theory.* Ann Arbor: University of Michigan Press.

Palmer, M. 2002. *The politics of the Middle East.* Itasca, IL: F.E. Peacock Publishers, Inc.

Patterson, T. E. 2002. *We the people: A concise introduction to American politics.* New York: McGraw-Hill Companies.

Petit, P., and L. Soete. 1999. Globalization in search of a future. *International Social Science Journal* 165-81.

Richardson, J. 1996). ed. *European Union: Power and policy-making.* New York: Routledge.

Rodman, K.A. 2001. *Sanctions beyond borders: Multinational corporations and U.S. economic statecraft.* Lanham, MD: Rowman and Littlefield Publishers.

Sagini, M.M. 2001. *Organizational behavior: The challenges of the new millennium.* Lanham, MD: University Press of America, Inc.

Sino, O. and Ndichu, L. 2003. *Kenyan MPs blast Bush, Blair.*

Skalnes, L.S. 2000. *Politics, markets, and grand strategy: Foreign economic policies as strategic instruments.* Ann Arbor: University of Michigan Press.

Steinbruner, J.D. 2002. *Principles of global security.* Washington, DC: Brookings Institute Press.

Stoessinger, J.G. 1990. *Why nations go to war.* New York: St. Martin's Press.
Thomas, D.C. 2001. *The Helsinki effect: International norms, human rights, and the demise of communism.* Princeton, NJ: Princeton University Press.
Thomas, K.P. 2000. *Competing for capital: Europe and North America in a global era.* Washington, DC: Georgetown University Press.
Thompson, G. 1999. Introduction: Situating globalization. *International Social Science Journal* 139-152.
Tickner, J.A. 2001. *Gendering world politics: Issues and approaches in the post-cold war era.* New York: Columbia University Press.
Valaskakis, K. 1999. Globalization as theatre. *International Social Science Journal* 153-64.
Wallace, H., and W. Wallace. 1996. eds. *Policy-making in the European Union.* New York: Oxford University Press.
Weber, K. 2000. *Hierarchy amidst anarchy: Transaction costs and institutional choice.* Albany: State University of New York Press.
White, J.W. 1998. Book reviews. *The Journal of Politics* 60, 4: 1202-73.
Wirtz, J.J., and J.A. Larsen. 2001. *Rocket's red glare: Missile defenses and the future of world politics.* Boulder, CO: Westview.
Woods, T.P. 2002. *American Studies* 43, 1: 127-53.
__________. 2002. Globalizing social violence: Race, gender, and the spatial politics of crisis. *American Studies* 43, 1: 127-53.

# Chapter IV
# Iraq: Reconstruction and Regional Geopolitics

Iraq is ancient *Mesopotamia*, a civilization that grew on confluence of the Tigris and Euphrates Rivers. The Sumerians of 2900 – 2500 BC, Akkadians of 2530 – 2159 BC, and Babylonians of 1894 – 1594 BC have all been the ancient imperial evolutionary roots of contemporary Iraq society. During his lifetime, Saddam was, and just as many Iraqis are proud of their ancient civilization from which modern Western society has inherited its philosophical, artistic and scientific values. With the emergence of Mohamedanism in sixth and seventh centuries, Arabs conquered Mesopotamia and Islamized Iraq in 633 AD. In successive imperial Administrations, such as those of the ancient Syro-Egyptian, Persian, the Abbasid, Umayad, Ottoman, British, Russian, and lately American influences have all historically shaped Iraq to be what it is today (Palmer 2002). More importantly, President Bush's unclear linkage of Bin Laden with Saddam Hussein in international terrorism and the failure of diplomacy to distinguish the motives of the two men contributed to the spring 2003 U.S.-Iraq war which lasted for 7.5 years.

Guided by neoReaganite and protestant Republican ideology, and reinforced by propagandistic and geostrategic ideologies and agitators in the pentagon, the United States used the doctrine of preemptive unilateralism and conventional strategic forces to remove Saddam Hussein from power. By using a faulty legal framework, the Bush administration painfully used the U.S. military for Iraq disarmament, regime change, and reconstruction. Immediately after the attack and removal of Saddam's Pan-Arabist Baath Party from power, the European Union, Russia, China, and the United Nations reaffirmed their opposition to this unilateral action by the U.S. The United States overlooked the Security Council's proper procedures and the U.N. Charter – the only legal, political and universal diplomatic document for international law, international security, and regime stability of the member states (Sagini 2004).

## LEGAL FRAMEWORK FOR WAR AND OCCUPATION

The Bush administration justified military action against Iraq because of its internal repression of its people, particularly the northern Kurds and the southern Shiites. In addition, Iraq's military arsenal made it an aggressive state that threatened the security of its neighbors, such as Israel and Saudi Arabia – the oil capital of the world. With the pressure used as a result of faulty intelligence concerning Iraq's possession of WMD, the decision to go to war was formulated as a disarmament strategy. Unfortunately, this preemptive, and unilateral action lacked the mandate of the world community and viable strategic thinking about post-conflict reconstruction.

Further still, on May 22, 2003, the U.N. Security Council adopted the renewable Resolution 1483 which gave the United States interim power to govern Iraq indefinitely. The resolution empowered the U.S. to control the collection and disbursement of Iraq oil revenue and share it with the coalition partners with whom the U.S. had entered the conflict in a unified command. Through resolution 1483, UNSC ruling made the United States an occupying power. The resolution also gave the U.S. and its partners' power to create a Development Fund for Iraq held by the Central Bank of Iraq that received oil revenue for Iraq reconstruction. The funds were allocated at the discretion of the Bank's authority in consultation with Paul Bremer (the U.S. Chief Administrator in Iraq) who was the facilitator for the creation of a transitional government and general reconstruction of the country. The fact that pro-Saddam royalists and other terrorist groups had attacked the U.N. agencies, facilities, diplomats, and U.S. forces indicated what was interpretively self-explanatory in terms of what was anticipated.

## FUNCTIONAL OBLIGATIONS OF COALITION FORCES – OCCUPIERS

The reconstructive role of the U.S. and the coalition forces was to "respect the human rights of the local population" and treat the population as "protected persons" pursuing the "right of self determination" (*Open Society Institute and the United Nations Foundation* 2003, 6). It must "ensure public order and safety" by recognizing the "laws in force in the country" (p. 6). It must "ensure and maintain public health and hygiene" (p. 6) of the occupied territory. It must "provide food and medical supplies" of the population (p. 6). It must "protect property and resources" (p. 6) including public buildings, real estate, forest and agricultural estates and the capital of the property in question. It must permit the facilitation of humanitarian and relief operations. It was to "refrain from making changes to the institutions of the government of the occupied territory that deprived the population of their rights" (p. 6). It was not going to "change penal laws" nor was it going to "selectively transfer or deport" persons (p. 6). The obligations were reconstruction measures which did not interfere with customary, traditional and religious laws practiced as Islamic law.

## U.S. PLANS FOR RECONSTRUCTION

After the initial victory over Iraq (April nineteenth, 2003), Lieutenant General Jay Garner, a retiree, was appointed by President Bush to become the Chief Administrator of the reconstruction process. His lack of public administration experience and his inability to formulate public policy and implement it quickly portrayed him as an ignorant, insensitive, and uncaring person. Within less than a month, he was replaced by Paul Bremer III, a career diplomat. Absence of a reconstruction strategy prior to the war against Iraq made the reconstruction process extremely difficult. This shift in leadership moved power from the military to the civilian control though the command line for reconstruction was controlled by the department of defense. As we witnessed, Bremer's role, that of the office of Reconstruction and Humanitarian Assistance had created tensions between the "Executive branch, the Department of Defense and the State Department. This triangular struggle for the dominance of policy formulation machinery can be described as follows:

> The National Security Council (NSC) which is part of the Executive Office of the President coordinates advice on foreign and military issues. Chaired by the President, the NSC includes the vice President and the secretaries of the state and defense as full members and the director of CIA and the Chair of the Joint Chiefs of Staff as advisory members. Since the State Department, the Department of Defense, and the CIA often have conflicting and self centered views of national security, the NSC acts to keep the president informed by providing a more comprehensive perspective. The NSC's staff of experts is directed by the president's national security advisor (Condoleezza Rice) She and her office in the White House had access to defense, diplomatic and intelligence sources that enabled her to become an important formulator of American foreign policy (Patterson 2004, 547-548).

While the State and Defense departmental chiefs are involved in a variety of complex, internal and external issues, the NSC tries to logistically coordinate and orchestrate them for presidential action. As commander-in-chief of the U.S. Armed forces, the President receives military advice from the Joint Chiefs of Staff (ICS) Chair and Vice Chair and a member from each of the uniformed services (Army, Navy, Air Force and Marine Corps).

Traditionally, post-conflict reconstruction was carried out by the United Nations system rather than by the military wing of the U.S. federal government. This departure from pre-reconstruction tradition may have intensified the cleavage between the United States and the International system whose reconstruction role had become peripheral rather than central. The 1483 Resolution limited the role of U.N. except in humanitarian matters and independent special representation to the secretary General. Also, the International Monetary Fund, the World Bank and the Non Governmental Organizations (NGOs) had more power than the U.N. in the reconstruction of Iraq (*Open Society Institute and United Nations Foundation,* 2003).

## Plans for Leadership in Iraq: Ethnic, Religious and Political Diversity

Iraq has 26 million people that are ethnically, religiously, and politically diverse. Of these 26 million, 97% are Muslims while 3% are Christians, Jews and other religious minorities. Religiously, 65% of the people are Shiites that receive their inspiration from Iran while 32% of them are Sunni Muslims who had for 85 years dominated the economic, political, bureaucratic, social, military, intellectual and legal sectors of the Iraq society within the context of Saddam's Pan-Arabist Baath Party. Overall, ethnic Arabs (75%) of the population, particularly the Baath Party, dominated Iraq before the 2003 war. The northern Kurds form 15% of the population. Worldwide, 90% of Muslims are Sunnis while 10% are Shiites. In Iraq, 18 million are Arabs. The Shiites are farmers who are the largest religious group that want an Islamic rather than a democratic, and secular republic. Recent conflict between the Shiites and the U.S. and UK were largely articulated by the younger clerics who wanted an Islamic rather than a democratic and secular republican system of government. The Sunnis resist that aspect of Shiite thinking. The Sunnis live in the North and West of Baghdad named the Sunni triangle. Under Saddam Hussein, Iraq was a secular republic. Islamic, Democratic and Secular visions of the future of the Republic are competitively controversial.

## Political Groups

In 1990/91, Iraq annexed Kuwait and threatened to control the Gulf States and Israel. With the removal of Saddam's regime from power, a strategy that was realized after planning to remove him for 12 years of his regime's isolation from the world, (U.N. oil embargo) and the U.S. and U.K. containment of the regime, the deBaathification of Iraq was carried out as planned. After the passage of Iraq Liberation Act in 1998, the Defense and State departments were empowered with resources for training democratic opposition and other subversive elements in Iraq. Seven major groups were funded by the U.S. state department to create prodemocracy parties in Iraq. These new parties included but were not limited to:

1. Iraq National Congress – Founded in 1992 by Ahmad Chalabi.
2. Iraq National Accord – It was weak and based in Jordan and its leader is Iyad Allawi (a Shi Baathist).

3. Kurdistan Democratic Party – Severed ties with Iraq and is now supported by U.S. It was founded in 1946.
4. Patriotic Union of Kurdistan, was founded in 1969 – based in Iraq, it was reformed in 1994 and works with U.S.
5. Supreme Council for the Islamic Revolution in Iraq, is based in Tehran and was led by Mohamed Baqir al-Hakim.
6. Islamic Movement of Iraq Kurdistan, was a minority splinter group, and
7. Constitutional Monarchists – was based in London and influenced by Britain.

These newly forged democratic elements were externally controlled, opposed each other philosophically, and lacked a nationalist mechanism for policy coordination. This position undermined their nationalistic, cohesive and reconstructionist influence.

## GOVERNANCE: PRINCIPLES FOR BUILDING A DEMOCRATIC IRAQ

Through the influence of Paul Bremer (Chief U.S. Administrator), the Military's, wing of coalition forces, and the United Nations (whose role was largely humanitarian), 15,000-30,000 Iraq Baathists were to be excluded from major positions of influence in society. On April 15, near the city of Nasiriyah, the U.S. and 100 leading Iraqis established eleven principles which constitute the theoretical and philosophical foundation for a post Saddam and new democratic government in Iraq. They formulated a constitution which would be democratic, federal and devoid of communal identity. The constitution rather than the president, parliament or parties was to be supreme. The country's new national culture would value ethnic, racial, religious, gender, and political diversity. Iraqis had to choose their leaders through an electoral process of voting. Voting was conducted through the secret ballot. The people were asked to reject political violence by getting involved in the task of national reconstruction. Iraqis and the coalition forces worked jointly in order to restore the security of basic services of the country at large. DeBaathification was employed to eliminate and eradicate Husseinism from Iraq political vocabulary. All national political groups had an open discussion in searching for solutions to problems. It was interesting to wait and see whether, a society that is closed, fundamentally Islamic and essentially tribal could be united to accept these democratic and largely Western values that flourish in open societies rather than in the desert and Middle Eastern culture.

## ACTUAL RECONSTRUCTION

It was difficult to asses the reconstruction needs for a country that is as large as the state of California. The creation of a strong and an acceptable governance system, it was believed, would be instrumental to the future security, justice and socio-economic well-being of Iraq. The nation's needs were to be examined in the light of short-term, medium-term and long-term strategic continuum. In terms of security police, Paul Bremer (U.S.. Chief Administrator) in consultation with the Department of Defense, trained and hired more than 100,000 Iraqis who were charged with the responsibility for civil defense, border patrol, police, and intelligence services. Since the country had no defense army after the overthrowal of Saddam, 130,000 U.S. military and 30,000 coalition forces largely from U.K., Spain, Poland, Italy, and Australia supplemented the U.S. and Iraq forces. Some Saddam loyalist elements may have been recruited into the security forces in order to perpetuate their revolutionary and violent tendencies. This inability to undermine the former regime's rise to power could have made the reconstruction role more difficult if not impossible. This very issue may have contributed to the prevailing difficulty of choosing a coalition government.

Initially, it was expected to cost $56 billion to rebuild Iraq for the next four to five years. In 2003, only $33 billion was available for the reconstruction. Of these, $33 billion, the U.S. pledged to give $20 billion, Japan had pledged $5 billion, Saudi Arabia $1 billion, the European Union $1 billion, and the IMF, the World Bank and NGOs would give the rest. The $20 billion was to be used as follows: $6 billion for electricity, $3 billion for restoration of oil refineries and wells, $2.5 billion for sewage system reconstruction, $3.1 billion for water, telephone and housing, and $5 billion or $6 billion for police work. All this money was to be given as loans because Iraq oil revenue would largely be used to finance the reconstruction. In 2005/06 congress approved $87.5 billion of which, 65 billion was used to maintain the American military and coalition forces in Iraq as they carried out the reconstruction work indefinitely. About $1.5 billion was to be used in Afghanistan reconstruction. By 2009/2010, based on the direct and indirect cost of the war in the Middle East, the U.S. had spent about $3 trillion which significantly contributed to the 2007-2009 recession in both the U. S. and around the world.

## CHALLENGES OF THE RECONSTRUCTION

The humanitarian aspects of the Reconstruction was commissioned and directed by the defense related Office of Reconstruction and Humanitarian Assistance in Consultation with the peripheralized U.N. agencies. Also, 70% of Iraqis lived in urban areas. The centralized systems of water, e.g. boiling, purifying, adding chemicals etc., the waste disposal (systems) and food especially for children who had been malnourished for 20 years during Saddam's rule needed to be restored. Refugees and internally displaced persons were to be rehabilitated. Public health issues had to be dealt with professionally and strategically by competent people. Raw sewage may have entered the Euphrates and Tigris Rivers because treatment plants were dislocated during the war. The treatment plants were to be repaired for effective service. Some people needed social, physical and psychological rehabilitation in order to reduce or eliminate the post conflict and post traumatic stress disorders. Over 3500 U.S. organizations had been given contracts by the department of defense in order to enhance the reconstruction efforts. Because the Europeans, Russians and Asians had not been given the contracts, the reconstruction process remained to be largely a unilateral action by the United States.

One of the enigmatic elements in the reconstruction was the fact that the other super powers in the international system, i.e., (German, France, Russia and China) etc. did not only refuse to provide resources for reconstruction, but the refusal was associated with the feeling that Iraq may have been attacked illegally. If Bush went to war because Iraq had WMD e.g. (Sarin, Anthrax, VX, etc,) and other nuclear weapons, then there is legitimacy in what happened. But if Iraq did not have biological, chemical, nuclear and radiological weapons, as it turned out to be, then the U.S. had no case attacking a follow member of the international system. Since both WMD and nuclear weapons were not found by the U.N. agency for disarmament or by the coalition forces, then American intervention in Iraq held no water. The U.S. spent billions of dollars weakly to enhance the reconstruction efforts. Also, more than 26,300 Iraqis had died although Bin Laden was still at large. Also, seven years since the inception of the war, 4440 Americans had died and over 20,050 were wounded. The security system, reconstruction teams, U.N. and American officials became targets of assassination coordinated by Saddam Hussein and supported by all former Saddam loyalists and a variety of Middle Eastern terrorist groups particularly the radical Islamists. Evidently, it appeared that evidence for going to war was circumstantial. The case for the war was overstated. Post-conflict Iraq reaction was underestimated in terms of the search for U.S.'s way out. The intelligence community, the President, and NSC office may have "hyped" the intelligence. If the lives of Americans were risked for bad intelligence and incompetent institutional officials, everybody had the right to ask why that happened. And many people are still asking the NSC, CIA and DOD why evidence for going to war was lacking. All the people were required to give answers including those who were subpoenaed.

According to Peterson (2003), the American war situation in Iraq paralleled the U.S. Vietnam crisis of the 1960s or the Soviet-Afghanistan debacle of the 1980s. In either case, each superpower lost the guerilla wars into which they had been entrapped and from which they found it lamentably difficult to disentangle themselves. In both cases, it was easy to start the war but difficult to exit because the superpowers underestimated nationalistic and external elements of the conflict. They had fewer military men in divisions. They lacked genuine knowledge about local cultures, physical terrain, and the significance of strategic forces in such conflicts. In Vietnam Americans had one-tenth of the resources they needed to win the war. In Afghanistan, the Russians had between one- seventh and one- eighth of the resources they needed to suppress their client state. And surprisingly, the U.S. had one-third of the resources it needed to control the situation in Iraq and mould it the way it saw fit. We were not "welcomed with flowers," as pre-conflict official propaganda had alleged. We were welcomed with bullets, rockets, air-to-surface missiles, and motors. We were not used to urban and arid guerilla warfare. We had a long way to go. Only "56,000 of the 130,000 American troops were combat trained…in a nation of 24" (p. 1) million people. We are not used to the "hit-and-run bands of guerillas" (p. 1). Iraq resistance was underestimated. The resistance was formidable.

Like the Soviets, said Oliver Roy of the National Center for Scientific Research in Paris, who is also an expert in Islam, "Americans neglected one vital element: nationalism" (p. 1). However, in favor of the U.S. resistance essentially, was a major characteristic within the Sunni Triangle while for the Soviets, such resistance was "spontaneous and universal" (p. 2). In addition, a large number of Iraqis, particularly those who were oppressed by Saddam in the North and South of the country, were generally happy with the U.S. reconstruction. Despite these favorable overtures, winning Iraq was difficult and dangerous though Americans had enough time to get out and safe their faces.

The process of "deBaathified Iraqification" was being expedited before Iraqis had the chance for potential nationalistic and political cohesiveness. Guerilla intelligence units may have penetrated the new Iraq police force. The disbanded army of special forces, which was well trained, well armed, well fed, and which never fought against the U.S. strategic forces had "stockpiles of weapons all over the country" (p. 2). No wonder their sophisticated operations had been instrumental to high U.S. casualties since the end of the major combat. Drawing from Soviet experience in Afghanistan, and enigmatically so, the U.S. should not have placed too much emphasis on democracy instead of "good governance and rule of law" (p. 2). Worse still, the U.S. was "a perfect machine for waging war … rather than a good machine for imperial policing" (p. 2) because it lacks a culture for policing. Historically, since occupation powers have never been legitimately popular, their illegitimate control of territory became a pervasive pattern of successes which did not tangibly lead to strategic leaps and gains. The U.S. needed to be vigilant and make sure that its forces did not become captives of our own propaganda through the usage of masked versions of truth in the theatre to rationalize our own performance.

Notwithstanding the challenges of the reconstruction, the patriotic and nationalistic aspects of Iraq resistance needed to be counteracted with well trained corps, a professional bureaucracy, an educated and elected legislature, an independent judiciary, and a free press which took the principles of Islamic law into perspective. Joseph Nye of Harvard's Kennedy School of Government concluded that such minimalist perspective, particularly the neo-Jacksonian model of conducting "quick fixes and running out" did not contribute to social order (Etzioni 2003). Professor Nye was vindicated.

## IMPLICATIONS

If the motive for attacking Iraq was materialistic and geostrategic, rather than Iraq's possession of the WMD, then the nature of the resistance and the expanding training camps for strengthening all fundamentalist and Islamist elements, including the madrassas, may have created the predicted quagmire that reinforced, according to this author, the "Vietnam Syndrome." If the Iraq reconstruction had become a quagmire, then the security of Israel would have been jeopardized because the entire region could use Iraq as a base for challenging Islamist discontent against Israel, which is viewed as an anomaly in the region. Since American reasons for going to war in Iraq were delegitimized by the world community and the Arab world, it was expected that the U.S. Was going to have difficulty in securing security support in order to deal with other strong "rogue states" particularly Iran and the well armed North Korea, unless the U.S. engaged others multilaterally in future. In addition, President Bush and the U.S. in general could have difficulty to defend Taiwan against potential Chinese unilateralism. Even though, the President had given mixed messages about it. Consistent with American attitudes in regard to Iraq, American prewar unilateralism paralleled its post-conflict unilateralism in the reconstruction process. While that was a source of contention due to American monopolistic deals of the reconstruction process, this essential element of American hegemonic and imperialistic power was the single most factor that enabled the United States to satisfy its materialistic instincts for going to war at the detriment of its obligations to the U.N. charter and the independence, security, and territorial integrity of its member states. Finally, in this conflict, President Bush had been criticized by the Democrats, some Republicans, the European Union, and even the Middle Easterners for being simple-minded, unfairly and institutionally irresponsible, insensitive, psychologically neurotic, and managerially incompetent in terms of not being in charge particularly when dealing with NSC facts. In spite of these charges, some of which were legitimate, he had "stuck to his guns," remained strategically persistent and rigidly decisive. Such criticisms, persistence and rigidity could have created a momentum for his defeat in the 2004 presidential election that following year. Alternatively, because the domestic and foreign policy conditions improved in his favor, He was reelected at the detriment of Democratic fortunes.

Speeding up Iraq take over from the Governing Council was partially be viewed as a form of liberation. During that time, the Governing Council was viewed as a mafia because it was not representative of the country's diverse political, religious and ethnic realities. Perceptually, the Governing Council was selected with flaws and had no legitimacy. To legitimize the process of reconstruction, the political structure of Iraq needed to be expanded with an elected executive, independent judiciary and an elected legislative assembly. At the provincial level, the people should have elected representatives some of whom could have chosen to join the national legislature. However, in a country where there had never been a census since 1957, it was difficult to hold elections of this magnitude without knowing the right number of people who lived in the country and what major issues were at stake and likely to become the focus of local and national elections. Second, perpetually, there was a lot of corruption within the Governing Council itself. This made many Iraqis to be further resentful of the American occupation. Although local governments had flourished everywhere in Iraq, these parochial institutions were afraid of the "tyranny" of the Governing Council and the implications of that kind of behavior on the national consititution and the potential electorate.

On the contrary, giving more power to Iraqis could have increased resistance against American occupation because this action would have reinforced the country's lack of democratic experience. By its very nature, and in the context of the desert mind, democracy is associated with western imperialism, colonialism and Hegemony reflective of early twentieth century Imperial policy of divide and rule practiced by the British. In this reconstruction process, the U.S. used democratic rhetoric as a stick rather than as a genuine attempt to introduce a system that would make a difference in Iraq's political life and future.

The reconstruction was conducted rapidly particularly in the areas of intensive social and economic infrastructure. It was hoped that the reconstruction would restore intellectual, economic and political life for the Iraqi people. Systematic deBaathification of Husseinism was enforced considerably. The security system was put in place to counteract the confusion and potential for further conflict emanating from the internally repressed and displaced people of Iraq or the externally related fundamentalist elements. Although extreme elements of violent militias and external terrorists had emerged, they were dealt with systematically and accordingly. In spite of the fact that the Bush administration had underestimated the power of conservative religious groups, groups which had been emboldened because they were nationalistic, ideologically revolutionary and in some ways Islamist, their traditionally and religiously prescribed dynastic and autocratic rule was analyzed, understood, and creatively managed in the context of prevailing conditions in order to control, coordinate and effectively communicate the reconstruction process in the midst of chaos.

Third, Mr. Paul Bremer and his implementation team became conversant with the idea that Islamic political theory relies on consultation, consensus, and the rule of law. Such knowledge which constitutionalists and Arab nationalists understand became the basis for the formulation of the constitution and introduction of democratic rule in the Middle East particularly in Iraq. Such a strategy was consistent with the introduction of a secular political Republic which could undermine the intolerance of extreme religious and revolutionary sectarian elements within the Iraq society.

Fourth, the system the U.S. created in Iraq was to be capable of being reinterpreted, in the face of Islamic doctrine, as a fair and legitimate system of government that was rooted in a new social structure that was orderly and stable. It could enable the people to revive and ideologically secularize the political culture of Iraqi society. It would enable the Iraqis not to lose faith in Bremer's long-term picture of a truly democratic and prosperous Iraq which could become an American ally rather than an oppressed colony whose seeds of rebellion would attract perpetual anti-Americanism around the World.

Fifth, initially,the U.S. government had committed $18.6 billion to be used by the contractors in the reconstruction process. This money was used by the United States and the coalition countries which removed Saddam from power. Some small countries like Iceland which had no significant role to play in the conflict were allowed to use some of this money for reconstruction. Major countries which were opposed to the conflict, particularly France, Russia, Germany and Canada were excluded by the United States for obvious reasons. These countries had been further peripheralized because they opposed American unilateralism of the conflict. These powers felt that they were slighted and had decided to take this case to the World Trade Organization for their exclusion from reconstruction contracts. The U.S. defended its exclusionary decision on the grounds that these moneys for reconstruction belonged to the U.S. tax payers rather than the taxpayers of these nations which never supported the United States to remove Saddam from power. What this showed is that the United States would continue to rely on its unilateralist approach to the solution of international conflicts. In the long run, this strategy could hurt the United States if other conflicts crop up elsewhere in the world. In the short run, the strategy benefited the United States but weakened its moral standing in the world as it did not immediately contribute to ironing out the differences between the United States and its traditional allies.

## AYATOLLAH SISTANI'S PERSPECTIVE

Ayatollah Sistani, an elderly Shia Cleric whose views about the occupation and elections were moderate, advocated immediate and popular electoral sovereignty for Iraq. Though elections would provide legitimacy, it was feared that the Saddam elements would be sizably elected into the provincial and national assemblies. The Governing Council was expected to have a dominant influence on those who would be elected. The regional caucuses were to elect people from 18 provinces and the Governing Council selected those who would form the government. Former Baathists' were selected into the regional councils and an unknown but sizeable number was recruited into the police systems. Ayatollah Sistani wanted Islamic identity to be preserved. He also wanted clerics to stay in the seminaries and mosques rather than in the structure of the new and future government. He emphasized that Islamic law would be the law of the land that is legislatively, constitutionally and legally consistent with Islamic principles, traditions and culture. He called constitutional issues (Fatwa) as his motto. This motto (fatwa) showed that Islamic law, religion, government and leadership are a unified quartet that is inseparable in the light of:

A legal opinion on an issue of Islamic ritual or conduct or on issues of jurisprudence. The person who issues a *fatwa* is one who is versed in Islamic Law, a jurist (mufti). Their legal opinions are based on religious principles that are applied to the specific problem which is addressed to the *muft*.

There can be a clear difference in the character of the *fatwa* described above and the *fatwa* rendered in Shiism. A *fatwa* is usually conceived as a legal opinion that has no binding effect. It can be ignored. This conforms to the character of Sunni Islam where consensus (*ijma*) among religious scholars is one of the sources of Islamic law. In Shiism where a hierarchical system of religious authority prevails, a *fatwa* at times can take on the character of a judgment.

In the twentieth century, the role of the *mufti* in the judicial process has declined considerably owing to the adoption of European legal codes by secular governments in the Islamic world. In recent years, however, with the renewed interest in Islam and the *Shari'a* (the body of religious law contained in the *Qur'ān* and the traditional sayings of Mohammed), the role of the *mufti* has been rejuvenated (McLean 1996, 178-179).

Sistani did not call demonstrations. If the Council went against his legitimacy, there were to be problems later. He was cooperative with the American occupation. He refused to talk directly to Paul Bremer because Paul had an American rather than an Iraq agenda. Islamistically, "those who talk to princes" are not the legitimate rulers of the people. He wanted moral guidance to be dominant in helping the country to overcome its problems. On the other hand, if such moral conversation was of an extreme nature, it would come into conflict with the residents of the "Sunni Triangle" most of whom were former Saddam loyalists.

## THE SECOND RECONSTRUCTION-NEW CONSTITUTION IN IRAQ

Iraq's top Shiite cleric maintained his demand for national elections, according to a U.N. envoy trying to work out differences over U.S. plans to transfer power to Iraqis. The handover had been further threatened by accelerated attacks against American forces and those who cooperated with them. Iraqi's U.S. administrators had been looking for a way to soothe opposition to their plans for creating a new provisional government in time for the June 30th target date. Iraqi's top Shiite cleric, Grand Ayatollah Ali al-Husseini al-Sistani, had shaken those plans with his insistence that national elections needed to be held to create a new legislature. He criticized the U.S. plan to delay the election by ballot and instead advocated for regional "caucuses" to organize the legislatures undemocratically and call for elections. This plan prompted demonstrations by tens of thousands of his supporters in January forcing Washington to request the U.N. mission to suspend its duties in hopes of assuaging the cleric.

The 75year old cleric refused to meet with U.S. officials, including the top American administrators. Paul L. Bremer – also demanded that an elected legislature approve a temporary constitution still being drawn up, rather than the U.S. –picked Iraqi Governing Council of twenty-five (Keath 2004).

Iraqi's current top official had demanded that Islam be the principal basis for Iraq's law, a move that breached a previous agreement among the framers of the interim constitution and created the possibility that Islamic law could rule the land. If approved, the proposal could have broad effects on secular Iraq, taking away rights of women in divorce and inheritance cases, shuttering liquor stores and banning gambling. Elements also run counter to President Bush's goal of turning Iraq into a beacon for democracy in the Middle East. "There could be changes on the Iraqi state," said Salem Chalabi, a legal advisor to the Governing Council and a member of the 10-member committee framing the basic transitional law, which acts as an interim constitution and is to take effect at the end of the month. Chalabi was later discredited for being a double dealer for both for the U.S. and Iran.

Article 22 of the constitution allows citizens whose rights have been abused to contest those rights in court. This is a liberal bill of rights which does not isolate itself from religion. In this political, legal and cultural context, no law can be passed by Parliament against the Islamic Code. This provisional constitution was accepted by more conservative elements who signed it. Ayatollah Sistani believes that if 3/18 of the provinces have veto power over the constitution. This is autocracy which he will try to change. However, since compromises have been made and the Bill of Rights was passed without dissent. No huge compromises were made. No one walked away (as in the U.S. case) between (1787-1791). Contextually, there will be no laws that contravene Islamic democracy with the Bill of Rights on which there is universal consensus (Islam). The security situation is a problem which draws a wedge between Shiites and Sunnis. A demagogue could take over and plunge the country into trouble. The document is still a status-quo constitution. It is supported by more fundamentalist than secular judges. It advocates separation of religion and state within the nation and the regions (state and provinces). Internal and external elements who disagree with it angrily expressed or threatened to kidnap foreigners and wage a civil war. The marginalization of the Sunnis and empowerment of the Shiites and Kurds (groups that were formerly dominated by Saddam's regime) has been achieved.

Iraq's interim constitution faces powerful critics: two influential ayatollahs, the leader of a Shiite party and other Iraqis who dismiss it as the work of the United States and its Iraqi allies.The criticism again places post-Saddam Hussein Iraq at the crossroads – whether to allow sectarian politics to prevail and put the nation's unity at risk, or close ranks and continue toward democratic rule.

Grand Ayatollah Ali al-Husseini al-Sistani, the most influential cleric for Iraq's Shiite Muslim majority, initiated the latest political wrangling. His objections to the interim charter prompted his supporters on the 25-seat Governing Council to refuse to sign it as scheduled for March 6. Citing a pressing needed to safeguard national unity and push forward the political process, they signed the constitution but made clear they had reservations about parts of the document and their wish to change it.

Handpicking Iraq's interim leadership to reflect its ethnic and religious make up seemed like the right thing to do at any coast. But communal tensions were on the rise, deepening the country's ethnic and religious faultlines and casting doubt on prospects for installing a peacefully elected government the following year. While Iraqis wallow in their newfound freedoms to speak, worship, publish and broadcast as they please, their future as a unified state is being tested by rivalries among Sunni Muslims, Shiites and Kurds, jockeying for power after the overthrow of Saddam Hussein.

Cobbled together by colonial Britain less than a century ago, Iraq has struggled for years with ethnic and religious rivalries. The prospect of national dismemberment may seem remote, but that possibility has been solved for Saudi Arabia, Syria and Turkey; to warn publicly against steps which might lead to the division of this nation of 27 million. Clashes between majority Shiites and minority Sunnis are not uncommon. Attacks on the offices of Kurdish political parties are increasingly common as was the squabbling among members of the Governing Council. The Iraqi interim administration of 13 Shiites, five Sunni Arabs, five Kurds, one ethnic Turk and one Christian – over whether to adopt a federal system in which the Kurds would retain substantial self-rule they had enjoyed in their northern provinces since the end of the 1991 Gulf War, remained workable.

Iraqi politicians routinely explain their differences as part of the country's new-found democracy and assure Iraqis that only dialogue, rather than violence, would be used to settle their differences. "There is no such thing as a 'representative' of Sunni Arabs," said Samir Shakir Mahmoud, a Sunni, when asked about his role on the Governing Council, "I consider myself an Iraqi citizen first … and I try to serve Iraqis, all Iraqis – Sunnis, Shiites, Arabs, Kurds and others," he said in a newspaper interview during the war. But for Sunnis, the prospect of minority status in a future, Shiite-dominated government is unsettling, given their long ascendancy under the British and then under Saddam. Now, for the first time in the modern era, Iraqis are free to speak out and form political parties. The long-oppressed Shiites and Kurds have been empowered and the Sunnis have lost their privileged minority status.

"I think what is happening in Iraq is natural," said Mahmoud Othman, a Kurd on the Governing Council. "Now we have new problems and conflicting views but at least we are free." Bush has surrendered his incompetence by giving in to politically nationalistic, universally moral and constitutionally legitimate demands. Chalabi was marginalized because he is an agent for both the U.S. and Iranian camps. The United Nations increased its influence in gorvenance matters. Brahimi negotiated the setting up of a government. In January 2005, Iraq held its elections in order to chart new directions for transitional democratic governance. The political reality the U.S. conferred to Iraq or on Fallujah and the southern Shiite world was consistent with world opinion. The transfer of political power and moral authority to Iraqis happened. U.S. gambled on the legitimacy of the internationally recognized system to take control while Americans relinquished theirs role. Pacification in Fallujah and the Sunni Triangle helped to stabilize the chaotic state in Iraq by helping to quench the thirst for its political temperature. Lots of problems and risks were part and parcel of the new reality that Iraq dictates.

According to Brzezinski, Bush wanted Iraq to be friendly to the U.S., but also called Iraqis terrorists and enforced limited sovereignty on the same state. Given this scenario, the longer the U.S. stayed in Iraq, war would continue because Iraq and America did not respect the sovereignty President Bush talked about. For effective governance in the region, the U.S. must address the Palestinian question in terms of completing the road map to peace between the PLO and the state of Israel. More authority for U.N. was needed to stabilize the situation. Prime Minister Blair thought in terms of "control and regulation" while Bush talked about "Iraq sovereignty and freedom." This fundamental dialectic between the two Anglo-Saxon leaders was more rhetorical in semantics than in real differences. Patachi (elderly Sunni statesman) declined to be president. Alawi was elected to be the president but as a Shiite Baathist, he faced a lot of opposition and other challenges. The level of violence increased nation-wide because the U.S. helped install a government that was not popular in non-democratic society.

## NEW GOVERNMENT

Brahim (an Algerian mediating envoy) played a limited role in appointing the new government. Brahim was opposed to appoint Sistani. Mr. Bremer wanted Patachi but the governing council appointed Alawi, . Major Shiite groups felt left out because the new president was a Shia but Baathist and Saddamist in orientation. The Shia major parties and religions felt left out particularly the Southern radical movement of Al Sadh which was excluded from regional and national governance. Kurdish, Sunni and Shia farmers were left out because they were not well represented. The White House, the U.N. and the U.S. military supported Alawi's government. Kurds parties came out and voted well. It was feared that the expatriate nature of the new government would have problems. The governing council had some credibility in what happened but key positions were taken by former Iraq exiles who may have not been representatives of internal nationalist conditions and urban/rural realities. Security became a problem, jobs were coming back and laws and campaign promises were being fulfilled by the government which may not have had total legitimacy. The process of restoring the Iraq military was jump started and the U.S. military and advisory role had been gradually diminishing.

## Chalabi Issue

The CIA found that Chalabi told Iran that the U.S. had broken the code. The FBI suspected U.S. people in Iraq, in the U.S. and in the Pentagon. Chalabi's intelligence was suspected of being Iranian. Habib was interviewed and polygraphed about the code issue. Chalabi was not liked in the U.S. The allegation was made that an Iranian in Baghdad got information from Chalabi and relayed it to Iran. Always, and the fact was known that Chalabi was not going to deliver. Secretary of Defense Don Rumsfield, and Vice-President Dick Cheney approved him. But the rest of the top Bush insiders did not trust him. He was an exile with very little political base in Iraq. Chalabi scared people in Iraq. He represented the interests of Iran which fears America's strategic, regional and geostrategic dominance in the Middle East.In essence,Chalabi was a leader of the provisional Iraq government in exile that would rule the country in the postreconstruction future. He was dismissed by INC. Because of his identity, Chalabi may have driven the U.S. and others who were not ready to go to war. He subjectively fed them with information they wanted. The information lacked objectivity. Chalabi's comments in British papers were questioned, and as a result politics in congress and the INC. turned against him partly because of U.S. political fallout in Iraq.

## H. Zabari – Iraq Foreign Minister Commented on the New Government like this:

(a) This resolution is important for Iraq Society; it is clear and unambiguous because it is a clear departure from the occupation.
(b) U.S. led multinational forces need to stay but be organized to avoid misunderstanding, prevent external terrorist enemies and leave when asked to by the new Iraq authority.
(c) The new government will control Iraq resources – funds and assets.
(d) Iraq needs to have a legal constitution that can help the nation to transfer authority from the U.S.-led occupation. The transfer should be real and genuine. Response has been positive at the U.N. The reconstruction should continue. (China, Russia, France and Germany) have pushed for the Iraq transfer of power – positively without jeopardizing the essence of the U.S./U.K. resolution for the transfer of power.

## How Ministers Were Chosen

The process of choosing ministers was a collaborative process. This process involved U.N. special envoy, Brahimi, Iraqi governing council and the Security Council. All ministers were 33 and 6 of them were women. They were talented and qualified individuals, 25 of them were members of Sadam's government.

This government had limited as opposed to full sovereignty largely due to what was viewed then, as relatively constructed colonial American occupation of the country. To some extent sovereignty was internationalized. Ayatollah Al-Sistani indulged the policy of limited sovereignty which made the American position unpopular although it positively staved the course of reconstruction.

## THE CHALLENGES OF THE SECOND RECONSTRUCTION

The U.S.'s unilateral action in Iraq made the reconstruction process difficult because this foreign occupation and its subsequent relative disengagement had been internationally delegitimized. It was condemned as illegal because the grounds for going to war against Iraq were based on the assumption that Saddam had weapons of mass destruction, he intended to use them against the U.S. and the West in general, and that he collaborated with al Qaeda terrorists against the U.S. in the 9/11/2001 terrorist attack. Evidence based on U.N. inspectors, David Kay, the Nine Eleven Commission, and Mr. Paul Bremer showed that the U.S. President lied to the American people in order to unilaterally and preemptively attack Iraq for economic (oil, gas) and strategic purposes rather than the alleged issues of WMD and terrorism.

The reconstruction process can retrospectively be viewed from the broader U.N., European, Russian, Middle Eastern and U.S. perspectives. Given the scope, breadth and depth and its global implications, the reconstruction process had a lot of challenges. First, the United States occupation and temporary disengagement lacked legitimacy in Iraq. The European Union, China, France, and Russia, with the exception of Britain, Spain, Australia and Italy, never got involved in the war. As a result, of the big powers, only the United Nations has legitimacy and experience to lead the reconstruction process. However, given the differences between the United Nations and the United States, the former was bound to be excluded from leading the reconstruction process. Based on the pressure put on the United States occupation forces from both internal and external environments, the U.S. was not only forced to modify its perceptions on the occupation, but it was also influenced, given its military, political, strategic, and moral limitations, to accept the creation of a machinery for establishing not only the constitution of the country but also its new government. Some of the pressure directed at the United States had roots in the Middle East, Russia, the European Union, Third World nations and the United Nations all of which condemned the United States for its unilateral and preemptive action against Iraq. Second and internally, a variety of new, radical, revolutionary and subversive groups continued to work hard against the U.S. military and the reconstruction process in Iraq. Some of these groups included but were not limited to Iraqi nationalists, Saddam royalists, al Qaeda supporters, foreign fighters and young tribal radicals particularly the Sunnis in the Sunni triangle and the Shiites in the south and central Baghdad. These forces were a great hindrance to the reconstruction process. They killed Iraqi Security forces, they killed American and coalition occupation forces, they kidnapped non-civilian contractors who managed the reconstruction process, they killed the United Nations diplomatic and the reconstruction engineers, they abducted, hurt and intimidated all Westerners, the kidnapping and killing of Johnson and Henseley are examples of their victims they heinously victimized. Hans Blix, the U.N. appointed scientific analyst said that there were "monumental intelligence" failures that disinformed and distorted reality . The rumor concerning Saddam's forgery of uranium from Niger for the the construction of a nuclear bomb was "Scandalous blunder." Justification for war was a myth and the U.S. has paid heavily in blood, treasure and reputation. The war caused the Great Recession in the US.

Four Principles (Senator John Kerry) put forward for dealing with Iraq included the following five principles:

a. "America should walk softly and carry a big stick" (FDR).
b. Launch and lead new alliances which terrorism requires.
c. We need a coalition of the able.
d. The U.S. leaders should listen to the views of military leaders in the field.
e. Beyond military power, we must deploy fully before the war.

Iraq police had not been paid and those who were injured had not been adequately hospitalized for treatment. American reconstruction police were scared because after the bombing in Tikrit, Iraq police left the area they were expected to patrol and protect. The U.S. deaths in Iraq experienced horrific images in which dead bodies were chained and pulled behind cars and hanged on the Tigris Bridge. A vast majority of Iraq's opposed the war. Economically, Western companies doing the reconstruction did not save much money. Theoretically, the companies saved money at a high cost. For instance, 30-50 contractors had died around the country and their deaths were, for security reasons, not instantly made public. Private companies could hardly hire locals to do the job. Lack of resources, security, trust, and motivation made it difficult for Western companies to hire locals for service. Private company's army, paramilitary police,and security for CPA orders were doing the work and needed more training. Private military companies made it difficult for the U.S. to send more soldiers for the war. This behavior could have caused negative economic and political implications. The behavior forced Allies, the U.S. and Iraqis to come in through the private companies and military forces. The companies were not under the U.S. commander. This private sector provided critical services regardless of the risks it underwent. Their mission was not centralized but decentralized as organizations. Firms' extraterritorial laws did not work for the defense department. If they committed malfeasance or felony, it was difficult to bring them to court in a foreign country during war time and in the absence of civilian jurisdiction. More coordination was needed between companies and military which controlled what the companies carried in terms of weapons for self-defense and the defense of Iraq national population groups or civil society which could have behaved like the Hutu majority which wiped out the Tutsis minority in Rwanda. Sunni hostilities against Shiite doubled dialectically. The U.S. provoked both the Fallujah shootings and the southern Shiite area of shootings that shut down their press. Fallujah was the center of foreign fighters that were coming to Iraq from Jordan. Five coalition countries had left before the end of 2004. The balance of forces had turned against the U.S. There was no strategy on the table that was workable. Iraq police joined the insurgents. Either way did not help to solve the problem. Analysis, judgment and assessment of the climate of war were badly inaccurate, distorting and propagandistic.

## WHY PEOPLE COMMIT ATROCITY

People commit crimes of murder during war time because of pressure from counter insurgency, war, fear, and frustration. The group process for carrying out atrocity corresponds with instructions given from military intelligence, higher military planners, foot soldiers and MPS. All sources of instructions have potential for causing brutality of one kind or the other. Human nature can be evil in an evil battle. People can do sadistic acts in prison or in private in order to exercise power even for a short time or in order to release certain forms of psychological tension. In times like these, both officers and ordinary soldiers and war prisoners are capable of committing atrocious activities. When all those involved come from the top of the system, ordinary or extraordinary people can do that, the logic of war produces what you see. Every soldier is trained about an illegal act. This is not the first in human history in which the army has been trained to disregard the law and damage the American reputation. The process released sadism whose sadistic behavior was a "doubling" form of a "second self" of killers who go for holidays and later come to kill as a profession. National Guard and reserve units are less trained and less disciplined. In that Iraq Prison, they behaved like American terrorists who committed lynchings to release tension or exercise power as fearful momentary experience. Atrocity entrapped Americans in that Iraq prison. If such acts are allowed to continue, they will become destructive to society because they violate the law, weaken military discipline, and bring a collective sense of shame to the whole nation. The good thing brought about by the media is that such bad incidents can be reported. Violations of Geneva Convention tend to dictate Violators to be court martialed and punished.

In one sense, administrators may have created an atmosphere of legal ambiguity. The American military allowed, in the absence of enough military professionals, to practice interrogative interviewing techniques in their search for terrorists and foreign fighters in Iraq. Civilians were now doing the work without training. Accountability was put under law with the state of impunity. However, the military leadership's mission was to extract better intelligence from Iraq underdogs by using sadistic acts and sensory deprivation. Sleep adjustment rules of engagement were abused. The abuse was a form of coercion in which pain was inflicted contrary to Geneva Convention regulations that govern how war is conducted.

## INTERPRETATION

Holistically, the U.S.'s unilateral action against Iraq, was legally, morally, politically and economically unjustified. This is why it was opposed by the coalition of the unwilling's world majority. There was no clear and conclusive evidence to warrant the attack. The shia are in power, the Kurds have internal autonomy and the Sunni have been relatively alienated and silenced because of systematic debaathification and Saddam's dethronement and decapitation. The internal and external insurgency problem was eliminated because a new constitution that has potential to reconcile differences between former enemies had been accepted. People have jobs and the four US managed elections have helped the secular and succesive political regimes to gradually transfer power from the occupation forces to the legitimately elected local, provincial and national institutions of government. Since national leaders are in power and the case for foreign terrorists has relatively lost its validity, then "the war against all" has been replaced by nationalistic sentiments such as pride and territorial sovereignty of Iraq. To a large degree, "this outcome depends on the extent to which the members of the Sunni community feel empowered, optimistic about the future, and secure enough to seek peaceful solutions to the political problems of modern Iraq" (Moaddel, et al. 2008/09, 644) that has turned out to be tentatively and uniquely democratic.

Geopolitically, several scholars have interpreted this conflict between the East and West in different and interesting ways. First, Brigitte Gabriel, in her book, *They must be stopped: Why we must defeat radical Islam and how we can do it (2008)*, argues that the West has been surrounded by radical Islam, in every way, for potential global conquest and domination. If Islam triumphs, it will do so because of its fundamentalist ideology that is undemocratic and inegalitarian. Gabriel sees that since the infidels are Islam's traditional enemies (rivals), the latter should be conquered with the use of the madrassa strategy. They can do that effectively because they utilize Western law, values and religious freedom to spread hatred. In the light of this kind of calculus, the West should employ the unified strategy of political correctness for protection and self-defense.

Second, Robert Baer has logically, synthetically, and analytically argued that Iran is a regional superpower that has used its oil and gas money, Shia political and Islamic ideology, and ancient traditional knowledge to establish a regional empire in the Middle East. This empire cannot be destroyed by either Israel, or the U.S. or both. The best alternative for the two countries is to construct a U.S.-Iranian diplomatic entente which recognizes their differences, respects their interests, and ascertains their strengths and weaknesses. However, if war against Iran were to break out, it would be catastrophic because the victim will destroy all oil sites and pipelines by setting them a blaze, attacking all

Western allies and interests in the Middle East in order to destroy the global economy and Western dominance in the region. The motive for such destruction would be to regain the "base" which the Industrial Revolution helped to destroy. At that juncture, and through Allah, they will be vindicated to inflict havoc and destruction on the infidels. Above all, while Americans are fighting and dying in Iraq and Afghanistan, Chinese are doing business uninterrupted and unprotected. It is difficult for the West to understand that the East cannot develop via the Western paradigm of rationalism, democracy, and freedom devoid of the canons of Koranic and other regionally and traditionally established cultural and socio-political dynamics.

Third, Lee Harris' *Globalization and its enemies: The next stage of history* (2008), asserts that Islamic fanaticism is a problem Western societies do not understand well and are ill-organized to fight. The West's system of negotiation, rationality, and tolerance is not prepared to deal with people who are adamant to modern methods of conflict resolution such as negotiation, economic sanctions and conventional warfare. The societies are relatively ignorant and poorly organized to understand the East because of the "intoxicating" spirits of the Renaissance, Enlightenment, and Modernity. Unless the West is "detoxified" of these spirits which have warped and desensitized its intelligence, it can hardly be triumphant in the context of a liberal, international, and regionally driven globacentric, geopolitical, and geostrategic environment.

For instance, and in comparison with the height of the Cold War, military expenditures in the 1985 budget was $1.2 trillion, the 2009 world military expenditure was $1.53 trillion. The expenditure was an increase of 6% since 2008 and 49% since 2000. As demonstrated, the current global military expenditure is 2.7% of world gross domestic product (GDP). Globally, the per capita income of this expenditure would be $225. Continentally, North America spends $684 billion or 44%, Europe S424 billion, or 27%, Asia $275 or 18%, Middle East 94 billion or 6%, Central & South America & the Caribbean $59.2 billion or 4%, and Africa $27.7 or 2%. Overall, $2.4 trillion or 4.4% of the global economy is dependent on war and military violence (*Global Peace Index 2008*). In the light of these statistical figures, military power produces geopolitical supremacy while peace produces economic prosperity and political stability ( Shah 2010).

In this political environment, the worst enemy of liberty is war. James Madison elaborated that war is the parent of armies that create debts and citizen taxation in order to empower the few who dominate the many. As a result, nations cannot sustain their freedoms in the "midst of continual warfare" (Madison 1795). Because President Barack Obama understands the long-term implications of the war in the Middle East, his strategic reasons for responsibly and immediately ending it are not only popular with the electorate, but they are different from those of his conservative hawks and counterparts whose views are largely influenced by the U.S.'s interest in its military industrial complex.

The U.S. military spends $712 billion or 46.5% annually while China spends $100 billion or 6.53% annually. This expenditure is seven times more than that of China, 13 times more than that of Russia, and 73 times more than that of Iran. The U.S. militarily spends more than the top 14 countries and 44 times more than the six known "rogue" states of Cuba, Iran, Libya, North Korea, Sudan and Syria. The U.S., its NATO allies, Japan, South Korea and Australia spend about $1.1 trillion (72%) of the world's total military budget. The six states, Russia, and China spend $169 or 24% Of the U.S. military budget (Shah 2010).

As far as the question of war in history is concerned, Edith Foster (2010) has logically compared two major works of Thucydides on the Peloponnesian War during the administration of Pericles. Her analysis concentrated on warfare and war equipment provided by Pericles the Athenian. Thucydides' narrative and logical explanation on the subject proves that any aggressive deployment of the military is frequently unproductive at most and counterproductive at best because the attacker is always limited by unintended consequences some of which tend to be unpredictable and unmanageable. For Pericles therefore, his assertive eloquence, knowledge and vision of war reality upon which his power, glory, and prudence were based, were, in essence, hubristic, myopic and imperialistically intransigent (Foster 2010). There is no better and comparable parallel than the "Dick Cheney's" U.S. war with Iraq between 2003 and 2010.

Contextually, the relatively strong Sino-Russian backed Iranian buffer has made the latter, in the wake of the elimination of Saddam Hussein from the political equation, the strongest regional power in the Middle East. Given the scenario in question, two powerful geopolitical conditions are likely to determine whether the Middle East oil could enhance the global oil security or could lead to oil supply disruptions, instability, and conflict in the Asia-Pacific region. The two inherently and diametrically opposed security conditions include but are not limited to the U.S.'s growing dependence on gas and oil from the Middle East and the Asia-Pacific region's thirst for these resources from the Middle East. The Asia-Pacific countries are steadily concerned about their ability to produce sufficient oil and gas to fuel future economic development. The region's immense recovery after the 1997/98 economic crisis, and its unsustained and rising energy needs makes it necessary for the region to devise strategies for addressing the challenges of energy insufficiency. Future planning, on the part of Western and Eastern global regimes requires an objective analysis of the growing dependence on the Middle East oil, on the potential for continuous oil supplies, the price of oil, and the nature of global oil security. Evidence suggests that continuous dependence on a volatile region such as the Middle East and the perception of the increasingly decreasing energy resources in the Asia-Pacific region, has potential to generate conflict in both global regions. To minimize conflict, world and globally seasoned leaders should creatively address the issues that matter most by dealing with geoeconomic rather than geostrategic interests (Salameh 2003). Also, potential and regionally based global conflicts can be resolved through markets and investment as opposed to the blatant use of force. In addition, regionally established global competitors should diversify the sources of energy and promote alternative energy development solutions and their usage.

## RECOMMENDATIONS

Under current circumstances, a new Iraq has been formed out of the old one. The Iraq people and their political elites should create necessary conditions for gradual, constructive and permanent political, economic, and constitutional systems. They should employ the newly created systems, values, and paradigms to chart new directions in the reconstruction of their great country and its legitimate return into the family of nations. To do that effectively, the Iraq political elite should rise above the "Saddam Syndrome" which paralyzed the past political system because people who had been governed under tyranny found it very difficult to accept instrumental coalition(s) for self-government. Interestingly enough, Iran could influence Al Sadah's parliamentary caucus to join Prime Minister Malik's minority group in order to form a governing majority. This prediction was realized. Alawi's leading faction was forced to accept defeat because the brilliantly designed Iranian strategy worked. Second, Ramadan's moderate views needed to be supported diplomatically and regionally in order to minimize and dispel extremist fundamentalism in the Middle East. Third, moderate Arab nations need to take the lead to build bridges between the East and West by discouraging all forms of extremism, hatred and warfare in order to enhance security. Fourth, President Barack Obama's policy of diplomatic engagement should regionally and globally be promoted for the purpose of eliminating diplomatic isolation, preemptive unilateralism, and regime change theory articulated by the neoconservative strand of the Bush administration. Fifth, more nations should be encouraged to do business with Iraq for the promotion of national unity and economic development. Sixth, bilateral, multilateral and supranational global institutions should help Iraq and Afghanistan reconstruct themselves so that they can be able to positively deescalate belligerent hostilities by learning to use constructive instruments of civil governance. Some of the instruments include but are not limited to democracy, security, self-reliance, transparency and elimination of corruption. Seventh, The Iraq political regime should be inclusive of all its major segments of the population and thereby try to minimize corruption and the temptation for sectarian exclusivism at the local, regional and national levels. Eighth, President Barack Obama and other world leaders should responsibly end the war in the Middle East and lay a strong foundation for constructive bilateralism in a global, multilateral, geopolitical, and geoeconomically sensitive strategic environment.

## REFERENCES

Abernethly, D.B. 2001. *The dynamics of global dominance: European overseas empires 1415-1980*. New Haven, CT: Yale University Press.

Appadurai, A. 1999. Globalization and the research imagination. *International Social Science Journal*: 229-38.

Barnett, M.N. 1997. Bringing in the new world order: Liberalism, legitimacy, and the United Nations. *World Politics* 49:526-551.

Betts, R.K. 1997. Should strategic studies survive? *World Politics* 50:7-33.

Boer-Ashworth, E. 2000. *The global political economy and post 1989 change: The place of the central European transition*. New York: St. Martin's Press.

Chernoff, F. 1996. *After bipolarity: The vanishing threat, theories of cooperation, and the future of the Atlantic Alliance*. Ann Arbor: University of Michigan Press.

Esman, M.J., and S. Telhami. 1995. *International organizations and ethnic conflict*. Ithaca. Cornell University Press.

Etzioni, A. 2003). *A sociologist's Iraq exit strategy*.

Famke, M.F.N. 2001. *Global limits: Immanuel Kant; international relations and a critique of world politics*. Albany: State University of New York Press.

Foster, Edith. 2010. *Thucydides, Pericles, and Periclean imperialism*. Cambridge University Press.

Ghanem, A. 2001. *The Palestinian-Arab minority in Israel, 1948-200 a political study*. Albany: State University of Washington Press.

Ginsberb, R.H. 2001. *The European Union in international politics: Politics by fire*. Lanham, MD: Rowman and Littlefield.

Grant, R.W. 1997. *Hypocrisy and integrity: Machiavelli, Rousseau, and the ethics of politics*. Chicago: University of Chicago Press.

Howard, R.D., and R.L. Sawyer. 2003. *Terrorism and counterterrorism: Understanding the new security environment*. New York: The McGraw-Hill Companies.

Jackson, R. 2000. *The global covenant: Human conduct in a world of states*. Oxford: Oxford University Press.

Kappen, T.R. 1995. *Cooperation among democracies: The European influence on U.S. foreign policy*. Princeton University Press.

Kegley, C.W. 2002. *World politics: Trends and transformation*. Manuscript.

Kegley, C.W. Jr., and E.R. Wittkopf. 2003. *World politics: Trends and transformation*. Thompson Wadsworth.

Kolodziej, E.A., and R.R. Kanet. 1996. *Coping with conflict after the cold war*. Baltimore, MD: Johns Hopkins University Press.

Kolowski, R. 2000. *Migrants and citizens: Demographic change in the European state system*. Ithaca, NY: Cornell University Press

McMahon, R.J. 2001. The cultures of empire. *Journal of American History* 88, 3: 888-92.

Makinda, S. 2003. Comment: Gulf attack has no legal backing.

Matarese, S.M. 2001. *Foreign policy and the utopian imagination*. Amherst: University of Massachusetts Press.

Miller, Ken. 2010. Coping with China's financial power: Beijing's financial foreign policy. *Foreign Affairs* July/August: 96-109.

Mlyn, E. 1995. *The state, society and limited nuclear war*. Albany: State University of New York Press.

Moaddel, M. et al. (2008/09). Saddam Hussein and the Sunni insurgency: Findings from Value Surveys. *Political Science Quarterly: The Journal of Public and International Affairs* Winter: 644.

*New Webster Dictionary and Thesaurus of the English Language*. 1992. Danbury, CT: Lexicon Publications, Inc.

Nincie, M., and J. Lepgold. 2000. *Being useful: Policy relevancy and international relations theory*. Ann Arbor: University of Michigan Press.

Palmer, M. 2002. *The politics of the Middle East.* Itasca, IL: F.E. Peacock Publishers, Inc.

Patterson, T.E. 2002. *We the people: A concise introduction to American politics.* New York: McGraw-Hill Companies.

Peterson, S. 2003. Afghanistan's lessons for Iraq.

Petit, P., and L. Soete. 1999. Globalization in search of a future. *International Social Science Journal* 165-81.

Richardson, J. 1996. ed. *European Union: Power and policy-making.* New York: Rouletdge.

Rodman, K.A. 2001. *Sanctions beyond borders: Multinational corporations and U.S. economic statecraft.* Lanham, MD: Rowman and Littlefield Publishers.

Sagini, M.M. 2003. International Diplomacy and the U.S. vs. Iraq Conflict. A paper presented at the LUISSO conference at Langston University OKC campus in spring.

__________. 2001. *Organizational behavior: The challenges of the new millennium.* Lanham, MD: University Press of America, Inc.

Salameh, Mamdouh G. 2003. *Quest for Middle East oil: The US versus the Asia Pacific Region.*

Shah, Anup. 2009. Social, political, economic and environmental issues that affect us all. *World Military Spending.*

Skalnes, L.S. 2000. *Politics, markets, and grand strategy: Foreign economic policies as strategic instruments.* Ann Arbor: University of Michigan Press.

Skinner, Richard M. 2008-09. George Bush and the Partisan Presidency. *Political Science Quarterly: The Journal of Public and International Affairs* Winter, 605-22.

Steinbruner, J.D. 2002. *Principles of global security.* Washington, DC. Brookings Institute Press.

Stoessinger, J.G. 1990. *Why nations go to war.* New York: St. Martin's Press.

Thomas, K.P. 2000. *Competing for capital: Europe and North America in a global era.* Washington, DC: Georgetown University Press.

Thompson, Drew. 2010. Think again: China's military, it is not time to panic yet. *Foreign Policy: Global Politics, Economics & Ideas* March/April: 86-90.

Tickner, J.A. 2001. *Gendering world politics: Issues and approaches in the post-cold war era.* New York: Columbia University Press.

Valaskakis, K. 1999. Globalization as theatre. *International Social Science Journal:* 153-64.

Wirtz, J.J., and J.A. Larsen. 2001. *Rockets' red glare: Missile defenses and the future of the world politics.* Boulder, CO: Westview.

Woods, T.P. 2002. Globalizing social violence: Race, gender, and the spatial politics of crisis. *American Studies* 43, 1:27-53.

# Chapter V
# Transnational Terrorism: Islamic and Western Views

Unlike the Western way of defining Islamic views on terrorism, the Saudi Arabian Islamic Fiqh Council has defined terrorism in the *Muslim World League Journal,* Jumad Al-Ula '1423/July 2002 CE. The council says that

> Terrorism is an outrageous attack carried out either by individuals, groups or states against the human being (his religion, life, Intellect, property, and honor). It includes all forms of intimidation, harm threatening , and killing without just cause and everything connected with any form of armed robbery, hence making pathways insecure, banditry, every act of violence or threatening intended to fulfill a criminal scheme individually or collectively, so as to terrify and horrify people by hurting them or by exposing their lives, liberty, security or conditions to danger; it can also take the form of inflicting damage on the environment or on a public or private utility or exposing a national or natural resource to danger (http:the true religion.org/modules)

In other words, though extremism, violence, and terrorism have not been emphasized in the *Qur'anic Shariah* (Islamic Law) and the *Sunnah* (prophetic teachings and traditions about Muhammad), Allah does not love those who commit "mischief "in the land (28:77). In addition, Allah did not only enact deterrent punishment against terrorism, aggression, and corruption, but according to the Qur'an, these types of actions are viewed as a declaration of war against Allah and the prophet. Parenthetically, the punishment for those who commit such type of mischief in the land is execution, crucifixion, or cutting off of hands, feet from opposite sides, or exile from the land; "that is their disgrace in this world and a heavy punishment in theirs in the hereafter" (5:33). In the light of this understanding, it is not surprising for Muslims world wide, to perceptually interpret the relations between Muslims and their neighbors in Palestine, Bosnia, Herzegovina and Kosovo as provocative elements of terrorist activity against Allah's people. The Qur'an (Islam) protects human life, honor, property, religion, and intellect. It condemns the unjust and the arrogant who commit crime because they do not fear Allah. Of such, "Enough for him is hell- an evil bed indeed to lie on" (7:33 and 2:205-206). To avoid retributive punishment from Allah, Both the individual and the communities are encouraged to practice moderation, eliminate destructive extremisms, and religious intolerance.

Quaranic Islam condemns intimidation, terrifying, horrifying, and the groundless killing of human beings. Non-Muslims and minorities are protected under Islamic law in all Muslim countries. They are expected, according to the Koramic Suras, to be treated with justice and whoever kills them will not go to Paradise. They deserve charity, mercy, love, and justice (60:8). Justice and pity are better than hatred (5:8). Those who are extremist in breaking the law will be retributively punished by the ruler rather than the individuals or groups.

This is the position Saddamists advocated and defined in order to exonerate Saddam Hussein. In accordance with the culture of Islam, the Jihad is prophetically ordained to make or uphold right, repel injustice, and establish justice, peace, and clemency by serving human kind in the separation of light from darkness. Specifically, Jihad has been ordained to eliminate all types of terrorism, defending the homeland against occupation, plundering, and colonialism. It is carried out against those who drive people out of their homes, are in conflict with Islamic covenants particularly their faith, religion, and the law and how, why, and where they propagate them.

The culture of Islam has a mandate in terms of rules and provisions that forbid the killing of non- combatants, innocent persons who have surrendered in conflict, mutilating the bodies of the dead, or wantonly destroying physical structures that are not connected with the issues in conflict. If these innocent, helpless and "unprotected" people are physically attacked and sexually violated or abused in any way, the attacks or abuses are not only Islamistically condemned in the strongest terms, but such behavior is universally recognized as a breach of international law. Was 9/11/2001 irrelevant in the Muslim world? The culture of Islam and Muslims in general and on the basis of the teachings of the Qur'an, the meaning of Islam is (peace). This contemporary and theological meaning is different from the aspirations of Muslims whose ancient civilization is colored with conceptions of imperialistic messianism whose roots radiate from medieval glorification of their philosophical, scientific, commercial, and political accomplishments. The aspirations of Islamists, who in a way, are reactionary and cotemporary worshippers of ancient glory, splendor, magnificence, and imperial majesty of the Islamic medieval empire whose spatial distribution spread from Spain to India, "lies in waste," but new dreamers are trying to resuscitate that phenomenal, global, and ancient model. The dream concerning the revival of Islamicism (Islamism) by activist political and philosophical reformers started in the nineteenth century and has been going on ever since although some of the movements, associations and groups had and have been coopted to the Western thought. The reformers criticize the secular rulers and governments in the Middle East for copying Western lifestyles at the detriment of the Umma (Community of Believers) and "for not fulfilling Islamic obligations to the Islamic community, or for corruption" (McLean 1996, 251). These activist reformers are reactionaries who condemn Western materialism, imperialism, colonialism and socialism as failed, exploitative and corrupt systems perpetrated on their civilization by infidels. Osama Bin Laden is a leading contemporary proponent of the reform school. The two prominent originators of the nineteenth century reform movement were Jamal al-Din al-Afghani (1839-97) and Muhammad Abdul 1849-1905. These two fundamentalist intellectuals were Islamists who were inspired by primordial values and leaders of the Medieval Islamic society. They sought to reform their society challenging European and Western thought which was perceived to threaten the purity and viability of Islamic lifestyle. They wanted to reform Islam in two ways. First, they wanted to incorporate many of the characteristic features of Western rationalism. Second, they wanted to look deep into the original authenticity of the Islamic civilization in order to "purify, expunge, and renew it by focusing on the principles of the earliest generation of Islam" (the base) (p. 251). This type of analysis has enabled the Islamist fundamentalist school to discover the essence of new voluntary and benevolent associations whose mission has not only been affirmed, but it has also been asserted by the umma. Fundamentalist beliefs, ideals, and practices are attractive because modern Arab nationalism as an ideology of power has lost its effectiveness and resolve in enabling the Muslims to win the 1967 Israel-Arab war, the 1980-88 Iraq-Iran war, the 1990 Gulf war and the subsequent use of Western victories over the Muhammedans have reinvigorated them to relate Islam to state power in challenging the West-hence transitional terrorism (McLean 1996). Simon Rushde's critique of Islam, The Dane's Cartoons about the Prophet and the Pope's assertion that Islam is a violent religion are episodes that fuel terrorism. Terrorist behavior in terms of thoughts, feelings, training objectives, strategies, tactics, methods, action, and rhetoric have been globalized. Islamists use worldwide networks which have been globalizationally institutionalized for "Coordination of resources, information, technology, and sources of social power across national borders for political, cultural, and economic purposes" (Kasloryano 2001:1). In addition, "increasing mobility and development of communication have intensified such transborder relations, leading to social and political mobilizations beyond boundaries" (p. 1). The mode of transnationalism is territorialization whose rhetoric of mobilization of intense and collective diasporic transnational mobilization has come to be associated with a new form of nationalism. Transnationalism can be different from established diaspora nationalism. However, contemporary diaspora nationalism

> may transform into movements for re-territorialization' and statehood. Transnational nationalism takes form after nationalism and nation-states have become realities; it may extend state nationalism in ways, producing exclusionist dis-

> courses based on national membership that is 'deterritorialized'....'Umma'. Transnational nationalism arises therefore as a species of globalizing communitarianism that reinvents crucial features of nationalism beyond boundaries. It does not make claims on behalf of territorial self-determination. It fashions new power relationships with states which are currently engaging the process of globalization through economy and culture. Thus the paradox: transnational nationalism challenges older historical notions of territory and national boundaries – indeed, the nation- state per se, but at the same time it situates itself towards and over states (p. 1).

The events of 9/11/2001 are reminiscent of the idea, behavior, and actions of transnational nationalism. The terrorists strategically targeted the most powerful and global symbols of American imperialism,economic power (twin towers), military might (pentagon), and political centricism, the White House (target failed due to the plane crash in Pennsylvania). Because terrorists were well educated and integrated in American society, their socialization had contributed to their institutional assimilation-hence naturalization. However, since they are politically transnationalistically deterritorialized and culturally and socioeconomically marginalized, they have psychologically developed multiple national identities for instrumental and expressive multinational and transnational nationalism. Largely due to historical and economic conditions, European minorities, particularly those who come from the Middle East and Africa, are more marginalized than American minority populations. Because the U.S. has institutionalized its multicuturalism in the land of immigrants, and due to its strong constitutional civil rights and civil liberties protections of the individual, American minority populations have more opportunity to compete in society and succeed or reach organizational echelons than their counterparts in Europe. It is unbelievably interesting that the Islamic or Islamist minorities had to take courage and attack the united states, even if there are geopolitical, economic, religious, and historically established civilizational differences between the East and the West (Huntington 1997). Peter Alexander Meyers, who is a political sociologist in Paris has argued that transnational terrorism has emerged and started to proliferate due to Western acceptance of "relativism, multiculturalism, and social construction" of societies. He asserts that while such noble forms of liberalism are defensible in the polities, sometimes they lead to situations in which good and evil cannot coexist largely due to the desire of both or either's search for security or escape due to insecurity respectively. In the light of such behavior, nations should re-evaluate their public policies as they utilize unimpeachable knowledge to examine with certainty, the role, scope, and purposes of certain liberal projects. Obviously, it is only the human race which is tolerant of such social projects for living together largely due to the fact that they use language, utter words that are a form of speech and that can be meaningfully interpreted for communicative and interactive competence. The degree with which the people understand such communication depends on their "ethos" or character and the type of friends they surround themselves with. Uniquely enough, Micheal

Mayer has theoretically argued that effective language use needs to encompass the three thematic aspects of classical rhetoric- logos, ethos, and pathos.

## How Sectism, Doctrine and Tradition Influence Terrorism

The dominant Sunni brand section of Islam has four historically established schools whose authority is valued in their analysis, interpretation and ideological nationalization of the Koran which is God given law to all Muslims. The Quran is the ultimate authority of Islamic culture; metaphysics, … theology to sacred history to ethics and law, to art (Seyyed 2005, 2). The religious law of Islam which schools rationalize is called al-Shariah. Al-Shariah is comparable to Christianity and Hadith in judism. The Shariah is based in the Quran and Hadith (Sagini 1996). These schools are the Hanafi school in Turkey, Pakistan and Islamic India; The Shafii school in Egypt, Indonesia and Malaysia; and the Hanbali school in Syria and Saudi Arabia.

The core beliefs of Muslims are based on the Quran and the Sunna of the Prophet Muhammad and central concerns about God, Muhammad, and the Umma. By the thirteenth century, a consensus on these beliefs had emerged. Common to these core beliefs, within Sunni Islam, is a diversity of interpretations and perspectives. While indicating what is meant by this diversity, it should be remembered that Islam is strictly monotheistic. The Quran is clear about God and his Oneness. As the question about the relationship between God and man, the Quran is ambiguous. Exploring the oneness of God and his relationship with man, the Sunni focus on the immanence of God or the transcendence of God. One response is the Sufi (mystic) tradition which expresses a yearning for personal communion with, and love for, God. In contrast, the answer to this and less crucial questions which the Quran did not answer was found in hadiths which were used to elaborate the silent or ambiguous areas of the Quran. In this way, the Sunna of the prophet became a source of law. A legalistic response resulted from the search for answers or, produced a diversity of schools to the number of four that were equally accepted by all Sunnis. These schools of law- the shari'a, the hanafi school of firmly othordox beliefs. It allows the use of customary and secular law which made it more flexible and accommodating to secular needs (officially recognized by Ottoman and Moghul sultans and many other major states). The Maliki shool of law rejected rational interpretation of the Quran though it allows a limited use of logic and analogy; it is dominant in much of Africa. The Shaf"i school of law indicates a methdology or roots of jurisprudence whereby the sacred sources) can be safely ... analogy via this methodology (this is common in Arabian coastline, southern India, which adhere to strict observance of the terms of the Quran and hadiths (McClean 1996, 486).

Throughout Sunni Islam, the central core beliefs are fragmented and diverse. Such fragmentation of religion provides the flexibility, as opposed to the rigidity, for toleration of ideas and debates- attributes the population has inherited and institutionalized for centuries. The second brand or sect in Islam is Shiism. The Shia are 10-15% of the Muslim population worldwide. Most of the Shia Muslims are located in Iran, Northern Yemen, Iraq, and Lebanon. Also, quite a few of the shia minority population are found in other Muslim countries.

The Shiites believe in the significance of "Ali the fourth caliph (successor) in 656-61, who died in 632. 'Ali was cousin and son-in-law to the Prophet, married to Fatima, the Prophet's wife, and those that supported him were referred to as the Shi'at 'Ali (party of 'Ali). While this was part of the politics of the time, it later became elaborated into theology ... and religious doctrine complete with theology. At the time, though, the first civil war in the Islamic community occurred between 'Ali as Caliph and Mu'wawiyah, the leader of the Umayyads. The Umayyads won, establishing their dynasty and caliphate. Hussein, 'Ali's second son and, ... In the Shi'i chronology, regarded as the third caliph or imam, was killed at Karbala (Iraq) by the forces of Yazid, the son of Mu'awiyah and successor to the umayyad caliphate. This event contributed to the annual Shi;i remembrance of the martrydom for Hussein, and his place of death and tomb at Karbala, became a point of pilgrimage. These events form the political background to the later theological development of Shiism. According to Shiism, the first Imam (divinely inspired leader) after Muhammad – as the Shi'i designated the legitimate leader of the Umma- was regarded to have been 'Ali, the fourth Caliph, and the proper succession should have been Muhammad to 'Ali and then to his descendants according to the possession of those qualities of seniority and reputation such as charisma, experience, and other necessary attributes for carrying out the duties of the commander of the faithful (Amir al-Muminin) and head of state. In the view of the Imams, the largest subdivision in Shi'ism, there have been a succession ... becomes a matter of contention among the Shi'i leading to fragmentation of the Shiites. The other two major subdivisions resulting from this contention are Isma'ilis and Zaidis. The Shi'i believed that Muhammad had designated 'Ali as successor and, in this way, a special quality was transmitted through the succession. Only the Imam, in effect is the final interpreter of the law on earth. In the doctrine of occulation, the twelfth

In AD 878, in effect, suspending the Imamate, the mujtahida, a scholar learned in Islamic law- may interpret the law. The Shiites have their own sunna (traditions) of the prophet and their (sayings and doings of the prophet). Each Shi'i subdivision developed separate schools of legal jurisprudence or interpretation and within these, there can be differences of opinion. Within the Ja'fari law school of the Imami, during the seventeenth century, two schools of thought emerged: the Akbari (traditions) which took a restrictive approach to ijtihad (independent interpretations in legal and theological matters), and the sacred sources as an intermediary of guides to the community. This meant interpretations were flexible to take account of changing conditions and times. The latter (Usuli), developed in the eighteenth century and it is within this revolutionary school that the Ayatollah Khomeini was located (McLean 1996, 450).

## Wahhabism

Wahhabism is a form of Salafism? The foregoing analysis has attempted to answer the question at hand. In Asia, Wahhabis live mostly in Pakistan and Afghanistan. Muhammad ibn Abd Al-Wahhab (1703-92) was a member of the puritanical sect of Islam that was founded in 1744 in the village of Nejd, Saudi Arabia. His movement conquered them in 1803 but the Ottomans beat them in 1819. Though al-Wahhab was not a gifted or prominent writer, he was a firebrand who preached the Wahhab sectarian doctrine that he adopted into the political friendship of the Saudi royal family for ideological and dynastic military protection of the regime (Mamdani 2005) *and( New Webster's Dictionary and Thesaurus of the English Language,1992).* In Wahhabi's school of thought, which is allied to the Egyptian-based Muslim Brotherhood, there is only one version of Islam-Wahhabism. This rigid Islamic legalism rejects sufism for its mystical, Pietetic and inner spirituality. It also rejects other spiritual, religious and theological interpretations of the Quran. Osama Bin Laden believes in this brand of Islam of one God, one prophet, one book, and one Qible all of which are sanctioned by the Sunna tradition and the faithful Umma. Muhammad Ibn Abd al—Wahhab's point creed that is dialectically constructed to separate "his" Muslims from non-Muslims. This creedal element of dialectical nullification of Islam has ten nullifiers: (1) not associating other deities with God; (2) not allowing for intermediaries between the Muslims and God; (3) calling unbelievers infidels (kuffar) or doubting their infidelity; (4) believing that a revelation other than that which accorded to the one Muhammad taught or did not teach; (6) having contempt for any part of the religion of Islam; (7) engaging in magic; (8) helping infidels against Muslims; (9) believing that any part of the Muslim community could leave the bounds of the Shariah and still be Muslim; and (10) turning away from the religion of God (Cook 2006, 39). As an ardent follower of Ibn Abd al-Wahhab, Osama Bin-Laden asserts that Saudi Arabian political and dynastic regime is guilty of three nullifiers 3, 8, and 9. This guilt makes the regime to be viewed as non-Muslims (takfir) or ignorant Muslims who suffer from Jahiriya (ignorance) discussed elsewhere by Qutb. Such ignorance has made them to allow foreigners to amass their militaries on Muslim lands which contain the three Holy sites at Karbala, Medina, and Mecca. In addition, diplomatic, commercial and political contact between Israel versus the Muslim countries is therefore, hypocritical Ulama- religion of Islam and un-Islamic. Since they undermine the knowledge of Islamic tradition and the interpretation of Islamic history, modern Arab political elites and their regimes should be overthrown and get replaced by fundamentalist, puritanical and uncorrupt ones. The new regimes, it is hoped, will restore the authenticity and legitimate historicity of the base's genuine, classical, Pristine and Primordial Islam. Bin Laden is an ascetic who believes in the tradition of jihad fighting modeled on Abdallah bin al-Mubarak (d. 797) and Abdallah bin-Mubarak (d. 1414). Both men abandoned a privileged and successful lifestyles as Bin Laden did, to dwell in caves of coastal Syria and Egypt, using them as bases for attacking and overthrowing non-Muslim controlled governments with the use of aggressive jihad. Due to his lack of knowledge about Islam and the role of Jihad, Bin Laden has been criticized for lacking understanding and authority to sanction the jihad. Classical Islam placed that authority in the Caliph other than in standard Wahhabi teachings.

Other than standard Wahhabi teaching, Bin Laden is most influenced by the medieval Islamic doctrine of al-wala (roughly, "love-loyalty and hatred-disassociation"), which polarizes all social relations as those who either love or hate Islam. It has two ideological precedents in Islam. One precedent, ironically, is Shiism. AL-Wala' was first developed by Shiites because there was stark distinction between the words that they were required to say in public and what they truly believed in private. Therefore, one had to manifest love or loyalty toward the imams and hatred or disassociation for the enemies of the imams in one's heart. This doctrine was never important in classical Sunnism until the thirteenth century because there was only rarely a divide between one's true beliefs. For the most part the Sunni could rely on being part of the majority and could express their faith openly. However, starting with Ibm Taymiyya (1328), we find the beginnings of the Sunni doctrine of al-wala', which is more important for Bin Laden's thought. According to Ibn Taymiyya, it is not necessarily (or merely) one who recites the shahada but rather, one who manifest loyalty and love for the Muslims and disassociates himself from any aspect of the unbelievers. It is easy to see why this doctrine is central to radical Islam; those who have written on the subject are veritables whose globalism radicalizes Muslims. According to the contemporary interpretation of this doctrine, those who imitate an unbeliever or maintain positive social relations with an unbeliever are themselves non-Muslims (42 and 43).

On the basis of this analysis, Bin-Laden's beliefs are an authentic product of Islamic traditionalism (hadith) and Quranic originality. Given the fact that he had not been tainted as other Muslims, and since he was not controlled by any political authority, and as his main goal of fighting to elevate Islam rather than himself or his friends, he had become a popular figure whom contemporary Scholars may compare to Muhammad the prophet of Islam. His magnetic appeal had made him transcendent. This transcendence reinforced the "World Islamic Front Declaration of War against Zionists and Crusaders' and the "Proclamation" which traditionally starts with the Quran's verse 9:5 - "Verse of the Sword" and two radical and traditional sayings-"Behold! God sent me (Muhammad) with a sword, just before the hour of Judgment ... and the Hadith of Thawban" (p. 44) which referred to the global conspiracy against Islam for which the Jihad is the only counterbalancing panacea. Bin Laden was farther inspired by several Medieval, contemporary and legal authorities whose writings, advice and wisdom he relied on. Of these main stream Sunni authorities, Ibn Qudama al-Maqdasi (1223), al-Kasani (1191), al-Qurtubi (1273), and Ibn Taymiyya- all from the Crusader-Mongol period. Probably this attempt to ground himself in the Muslim legal tradition was the result of criticism that he had faced for his prior forays into the world of fatwas. Most of the contemporary authorities mentioned by Bin Laden are Saudi, including Hamud bin 'Uqla al-Shu'aybi (2002), Sulayman al-'Ulwan (who wrote on the "nullifiers of Islam"), and Yusuf al-'Ayyiri (killed in june 2003); but there are several others, such as the Egyptian 'Umar 'Abd al-Rahman and the Pakistani Nizan al-Din Shamzi. They all have impeccable radical credentials, and he never cited anyone who was not fully committed to the cause (p. 44)

This radical and ascetic scholar believed that God would vindicate the weak (Mustada' fin) as the prophet's people and the prophet himself through fight's against the Pagan and corrupt Western infidels who dominated the Muslim lands and usurped their substance. Since he represented common people, Bin Laden's writings are clear and easier to understand. The writing "Talks About traditional ideas of self-sacrifice, asceticism, honor and vengeance" (p. 46). He scorns the West, uses poetic imagery and deep descriptions to assert that Muslim's faith in God will enable them to defeat Westerners and Israel in spite of their dependence on the superiority of military technology. Since his ideas are couched in pan-Islamic and egalitarian strain, they resonate with a powerful sense of universality rather than narrowly written, parochial, and exclusive sentimentality. The Staunchest critics of Bin Laden are the Ulama (religious leaders of Islam) who do not buy his doctrines because they think he misrepresents the purpose of Islam. They criticize him because he indirectly calls them infidels and Western dominated Muslim elites and their political regimes. His Wahhabist beliefs come into conflict with Sufist doctrine which most Muslims, particularly those in India, Africa, and Indonesia who cherish the Sufi mystic tradition as practiced by both Sunnis and Shiites.

Sufism is a "popular form of informal Islam" (Palmer, 2002:21) that is experientially and mystically internalized as a form of inner piety that "Shapes Muslim values, worship, theology, conversation and social order which is similar to the Ulama tradition" (Sagini1996, 96) as tension in the Ummah arises from sectal and intersectal (Sunni-Shia) interpretation of Quranic Shariah. Many "Sufis criticize the Shari (Muslim vision of life lived according to the dictates of Islamic Law (shariah), for its superficiality and lack of impact on internal spirituality" (p. 96). Sufism originated in Persia (Iran) and Iraq between the 9$^{th}$ and 11$^{th}$ centuries before it became institutionalized into Islamic orthodoxy. The writings of al-Ghazzah (1058-1111) enabled sufism to be accepted in conservative circles. This acceptance reinvigorated the arid scholasticism of the religion of Islam. Conflictually and comparatively speaking, while there is tension between Sunnism and Shiism, in broad prospectives, this tension is a product of how each sect uses the Koran's theology, the Ulama tradition, tradition lineage, hadith, isnad and the Shariah to interpret their legitimate claims to power and authority in Islam as demonstrated in the ascendant conflict between Muawiya's and Ali's Sharifism. Based on Shii communities and Sufi orders, prophetic Sharifism is "interpretation based on the light of traditionally related economic, aristocratic, tribal, political, and spiritual aspects that strengthen certain claims to leadership or special privilege on earth" (p. 97).

There is tension also between Wahhabism and Salafism. A comparative analysis between the two movements is instructive. The former is an aggressive, desert, and populist movement whose roots have a thin intellectual base for cultural interpretation and reconstruction. However, its radical and political beliefs, which are based on extrapolations and excepts from their spiritual regurgitation of Islamic law and Quranic interpretation, tend to resonate well with Islamic groups which have less political, economic and religious power and influence at home and abroad. While the terrorism of these fundamentalist Islamicists tends to create risk and uncertainty world wide, their violent, reactionary and political behavior tends to become a liability to the faith of Islam particularly in Muslim enclaves (McGregor 2006). Though the nineteenth century Ottoman Empire and Pasha of Egypt effectively suppressed their influence, twentieth century British and American imperialistic and economic interest in the region allied themselves with the Saudi Arabian aristocratic and dynastic political elite helped to institutionalize their interests which paid off in helping the West to neutralize Soviet expansionism in the Middle East during the Cold War. Also, the gradual decline and paucity or lack of professional magistrates and jurists was replaced by wahhabists. This replacement caused the latter to reorganize religious constituents, exercise mysticism, discard historically and traditionally well established Quramic commentary, make Hadith a unidimensional source for validity of the revised version of Sharriah-Islamic law and persistently attack and humiliate the Shia whom they despise because they question the latter's authenticity of their Islamic beliefs. To display their dislike of the Shia, the contemporary Saudi State uses its oil gotten wealth to "export Wahhabi ideology through its funding of religious schools and literature, especially in the poorer parts of the Muslim World". This form of behavior has "exacerbated Shi'a resentment" (p. 2).

Because Wahhabism as a practice has a darker side, it tends to exist outside the mainstream of Islamic traditionalism. When it proscribes all Muslims who reject its intellectual historical traditionalism, it marginalizes itself. Due to its intellectual thinness and for its own survival, it clings to an elaborated preindustrial and primordial (pristine) past which is legally structureless, theologically bankrupt and mystically demystified. It relies on the literal Quran and the Prophet as the model. Worst of all, Wahhabism censures others for its intrinsic survival. For instance, Wahhabism condemns praying for someone at the grave side- a practice initiated by the prophet. This doctrine has contributed to the destruction of Arabian graves of early Muslims they disagreed with. They also attacked their institutional mysticism (Sufism) everywhere. Unlike the Wahhabists, Salafists are "ultra strict and quietistic" (Mamdani 2005, 148). The salaf (pious forbearers) were the original writers, transmitters and guarantors of Quranic Mohammedanism in terms of the Prophet's words, faith, and practice. In other words, Salafism (salafiyyah) is a puritanical and fundamentalist Islamic movement whose revivalist vision of Islam rejects contemporary Jahiriyyah because they favor a return to an Islamic past lived by the first three generations of

Muslims (7th and 8th centuries A.D.). (Shabah, Tabi'in and Taba' at Tabi'in) Salaf. Classic traditionalism is rooted in their spiritual, philosophical and intellectual vivification and connectedness with original community- the Ummah. Though they agree with the Wahhabis in most philosophical outlooks, they radically differ in one important way. First, the Wahhabi reject modernization which they view as a form of Westernization. In their opposition to Wahhabist thought, the Salafi attempt to reconcile Islam with contemporary notions of modernization (Sagini 1996). The term Salaf is also used by many Islamic groups especially those who worship venerables of early Islam and political Islamists. Salafis "idolize an uncorrupted bygone religious community that declined due to foreign innovations....They seek an Islamic revival through the purging of these influences and the emulation of early generations" (Wikipedia.com). Because Salafist thinking originates in the Quran and the Sunnah, it elevates monotheism by condemning polytheistic traditionalism such as shirkism. The revivalist tradition of Salafism was initiated by al-Azhar' University's activist intellectuals of the nineteenth century. These four major intellectuals who led the reform movement were influenced by the European Enlightenment tradition. These prominent Egyptian Scholars of Cairo (al-Azhar University) were Ali Khan-lawyer, Muhammad Abduh- educator (1849-1905) Jamal al-Din, al-Afghan-political activist (1839-1897) and Rashid Rido (1865-1935). Their revivalist vision and tradition is called the Second Era of Ijtichad (1875-present). The nature and character of their reformist ideas is dialectical; and it ranges from violence to powerful, public, radicalized and highly politicalized forms evangelism. The trinity of Wahhabism, Salafism and al Qaeda originate in Saudi Arabia and their terrorist influence radiates worldwide. It is interesting to note that in their theological, philosophical, ideological and political activism, their competitive rivalry for power, leadership and influence has been towered by al-Qaeda largely because of Bin- Laden's economic, ideological, and military influence. Though Salafism appeals to be doctrinally and peacefully rigid, by itself, it is less equated with violence, terrorism and ultra radicalism. However, within these three stands of doctrinaire elements of Sunnism/Shiism, exist four subgroups that change their behavior concentrically. First the Jihadist Salafis are local groups who advocate al-Qaedaism. Second, the Salafis are those who initiate the behavior of the Salaf (saliheen) who were the Prophet's companions whose model and traditionalism should be evaluated by contemporary society. Third, the Islamists think that any Muslim or Islamic ideas, regardless of their interpretation, should be fundamental to the political and social order of all Musmims in the world. Fourth, the discontented Muslims are those who are unhappy with their station in life, with the life as it is lived in the world. The first group or movement has recruited rootless, committed and internationalist zealots who fight jihad for the recreation of the fundamentalist Ummah and Shariat for building an Islamic Society. These Jihadist salafists are so conservative and radical enough to form celled global networks of Islamist fighters that have conducted jihad in Kashmir, Bosnia, Chechnya, Afghanistan, and the Philippines.

Its influence in Central Asia and the Caucasus is less dynamic because the movement is largely localized as an expression of identity in Ferghana, Daghestan, and Uooer Gharm valley.

Professor Seyla Benhabib, who teachers political science and Philosophy at Yale University, argues that the global terror network of Osama bin Laden is a very entrenched and sophisticated Islamist group that has Neo-Nazis and White supremacist supporters in Europe and the U.S.A. In the U.S., they can further terrorize the civilian population with the use of anthrax. Both Islamic terrorism and Western biological terrorism of which, anthrax and HIV/AIDS are classic examples, are new paradigms of violence that challenge state-centric politics and the foundations of Western imperialism and hegemony which have failed Muslims by interpreting these events along the tired paradigm of anti-imperialist struggle by the 'wretched of the earth;' neglecting the internal dynamics and struggles within the Islamic World, and the history of regional conflicts in Afghanistan, Pakistan, India, and Kashmir" (Benhabib 2001, 1), and now in Iraq, Palestine, and Labanon. The internal and external dynamics which give rise to these incidents, conflicts, and war are not too complex to analyze. However, they are too difficult to interpret, mange, and control. In other words, our analysis of them is largely superficial, rather than substantial, journalistic rather than scholarly, performance intended to incite, humiliate, ridicule or star up Easterners for their politically consumable emotions. Such behavior could be inadmissible reflections of internalized inferiority that is suppressed in consciousness. For their wars against the West, Muslims use a variety of methods: they use guns and bullets to target buses, rail stations, street corners, and places where people gather. They kidnap, kill and torture Westerners at their pleasure. Most of their victims are journalists, soldiers, reconstruction service men and women, and international businessmen searching for fortune. Islamists use suicide bombings such as the proSaddamist Hamas experience with the state of Israel and the Hezbollah-Lebanon based confrontation with the state of Israel in summer 2006. They use bombs as those used in the World Trade Center in 1993, Oklahoma City in 1995, the East African (Kenya and Tanzanian Embassy bombing of 1998), the Madrid bombing in 2004, the London underground train (tube) bombing of 2005, the Bali bombing of 2003, the 2001 Transcontinental commercial airlines that destroyed the Twin Towers, and the Pentagon, the White House ill-fated flight that crashed in Pennsylvania and the 2013 Westgate Al-Shabaab attack in Nairobi, Kenya. They used 'total war' in which foreign terrorists united with the local pro-Saddam Baathists and the Shiite nationalist alliance against occupation by Westerners and humiliated them by destroying the normal daily life of the occupiers in cafes, markets, stations, and even in the Green Zone. Finally, they used the Jihad-holy war which proved to be distractive but fruitless and "Jihad-on-line" for highly resurgent and electronically globalized propaganda that was intended to isolate and humiliate "the enemy ... guilt, complicity, responsibility, conflict, combat and war" (Benhabib 2001, 2). Jihad also means the struggle of the soul with itself as it leads a virtuous life exemplified in the Koran. Islamic armies protected Islam during the seventh century. However,

> one of the most commonly heard contentions in the aftermath of September 11 was that even if the terrorist attacks upon the World Trade Center and Washington equaled war in the civilian and property damages they inflicted, the deliberateness and precision with which they were executed, and the brazenness with which they violate customary, moral, legal, and international norms, the U.S. Congress could not actually declare war, not because the enemy was as yet unknown, but because a state can declare war only against another state. The idea that a democratic nation-state would declare war upon a global network of loosely organized sympathizers of religious civilizational cause, strained all categories of international law with which the world has lived since 1945, and in which nation-states are the principal recognized actors. For this reason, the Congress has authorized the President to do whatever is necessary to fight the global terror network and to bring the perpetrators to justice, but congress has declared war neither upon the Taliban (whom most nations do not recognize as a legitimate regime) nor upon the Afghani people. It is as if the territory the terrain of Afghanistan is our enemy in that this terrain offers a sanctuary and an operational base for one of the great fugitives of out time-Osama bin Laden. Ironically, the people of Afghanistan have themselves fallen captive or prisoner to one who operates on their territory, and to whom the Taliban has granted refuge. Afghanistan is a decaying or failed nation-state, and this very condition of decay permits us to understand all the more vividly the principles of national sovereignty which have governed international relations since the Second World War (Benhabib 2001, 2).

In this context, Max Weber has provided a classic and modern meaning which suggests that Afghanistan has no 'legitimate monopoly over the territory' (Weber 1978, 904-05). The legitimate monopoly of violence by the political territorial association is not a primordial institutional order, but rather, an evolutionary rational consociation. A modern state is characterized by territoriality, administrative and military monopoly, the use of violence and the legitimacy to behave that way. However, when states decay, dissolve or secede, these four characteristics of the state cease to exist. Hence the natural inexistence of states may attract a zone for staging guerilla fighters, drug smuggling, weapons of mass destruction and contraband, and other illegalities. In such a situation, governance and military competence are towered by substate forces of terror particularly the regional or sectional and provincial war lords, commands, traditional chieftains who promote the interest of their fiefdoms and tribal or religious leaders who perpetuate a conservative and totalitarian theocratic order. As a result of disorderlessness, legitimacy like power may flow from the barrel of the gun or from supranational or subnational ideologically based world views that promote East-centric race, religion, region and civilizational agenda. Such disorderly, decayed and fragile nation-states are totalitarian systems whose lack of rule of law, absence of representative and democratic way of life, pervasiveness of violence against women and minorities, are characterized by their universalization of suicide, torture, murder, crime and fear. This behavior overrules bureaucratic efficiency and encourages the practice of radical and reactionary ideological systems reminiscent of twentieth century medieval feudalism noticeable in Afghanistan, Chechyna, Bosnia-Herzegovina, Rwanda, Darfur (Sudan) and lately Iraq. These substrates emerged with the dissolution of the administrative, territorial and military order of the states.

> As Hannah Arendt has shown us, totalitarian movements also had globalizing ambitions in that they touted supranational ideologies like pan-Germanism and pan-Slavism. Yet the global ideologies of today's terror movements are both larger and smaller in range instead of the ideology of linguistic or cultural unity among the Slavic or Germanic nations, for example, today we are dealing with ideologies aimed at tribes, ethnicities or at a vision of community of believers that transcends them all namely the Islamist ummah of the faithful. The new form of war is not just the destruction of the enemy but the extinction of a way of life. The emergence of non-state agents capable of waging destruction at a level hitherto thought to be only the province of state and the emergence of a supernational ideological vision with and indefinable moral and political content, which can hardly be satisfied by ordinary political tactics and negotiations, are the unprecedented aspects of our current condition (Benhabib 2001, 3).

Any form of state terrorism carried out by democratic states or non-state movements can be brutal, unjust, and merciless. But, democratic systems monopolize state power to control violence due to the fact that they exercise the rule of law that is democratically legitimized by the citizens. Internal controls on the use of legitimate use of violence are the prerogative of international organizations that are empowered to use it by sovereign states. These states bind themselves together in a form of pacts, associations and treaty signatories in order to stop or limit the use of violence on the international level. The terrorist movement is anon-state entity whose proliferation in a multipolar world emerged with the collapse of the bipolar world. This movement of non-state actors who are violent players are not subject to the conventional constraint of international law and treaties. The international treaties concerning the use of WMD are not applicable to this movement of non-state actors. In other words,

> The concept of an "internal enemy", which is now being promoted against "suspect groups" through surveillance, wiretapping and stricter immigration controls, is not one that democracies can live with. The category of the terrorist as an "internal enemy" as one who is among us, even if no one of us, strains the democratic community by revealing the rule of law is not all-inclusive and that violence lurks at the edges of everyday normalcy. Our thinking about foreigners, refugees, and asylees becomes colored by the image of others as potential enemies; the "other" becomes the criminal. We may be at a point in history when indeed the state-centric system is waning: global terrorism and the formation of a global economy and civil society are part of the by state-centric terms which presuppose the unity of territoriality, the monopoly over the use of the means of violence, and the attainment of legitimacy through representative institutions. It is.... of unilateralism and isolationism and who denounced "nation building", now finds himself supporting multilateral actions with allies like

> Pakistan, Saudi Arabia, and Syria, whose democratic legitimacy is highly questionable, and also reconstructing a post-Taliban government in Afghanistan. Can we find responses to this new challenge that will break the vicious cycles of violence, incomprehension, repression at home and by war abroad? (Benhabib 2001, 5)

After his authorship of *The clash of civilizations and the remaking of the world order* (1996), Harvard University's professor's bold, imaginative and provocative theory of the communist world politics argues that "civilizations have taken over, from nations and ideologies, as the shapers or driving forces in global politics and international relations. These makers of human destiny from Westernization and is producing neither a universal civilization in any meaningful way nor the Westernization of non-Westerns societies" (Huntington 1996, 20). If anything, modernizational Westernization may have contributed to the many divisions in the global society in which it is dominant enough to produce more interculturally based faultline conflict and chaos. Though nations will continue to be the most powerful actors in world politics, their associated major conflict will emanate from nations and groups of different civilizations (Huntington 1996) whose political, religious and economic animation may be the source for the destruction of empires or the source for exchange, cross fertilization, and sharing (Said 2001). Qutb, who is an Egyptian philosopher studied in France and may have been influenced by European philosophers such as Nietzsche, Heidegger, Adorno and Horkheimer. He severely critiqued the West for its extremely ungodly and anticommunitarianism, corruption, coldness, heartlessness, and individualism. The 9/11/2001 clash of civilizations was reactively caused by an externally (transnationally) clash-based terrorist movement, while the regional or state militarization of the bureaucratic elite in the oil kingdoms which protect "exploitative" and modernist western powers that imposed political regimes that are viewed to be ignorant of the local reality of Islam, Koranic Shariah and Jihad, have consolidated to form reactionary movements that are the voices of discontent that speak for the masses in order to replace modernized, irrelevant and autocratic western imposed kingdoms. These are internal clashes whose root cause is based in asymmetrically applied theories of democracy, exchange, cross fertilization and sharing. These theories are asymmetrical because their imposition lacked the ideological reservoir for reinforcing Nasserism, Marxism, capitalism, socialism, and Arab nationalism that were essential for assimilatory Westernization and progressive and social reintegration of the Middle East. In other words, the failure of these ideologies to fill the vacuum left by the collapse of USSR as a galvanizing and legitimating force in the Islamic world contributed to the proliferation of ungovernable, violent and disruptive Islamist movements of which al Qaida is the ring header. "Islamic values of these movements cannot be reconciled with political democracy. As a result, "Islamism emerges as a plausible civilizational project, not just against the West, but against the failure of Westernizing elites who have only managed to import a truncated modernity into their own societies" (Benhabib 2001, 8). In

Weberian perspective, he wonders which direction religious rejections of the world take and why. He sees that there is "a fundamental conflict between secular, capitalist, modernity, driven by profit, self interest, individualism and the ethical world views of the religions" (p. 8) which preach about a variety of "abstinence, renunciation of riches, the pursuit of virtue among members of the faith, and the disciplining of everyday life to do the work of the Lord" (p. 8) Weber discovered that in the spirit of Calvinistic economic theory of Christianity (Protestant ethic), Protestantism has an 'elective affinity' "to capitalism by transferring the abstinent and methodical pursuit of one's vocation in the service of God into the methodical, predictable, and disciplined pursuit of work and profit in this world..... millenarian movements which reject the capitalist control of everyday life for the sake of disciplined labor and profit accompanied by the rise of Western modernity" (p. 8)

> the protestant and more narrowly Calvinist-transformation of religious salvation into an earthly vocation of hard work in the service of an unpredictable God, is one among the many paths that the religious accommodation with the world can take. It is also possible to split the religious and mundane spheres in such a way that one altogether withdraws from engagement with the world; the religious abnegation of the world remains an option. A third option-besides engagement of withdrawal is to compartmentalize by separating the spheres of life which do not. Throughout the Islamic world, such a strict separation of religious observance (in the domain of family life and the "bazaar" (the marketplace) was practiced. This separation of the home from the market was made possible by the practice of Islamic tolerance toward the other Abrahamanic religions, like Judaism and Christianity. The Ottomans adopted these "separate Spheres" model, and permitted the wide array of ethnic groups, and peoples whom they dominated to govern themselves in their own communal affairs according to their own religious and customary traditions (the so-called millet system.) Global modernization is destroying the fragile balance between these separate spheres; this may explain in turn the obsessive preoccupation with controlling female sexuality which all Islamist groups exhibit (Benhabib 2001, 8-9).

Modern technology, in all its gadgetry, threatens no Islamist groups or individuals rather than giving them opportunity to use it for communicative, vocational, electronic and peripatetic competence. The sharia has been capitalistically adapted to use the hawale way to transfer money across the banking systems. Through this way, wealthy Muslims contribute 5% of their wealth for the maintenance of Madrassas-religious learning institutions for orphans or for indoctrinating young Muslims to adhere to prominent Islamic causes and pressures that require Islamic girls and women to unveil their heads and become a threat to the separate spheres model that threatens family and personal life. Further still, threats to family and personal life accompany global capitalism whose images of sexual freedom and promiscuity and Hollywood liberalism undermine clan, tribal, and cultural values of the preindustrial desert and religious communities. Their patriarchal and authoritarian lifestyles, which the Koran sanctions, are challenged by the globalization projects. There are about 13-20 million Muslims in Western Europe and about 8 million in North America. These immigrant communities have many challenges of which the following are paramount:

> They try to practice the separate life spheres model in their new homes. But the children of Muslim migrants are caught between two worlds, though educational institutions or the influence of mass culture, if not the parents, between the authoritarian and patriarchal family structures from which they emerge and the new world of freedom into which they enter. There is a continuous renegotiation of clashing moral codes and value orientations in the minds of this younger generation, and particularly women. If we want to understand why so many educated, relatively well-off Muslim males from Hamburg and Paris would participate in the actions of September 11, we have to understand the Psychology of Muslim immigrants in their encounters with secular liberal democracies of the West. Given the failure of their own home- grown versions of modernity like Nasserism and the Ba'ath movement, given the profound assault on their identity as Muslims which the global entertainment industry brings, and given the profound discrimination and contempt which they experience in their host societies as new immigrants who are perceived to have "backward" morals and ways of life, many young Muslims today turn to Islam and fundamentalism. (Benhabib 2001; http// www.ssrc.org/sept11/essays/benhabib.htm)

Obviously, though these struggles may be unique to Muslims in the West, they are not unique to the story of human history and human civilization both in the past and perhaps in the present and wherever cultures differ. The rhetoric of vengeance associated with apocalyptic manifestations should be deemphasized in the democratic world. Since the viability of democracies is inconsistent with Jihadism, the former need to try to reach out to the latter with the use of rationality, empathy, compassion, respect for the religious and cultural institutions of other people, justice and pragmatic prudence. An international and multilateral diplomatic approach for reconciliation should be set up by the U.N. The agency should strive to bridge the bitter differences between the East and the West. Is the United States regarded as a terrorist nation by its own citizens? This is an interesting question which could only be answered by another question which reads as follows: What is terrorism? In this article the United States and Global Wars of Terror, Noam Chomsky, who is prominent linguist, philosopher and political activist and professor at MIT has answered the question. For over four decades Chomsky has remained one of the staunchest critics of U.S. "Hypocrisy, double standards and support for state terror" (Grover and Peschek 2006, 318) that is characteristic of the U.S. foreign policy. To quote him more extensively, he asserts that:

> The Bush doctrine of Preemption announced on September 20, 2002 .... explicitly extends a policy in a place since the end of WWII. Chomsky points out that the United States consistently has inflicted violence and state terror on numerous nations, either directly or more commonly, indirectly through economic and military support for client regimes who brutalize their own people to pro-

> tect the U.S. interests, as the case of Columbia, Turkey, South Africa, Nicaragua, East Timor, Panama and numerous other examples. In the Middle East specifically, U.S. and Israel state terror sets the context for today's unrest, with disregard for international law against the opposition of most of the rest of the world. Indeed, as he shows with ample reference to the U.S. foreign policy elites, the United States simply does not acknowledge international law when it might inconveniently interfere with the unfettered U.S. pursuit of its objectives and poorer interests, a standard which would be criticized with ferocity in the United States if another nation adopted such an arrogant posture. (p. 318).

Unfortunately for America, Middle Easterners have noticed, experienced and internalized American practice of hypocrisy, double standards, and terrorist behavior in their borders. They have decided to challenge its interests by setting and using goals that are al-Queida backed. "Their goal, in their terms, is to drive infidels out of

Muslim lands, overthrow the corrupt governments they impose and sustain, and institute an extremist version of Islam" (p. 325). Though Islamists engage in high risk and high cost activism including violent behavior, they tend to produce concessions from their enemies. Their tactics have logic, coherence, and rationality. In other words, although some radical Islamists are compelled by economic incentives or personal psychological needs that may have nothing to do with religious conviction. .... They need to revenge against perceived oppressors; a need for a sense of empowerment, or a desire for prestige, religion matters for many. In cases where individuals take spirituality seriously, they employ movement ideologies and strategies for fulfilling divine duties and maximizing the prospects of salvation on judgment day. In essence, "these ideologies serve as heuristic devices or templates that outline the path to salvation. Where individuals believe that the spiritual pay off outweigh the negative consequences of strategies in the here and now, high-cost risk activism is intelligible as a rational choice" (Wiktorowics and Kaltenhsler 2006, 2395). For these Islamist radicals, imposition of Western democratic institutions and lifestyles are not a collective good for their societies. However, the collective goods that will benefit Muslims are "establishment of the Islamic State, expulsion of the U.S. from Muslim lands, divine justice" etc. (p. 300). A cornerstone of their ideological templates is that individuals must face high risks and costs because God demands this as a condition for the spiritual payoff. In other words, radical Islamists choose to face great personal risks and costs because they pursue their self-interest..." Because individuals are judged as individuals on judgment day according to whether they personally followed the commands of God, free-riding jeopardizes salvation" (p. 301). This rational and activist behavior model is culturally informed by the values of the East which Samuel Huntington and Bernard Lewis have considerably written about. In brief, both Islamic culture and politics are the motivation for Islamist violence and religious fundamentalism" (Mamdani 2005, 148). This cultural explanation is more logical rather than conclusive form of evidence. Two other scholars, Giles Kepel who authored *The war for Muslims minds: Islam and the West* (2004), and Oliver Roy the author of *Globalized Islam: The search for a new ummah* (2004), have extended this culturalist model of Islamic activist rationality from generalist and descriptive semantics to particularist and doctrine- based religious, cultural and interpretivist explanatory argument. For instance, while Kepel looks at the problem from an intellectual and historical perspective, Roy's analysis focuses on Sociological conditions which influence Muslims to think, internalize, and act violently. Jihad in *Knights under the prophet's banner,* Zawahiri argues that Jihadism "requires new elitist leadership that is scientific, confrontational, and rational to attack the far away rather than the nearby enemy" (Zawahiri). Although the Jihad is the (Holy War) declared against an enemy power, there are many forms of Jihad in both Islamic and non-Islamic civilizations. For example, Benjamin R. Barber's (1996) *Jihad versus McWorld: How globalism and tribalism are reshaping the world* is a deconstructed metaphor concerning anti-Westernization, anti-universalism, and anti-disestablishmentarianism. In other words, though the Islamic civilization is not against democracy, it is against Western modernization for its "secular culture.... values" that are corrupting to and morally incompatible with its own (p.209). With the humanistic use of world conditions, it violently and forcefully uses its political and religious power for corrective, retributive, and judgmental role. In this respect, the teachings of the Koran are accountably legitimized for strengthening the "Ummah- community, Shura- mutual consultation and al-Maslaha-public interest" (p. 209). However, Jihad and McWorld are dialectical moral antimonies. These two represent consumerist capitalism that is inspired by the values of the Enlightenment on the one hand, and religious, rootless and tribal fundamentalism on the other. These "diametrically opposed but strangely intertwined forces are tearing apart-and bringing together- the world as we know it, undermining democracy and the nation-state on which it depends. On the one hand, consumer capitalism on the global level is rapidly dissolving the social and economic barriers between nations, transforming the world's diverse population into one uniform market. On the other hand, "ethnic, religious and racial hatreds are fragmenting the political landscape into smaller and smaller tribal units"(Barber 1996, back page). Though there are several moderate and liberal strands in Islam, its universalist and comprehensive nature, which is devoid of economical character, makes the militant strand 'more rather than less ascendant as the Jihadists fight with words and ideas or ballots or, in extreme cases, bullets' (p. 206). In other words, in *Jihad vs. McWorld*, Professor Barber has attempted to show how powerful and interdependent forces can be empirically, theoretically, and naturalistically paradoxical in their behavior as reflected in and by all major fundamentalist religious and philosophical traditions (Sunni, Shiite, Protestantism, Catholicism, Hinduism, Sikhs, Thervada Buddhism, Confucianism,Revivalism and Zionism). While these religious systems can be ratified in a political and nationalistic way, their provincial and parochial nature is chameleon like and rationally irrational. As a result, analyzing social and political theory in such a context doesn't easily affirm or contribute to its ultimate veracity and canonicity of its scientific validity. However, Jihad, which really represents the smaller elements of the market economy, while McWorld, which represents the larger elements of the market economy, are not only an interdependent and paradoxically inimical forces of the global market, but such interdependence is neither good for liberty or democracy because both are supplanted by McWorld whose global culture, ideology, and institutions it controls via information, communication, and entertainment industries. In the light of this scenario, McWorld's busy, absorptive and regulative power of the free, competitive and inscriptive market, tends to, and sometimes inadvertently so, marginalize and neutralize all forms of Jihads, in the long run. Jihads' singular or collective attempt and will to reinvent the past (wheel) lacks a sound economic, philosophical, scientific, and political foundation for bringing its ambitious dreams to reality.

## REFERENCES


Afrasiabi, Keveh, et. al. 2005. Negotiating Iran's nuclear populism. *The Brown Journal of World Affairs* XII, 1: 255-68.

Ahmed, Salman. 2005. No size fits all. *Foreign Affairs* 85, 1: 162-73.

Allison, Graham. 2006. Flight of fancy. *The Annals of the American Academy of Political and Social Science* 607: 162-6.

__________. 2006. Preface. *The Annals of the American Academy of Political and Social Science* 607: 6-9.

Alexander, Gerrad. 2005. There are no alternatives to the "western" model of democracy. *The Brown Journal of World Affairs* XII, 1: 155-66.

Anderson, Lisa. 2004. Review article – Shock and awe: Interpretations of the events of September 11. *World Politics: A Quarterly Journal of Internal Relations* 56, 2: 303-25.

Arendt, Hannah. 1979. *The origins of totalitarianism*. New York: Harcourt Brace and Jovanovich.

Aronoff, Myron J. 2001. Radical change in Israel: A review essay. *Political Science Quarterly: The Journal of Public and International Affairs* Fall: 447-53.

Baran, Zenyo. 2005. Fighting the war of ideas. *Foreign Affairs* 84, 6: 68-78.

Barber, Benjamin R. 1996. *Jihad vs. McWorld: How globalism and tribalism are reshaping the world*. New York: Ballantine Books.

Beeman, William. 2004. Elections and governmental structure in Iran: Reform lurks under the flaws. *The Brown Journal of World Affairs* XI, 1: 55-68.

Bellin, Eva. 2004-2005. The Iraqi intervention and democracy in comparative historical perspective. *Political Science Quarterly: The Journal of Public and International Affairs* Winter: 595-608.

Benhabib, Seyla, and Meyer Eugene. 2001. Unholy politics: 1-11.

Benjamin, Daniel, et al. 2006. The war of unintended consequences. *Foreign Affairs* 85, 2: 179-88.

Bergman, Edward F., and Renwick, William H. *Introduction to geography: People, places and environment*. Upper Saddle River, NJ: Pearson Prentice Hall.

Betts, Richard K. 2002. The soft underbelly of American primacy: Tactical advantages of terror. *Political Science Quarterly: The Journal of Public and International Affairs* Spring: 19-36.

Biddle, Stephen. 2006. Seeing Baghdad, thinking Saigon. *Foreign Affairs* 85, 2: 2-14.

Blinder, Allan S. 2006. Offshoring: The next industrial revolution? *Foreign Affairs* 85, 2: 113-28.
Brown, Seyom. 2002. American foreign policy and the limits of military might: A review essay. *Political Science Quarterly: The Journal of Public and International Affairs* Fall: 451-4.
Brumberg, Daniel. 2001. Dissonant politics in Iran and Indonesia. *Political Science Quarterly: The Journal of Public and International Affairs* Fall: 381-411.
Bunn, Matthew. 2006. A mathematical model of the risk of nuclear terrorism. *The Annals of the American Academy of Political and Social Science* 607: 103-20.
Bunn, Matthew, et al. 2006. Terrorist nuclear weapon construction: How difficult? *The Annals of the American Academy of Political and Social Science* 607: 133-49.
Byman, Daniel L. 2006. Do targeted killings work? *Foreign Affairs* 85, 2: 95-112.
__________. 2003. Al-Qaeda as an adversary: Do we understand our enemy? *World Politics: A Quarterly Journal of International Relations* 561: 139-63.
Calder, Kent E. 2006. China and Japan's simmering rivalry. *Foreign Affairs* 85, 2: 129-40.
Carothers, Thomas. 2006. The backlash against democracy promotion. *Foreign Affairs* 85, 2: 55-68.
Cha, Victor D. 2002. North Korea's Weapons of Mass Destruction: Badges, Shields, or Swords? *Political Science Quarterly: The Journal of Public and International Affairs* Summer: 209-30.
Chomsky, Noam. 2006. The United States and global wars of terror. In William F. Grover, and Joseph G. Peschek, eds. *Voices dissent: Critical readings in American politics*. New York: Pearson Longman: 318-29.
Cimbalo, Jeffrey. 2004. Saving NATO from Europe. *Foreign Affairs* 83, 6: 111-21.
Cirinocione, Joseph, et al. 2005. No good choices: The implications of a nuclear North Korea. *The Brown Journal of World Affairs* XII, 1: 269-77.
Cooley, Alexander. 2005. Base politics. *Foreign Affairs* 84, 6: 79-92.
Cronin, Audrey K. 2005. Behind the curve: Globalization and international terrorism. In Spiegel Steven L., Jennifer M. Taw, Fred L. Wehling, and Kirsten P. Williams, eds. *Readings in world politics: A new era*. Thomason Wadsworth: 340-59.
Curtis, Charles B. 2006. Curbing the demand for mass destruction. *The Annals of the American Academy of Political and Social Science* 607: 27-32.
Deng, Yong. 2001. Hegemon on the offensive: Chinese perspectives on U.S. global strategy. *Political Science Quarterly: The Journal of Public and International Affairs* Fall: 343-65.
Deutch, John. 2005. A nuclear posture for today. *Foreign Affairs* 85, 1: 49-60.
DeVries, Hent, and Sullivan, Lawrence E. 2007. *Political theologies: Public religions in a post- secular world.*
Diamond, Larry. 2004. Transition to democracy in Iraq? *The Brown Journal of World Affairs* XI, 1: 45-54.
Dobbins, James. 2005. Iraq: Winning the unwinnable war. *Foreign Affairs* 85, 1: 16-25.
Dobbins, James, et al. 2005. Iraq: Get out now or later? *Foreign Affairs* January/February.
Doran, Michael. 2002. The pragmatic fanaticism of al Qaeda: An anatomy of extremism in Middle Eastern politics. *Political Science Quarterly: The Journal of Public and International Affairs* Summer: 177-90.
Drozdiak, William. 2005. The North Atlantic drift. *Foreign Affairs* 85, 1: 88-98.
Eizenstat, Stuart, et al. 2005. Rebuilding weak stress. *Foreign Affairs* 85, 1: 134-47.

Euben, Roxanne. 2002. Killing for politics: Jihad, martyrdom and political action in political theory. October 16.

_________. 1999. *Enemy in the mirror: Islamist fundamentalism and the limits of modern rationalism.* Princeton, NJ: Princeton University Press.

Fessenden, Helen. 2005. The limits of intelligence reform. *Foreign Affairs* 84, 6: 106-23.

Friedmann, S. Julio, et al. 2004. Out of the energy box. *Foreign Affairs* 83, 6: 72-83.

Fisher, Louis. 2003. Deciding on war against Iraq: Institutional failures. *Political Science Quarterly: The Journal of Public and International Affairs* Fall: 389-410.

Fukuyama, Francis. 2005. Re-envisioning Asia. *Foreign Affairs* 85, 1: 75-87.

Gaddis, John Lewis. 2005. Grand Strategy in the Second Term. *Foreign Affairs* 84, 1: 2-15.

Gallucci, Robert L. 2006. Averting nuclear catastrophe: Contemplating extreme response to U.S. vulnerability. *The Annals of the American Academy of Political and Social Science* 607: 51-8.

Garrett, Geoffrey. 2004. Globalization's missing middle. *Foreign Affairs* 83, 6: 84-96.

Garten, Jeffrey. 2005. The global economic challenge. *Foreign Affairs* 85, 1: 37-48.

Goldstein, Lyle J. (2003). Do nascent WMD arsenals deter? The Sino-Soviet crisis of 1969. *Political Science Quarterly: The Journal of Public and International Affairs* Spring: 53-79.

Golman, Robert. 2004. Putin and the oligarchs. *Foreign Affairs* 83, 6: 33-44.

Haddad, Yvonne Y. 1993. *Muslims in America.* New York Oxford University Press, Inc.

Harrison, Selig. 2005. Did North Korea cheat? *Foreign Affairs* 85, 1: 99-110.

Hecker, Siegfried. 2006. Toward a comprehensive safeguards system: Keeping fissile materials out of terrorists' hands. *The Annals of the American Academy of Political and Social Science* 607: 121-32.

Herbest, Jeffrey. 2005. Mbeki's South Africa. *Foreign Affairs* 84, 6: 93-105.

Herzog, Micheal. 2006. Can Hamas be tamed? *Foreign Affairs* 85, 2: 83-94.

Hoodbhoy, Pervez. 2004. Can Pakistan work? *Foreign Affairs* 83, 6: 122-29.

Horvat, Andrew. 2004. Overcoming the negative legacy of the past: Why Europe is a positive example for East Asia. *The Brown Journal of World Affairs* XI, 1: 137-48.

Hulnick, Arthur. 2004. Espionage: Does it have a future in the twenty-first century? *The Brown Journal of World Affairs* XI, 1: 165-74.

Huntington, Samuel P. 1996. *The clash of civilization and the remaking of the world order.* New York: Simon and Schuster.

Hynes, Micheal V., et al. 2006. Denying Armageddon: Preventing terrorist use of nuclear weapons. *The Annals of the American Academy of Political and Social Science* 607: 150-61.

Indyk, Martin. 2004. Timing the trusteeship: Iraq and the opening window of opportunity. *The Brown Journal of World Affairs* XI, 1: 217-24.

Jackson, Sherman A. 2005. *Islam and black America.* New York: Oxford University Press.

Jackson, William D. 2002. Encircled again: Russia's military assesses threats in a post-Soviet world. *Political Science Quarterly: The Journal of Public and International Affairs* Fall: 373-400.

Jacobson, Gary C. 2003. Terror, terrain, and turnout: Explaining the 2002 midterm elections. *Political Science Quarterly: The Journal of Public and International Affairs* Spring: 1-22.

Jacoby, Tamar. 2001. The other Muslims. *The Wall Street Journal* 238, 93:17.

Jenkins, Bonnie. 2006. Combating nuclear terrorism: Addressing nonstate actor motivations. *The Annals of the American Academy of Political and Social Science* 607: 33-42.

Jervis, Robert. 2002. An interim assessment of September 11: What has changed and what has not. *Political Science Quarterly: The Journal of Public and International Affairs* Spring: 37-54.

Jones, Toby. 2006. Shifting sands. *Foreign Affairs* 85, 2: 164-70.

Joseph, Edward. 2005. Back to the Balkans. *Foreign Affairs* 85, 1: 111-22.

Kagan, Robert. 2005. A matter of record. *Foreign Affairs* 85, 1: 170-3.

Kalugin, Oleg. 2004. Terrorism and human intelligence: The Soviet experience. *The Brown Journal of World Affairs* XI, 1: 183-8.

Kaye, Dalia D. The Israeli decision to withdraw from southern Lebanon: Political leadership and security policy. *Political Science Quarterly: The Journal of Public and International Affairs* Winter: 561-85.

Kokoshin, Andrei. 2006. A nuclear response to nuclear terror: Reflections of nuclear redemption. *The Annals of the American Academy of Political and Social Science* 607: 59-63.

LaFeber, Walter. 2002. The post September 11 debate over empire, globalization, and fragmentation. *Political Science Quarterly: The Journal Of Public and International Affairs* Spring: 1-17.

Lewis, Rand. 2004. Espionage and the war on terrorism: Investigating U.S. efforts. *The Brown Journal of World Affairs* XI, 1: 175-82.

Lieber, Keir, et al. 2006. The rise of U.S. nuclear primacy. *Foreign Affairs* 85, 2: 42-54.

Lutrrwak, Edward. 2005. Iraq: The logic of disengagement. *Foreign Affairs* 85, 1: 26-36.

Mamdani, Mahmood. 2005. Whither political Islam? *Foreign Affairs* 85, 1: 148-55.

Maugeri, Leonardo. 2006. Two cheers for expensive oil. *Foreign Affairs* 85, 2: 149-63.

McCartney, Paul T. 2004. American nationalism and U.S. foreign policy from September 11 to the Iraq War. *Political Science Quarterly: The Journal of Public and International Affairs* Fall: 399-423.

McGregor, Richard. 2006. *Muslims Christian Century* 123, 24:24:36-45.

McLean. I. 1996. *The concise Oxford dictionary of politics*. New York: Oxford University Press.

Molavi, Afshin. 2005. Dubai rising. *The Brown Journal of World Affairs* XII, 1: 103-4.

__________. 2004. Buying time in Tehran. *Foreign Affairs* 83, 6: 9-17.

Mueller, John. 2005. The Iraq syndrome. *Foreign Affairs* 84, 6: 44-54.

Nacos, Brigitte L. 2003. Terrorism as breaking news: Attack on America. *Political Science Quarterly: The Journal of Public and International Affairs* Spring: 23-52.

*New Political Science*. 2003. Wars of Terror 25, 1: 113-27.

Nicolaidis, Kalpso. 2004. We, the Peoples of Europe. *Foreign Affairs* 83, 6: 97-110.

Nunn, Sam. 2006. The race between cooperation and catastrophe: Reducing the global nuclear threat. *The Annals of the American Academy of Political and Social Science* 607: 43-50.

Nye, Joseph S., Jr. 2002-2003. Limits of American power. *Political Science Quarterly: The Journal of Public and International Affairs* Winter: 545-59.

O'Connell, Kevin. 2004. Thinking about intelligence comparatively. *The Brown Journal of World Affairs* XI, 1: 189-202.

Odom, William. 2004. Understanding America's empire (If it really has one). *The Brown Journal of World Affairs* XI, 1: 203-216.

Owen, John M. 2005. Iraq and the democratic peace. *Foreign Affairs* 84, 6: 122-7.

Palumbo, Gaetano. 2005. The state of Iraq's cultural heritage in the aftermath of the 2003 war. *The Brown Journal of World Affairs* XII, 1: 225-38.
Pape, Robert. 2003. The strategic logic of suicide terrorism. *American Political Science Review* 97: 343-62.
Payne, Leigh. 2004. In search of remorse: Confessions by perpetrators of past state violence. *The Brown Journal of World Affairs* XI, 1: 115-26.
Perry, William J. 2006. Proliferation the peninsula: Five North Korean nuclear crises. *The Annals of the American Academy of Political and Social Science* 607: 78-86.
Pillar, Paul R. 2006. Intelligence, policy, and the war in Iraq. *Foreign Affairs* 85, 2: 15-28.
Rayburn, Joel. 2006. The last exit from Iraq. *Foreign Affairs* 85, 2: 29-41.
Rich, Georg. 2004. The Euro after five years. The *Brown Journal of World Affairs* XI, 1: 241-51.
Ross, Dennis. 2005. The Middle East predicament. *Foreign Affairs* 85, 1: 61-74.
Ross, Robert S. 2006. Taiwan's fading independence movement. *Foreign Affairs* 85, 2: 141-8.
Rubin, Barry, et al. 2004. Anti-American re-examined. *The Brown Journal of World Affairs* XI, 1: 17-26.
Russell, Richard L. 2002. CIA's intelligence in Iraq. *Political Science Quarterly: The Journal of Public and International Affairs* Summer: 191-207.
Sagini, Meshack M. 2001. *Organizational behavior: The challenge of the new millennium.* Lanham, MD: University Press of America, Inc.
Saradzhyan, Simon. 2006. Russia: Grasping the reality of nuclear terror. *The Annals of the American Academy of Political and Social Science* 607: 64-77.
Schauble, Wolfgang, et al. 2004. Talking Turkey. *Foreign Affairs* 83, 6: 134-7.
Segal, Adam. 2004. Is America losing its edge? *Foreign Affairs* 83, 6: 2-8.
Sen, Amartya. (2006). The Man Without a Plan. *Foreign Affairs*, March/April 85, 2, 171-178.
Shain, Yossi. 2002. Jewish kinship at a crossroads: Lessons for homelands and diasporas. *Political Science Quarterly: The Journal of Public and International Affairs* Summer: 279-309.
Shikaki, Khalil. 2004. The future of Palestine. *Foreign Affairs* 83, 6: 45-60.
Slater, Jerome. 2001. What went wrong? The collapse of the Israeli-Palestinian peace process. *Political Science Quarterly: The Journal of Public and International Affairs* Summer: 171-99.
Smith, Tony, et al. 2004. Was Iraq a fool's errand? *Foreign Affairs* 83, 6: 130-3.
Straus, Scott. 2005. Darfur and the genocide debate. *Foreign Affairs* January/February: 123-133.
Tangugi, Laurent C. 2005. The end of Europe? *Foreign Affairs* 84, 6: 55-67.
Tinaz, Nuri. 2006. Black Islam. *Journal of Muslim Minority Affairs* 26, 2:151-70.
Tucker, Robert, and David Henderson. 2004. The sources of American legitimacy. *Foreign Affairs* 83, 6: 18-32.
Urquhart, Brian. 2004. New demands and old constraints: The role of the UN in the modern international system. *The Brown Journal of World Affairs* XI, 1: 225-30.
Van Evera, Stephen. 2006. Assessing U.S. strategy in the war on terror. *The Annals of the American Academy of Political and Social Science* 607: 10-26.
Wedgwood, Ruth. 2002. Al Qaeda, military commissions, and American self-defense. *Political Science Quarterly: The Journal of Public and International Affairs* Fall: 357-72.
Wieck, Hans-Gerog, et al. 2004. Spies like us. *Foreign Affairs* 38, 6: 138-41.

Wikipedia. com

Wikotorowicz, Quintan, and Kaltenthaler Kar. 2006. The Rationality of Racial Islam. *Political Science Quarterly* 121, 2: 295-319.

Wolfsthal, Jon. 2005. The next nuclear wave. *Foreign Affairs* 85, 1: 156-63.

Wood, Daniel B. American black Muslims. *Christian Science Monitor* 94, 57:3.

Yergin, Daniel. 2006. Ensuring energy security. *Foreign Affairs* 85, 2: 69-82.

Zenko, Micah. 2006. Intelligence estimates of nuclear terrorism. *The Annals of the American Academy of Political and Social Science* 607: 87-102.

# Section Two: Comparative Foreign Policies of the Great Powers of the 21st Century

Section two consists of chapters six through ten. The chapters discuss the evolutionary, historical and imperialistic foreign policies of the U.S., EU, and China. Each region's (country's) foreign policy is a product of its own people, region or continent. Because each foreign policy type belongs to a different cultural system, the systemic differences in foreign policies are continental, transcontinental, and regionally triadic in their projection of power differentials and influence. In this arena, the speed, volume, and impact with which interactive diffusion globally takes place has tremendous potential for the generation of conflict. Such conflict is inevitable because the systems are inherently prone to dealing with issues of competitive and comparative advantage at the regional, global, and international levels. The realization for potential conflict calls for thorough reexamination of the motives, fortunes, and vices of globalization in order to minimize potential for anarchy, massive deglobalization, and deenlightment. The same reevaluation of globalization should critique the nature and character of laissez-faire liberalization and bureaucratically bloated technocratic forms of institutionalism. To initiate reforms of this kind, reformers should place emphasis on interdependence, democracy, and scientific uplift of the underdeveloped regions that experience persistent gloדal explotation, control, and marginalization.

# Chapter VI
# U.S. Foreign Policy

## INTRODUCTION

As an historical product of the evolution of public policy, American foreign policy is rooted in its revolutionary Enlightenment ideas of natural rights, the Declaration of Independence and, the Constitution. Second, the synergistic influences of the Greco-Roman world, and Judeo-Christian Western Civilization have provided it with its core ideals. Third, contemporary ideas concerning globalization, regionalism and the unknown quest for its future in the world, tend to drive the dynamics that help it to chart new directions and old ones in new ways. The contemporary period spans from the nineteenth century notions of Western expansion and twentieth century rationalization of decolonization, containment, and globalization.

American foreign policy of the realist, centrist, and Kissingerian or Kenanist school of the Cold War was hijacked by the Neoconservative movement during the presidency of George Bush the second. Their intellectual roots were based on the Chicago School. The School's influence produced a cadre of anti-communist and ultra conservative intellectual ideologues who dominated American foreign policy agenda during the first decade of the new millennium. Neoconservatism is one of the four different approaches to American foreign policy. "There are, in addition to Henry Kissinger, those who respect power and tend to down play the internal nature of other regimes and human rights concerns; there are liberal internationalists who hope to transcend power politics altogether and move to an international order based on law and institutions; and there are what Walter Russell Mead labels 'Jacksonian' American nationalists, who tend to take a narrow, security-related view of American national interests, distrust multilateralism, and in their more extreme manifestations, tend toward nativism and isolationism" (Fukuyama 2006, 7). The neoconservative alliance, with the support of Jacksonian nationalists, used diverse logics to solidify their move for regime change in Iraq. Centrist realists such as Henry Kissinger, James Baker, and Brent Scowcroft were ignored because the neoconservative school is diametrically opposed to the centrist ideological tradition of the realist philosophical thought. The main problem is that none of the "neoconservative, realist, 'Jacksonian' nationalist, or liberal internationalist properly define the approach to the world that the U.S. needs to follow in the aftermath of September 11 and the invasion of Iraq" (p. 8).

American foreign policy needs to employ soft rather than hard power, rationalize realism as opposed to neoconservative extremism and enculturate realist Wilsonianism as opposed to classical realism. Foreign policy think-tanks and its bureaucratic and technocratic implementers should lessen their social engineering aspects, work to promote democracy in failed states that have become the source of global instability, and restore the traditional moral purpose of American foreign policy by promoting democracy and economic development as opposed to promoting unilateralism, preemptive innovations, and antimultilateralism in an economically, technologically and socially interpenetrated global society.

The main varieties of American neoconservatism which cannot be disentangled include "small government libertarianism, religious or social conservatism, or American nationalism" (p. 38). Determining who is qualified as a neoconservative is difficult because mainstream population has accepted all these strands of the neoconservative movement- economic, religious, nationalist, and libertarian due to the fact that all these brand adherents started life as socialists. It is self- evident that after the collapse of the U.S.S.R., "these former socialists" experienced an intellectual and ideological flight from traditional and historical structuralism by discovering an acceptable ideological niche (neoconservatism) they fervently cling to in order to rationalize their own foreign policy agenda. The rationalization of this agenda is promoted through the media, public opinion polls, political parties, interest groups, and a variety of organizational and institutional think-tanks.

Douglas Murray (2006) wrote a book called *Neo-conservatism: We need it.* Like President George W. Bush, he believes that the Islamist movement is a form of extreme and fanatical fascism that has attained the malignancy of its Medieval fundamentalism. The neoconservative movement of the neocons emerged before Bush II became the president. They believed in the enlightenment ideas, in virtue, the Constitution, the Declaration of Independence, imperialism, but distrusted philosophy. They did not like change. These extremists whom the liberal establishment despised, goaled Bush to invade Iraq and were for strategic reasons, adamant to see the war ended. The "neo-cons" movement had intellectual roots that radiated from Leo Strauss although its godfather was Irving Kristol, the editor of the *Weekly Standard* and founder of William Kristol cable news talk show. The prominent "neo- cons" included but were not limited to Daniel Patrick Moynihan, Jeanne Kirkpatrick (both were democrats when they accepted the philosophy), Tony Blair, Charles Krauthammer, Allan Bloom and Paul Wolfowitz. Wolfowitz had a dominant influence on the president's foreign policy and defense strategy. The former's chief interest in all this was, other things being equal, based on the security of Israel which had been enhanced or retrogressed by the evolving post Saddamist politic-economic and geostrategic calculations of the three superpowers (E.U., Russia and China) that have a stake in the region with which the U.S. interests converge.

Neo-conservatism is not traditionally conservative enough. It's unintellectual polemic or way of thinking rationalizes domestic and foreign policy in the light of republican perspectives particularly in the areas of tax policy, welfare reform, and the refinement and diffusion of domestic ideals around the globe. In this crisis, they saw Arabs to be not only the aggressive combatants who also see themselves as victims, but they challenge them to search for the truth also. In the wake of the collapse of the USSR and disintegrations of the Soviet empire, the neo-cons, some of whom have an evangelical zeal for missionary and democratic evangelization of the Middle East, acted opportunistically in order to reshape the world in the American image. This group advocated the strategies of conflict, Unilateralism, preemption, and confrontation. The second group of less assertive republicans advocated corporatism, multilateralism, and peaceful stability in a changing and global environment. During 9/11/2001, the Eagles response to these events caused it to "crash land," become a global policeman and got entangled in an explosive, and anti-American (antiglobalization), Islamist and global environment. This powerless superpower should needed to rethink strategically; avoid "shock and awe" (Gaddis 2005) tactics and reshape a new foreign policy in order to alleviate its Bushistic isolationism. No hegemonic power could manage a world empire by using an ambitious foreign policy agenda that is rationalized with the use of insufficient means and resources. However, the insufficiency of means and resources is traceable way back to the day of Woodrow Wilson (Dueck 2003/2004).

Though the neo- conservatives had modeled their foreign policy choices on those of President Ronald Reagan, their over interpretation of the Bush Doctrine had contributed to undercutting its strategic effectiveness (Lowry 2005). In the light of the nation's decline in economic, political, and military power, factors that made the United States the hegemonic power for over 100 years, its loss of them may have caused the Eagle to crash land (Wallerstein 2002) rather than descending systematically and gracefully. The preemptive action against Iraq could have exacerbated the speed with which descent took place if Obamarian and immediate measures to contain it had not effectively been implemented. Given the fact that the U.S. acted unilaterally and preemptively rather than multilaterally (Tepperman 2004), it had no choice.

In terms of the domestic side of American politics and foreign policy, American nationalism is quite paradoxically rooted in the faith and superiority of American ideas rather than in the knowledge of its ethnic superiority. As a result, the rejection of ethnic nationalism contributes to America's inability to understand the continuing power of nationalism in world affairs and the perceptions of America illegitimacy in conducting foreign policy (Pei 2003, *America*

*Foreign Policy: Annual Editions: VII*). In addition, this nationalistic element which advocates the superiority of American ideas as opposed to its ethnocentricity is farther weakened by the doctrinal division of the politics of U.S. military interventions (Western 2004). Western tries to show that since the American public has unrealistic expectations about the effectiveness of military interventions, the rhetoric of political campaigns and the challenges associated with post-war reconstruction tend to erode the superiority and viability of the ideas in question. Speaker
Nancy Pelosi's attempt to conduct American foreign policy in the Middle East was reminiscent of the weaknesses of the idea in question, about which President Bush had failed to understand why we were in Iraq although he took us there in the first place.

## U.S. FOREIGN POLICY: PRESIDENTIAL INVOLVEMENT

Between 1789 and 1898, i.e. for about one hundred and ten years of the republic, American foreign policy, particularly during the administrations of George Washington, who believed in "temporary rather than permanent alliances," Thomas Jefferson who in 1801 talked about no entangling alliances and the 1823 Monroe Doctrine through which president James Monroe warned Europeans against interference in the Western Hemisphere- the Americans, were largely isolationist rather than activist, engaged, or interventionist in character. However, throughout the twentieth century and at the down of the twenty-first century, American domestic, military, economic, institutional and global interests have jointly and powerfully consolidated and solidified in their use of diplomatic instruments to dictate the demand for the era of trade, diplomacy, peacemaking and peace keeping. Such interventionist peacemaking and aggressive foreign policy has been influenced by many thinkers particularly those from the realist and neorealist intellectual traditions especially Hobbies, Thucydides, Machiavelli, E.H Carr, Hans Morgenthau, Kenneth Waltz, and Henry Kissinger (Sagini 2004). The writings of these great men have, both in the past and present, inspired world leaders particularly those of the United States, to craft imperialistic notions of American colonialism, containment, détente, globalization and fragmentation. In the era of globalization, what is needed most for the U.S. to successfully "reinvent itself" globally and particularly in foreign and domestic matters is the positive promotion and reconstruction of "universal human values" and progressive disengagement of the bureaucratic and foreign policy elitist mentality of maintaining "class struggle" notions in domestic and international otherness. Second, the U.S. should reinvent its inferior popular culture (Markovits 2007) in order to promote its peoples' moral and economic power (Starr 1991). American leaders have lost influence in spite of their "superior ability, sound training and high ideals" (Thompson 1999, 241).

On July 4, 1821, the then secretary of state, John Quincy Adams opposed sending the U.S. Navy to interfere in the internal affairs of the newly independent Spanish colonies of Columbia and Chile. He asserted that "America does not go abroad in search of monsters to destroy. She is the well-wisher to the freedom and independence of all. She is the champion only of her own." However, in 1823, President James Monroe proclaimed the Monroe Doctrine which asserted that the United States would not interfere in European colonies in the Western Hemisphere, the U.S. would not interfere in the European affairs either. Logically, this isolationist position meant that if a European nation were to meddle itself in the Western Hemisphere, the U.S. foreign policy machinery had the right and power to attack that nation. Interpretively, the U.S. foreign policy, as President Monroe stated, had became the defender and protector of the Western Hemisphere.

In 1898, President William Mckinley asked congress to declare war on Spain for its abuse (mistreatment) of Cubans' human rights. The President argued, "It is no answer to say this is all in another country, and is therefore none of our business. It is especially our duty, for it is right at our door." The Spanish American war enabled the U.S. to fight and defeat Spain for the freedom of Cuba, the Philippines, and Puerto Rico. Cuban revolutionaries fought on the U.S. side. The Spanish fleets were defeated and by the treaty of Paris (1898), the Philippines, Guam, and Puerto Rico were ceded by Spain to the U.S. Spain lost control of Cuba whose provisional occupation by the U.S. military became a triumphant American foreign policy affair. In the wake of the War between the U.S. and Spain, Ambrose Bierce, a satirical novelist, observed that "War is the God's way of teaching Americans geography". The U.S. left Philippines in 1946 but its military base was maintained until 1990 and renegotiated for an indefinite period shortly afterwards.

President McKinley was succeeded by President Theodore Roosevelt who reinforced the Monroe Doctrine (Roosevelt Corollary) which reasserted that "chronic wrongdoing may...require intervention by some civilized nation, and in the Western Hemisphere the adherence of the United States to the Monroe Doctrine may force the United States however reluctantly, in flagrant cases of wrongdoing of impotence, to the exercise of an international police power."

For almost a century, the Monroe Doctrine made the United States and the entire Western Hemisphere to experience diplomatic isolationism which enabled it to remain politically stable but economically, scientifically, technologically, and militarily ascendant. Between 1914 and 1918, the negative impact of WWI in the world influenced President Woodrow Wilson (1913-21) to repudiate the isolationist stance of the U.S. in world affairs. Wilson announced that he was ready to let the United States join a permanent association (alliance) of nations. However, his administrative tactlessness and inability to compromise with congress resulted in the United States' failure to join the League of Nations. Subsequently, and twenty years later, the lack of strong and dynamic statesmanship in world leadership drove the world into the Second World War (1939-1945). Hitler had almost conquered the entire European continent. However, in 1944, the allies (U.S.; UK; USSR; and France) decided to divide Germany and Austria into four occupations zones respectively. In February 1945, the Allies "smelled" victory and the three leaders (Roosevelt, Stalin, and Churchill) met at the Ukrainian City of Yalta and planned how the postwar world would look like. Almost without protest, the two Western leaders allowed Stalin to demarcate and control Eastern Europe and declare war against Japan in the Pacific and Mancharia (N. Korea) in order to save American lives. During the spring of 1945, Stalin agreed to join the U.N.O which was founded in San- Francisco. On April 12, President Roosevelt died from cerebral hemorrhage. Truman, at a British-Soviet-American conference at Postdam (German) said, "the leaders endorsed the expulsion of ethnic Germans from eastern Europe and moved the borders of Poland 100 miles into historically German territory. Truman also made it clear that the United States expected to dominate the occupation of Japan. Its goal was to democratize the Japanese political system and reintroduce Japan into the international community, the policy succeeded" (Abbott 2007, 836). When the Potsdam Declaration failed to fully convince Japan to surrender to the United States, the latter detonated two atomic bombs on Japan in August 1945 at Nagasaki and Hiroshima, instantly kill 40,000 and 80,000 people respectively. The decision to use the bomb was dictated by circumstances that surrounded military necessity, economic diplomacy, and domestic politics concerning secretly using billions of the Manhattan Project. Finally, the decision to bomb Japan was a military tactic through which the massive destruction of Japanese cities would make the war's momentum attain ultimate resolve (Abbott 2007), even scaring Stalin as well. Although this action could have been avoided since the war had ended, the decision to use the bomb was an act of strong presidential leadership. As a foreign policy decision, President Jimmy Carter emphasized the importance of protecting and encouraging all countries to observe the significance of human rights in all countries during the Cold War period. When Russia attacked Afghanistan in 1980, Carter retaliated diplomatically by nullifying American participation in Olympic Games in Moscow and by urging allies to do so.

The 9/11/2001 attack on the United States changed America's relative isolationist world view because it ended the United State's willingness to respect terrorist states and the states which harbor terrorists. On September 20, 2001, President W. Bush addressed Congress as follows:

> We will drive ... terrorists from place to place, until there is no refuge or no rest. And we will pursue nations that provide aid or save haven to terrorism. Every nation, in every region, now has a decision to make. Either you are with us, or you are with the terrorists. From this day forward, any nation that continues to harbor or support terrorism will be regarded by the United States as a hostile regime. The president reiterated that "every nation has a choice to make. In this conflict, there is no neutral ground. If any government sponsors the outlaws and killers of innocents, they have become outlaws and murders themselves. And they will take the lonely path at their own peril (Abbott, et al. 2007, 579).

Many critics and observers think that the president's diplomatic warning repudiated many systems including the 1648 Treaty of Westphilia signed on October 24, by the "Holy Roman Empire, France, Sweden, and the Protestant States of the empire, ending the Thirty Year's War. The Holy Roman Empire was greatly weakened by the recognition of the German States" (*New Webster Dictionary Thesaurus of the English Language* 1992, 1118). In the provisions of the treaty, France gained Alsace, and became the dominant power in Europe. Sweden gained the western part of Pomerania. Switzerland and the Netherlands became independent while Calvinists were religiously tolerated. In other words, the historical, constitutional, and diplomatic standards upon which the foundation of the modern European nations is rooted were, indirectly speaking, repudiated by President Bush.

Senior advisor to President Nixon, Ford, George H. Bush, and Reform Party's presidential candidate, Patrick Buchanan, in 2000, asserted that what happened on 9-11-2001 "was a direct consequence of an interventionist U.S. policy in an Islamic world where no threat to our vital interests justifies our massive involvement. We are a republic, not an empire. And until we restore the foreign policy urged upon us by our founding fathers of staying out of the other nations' quarrels we shall know no end of war and no security of peace in our homeland" (Abbott, et al. 2007, 579). Although Buchanan's comment cannot credibly be contextualized historically, the comment is a cautionary statement.

During the U.S.-Iraq War, and in contradistinction to the isolationist character of American foreign policy, the United States had arrogantly become the world's policeman that destroyed monsters. In his *Wars and peace: The future Americans, 1861-1991 (1998),* David Mayer's analysis of American foreign policy reflects on the five major wars of the twentieth century. In this analysis, he is concerned with the consistent "failure of American leaders to provide a coherent set of principles that could be used to guide the nation in the chaotic post- Cold War years of the 1990s" (Heston, 200: 204) and beyond. These major global conflicts have not, as a common theme that emerges from this analysis, enabled the nation's leaders to realize war time visions and missions. For instance, Reconstruction proved to be a far cry from Lincoln's plea for peace and reconciliation to bind up the nation's wounds. The U.S.'s desire to free Cuba ended up with that island's becoming an American protectorate, and eventually an anti- American communist nation "as well as with the acquisition of the distant Philippines." Wilson's call for peace without victory in the vindictive treaty of Versailles and another world war just 20 years later. FDR's appeal for a world based on the freedom from fear led instead to the Cold-War, which ended in an apparent American triumph with the disintegration of the Soviet Union, followed by the Persian Gulf War and the subsequent Middle East War from which America hardly failed to disentangle itself and in which she was the big loser particularly in issues related to "massive ethnic violence in Africa (Ruanda, Congo, Liberia and Sudan), and in the brutal civil war in Bosnia" (p. 204).

Mayers (1998) argues that since the U.S. history is a story that is "chastised by conscience" whose latent imperialism tends to produce challenged "democratic universalism," each solution produces new and greater challenges for the nation. For instance, "Infighting to right a wrong, whether slavery in the south, Germany attempt at European hegemony, or Soviet totalitarianism, we end up with new challenges that are equally difficult to resolve" (p. 205) such a form of fighting and losing, even in Somalia, is an element of futility that tends to animate American isolationism.

To a large extent, the nature, structure and texture of contemporary American foreign policy in terms of how it is "constructed, historical and cultural texture that informs it, the ideologically oriented political and economic culture that animates it, the political texture that sustains it, and the legal ideas and interests" that dynamically and inherently drive it (Sagini 2004, 38) has its evolutionary roots in the post World War II and Cold War realities of the twentieth century. For instance, while the 1989 collapse of the U.S.S.R was largely caused by internal and external forces in terms of "economic exhaustion, failure of leadership, intervention in Afghanistan, triumph of democratic ideas and power of nationalism" (Abbott, et al 2007, 965) and Western geostrategic containment (Sagini 2001), the 1945 defeat of the Axis by the Allied forces enabled the latter to dictate a post war economic trading structure that did not only favor its interests, but also proved to be effective during the twentieth century largely, because it contributed to the development of a vast industrial, technical and capitalistically managed regional and global economy. The powerful, popular, and central powers (U.S. and U.S.S.R) were naturally antagonistic to each other, were not only and inherently challenged by ideological differences between capitalism and socialism/ communism on the one hand, but, the zealous, massive, and destructive ability to develop nuclear weapons which made relative parity of power existing between America and the U.S.S.R ... direct superpower made war mutually suicidal" (Feste 1990,1). The massive development of these weapons by both powers became a deterrent of their use because the major civilizations learned that if they were to use them against each other, they would be changed into nuclear winter. As a result, their spheres of influence in the periphery bore the brunt of the interventionist and confrontational policies in the Third World. Some of these colonial policies, in particular, caused the European powers to lose their colonies and therefore disintegrate by losing Superpower status. The only existing superpower (U.S.) continues, in its interventionist character, to use the same relatively similar foreign policies particularly in the Middle East. Superpowers particularly the United States articulate their foreign policy, as a form of intervention in other countries. In this case the U.S. uses "military and economic intervention on as a tool of statecraft" (p. 2).

## WHAT IS THE MEANING OF INTERVENTION?

> Intervention is the dictatorial or coercive interference by an outside party or parties in the sphere of jurisdiction of a Sovereign State, or more broadly, of an independent political community. It may be forcible or nonforcible, direct or indirect, open or clandestine; the jurisdiction may refer to as State territory, its citizenry, the right to determine its internal affairs, or the nature of interference might involve the use of military or paramilitary instruments, or economic or diplomatic sanctions by the outside party … intervention overlaps with international politics in general, constituting another perspective in grand conceptual analysis for understanding foreign policy" (Feste 1990, 3).

Both Bull (1984) and Rosenau (1969) have argued that intervention is a form of behavior which changes the relationship between the two states (the attacker and the attacked). Such behavior is aimed at changing or preserving the fundamental grain of political values in the attacked country. If the nature of the attack is unilateral, as it evolved to be in Iraq, the attack or intervention is viewed as irrelevant, illegal and immoral by the world community. In spite of "wide spread disapproval and numerous legal prohibitions, restraining it, coercive intrusion by one state into another continues to be a common feature of contemporary international affairs; both the rules of non-intervention and mutual respect of sovereign jurisdiction are remote from the realities of current events" (Feete 1990, 3). There are several theories that explain the interventionist nexus (as covert action, intelligence, propaganda, and peacemaking). Intervention is an instrument of foreign policy and as a realist theory of international relations executed by the superpower(s), is rooted in the rational actor model. First, based on the model, a superpower, like any country, tends to make choices on the basis of "structured interactive processes of inputs and outputs and constraints and opportunities" (p. 4). Second, Allison and Valenta advocate the use of the bureaucratic model which emphasizes the significance of shifting policies of loose heterogeneous coalitions of key bureaucratic interest groups" (p. 4) which will be discussed later. Third, general, imperialistic theories that are a display of superpower foreign policy intervention advocate aggressive, expansionistic policies and containment based objectives reminiscent of post Cold War expansionism. Fourth, and in respect to American intervention in Latin America and its unilateral and preemptive intervention in Iraq, U.S. security needs are the main factors for its coercive involvement in this area. Fifth, other scholars argue that U.S. interventionist interference is grounded in 'domestic political factors, interested groups and bureaucratic competition between the hawks and the doves and their unrealistic suspicions, that arise from the demand for gas, oil, and minerals do influence the foreign policy imperialistic elite groups to pursue their interest(s) in the name of the national interest. Finally, bureaucratic and strategic thinkers who feel the national interest is not well served when coercive and economic instruments are applied tend to use diplomacy rather than" the stick and the carrot or any of the above described theoretical approaches. In essence, most intervention strategies tend to be ineffective as evidence based on experience in Vietnam and the twenty-first century U.S. vs. Iraq War has demonstrated. However, when intervention policies become "more economic, political, and diplomatic and less military" (Hart 1990, 11) the national interest is better served. In addition, bureaucratic leaders and political regimes should de-ideologize their diplomatic, and foreign policies in order to enhance interstate relations, reduce class, or interstate conflict rather than" senselessly remaining stubborn and clinging to counter productive and enmity promoting theories of fictional messianism" (Woodly 1989, 17).

Lawrence R. Jacob and Benjamin I. (2005) have, by analyzing the literature on international relations, identified people and social forces responsible for influencing the construction of American foreign policy. These people and forces include but are not limited to "experts and epistemic communities, organized interests ... especially business and labor, and ordinary citizens or public Opinion" (p. 107). However, a comparative set of studies on who influences American foreign policy in terms of a variety of academic, cross section and demographic studies concluded that "U.S.. foreign policy is most heavily and consistently influenced by internationally oriented business leaders, followed by experts (who, however, may themselves be influenced by business). Labor appears to have significant but smaller impact. The general public seems to have considerably less effect except under particular conditions. These results generally hold several different analytical models (including two- observation time series) and different clusters of issues (economic, military, and diplomatic), with some variation across different institutional settings (the U.S. house, Senate, and executive branch) (p.107). Public opinion is a populist and less effective way of obtaining ideas on American labor or interest groups familiar with foreign policy ideas and networks. Knowledge- based "experts in the academy, think tanks, and other repositories of technocratic expertise" (Haas, 1992, 12; Hall 1989; Nelkin 1979) influence U.S. foreign policy. As far as epistemics are concerned, most of them are, in terms of professional training, prestige, and reputation for expertise, they are objectively valid and authoritative advisers of legislative and executive branches of the U.S. government. These technical experts tend to use comparative, classical, and contemporary theoretical paradigms to analyze and interpret the effect of international structure on contemporary political practice and international relations. Overall, however, while business and technocratic models are dominant, foreign policy decision making agencies and the mass of public opinion and interest groups have less influence while business influence is greater than the influence of the academic technocratic elite whose influence is only secondary to that of business elites because of the former's's competitive struggle over the national interest. The U.S. presence in and conflict with Iraq cannot be more underscored in respect to this argument. Though academic foreign policy experts such as Henry Kissinger, Zbigniew Brzezinski, Anthony Lake, Madeleine Albright, Joseph Nye, Condoleezza Rice, Stephen Krasner and their students do research on the subject, "the research they do tends to have less direct bearing to their foreign policy advisory responsibilities. The foreign policy debate is what scholars teach students, publish in policy journals, write in news papers op-ed, say on the media, advice political leaders with, and do when they are themselves in public office" (Bennett and Ikenberry 2006, 651).

The Central thesis of American foreign policy is rooted in the global society whose political, economic, technological, cultural, environmental, and other social forces have deeply and increasingly become inseparable from American domestic policy. The multiplicity of the challenges associated with that position has intensified the debate as to whether the United States should continue with the former President Bush II's apparently destructive global engagement, or disengage from it completely, or creatively and selectively become innovative rather than remaining stubbornly and strategically myopic in the global arena. The Obamarian strategic global engagement may have currently become the new vision with which the whole world is pleased. For instance, "the intensification of U.S. Interdependence with the world political economy that accompanied globalization increases domestic pressure on the nation's foreign policies and policy making processes. ... Interdependence comprises of the sovereign autonomy of the state, blurs the distinction between foreign and domestic politics, and elevates the participation of domestically oriented government agencies in the policy process … produces clear winners and losers within the American polity" (Wittkopf and McCormick 1999, XII) and even more so at the periphery. By doing so, the globalization process which is the chief raison detre of American foreign policy, has destructively, expansively and unrelentingly become extremely divisive in every sphere of life in the global community in which elitist, pluralist, bureaucratic, and majoritarian foreign policy decisions are made and influenced by domestic, societal interest groups, the media, political parties, public opinion, institutional culture, social structures and major ideologies. Michael J. Sordaro (2008) "refers to the growing interconnectedness of governments, non- state actors, and populations throughout the world through a variety of political, economic, technological, cultural, environmental, and other interactions" (p. 19). This multifaceted system of global interactions and interdependence is engineered by economics while being fueled by technology. "When the U.S. economy sneezes, the rest of the world catches cold." In spite of its merits, it critics contend that since it has afflicted millions of subsistence based economic systems in the south and contributed to "poverty, child labor, the marginalization of women, environmental degradation and etc." globalization could be "imperiled" (p. 17).

American hegemonic power was built on the basis of post war tacit agreement and institutionalized arrangements that were compellingly envisioned as liberal hegemony that was constructed to enfoıce the "containment order" of the Cold War. That order maintained "a wary balance of power backed by nuclear deterrence and maintaining that order, the U.S. policymakers succeeded because "they were able to make the case… for free trade, an open trading system, and a set of Western democracies" (Ikenberry 2006, 111). The containment and orderliness of free trade and open trading system of the capitalist and free enterprise system was "sold convincingly to the Asian and European partners" (p. 111) for stability and predictability. Ikenberry asserts that the U.S. managed to exercise 'strategic restraint'- and "persuaded potential partners of the commitment to the principles of the non-coercive and multilateral postwar order-that was essential to achieving a settlement that was mutually acceptable to a group of states with huge power asymmetries" (p. 111).

## IS THE U.S. AN EMPIRE OR NOT? THEORETICAL INSIGHT

To answer this question effectively, it is important to analytically define unipolarity, hegemony, and empire in relational and structural terms that have network properties (Wellman 1983; Simmel 1971). Two scholars, Daniel H. Nexon and Thomas Wright (2007) of George Washington University have addressed this question from an interdisciplinary and rigorous theoretical and analytical perspective. Conclusively, they have asserted that:

> Scholars of World Politics enjoy well- developed theories of the consequences of the unipolarity or hegemony, but have little to say about what happens when a state's foreign relations take on imperial properties. Empires, we argue, are characterized by rule through intermediaries and the existence of distinctive contractual relations between cores and their peripheries. These features endow them with a distinctive network-structure from those associated with unipolar and hegemonic orders. The existence of imperial relations alters the dynamics of imperial international politics: processes of divide and rule supplant the balance-of-power mechanism; the major axis of the relations shift from interstate to those among imperial authorities, local intermediaries, and other peripheral actors; and preeminent powers face special problems of legitimating their bargains across heterogeneous audiences. We calculate observations about the American empire debate, including that the United States is, overall, less of an imperial power than it was during the cold war (Nexon and Wright 2007, 253).

An empire is a sovereign country that has immense military power for economic conquest of the less powerful states, which it colonizes or converts into federal systems. The conquered areas may include countries or/and territories that formerly were independent of it. The empire's commercial, industrial, financial wealth and military power are equal to its size. Though most Americans do not see themselves as an imperial nation, for fear of "politics that maintain, enhance, or erode its security" (p. 253) its "unipolar" stature and other values make it the leader of the hegemonic order 'that' shapes the basic dynamics of international politics (Ferguson 2003).

There three major types of empires include ideal- typical empires (systems), unipolar orders, and hegemonic orders (pp. 253-261). First, *ideal–typical empires* are different from hegemonic and unipolar orders because the former "rule through intermediaries and heterogeneous contracting between imperial cores and constituent political communities" (p. 253). These ideal- typical empires "comprise of a 'rimless' hub-and- spoke system of authority, in which cores are connected to peripheries but peripheries themselves are disconnected- or segmented- from one another" (p. 25; Galtung 1971; Motyl 2001; Tilly 1997). As imperial relations are established, several changes take place in the fundamental dynamics of international relations and world or global politics. Of these relations the: "dynamics of divide- and- rule supplant traditional balance- of- power politics. Imperial control works, in part, by preventing resistance in the periphery from spreading to other peripheries. Some of the most important challenges to imperial rule arise, therefore, when imperial policies, exogenous shocks, transitional movements, or other developments trigger uncoordinated or coordinated simultaneous resistance in multiple peripheries" (Nexon and Wright 2007, 253).

Iraq is a classical example in this regard. The U.S. did not adhere to the maxim of "honesty is the best policy" when it bluffed the world that because Iraq regime had weapons of mass destruction, it needed to be unilaterally and preemptively removed from power. In the field of game theoretic modeling, deterrence against resistance in spite of the U.S. application of will and "muscular" capabilities for resolve went down to the drain largely because the challenger (U.S.) underestimated the honest beliefs of the defender (Iraq) (Sartori 2005). In this business, imperial capability and credibility undermined deterrence for revealing too much. As a result, America lost its case in Iraq' because Iranians were better geostrategic and georegional thinkers and planners. Both unilateralism and preemption were undermined by nationalistic uprising and the reliance on private contractors, absence of the State Department experts and insufficiency of Arabists in the reconstruction process (Phillips 2005).

In addition, Jon Western (2005) has rigorously examined competition among American foreign policy elites in the executive and congressional institutions and their support for military intervention during the 1954 French Indochina conflict, the 1958 military involvement in Lebanon and its subsequent involvement in Grenda, Somalia, Bosnia and Iraq. Western argues that though presidents and their followers orchestrate campaigns for military support, eight categories of foreign policy elites (hardliners, selective engagers, reluctant warriors, neo- isolationists, liberals, pacifists, anti-imperialists and humanitarianists) tend to monitor public attitudes and perceptions before they influence the public's opinion into thinking about military intervention.

As far as the behavior of the empire is concerned, if the main axis of political relations change from interstate to intersocietal ones,

> Imperial cores exercise rule through local intermediaries over various actors within the domestic sphere of constituent political communities. This structure creates endemic tradeoffs between, on the one hand, the advantages of indirect rule and, on the other, the principal- agent problems that stem from intermediary autonomy. Imperial control of particular peripheries also involves local processes of divide-and–rule. Imperial authorities utilize various strategies that, through accident or design, succeed by preventing various local actors from forming widespread coalitions against the terms of imperial control (Nexon and Wright 2007, 253-254).

The strategies are called 'pivoting' or 'binding' and are imperialistically sanctioned by costs and benefits or merits and demerits. Afghanistan is a case in point.

Alternatively, ideal-typical empires may face "problems of legitimating their control" (p. 254) as the Iraq experience had demonstrated. In this case, ... Imperial rule involves heterogeneous contracts that specify varied rights and privileges to different peripheries; empires function most over extremely diverse audiences who, in turn, place differing demands on imperial authorities. Empires often best navigate these cross pressures by engaging in 'multivocal' or 'polyvalent' signaling: "by projecting different identities and commitments to discrete audiences" (p. 254)

Under these circumstances, the stakes of American imperial claims remain high because other states understand their anarchical position in international relations where the "balance of power and hegemonic-stability theory" (p. 254) is challenged (Waltz 1979). The three major categories that are preeminent frameworks for analyzing "ideal-typical network structures" (Nexon and Wright 2007, 254) are unipolarity, hegemony and empire" (p. 254). This analysis will expound the circumstances through which the social network arrangements of imperial orders "produce a set of dynamics and processes that distinguish the logics of empire from the logics of unipolar or hegemonic systems" (p. 254) and their implications on U.S. foreign policy in the global arena.

Unipolar systems are conceptualized as systems with preeminent powers that are unitary actors that operate within an anarchical environment that is "Unstable" (p. 254) due to the fact that power is concentrated in a single political community which may be counterbalanced (Waltz 2000) or remain "stable" (p. 254) largely because "no state or coalition of states will be able to challenge the preeminent power... in balancing behavior" (p. 254 and Wohlforth 1999). International relations theorists assert that 'unipolarity' "is the existence of a single great power in the absence of a common authority and 'hegemony' as a condition in which a single great power establishes rules of the game' for economic and political cooperation" (Nexon and Wright 2007, 255; Mastanduno 2005, 179).

In the light of unipolar orders or systems, their authenticity is contextually explained in structural- realist paradigm, which theoretically views "states...as unitary, and anarchical environment" (Waltz 1979, 104-105). These ideal typical unipolar orders are characterized by weak and sparse but interstate relations whose vectors are weak in authority (Waltz 1979). As a result, the absence or presence of "multiple channels fail to 'connect societies' as they rationalize their 'interstate, transgovernmental' or 'transnational' (Nexon and Wright 2007, 256) relations. To say it in another way, "the relations among states is one of 'billiard balls colliding' against one another" (p. 256). In this regard, "ties with states are characterized by the "division of labor across nations... is slight in comparison with the highly articulated division of labor within them integration draws the parts of a nation together"... "strong collective identification within states contrast with weak (or nonexistent) collective identification between units. States identities, at least implicitly, are heterogeneous with respect to on another: each state claims to represent a different national or ethnic group" (p. 256; Lapid and Kratochwil 1996).

Second, since ideal-typical unipolar orders are by nature unstable and at times counter- balanceable, "collective mobilization among actors will be subject to strong Prisoner's Dilemma logics in the absence of dense ties and cross-unit identification. Heterogeneous identities work against trust, whereas sparce networks prevent effective monitoring of cooperation and defection" (Nexon and Wright 2007, 256). Evidently, because collective action is, comparatively speaking, very easy within units than between the states, nations or regions, there is "a strong bias toward within–unit provision of collective goods, such as security. The ubiquity of standard collective action problems among political communities, as many realists argue, is one of the key factors that determine whether unipolar systems will generate counterbalancing" (p. 256; Wohlforthy 1999) that will overthrow them.

Third, unlike ideal-typical unipolar orders, ideal-typical hegemonic-order theory "covers a broader array of approaches" of which, "hegemonic stability theory, power- transition theory, and constitutional order theory" (p. 256) are paramount. In this regard, "The fate of hegemonic systems depends largely on the interaction of three factors: the ability of the hegemony to sustain its economic, military and technological leadership; the degree to which potential challengers perceive themselves as benefiting from the existing hegemonic order; and the propensity for hegemonic overextension. Hegemonic order theorists tend to treat states as unitary actors, although their vision of hegemonic systems involves elements of both anarchy and hierarchy" (p. 256; Gilpin 1981, 26-27; Ikenberry 2001).

A variety of scholars with different intellectual perspectives particularly Michael Doyle (1986), Lake (1996), Snyder (1991), and Hui (2005) have tried to show why empires rise. Using International relations theory, unipolarity and hegemony as structural arrangements, empire(s) rise(s) "either as a question of the domestic organization of units operating under anarchy or as a particular outcome of state expansion. Lake has explained why empires expand. Snyder has analyzed the conditions which account for the rise of empires. Although President Bush (2000 - 2008) does not believe that America is an empire (Kagan 2002, 16) his definition of an empire may be different from that of other individuals. In addition, American policy makers also argue that U.S. Policy makers have different goals from those of their Roman counterparts. For instance, U.S. policy makers subjectively "seek peace and prosperity among sovereign states rather than the annexation and direct domination of independent polities" (Nexon and Wright 2007, 255) though their behavior in terms of the preemptive and unilateral American occupation of Iraq between 2003 and 2008 speaks to the contrary.

In other words, the American empire debate may call attention to "imperial orders as multiple realizable structural arrangements ... may be unplanned or planned; they may emerge through conquest or voluntary amalgamation. They may, in turn, involve a wide range of ideologies and norms" (p. 255; Lake 1996, 8; Motyl 1999, 133-136). As always, the motives of political elites and the causes of imperial enlargement determine the nature, rise, dynamics, and decline of imperial orders. Gilpin (1981) and Kennedy (1987) show that empires and great powers relate to each other as fundamental continuities that rationalize their existence in terms of "hegemonic cycles" (Nexon and Wright 2007, 255). Although Gilpin sees contemporary hegemony as a crucial break from the older pattern of imperial formation and decline, his decision to place both empires and hegemonies within a similar theory of international political change continues to shape many contemporary treatments of empire" (p. 255). Sometimes, and an analytical definition of the term empire, particularly in the context of U.S. foreign policy, tends to "elude the distinction between imperial and hegemonic systems" (p. 255, Cohen 2004, 56).

Imperial orders or empires are difficult–to define because of the complex nature of their differences in space over time (Howe 2002). In spite of the difficulty, scholars view empires to be multiethnic polities that involve the dominance of one polity that involve the communities, and that core- periphery relations are an important component of empire" (Spruyt 2005, 3-4). Using comparative historical scholarship, Galtung (1971) has authoritatively argued that "empires involve a distinctive core-periphery structure from those found in other institutional forms. Imperial cores are not merely differentiated from peripheries, but peripheries are differentiated-or segmented-from one another" (Nexon and Wright 2007, 2008). The most striking element of such a "structure is not the hub-or-spoke, but the absence of a rim ... of political and economic relations between and among the peripheral units or between and among them and non-imperial polities" (p. 2008).

The concept of rimless-hub-and-spoke structure of the ideal - typical empire is derived from the norms, style and structures of imperial governance. Imperial "cores rule their peripheries through the 'retention or establishment of particular, distinct compacts' and exercise power 'through intermediaries who enjoy considerable autonomy with their own domains' in exchange for 'compliance, tribute, and military collaboration with the center.' Empires combine heterogeneous contracting – the basic institutional bargain between the core and each periphery involves distinctive attributes – with some degree of indirect rule. The features, in combination, distinguish imperial structures from those associated with unipolar anarchies and hegemonic systems" (p. 258).

Empires are very powerful states in preeminence (Lefever 1999). They may also be viewed in terms of "unilateralism, preventive war, the promotion of market economics, and high levels of military spending" (p. 258). In their imperialistic behavior, empires provoke the emergence of countervailing coalitions that sometimes alienate allies (Snyder 2003). If such empires do not strategically reconstruct their behavior in relation to others and in relation to themselves, they may experience isolationism or collapse particularly if they have decayed from within (Sagini 2001). This is what happened to both the Roman and Soviet empires. The former was initially attacked by various military and effective nomadic Visgoths and Vandals before Christianity shattered it asunder due to the decline of the commercial wealth and scientific innovations of the empire. The soviet empire collapsed largely because its foundation was rooted in weak ethnic, ideological, economic and cultural base that could not sustain its survival in the wake of internal decay, nationalistic rebellion, costly and unnecessary military adventurism, geostrategically rationalized Western containment and China's disaffection with it.

The United States is a putative empire that comprises of juridically or jurisdictionally diverse regional states- the "informal imperial order" (Nexon and Wright 2007, 255). As a result, the "degree to which specific sectors of international politics reflect not principles of anarchy, but of the hierarchical domestic organization of empires" (p. 255) deserves clarification. Informal empires are forms of political structure that are conceptually reminiscent of "ideal- typical empires and hegemonic orders" (p. 255; Hurrell 2005). Imperial historiography shows that empires use either indirect or direct rule approaches to exercise Imperial governance. An "indirect rule" is the governance system in which "empires recruit intermediaries from peripheral populations, such as local chieftains or princes" (p. 258). Direct rule is the "administration by which officials are recruited from imperial core" (p. 258). In the twentieth century, the British used indirect rule while the French and Russians applied direct rule. French direct rule and governance mechanisms were reinforced by the policy of assimilation which politically, economically and culturally strengthened the relationship between the mother country and her former colonies in Africa. The internally self-governing English Colonial people of the North-American eighteenth century British Empire became the United States of America at Independence and, as new states, of the American empire, the informal empire, has now continued to exercise internal autonomy (self- governance) that is politically and constitutionally protected by federal structure of power and national norms and values that reinforce institutional constitutionalism. In the Russian Empire, imperial rulers protected the trade routes that supplied revenue to the "horde" (p. 258) and that also provided "populations, livestock and resources" (p. 258). Local elites of the vassal states were powerless in French vassal states. In Korea, "Japanese governor-general functioned as imperial proconsuls, rather than mere agents of civil government" (p. 258; Keenam 1986, 131). In informal empires, Intermediaries are local rather than national elites involved in high levels of intermediary autonomy. The degree of intermediary autonomy in formal empires varies across and among peripheries within a particular empire.

## IMPERIAL GOVERNANCE

Governance is the political, legal and administrative authority of the state or core system to make decisions, regulations, policies and procedures for controlling, directing, determining, restraining or ruling the peripheries which are bound to accept such authoritative directives from the core. The core governs by indirect rule, direct rule, laissez- faire, dictatorship etc. In the age of globalization, imperial governance may indirectly be applied through democratization mechanisms, or through the six "cornerstones of the empire"- the U.N, the IMF, the WTO, The World Bank, OECD and NATO. These institutions were created after the II World War. Japan, protected by the U.S. military, became part of the Western alliance in order to succeed in having access to Western markets for her businessmen.

> Thus a system of U.S. military alliances emerged to provide a supra- national governance role; an enforcement backdrop for international political and economic cooperation. U.S., military and economic dominance gave Washington a strong advantage in guiding the decision- making processes within both the economic organizations and the military alliances, in which they were participants. Nonetheless, this authority was used moderately and only at critical junctures to prevent the kind of paralysis that killed the League of Nations. The direction of influence on power, however, was not just one way; U.S. policies were often modified at the urging of members of these organizations, even when America insisted on having its own way.... Choosing the lesser of the two evils they more often sided with America than against it (Odom 2004, 203).

This American led and largely Western alliance was a supra- national, political and military authority whose membership in the empire was an "empire by invitation" (p. 204). The empire was and is a hierarchical structure which protected its existential survival during the Cold War and after it. Contrary to the expectations of the realist theoretical paradigm of international relations, the empire did not collapse after the disintegration and disappearance of the U.S.S.R and the Warsaw Pact. Historically, the alliances collapsed because the very reason for their evolution and development no longer obtained. Since the Western alliance did not collapse, the reason for its survival may largely be explained in economic rather than military or political terms. "The economic payoffs had proven too high and unprecedented in Europe and Northeast Asia to end a relationship with the U.S. These economic achievements were possible not only because tariffs declined and international trade expanded, but also because a U.S. military force provided a security umbrella against traditional enemies now inside the U.S. military alliance system. Rising confidence in political and military stability within the Western order encouraged greater commerce and investment; transaction costs declined, and everyone declined" (p. 205). In addition, economic growth in Europe and Japan stimulated growth in the U.S. so much so that the latter come to control 30% of the World's GDP. The European and Asian markets benefited the U.S. as well as the countries in the regions. Liberal political institutions which acted collectively in major issues effectively enabled trade transactions and costs to be managed better and more efficiently. Less liberal states such as France, Japan and German gained less than the U.S. Destroying the military alliances would weakened the U.S. and destroyed the empire. In the context of the realist paradigm, "multilateral institutions are useful only if they provide strategic security and enhance the ambitions of their member states. That is why unilateralism tends to destroy empires

Russia's attempt to reconstruct itself and challenge Western dominance in global affairs is being exercised by Chinese resurgence which applies a different governance system. However, the American empire which survived cold- war rivalry between U.S. and U.S.S.R. has been scholastically defined as "Western identity and civilization ... democratic peach theory ... of democratic states. The liberal peace theory ... of mature constitutional states ... supranational institutions, which are composed of political, economic and security organizations ... and the role of U.S. military power as a supranational governance force" (p. 207). These institutions make the American empire to be radically different from those of ancient, medieval and modern civilizations.

The American empire is characterized by three major distinctions: first, the empire largely is ideological rather than territorial in which citizens and subjects are constitutionally categorized. Second, the empire was created to make rather lose money. Though it suffers from 'imperial outstretch' (Paul Kennedy 1987) it has not been counterbalanced because it "converted the core state from a 'discriminating monopolist' in extracting revenues into a 'third- party enforcer' that reduces transaction costs. This allows the 'rate of private return to stay.' This simply means that countries failing to qualify ideologically for membership in the American empire are condemned to poor economic performance" (Odom 2004, 208) in the long run. Oil, gas and mineral exporting countries are exceptions in spite of the fragility of their institutions. Poor countries which follow wealthy ones practice 'path dependence' and find it difficult to change. Third, in the past, countries that fought so hard to join the American empire never wanted to leave due to the promise of prosperity, wealth and military security. Membership in the American empire is loosely and ambiguously designed. It does not restrict countries that join or leave it. The member countries of the empire "differ significantly. In some countries the state is involved more directly in economic enterprise than in others, and the level of the welfare transfer payments varies greatly from country to country. These differences are the source of endless quarrels between continental states in Europe and the Anglo- Saxon countries that favor more flexible and competitive business rules ... vary costs and ... create troubles among the nations of the American empire and the countries outside it, who have unstable property rights, high levels of corruption, and large state ownership of economic firms" (p. 209).

If the empire makes decisions that enable it to act unilaterally rather than cooperatively or multilaterally, it weakens its case for accountability, counter-balancing and desire for collective security and defense both institutionally and diplomatically. Acting largely alone in the effort to overthrow Saddam Hussein and occupy Iraq increased President Bush's global American Isolationism and weakened the empire's ability to control events in Iraq and the Middle East whose conservative fundamentalism was provoked to become radical and revolutionary Islamism that has attained ungovernable manifestations in Iran, Lebanon, Pakistan, Iraq and Afghanistan. Isolationism is a form of global anti- Americanism. In the Middle East, anti- Americanism is closely linked with anti-Zionism largely because of the "elusive relationship of the Arab- Israel conflict through which 17 countries have experienced 30 year Israel repression that is supported by its ally- the United States" (Lebovic and Thompson 2006, 502-518).

Several 2008 presidential candidates suggested how to strengthen the U.S. in the wake of its global isolationism. Barack Obama, Democrat, argued that "America cannot meet the threats of this century without America. We can neither retreat from the world nor try to bully it into submission" (Obama 2007, 1). In a world where the U.S. is interdependent rather than dominant, America should renew its leadership in the area of recruiting competent and energetic visionaries who can restructure the military and intelligence for dealing with twenty-first century issues rather than those of the Cold War, build new global partnerships in multipolar as opposed to the unipolar world, whose beliefs are based on fear rather than on morality and hope. Mitt Romney (2007), Republican, argued that Americans did not need to lose faith in the then climate of relative isolationism. They needed to unite, renew their economic and military might, attain energy independence and reenergize civilian and interagency capabilities for creatively revitalizing alliances and their institutions. Also, at the end of the 2008 presidential debate, the American people rejected Senator John McCain's and Senator Hillary Clinton's ideas and elected Senator Barack Obama because his global engagement ideas made him more promising and competitive.

## Results of Imperial Structures

Realists who believe in international structure and those who believe in the existence of imperial relations differ in how governance is to be handled. The former emphasize the fundamentals of the balance of power phenomenon. The latter believe in the logics of divide- and – rule. Divide and rule maintains hierarchy while the balance of power works to sustain anarchy. In addition, divide and conquer ways create hierarchy which is used to disrupt the strategic balance of power (Hui 2005).

Whenever the asymmetrically controlled, or subordinate political communities try to secede from the core, empires try to repress the secession by "acquiring and maintaining technological, military and social organizational advantages of subordinated polities and peripherals." Also, core imperial authorities use imperial resources from all the peripheries of the empire that are connected to the core. In other words the core uses capabilities mobilized from the imperial network in order to suppress resistance to imperial rule and "imperial overextension. The factors that erode the across-periphery divide-and–rule strategy and destroy or weaken the empire include 'decreasing peripheral segmentation' and triggers of simultaneous resistance" (Nexon and Wright 2007, 262). These two anti-imperial phenomena were experienced by the Roman, Russian, and British empires; currently the U.S. maybe struggling with it. However, empires can be strengthened by applying the strategies of "heterogeneous contracting and peripheral segmentation" (p. 263). In addition, to making resistance more or less likely, it is important to legitimate the strategies of "multivocal or polyvalent" (p. 264) nature because they appeal to various segments and peripheral networks within the empire. To lessen further resistance against the empire, local structures should only use divide-and-rule strategy, as local intermediaries are allowed to exercise internal autonomy. The British used this mechanism in their empires. Indirect rule minimizes the costs of imperial governance because it "pumps resources to rulers without costly monitoring and repression" (Tilly 2003, 4).

Direct rule, which the French and Russians were known for tended to "turn central authorities into intimate participants in the local factional and political struggles, thereby eroding their ability to function" (p. 264) because the core functionaries became 'impartial' brokers of the conflicts in question. Within the Spanish empire, governors and viceroys accepted the blame for bad judgment in which resistance against the centre was at stake. However, these agents were rarely punished for it. Romans killed heavily by punishing their imperial agents if their activities provoked peripheral and segmental resistance against the empire. On the other hand, if these agents usurped authority, they were equally treated in kind. To avoid conflicts in the centre and the periphery, empires compromised by making tradeoffs. Some imperial authorities rotated their administrators and prevented them from developing strong ties (independent) with various actors in certain segments (Barkey 1994). In other words, the centre did everything to triangulate or navigate "the costs and benefits of using these forms of intermediary autonomy" (p. 205).

Unlike hegemonic or unipolar systems, imperial orders are characterized by the distinction between 'domestic' and 'international' politics. Imperial intermediaries are more autonomous than state centric models reminiscent of unipolar and hegemonic systems. Imperial orders have extensive peripheries that use peripheral coalitions to raise revenue, resources and acceptable political demands. Imperial authorities use different strategies for tradeoffs as pathways for intermediary autonomy as they configure and reformulate various pathways for imperial structural transformation. The major classes of actors in the divide- and-rule dynamic include central authorities, local intermediaries particularly the elite groups and either regional (provincial or state) and local (district) or municipal agents. The fewer they are the better off their index of efficiency and effectiveness. These local elites tend to rationalize binding strategies if they are allowed to accumulate materials and if their ideological orientation is parallel rather than antagonistic to imperial expectations. If the central authorities apply "pivoting strategies," they will be able to triangulate various local factions and uncooperative intermediaries in order to rationalize imperial rule. As always, the "empires" rimless hub-and-spoke structure is not only a product of divide- and – rule governance technique, but such a form of administrative tool is exploitatively enforceable to the extent of creating social differentiation in terms of "class, status, identity, religion, ethnicity" (Baumgartner, et al 1975, 422) and gender. That is why "binding strategies are easier to implement than pivoting strategies" (p. 265). In the global age, America's informal empire has more validity for viability than its global one largely due to the proliferation of multipolarity as opposed to unipolarity and largely due to the "decayance" of our own culture, intelligence, scientific and religious traditions.

## CHALLENGES OF U.S. FOREIGN POLICY

Currently, the preeminence of U.S. power is increasingly embattled both from within and from without. The internal and external challenges are globalizations "push and pull" forces whose dynamics will either destroy it or creatively force it to restructure, reinvent and reengineer its competitive survival in the twenty-first century (Sagini 2001). The plethoras of challenges include but are not limited to:

> open-ended war terrorism, but they have been unable to bring democracy or even order, to Afghanistan, or Iraq after invading and occupying both countries. The Iraq war … has revealed gaping holes in U.S., intelligence, military doctrine, and defense planning. The overthrow of Saddam Hussein, unsanctioned by the UN Security Council, strained U.S., diplomatic relations with key allies and the World body. This resentment is compounded by U.S. opposition, virtually alone among major powers, to global treaties on climate change, the testing of nuclear weapons, arms trafficking, land mines, and the International Criminal Court. Although U.S. economic production is by far the most robust in the world, the nation suffers unprecedented trade deficits and debts and was replaced in 2005 by Germany as the leading exporter of manufactured goods. Finally, the nation's 'soft power' has diminished in recent years. Surveys find the nation to be widely distrusted and feared overseas, even by the citizens of its closest allies (Hook 2008, XI).

In the wake of the Soviet imperial collapse, President Clinton was determined to influence the U.S., primacy for the service of global engagement. Foreign policy decision-making rivalry between antagonistic congressional conservatives and liberals contributed to the elimination of a variety of treaties and commitments in a post Cold-War climate whose institutions were and are still so unreformed to address contemporary issues of globalization. The cynical alienation of the electorate by its leaders withdrew from public and world affairs to the detriment of its unsolvable and poorly articulated issues of global warming, HIV/AIDS crisis, ethnic conflicts and wars in Africa, Europe, Asia and Central America and the Middle East especially. These problematic issues, cannot be solved easily because the nation has lost its mission due to internal economic, cultural, political, moral decay and imperial overstretch that lacks resources (skilled manpower, ethical beliefs, universal human brotherhood, respect for others and imperial soft sidedness as opposed to imperial cruelty) that exacerbates conflict, fear, chaos, disorder and social and cultural fragmentation at the periphery (Wittkopf and McCormick 1999). The loss of these resources has made the U.S. incapable of introducing viable forms of democratization, multilateral cooperation and universally acceptable economic globalization. The inability of the U.S. to resolve the existing global problems at home and abroad has not only made the U.S. to be viewed as a victim of its own success in ... "living standards, educational opportunities, scientific advances, cultural outlets, political and economic system" (Hook 2008, XII) but, they have made the nation to be viewed as a paradoxical beneficiary of its stupendous and imperial foreign policy whose elite participation in its construction is fundamentally conflicted, ideologically antagonistic, politically contradictory, and economically elitist. In other words, though the determination of U.S. foreign policy is less pluralistic than elitist, the media are prominent spokespersons of the elites because the former provide the "conduit through which public opinion is manipulated and molded to fit elite preferences" (Wittkopf and McCormick 1999, XVIII). The same media ... and because of its independence, is "less conspiratorial in pluralist than in elitist model" (p. XIX) settings.

The media helps to set foreign policy agenda and interprets it to the public. The political parties help to aggregate it into "ethnic, religious, economic, educational, professional, working class, and ...sociodemographic groups" (p. XIX) from which personnel for major policy making decisions are selected. The institutions of checks and balances contribute to the persistence rather than the innovation of U.S. Foreign Policy prescriptions. As a result, the policy is "incoherent, inconsistent" and at times, at odds with reality (p. XX) because many people in terms of (personality traits, perceptions, and psychological predisposition) institutions, and climates do not influence it. Some are crusaders, others are pragmatists, and still some may be ideological zealots. A president's personality ultimately, helps to explain the nature and character of U.S. foreign policy. Since foreign policy- making in the U.S. is organizationally a group rather than individual enterprise, its eventual results are inherently complex at most and enigmatically paradoxical at large. That is why the advocates of globalization do not know how to address the problems associated with fragmentation, "global uprising" associated with tribalistic and transitional instability.

## CONCLUSION

Throughout the last 220 years, American foreign policy, which is a product of many competing interests in society, rooted in institutionalist interpretations of American history, couched in putative notions of American hegemony, rationalized in benevolent but complex diplomatic jargon and dominated by the quest for materialistic prescriptions of the nation's economic elites, is a dynamic global force that cannot easily be meddled with. There are five fundamental dimensions of American foreign policy. The first dimension consists of the Bureaucratic secretaries of the departments of the State, Defense and Treasury, the Joint Chiefs of Staff (JCOS) the director of the Central Intelligence Agency (CIA) ... the National Security Council (NSC), Department of Homeland Security (DHS), composed of twenty-two agencies ..." and "the Federal Bureau of Investigation (FBI), the U.S. Citizenship and Immigration Services, and the Internal Revenue Service (IRS)" (Ginsberg et al. 2007, 702). Although Congress, the media and interest groups have a role to play in shaping U.S. foreign policy, all the ideas that come from various institutions in society are aggregated by the President who is viewed as the chief architect of American foreign policy.

The second shapers of American foreign policy are the nation's core values (Patterson 2008) of "individualism, unity, democracy, liberty, limited government and diversity" (p. 3). One of the ways for avoiding big national government (in terms of limited government) and "presidential supremacy" (Dye 2007, 753) was to avoid "foreign fragments that made foreign policy, diplomacy, secrecy, and presidential discretion necessary" (p. 735). For almost 150 years, Americans remained confined to the small and isolationist political tradition of its founding fathers. However, after the Second World War, and in some cases even before the war, "the intermingling of domestic and foreign policy institutions, unilateralism... when confronted with foreign conflicts" (p. 735) the nation was involved in foreign entanglements.

The third shapers of American foreign policy are what may be called "instruments: diplomacy, the United Nations, the International Monetary Structure (IMF and the World Bank), economic aid, collective security" (e.g. NATO) and Military deterrence" (p. 735). Presidents of either political party tend to use these Bretton Woods institutions in order to strengthen American foreign policy.

Fourth and fifth, in terms of the roles the Congress and the President play in the formulation and disformulation of American foreign policy, these two competing and adversarial institutions play their roles in the light of four categories that collectively contribute to the consistent and stable conduct of diplomacy for the nation- state and other nation- states. The four roles of American foreign policy have been identified by historians of diplomacy in Western countries. These roles are "the Napoleonic, Holy Alliance, balance of power, and throughout the Cold-War era, the United States and its allies- Western Europe and Japan, were a Holy Alliance. "This alliance will never allow the U.S. to run "foreign policy undiplomatically. This indicates that the United States is inextricably connected to the "perils and ambiguities" (p. 736) of the global and international community. If anything then, still, diplomacy is the best available instrument for the orchestration and articulation of American foreign policy.

Foreign policy is an intellectual, disciplinary, institutional and normative component of the nation's public policy. The parallel of foreign policy is domestic policy. Public policy, of which foreign policy is its component concerns what, when, why, where and how governments do or do not do certain things in society. These governments "regulate conflict within society; they organize society to carry on conflict with other societies; they distribute a great variety of symbolic rewards and material services to members of society; and they extract money from society most often in the form of taxes. Thus public policies, may regulate behavior, organize bureaucracies, distribute benefits, or extract taxes- or all these things at once" (Dye 2008, 1). In a globally interdependent and competitive environment, the major issues from which public policies will emanate include but are not limited to global warming, energy security, and global terrorism.Nuclear proliferation, drug trafficking, and natural and manmade hazards such as famine, earthquakes, diseases and other climate related issues are domestic policy considerations.

With the evolutionary emergence of the dynamic influence of the G20's Great Moderation (Goldstone 2010), a New World Order has surfaced on the declining sphere of the G7 and its archaic and weak global institutions and their questionable vision and development trajectory. President Barack H. Obama, unlike his predecessor George W. Bush, has established a viable machinery for working with the G20 and the rest of the global society. In other words, the President's analytically and pragmatically, as opposed to ideologically and dogmatically oriented approach to American foreign policy will articulate a centrally coherent worldview and significant geopostrategically essential and paramount issues:

- Islam is not an enemy and the global war on terror does not define the United States' current role in the world;
- the U.S. will be a fair-minded and assertive mediator when it comes to attaining lasting peace between Israel and Palestine;
- the U.S. ought to pursue serious negotiations with Iran over its nuclear program as well as other issues;
- the counterinsurgency campaign in the Taliban-controlled parts of Afghanistan should be part of a larger political undertaking, rather than a predominantly military one;
- the U.S. should respect Latin America's cultural and historical sensitivities and expand its contacts with Cuba;
- the U.S. ought to energize its commitment to significantly reducing its nuclear arsenal and embrace the eventual goal of a world free of nuclear weapons;

- in coping with global problems, china should be treated not only as an economic partner but also as a geopolitical one;
- improving U.S.-Russian relations is in the obvious interest of both sides, although this must be done in a manner that accepts, rather than seeks to undo, post – Cold War geopolitical realities; and
- a truly collegial trans-Atlantic partnership should be given deeper meaning, particularly in order to heal the rifts caused by the destructive controversies of the past (U.S.- Iraq War) (Brzezinski, 2010: 16-17).

## REFERENCES

Abborlt, Carl, et al. 2007. *The American journey: A history of the United States.* Upper Saddle River, NJ: Pearson Education.

Barkey, Karen. 1994. *Bandits and bureaucrats: The Ottoman route to state centralization.* Ithaca, NY: Cornell University Press.

Barnet, Michael N. 1998. *Dialogues in Arab Politics: Negotiation in regional order.* New York: Columbia University Press.

Bennett, Andrew, and John G. Ikenberry. 2006. The review's evolving relevance for U.S. foreign policy 1906- 2006. *American Political Science Review* 100, 4: 65-8.

Berger, Thomas U. 1998. *Cultures of antimilitarism: National security in Germany and Japan.* Baltimore, MD: John Hopkins University Press.

Bernstein, Richard and Ross H. Munro. 1999. The new China lobby. *In the Domestic Sources of American Foreign Policy: Insight and Evidence.*

Boydston, Jeanne, et al. 2004. *Making a nation: The United States and its people.* Upper Saddle River, NJ: Pearson Prentice-Hall.

Brzezinski, Zbigniew. 2010. From hope to audacity: Appraising Obama's foreign policy. *Foreign Affairs* January/February: 16-30.

__________. 1989. *The grand failure: The British and death of communism in the twentieth century.* Charles Scribner's Sons.

Ferguson, Niall. 2003. Hegemony of Empire? *Foreign Affairs 82: 5.*

Feste, Karea. 1990. *American and Soviet intervention: Effects on world stability.* New York: Craime Russak.

Fishman, Ted C. 2005. *How the rise of the next superpower challenges America and the world.* New York: Scribner.

Fukuyama, Francis. 2006. *America at the crossroads: Democracy, power and the neoconservative legacy.* New Haven, NJ: Yale University Press.

Geiss, Imanuel. 1968. *The Pan African Movement. A history of Pan- Africanism in America, Europe, Africa. New York.*

Gilpin, Robert. 1981. *War and change in world politics.* New York: Cambridge University Press.

Goldstein, Avery. 2005. *Rising to the challenge: China's grand strategy and international security.* Stanford, CA: Stanford University Press.

Gregory, Robert. 1971. *India and East Africa: A history of race Relation within the British Empire 1890-1939.* London: Oxford University Press.

Haas, Peter. 1992. Introduction: Epistemic communities and international policy coordination. *International Organization* 46: 1-35.

Hall, Peter. 1989. *The political economy of ideas: Keynesianism across national.* Princeton, NJ: Princeton University Press.

Henretta, James A., et al. 2006. *America: A concise history.* Bedford, MA: St. Martins.
Heston, Alan W. 2000. *The Annals of the American Academy of Political and Social Science.* 70: 1- 224.
Hill, Christopher, and Karen E. Smith. 2000. Eds. *European foreign policy: Key documents.* New York: Routledge.
Hook, Steven W. 2008. *U.S. foreign policy: The paradox of world powers.* Washington, D.C: CQ Press.
Ikenberry, John G. 2006. Liberal hegemony and the future of the American postwar order. In Joel Krieger, ed. *Globalization and state power: A reader.* New York: Pearson Longman.
__________. 2001. *After victory: Institutions, strategic restraint, and the rebuilding of order after major war.* Princeton, NJ: Princeton University Press.
Jacob, Lawrence R., and Benjamin I. Page. 2005. Who influences U.S. foreign policy? *American Political Science Review* 99, 1: 107-23.
Jeffries, Charles. 1948. *The colonial empire.* London: The Colonial Office.
Laquer, Walter. 2007. *The last days of Europe: Epitaph for an old continent.* Boston: St. Martins Press.
__________. 2007. So much for the new European century. *The Chronicle of Higher Education* May 11: B6-B9.
Layton, Azza S. 2000. *International politics and civil rights policies in the United States, 1941-1960.* Cambridge: Cambridge University Press.
Lebovic, James H., and William R. Thompson. 2006. An illusionary or elusive relationship? The Arab-Israel conflict and repression in the Middle East. *Journal of Politics* 68, 3: 502-18.
Legro, Jeffery W. 2005. *Rethinking the world: Great power strategies and international order.* Ithaca, NY: Cornell University Press.
Lenzer, Steven. 2003. Ed. Leo Strauss and the conservatives. *Policy Review* 118: 75- 82.
Leonard, Mark. 2005. *Why Europe will run the 21st century.* New York: Public Affairs.
Lugard, Frederick. 1922. *The dual mandate in the tropical Africa.* London: London University Press.
Markovits, Andrei S. 2007. Western Europe's American problem. *The Chronicle of Higher Education* 19: b6- b9.
Murray, Douglas. 2006. *Neo-conservatism: Why we need it.* Encounter Book.
Nelkin, Dorothy. 1979. Scientific knowledge, public policy and democracy. *Knowledge, Creation, Diffusion, Utilization* September: 106-22.
Nexon, Daniel H., and Thomas Wright. 2007. What's at stake in the American empire debate. *American Political Science Review* 101, 2: 253-71.
Obama, Barack. 2006. *The audacity of hope: Thoughts on reclaiming the American dream.* New York: Crown Publishers.
Odom, William E. 2004. Understanding America's empire: If it really has one. *The Brown Journal of World Affairs* XI, 1: 203-15.
Patterson, Thomas E. 2008. *We the people: A concise introduction to American politics.* Boston: McGraw Hill.
Phillips, David L. 2005. *Losing Iraq: Inside the postwar reconstruction fiasco.* New York: Basic Book.
Pickus, Noah. 2005. *True faith and allegiance: Immigration and America civic nationalism.* Princeton, NJ: Princeton University Press.
Prunier, Gerard. 2005. *Darfur: The ambiguous genocide.* Ithaca, NY: Cornell University Press.

Robinson, et al. *Africa and the Victorians: The official mind of the British imperialism.* London: Oxford University Press.

Rosenau, J.N. 1968. The concept of intervention. *Journal of International Affairs* 22: 165- 76.

Sagini, Meshack M. 2004. International diplomacy and the U.S.-Iraq conflict: The failure of unilateralism in multilateral context. *Journal of Scholar and Scientific Perspectives: An International Journal of Scholarly and Scientific Research* 1: 23-43.

__________. 2001. *Organizational behavior: The challenges of the new millennium.* Lanham, MD: University Press of America Inc.

Sartori, Anne E. 2005. *Deterrence by diplomacy.* Princeton, NJ: Princeton University Press.

Sodaro, Michael S. 2008. *Comparative politics: A global introduction.* Boston: McGraw Hill Higher Education.

Solana, Javier. 2007. *E.U. High Representative for Common Foreign and Security Policy: At the E.U Defence Ministers in the Framework of the General Affairs and External Relations Council-at Brussels.*

Staar, Richard F. 1991. *Foreign policies of the Soviet Union.* Stanford, CA: Hoover Institution Presses.

Vandiver, Frank E. 2005. *How America goes to war.* Westport, CT: Praeger Publishers.

Waldner, Ferro. 2002. *Common foreign and security policy (CFSP).*

Western, Jon. 2005. *Selling intervention and war: The presidency, the media, and the American public.* Baltimore, MD: Johns Hopkins University Press.

Williams, Walter. 2006. Should we copy Europe. *The Oklahoman.* Saturday November 25: 13A.

Williamson, J.W. 1949. *A short history of the British empire.* London: Oxford University Press.

Wittkopf, Eugene R. and James M. McCormick, eds. 1999. *The domestic sources of American foreign policy: Insights and evidence.* Lanham, MD: Rowman and Little Field Publisher, Inc.

Woodby, Sylvia. 1989. *Gorbacher and the decline of ideology in Soviet foreign policy.* Boulder: Western Press.

Zimmerman, William. 2002. *The Russian people and foreign policy.* Princeton, NJ: Princeton University Press.

# Chapter VII
# Chinese Foreign Policy

## INTRODUCTION

This chapter is an interdisciplinary analysis of Chinese foreign policy as viewed in the light of the disciplines of political science, history, sociology, and international relations. Throughout the analysis, China's classical and medieval history, Cold War as well as contemporary, diplomatic, security, and economic issues will be explained in order to elucidate the evolution of China's foreign policy agenda and its spasmodic development, modification, and implementation throughout history particularly during its post revolutionary era. Thirdly, the analysis will focus on the policy agenda from contemporary global perspectives in the light of western geo-strategic rationality and democratically inspired diplomatic trajectory. This nation of 1.5

billion people is 3.745 million square miles that is almost the size of both U.S. and Canada combined. Its diplomatic performance in unipolar and progressively advancing panoply of multipolarity has enabled China to chart new directions in the global market place and uncharted diplomatic terrain.

## HISTORICAL BACKGROUND

Chinese history is rooted in myths and legendary traditions concerning their original King (Son of Heaven) whose imperial origins contributed to the evolution and development of Chinese society on the Yellow River (Hwang – Ho) during the 3$^{rd}$ Chou dynasty between 1122 and 221 BCE. China's first (Qin) dynasty was established in 1875 BCE. Together, there are 22 dynastic periods in Chinese history. During the Chou dynasty, Chinese society experienced a high degree of intellectual and philosophical development associated with the evolution of "Confucianism, Taoism, Mohism, and Legalism" (*New Websters' Dictionary and Thesaurus of the English Language* 1992).

After Qin (Chin) dynasty (221-209 BCE), the empire created a strong legalist imperial tradition that permeated all facets of society just as the Confucian philosophical ethic before it had done. Between 206 BCE and 220 A.D; the Han empire created a professional intellectual bureaucracy which advanced Chinese diplomatic goals that enabled the country to establish strong political, economic, and cultural institutions that ensured the nation's stability, created mechanisms for controlling disruptive and belligerent barbarian neighbors, especially the Mongols and Turks, and eliminated diplomatic isolation of the empire. A stable social system whose empire had sound laws and an attractively and an absorptively suitable climate for new ideas allowed the introduction and development of Buddhism during the first century A.D. The externally introduced Buddhist religious and philosophical doctrine divided China into three kingdoms that dominated it from 220 to 589 A.D. Buddhism is naturalistic and practical atheism that opposed Indian Castism. The Empire was reunited during the Suis (590 – 618) dynasty and it became consolidated by the Tangs (618 – 906). The weak leaders of this period contributed to the philosophical, cultural and political fragmentation of Chinese society. However, between (960 – 1279), the Sung dynasty restored law and order. Peace and advancement of the arts flourished and refurbished the empire. Though the Mongols invaded China in 1210, the invasion was consequentially less significant given the complex heterogeneity of Chinese society. Genghis Khan established the Yuan dynasty (1279 – 1368). The activities of Mongols caused the people to revolt against its leaders and thereby encouraging Mongol oppression of the Yuan dynastic regime. The oppressive Mongol influence provoked the empire to solve its problems through the isolationist administrations of the incumbent Ming dynasty (1368 – 1644). The power and ability of the Mings to govern was weakened by the use of corrupt administrative practices and massive infiltration by foreigners whose influence destroyed the empire and from whose experience Americans are indebted to learn.

Between 1644 and 1912, the rulers of Manchu dynasty reestablished the Chinese empire. The Manchus were Mongolian people who came from Manchuria and, as referenced earlier, conquered China. The Manchu is also known as the Ching dynasty which introduced the Tungusic language of which Chicuas is spoken by the Heilungkian, Kirin and Liaoning provinces and a section of the Inner Mongolian autonomous region. All these areas were settled by nomadic tribes around c 1000 BC. These populations became part of the Chinese empire during the third century B.C. The Manchurian tribal influence was dominant in China between the tenth and fourteenth Centuries and under the Manchu dynasty i.e., between 1644 and 1912. Russia forced China (1858 – 60) to cede part of Manchuria, which was disputed in (1895-1905) during the Russo-Japanese War. Between 1932 and 1945, the puppet Kingdom of Manchukuo was put under the Japanese who surrendered it to China in 1945 largely due to the former's defeat during the Second World-War. The dominant ethnic group within the Manchu's was the Han. Manchu population was only 2% of the entire Chinese people. Their rule unified China, established a strong state by adopting existing bureaucratic authoritarianism. They governed China "through a judicious combination of military power and the cultivation of the leading elements of Chinese society; who in turn obligingly supported imperial rule" (Sodaro 2005, 656).

The Manchu imperial influence caused the Chinese to wear the queue (pigtail) as a symbol of submission to their new authority. These foreign masters never integrated themselves into the population. In order to govern China effectively, they allowed 1,000,000 Han Chinese to receive excellent degrees from Chinese universities and colleges for bureaucratic specialization, the most prestigious of which required 40,000 experts to run the empire whose population was 300 million.

## Buddhism

Buddhism is a collection of religious and philosophical ideas that originated with the life and teachings of India's Gautama Buddha during the sixth century B.C. Buddha did not approve of or advance the Hindu caste system of social segregation, animal sacrifice, and undue forms of asceticism. He founded the order of mendicant (begging) preachers or friers whose social organization consisted of both sexes. Some of his greatest ideas (teachings) include but are not limited to the four Noble Truths:

1) Sorrow is the universal experience of humanity.
2) The cause of sorrow is desire whose perpetual recurrence is the need for existence,
3) The permanent removal of desire is commendable.
4) Finally, desire can be systematically eliminated by following eight steps of nobility. Only after this has happened will the individual be transformed into a pure being who has attained Nirvana. Though Buddha's teachings are practically empirical, his critics and disciples associate his teachings with conceptions of naturalistic atheism.

The Noble Eightfold Path, the basis of the disciplines of Buddhism are not consecutively organized but they fall into three main groups: (1) Right understanding of Buddha! Basic teachings and right aspirations toward benevolence and renunciation; (2) right speech (no lying or abuse and right conduct (i.e. no killing, no stealing, no over indulgence), and right means of livelihood (i.e. nothing tending to the use or encouragement of wrong speech or conduct); (3) right striving (toward building up of good and the eradication of evil within oneself), right self-possession (involving self-knowledge and control of thought), and right contemplation (according to the traditional stages of meditation). This is also called the Middle Path-Buddhist way of life.

He (Buddha) taught that man's release from sorrow was not obtainable by any act of sacrifice or pilgrimage for godly favor. This release was the result of man's absorption of knowledge concerning the idea that his/her selfish desires are rooted in the dualistic delusions of the individual. Buddha's original teachings developed into two major conflicting brands of thought. The first is Theravada (Hinayana) that is largely found in Ceylon, Burma, Thailand and Malaysia while the Mahayana doctrine developed in China, Tibet, Korea, and Japan. The former strand lays emphasis on the development of monastic disciplines, and has resisted any attempts to compromise with theism. The latter has advanced the incorporation of the knowledge that Gautama is the incarnation of "The Buddha – Spirit" – bodhisattva. In Theravada tradition, the ideal "saint" is the arhat (man) who attains personal enlightenment (satori) which is available only when the subconscious is set free to resolve the false dualities of existence, which can not be rationally resolved. The Buddhist religious and philosophical tradition has about 600 million followers in Asia – The founder of this ethical philosophical tradition lived between 563 and 483 BC. He was an Indian son of a nobleman and member of the Kshatriya caste, the second of the four castes that rule. He started his public ministry at 29 and after 6 years he abandoned his asceticism. As a sage and a follower of truth, he established a strong ethical, religious and philosophical tradition which has for centuries influenced the life of millions of people particularly in the economic, political, academic, and cultural legacies of the Chinese and other Asian peoples.

## CONFUCIANISM

The founder of Confucianism was Confucius (c551 BC – c479 BC), the Chinese philosopher who was born and buried at Chufoo. He became a public administrator for 15 years (c532 BC – c517 BC). After that, he spent the rest of his life studying and teaching the Chinese classics and popularizing his philosophy-Confucianism. After his death, his sayings (Analetics) were recorded. Together with the classics which were edited, both works formed the corpus of traditional education of China. Confucianism is also a moral and religious philosophy. His contemporary, Mencius, edited the Analetics after the death of the sage during the fourth century B.C. The same philosophy was further developed and popularized by Chu His contemporary, during the twelfth century and by Wang Yang-Ming in the sixteenth century.

Confucianism is a system of ethical precepts such as benevolent love, righteousness, decorum, wise leadership, sincerity, etc., designed to inspire and preserve the proper management of family and society. Between the second century B.C. and the second century A.D. Tung Chung – Shu introduced a theological dimension with five virtues of the cosmic order that is governed by Shang-Ti (ruler of heaven to whom the emperor was accountable). All Chinese emperors were influenced by this aspect of theological and cosmological philosophy of Confucius. Confucianism became the official doctrine of imperial China during the Han dynasty for almost 400 years. Between the first century A.D. and 1949, ritual sacrifice was conducted in selected shrines that perpetuated the spirit and the theological genre of Confucianism.

Eclipsed by Taoism and Buddhism from the third to the seventh century, Confucianism was revived to become a state religion during the Tang dynasty (618 – 906). Subsequently, New – Confucianism became very strong between the tenth and the thirteenth centuries. For more than three centuries, Confucianism opposed the supernatural and quietist tendencies of Buddhism and Taoism. It advocated a humanistic rather than supernatural search for truth. Overall, between the second century B.C. and the twentieth century, Confucianism remained to be the distinctive and dominant philosophy of China that influenced and became the fundamental glue for social organization, education, and administrative management in the country, particularly in the foreign policy arena.

## Nineteenth and Twentieth Centuries Chinese History

Politically oriented administrative ineptitude, incompetence, and internal conflict during the eighteenth century and the continuous efforts of foreign nations to exploit trade and commercial relations during the nineteenth and twentieth centuries contributed to the proliferation of more than six major conflicts between China and other nations particularly England, France, U.S., Japan, and Russia. Of these conflicts, the (1850-65) Taiping rebellion, which was led by Hung Hsiu – Ch`uan, unsuccessfully tried to overthrow the Manchu dynasty. The uprising was suppressed with the American and British assistance under General Gordon. This disruptive, chaotic, and abortive invasion left China economically bankrupt and politically disorganized. Second, the Arrow War of (1856 – 1860) weakened China farther. Third, the two Sino – Japanese wars caused a lot of chaotic instability in Chinese development. The first War (1894 – 5) was waged for the control of Korea. The war spread into Manchuria and was concluded with the defeat of China in 1895. China was forced to recognize the independence of Korea by paying an indemnity and ceding Formosa, the Pescadores islands, and the Liotung Peninsula to Japan. In the Second War which was explained above earlier, Japan illegally occupied Manchuria (1937) and the eastern coastal region (1940). The 1941 Japanese bombing of Pearl Harbor merged the conflict with the Second World War in which the Allied forces defeated the Axis ones.

Fourth, the Opium War (1839 – 42) between Britain and China was caused by the English attempts to force China to import and consume opium from British Colonial India and to bring an end to the restrictions China imposed on foreign trade. Since China was politically and relatively weak but potentially important in the opium trade, the British action was an imperialistically designed rational form of diplomatic fiasco- (displeasure) with the Chinese. At the end of the war, China ceded Hong Kong to Britain and opened five ports. From the British perspective, coercive diplomacy worked. Fifth and sixth, the development of secret antiforeigner societies especially the Triad and Boxer Rebellions were problematic. In particular, the Boxer Rebellion of 1900 was organized by a Chinese Secret Society in Northern China. The Society besieged the legations on Peking. Legations are the official residences of middle level diplomatic envoys and missions for foreign countries. Since the secret society wanted to expel foreigners from China, the foreign nations united to use force and restore their diplomatic and commercial influence in China in 1901. Their restoration of order and diplomatic etiquette enabled them to negotiate and obtain increased foreign policy privileges. In the light of such circumstances, Russia extended its tutelage – to Manchuria, an action that precipitated the Russo – Japanese War of (1904 – 05). The War concerned, as implied earlier, Russian/Japanese conflict of interests in Masnchuria and Korea. The swift Japanese victories provided Japan with control over the two conquered areas and made Japan a world power. In the wake of Russia's defeat and loss of preeminence and prestige, this humiliation caused it to experience the 1905 internal Revolution.

In 1900 and afterwards, China was divided into several spheres of European influence that claimed ownership of it. Several attempts at reform were made and the Ching (Manchu) dynasty was overthrown in 1911. China became a republic under the Presidency of Sun Yat-sen. In 1912, an imperial military general, Yuan Shih – Kai became the president but his monarchical influence made policies that resulted in anarchy and the ascendance of war lordism after his death in 1916. In 1926, The Kuomintang (KMT) (Chinese nationalist political party) – founded by Sun Yat-Sen, based on democracy and socialism, ruled Chiang Kai-Shek's China between 1926 and 1949. This nationalist government withdrew to Taiwan (Formosa) after the military defeat by the Mao Zedong (Tsu-tung) Communist government in 1949. Although the second Sino- Japanese War (1931-45) stopped the conflict temporarily, civil war resumed at the end of the Second World War, and contributed to the eclipse of the nationalists and their flight to Taiwan whose independent nationalism and nationhood is dialectically and diametrically inimical to the PRC's one China policy.

## POST–REVOLUTIONARY CHINA'S FOREIGN POLICY

The People's Republic of China was founded on September 21, 1949. It laid a strong five year plan for its economic foundation while progressing rapidly between 1953 to 1957 and 1959 – 1962. In 1966, Chairman Mao Tse-Tung launched the Cultural Revolution which was an ideological purge intended to restore fidelity to Maoist political and military discipline of the Red Guards. The revolutionary elites denounced the revisionist elements that were hostile to the Communist Party of China (CCP). Although other people criticized its extreme excesses, Mao's charisma, personality, historic popularity associated with the "Sinification of Marxism" (Sodaro 2008, 660) and his well respected but antinationalist attack on Japan were variable elements of the "cult of Mao" that superstitiously became the driving dynamic of China's foreign policy and socioeconomic development in the country. Mao's extensive, literary and editorial skills enabled him to understand the history, politics and culture of China in order to champion the implementation of the Cultural Revolution without experiencing a paralyzing confusion and disabling backlash. He established a system for national unification by eliminating the influences of the Japanese KMT, the communist armies, and the derisive effects of war lordism. His Cultural Revolution was transformative in terms of the elimination of 15 million landlords and their replacement by the peasantry. The CCP nullified the marital traditionalism of arranged marriages with the introduction of a new marriage law. The laws enhanced the rights of women and destroyed the traditional power of clans and heads of families. It banned opium and prostitution by putting addiction and prostitutes in rehabilitation centers where they were medically taken care of and given new skills for productivity. Third, Mao used the five year plan, Soviet style model of central management and economic planning to reduce inflation; restore agriculture, and industrial production to pre-Sino-Japanese Second War Period. Chairman Mao wanted China to be recognized as a great power.

During the 1950's, the CCP transformed itself into a political party that could popularly govern not only the rural but also the urban centers of China. The dynamics for change and modernization were driven by the debate between the roles of the "Reds" versus those of the "experts." The Reds were old-fashioned "ideologically oriented revolutionaries, characterized by their political reliability and ability to mobilize the masses rather than by their technical, administrative, and scientific skills for governance" (p. 666). The revolutionaries wanted to bring change without modernization (Westernization). Experts, on the contrary, who were well educated wanted to create a sound economy that would strengthen the ultimate goals of communism. The Reds felt that experts were arrogant while the Latter felt that the Reds were intellectually and technically untrained for national modernization requirements. These debates were also interpreted in the light of economic development versus philosophical utopianism and collectivization (villagization) versus modern industrialization and marketization in the global arena. By the mid 1950's, "over 110 million private enterprises had been turned into 300,000 communist cooperatives" (p. 667). Capitalism was nonexistent. The peasants' land was taken away from them and collectivized in cooperative farms – directed by the CCP. This action was taken by following Confucius' dictum that 'Let a hundred flowers bloom, let a hundred schools of thought contend' (p. 667). This statement meant that exchange of ideas and planning strategies was both healthy and beneficial to the nation. Chairman Mao accepted criticism and input from experts, intellectuals and bureaucrats. This form of accessibility and openness to new ideas helped him to demystify the role of conservatism, bureaucratic, and cultural inertia in society. Shortly after words, Mao could not "Stomach" the criticisms from the "rightists" (Pro Western intellectuals) who advocated "democracy, the rule of law, free expression, and free scientific inquiry" (p. 667). Mao marginalized the rightist dissent for not respecting traditional authority and its contributions to society.

Wages went down, propaganda rather than scientific rationalism proliferated and persuasion was rampant. This was the Great Leap Forward of (1958-59) when communes were created. The G.L.F and the anti-rightist competition made the economy to crumble. A bad policy and no rains weather contributed to production failures. Between 1960 and 1962, over 30 million people starved to death.

The villagization of Communes, the elimination landlordism, other competitive private enterprises, and the suppression of dissent made the G.L.F policy a failure. Subsequently, proper planning, use of economic incentives, and introduction of minimal private interprice initiatives during the 1960's flourished and made the economy to come back. Inspite of these positive developments, Mao felt that he was being marginalized by the younger generation of Leaders such as (Liu and Dang) both of whom he had promoted to party leadership. Since he was very old and indecisive, his revolutionary vision in terms of leadership from bellow did not make the country economically self-sufficient. The capitalist ideas he hated for their promotion of class consciousness, a Marxist, Leninist, Stalinist, and Socialist philosophy that had temporarily succeeded in U.S.S.R., failed to materialize in China and made Mao's model of their implementation to flip-flop and irrelevant. He was delegitimized by his followers.

Finally, Chairman Mao tried the Great Proletarian Cultural Revolution (GPCR) by using the youth (Red Guards) as ombudsmen or whistle-blowers. These poorly educated, inexperienced, and hot-tempered anti-Rightist revolutionaries brutalized the bureaucracy, the intellectuals, the party, and all other organizations largely due to their nativity and mismanagement. They caused the party and the government to collapse and the nation's salvation found its niche in martial law. Utopianism, usurpation of power, and corruption proved the Great Leap Forward to be an economic catastrophe while the Cultural Revolution was politically disastrous. The implications of these economic and political failures on the nation's development trajectory were viewed negatively by the Chinese people and the rest of the world. The root source for their unsuitability was seen to be associated with not only the persistent failure to implement revolutionary zeal by using the less talented masses, but these orthodox ways of introducing socialist reforms were rooted in the implimenters' lack of understanding. The youth were not institutionally well organized because they were characterized by erratic, myopic, and philosophical populism. This model's template was transplanted from communist pantheism in the USSR, was viewed to be Chauvinistic and associated with revisionism in terms of "consciousness', reformism, and class violence ... that plagued the Communists at almost every turn in their quest for power" (Brzezinski 1967, 309) for the enhancement of their Marxist, Leninist, Stalinist, Moist and internationalist proletarianism and the permanent disembourgeoisement of the middle class. To achieve that objective, the human coast included the summary executions of opponents in the process of taking over power; extermination of all categories of people whose attitudes were hostile to the regime particularly the former military officials, bureaucrats, landowners, priests, and capitalists; liquidation of independent peasants, and those deported and forced for resettlement; labor camp deaths of the executed and communist purges; the physically and psychologically scarred due to prolonged imprisonment and forced labor; and last but not least, these errors and excesses of revolutionary consciousness created "a socially pervasive climate of fear ... and personal and political isolation" (Brzezinski 1989, 239-40) for the people and nation as a whole largely due to the failure of officialdom in its role to socially reconstruct an economically and politically successful communist society.

The political and economic failures of the Cultural Revolution was a failure of the CCP and the Communist government of Mao Tse-tung. Through experience, "People learned that it was acceptable to challenge authority and that it was necessary to think for themselves....should not, accept the prevailing political orthodoxy as truth. They learned too late that the C.R. was not about revolutionary goals at all, but just a cynical struggle for power – leaders do not always know everything and what they know can be very dangerous for their development if it is not openly analyzed, tested, and evaluated.

After the death of Mao Tse-Tung (1976), utopianism was abandoned in order to promote economic development. The party's ideology and the charisma of its leaders were no longer the basis of the party's legitimacy. A new generation of pragmatic intellectual leaders of whom Deng Xiaoping, Jiang Zemin and Hu Jintao, all of whom Chairman Mao had trained and promoted, successfully became the hope of modern Chinese economic, diplomatic, political, technological and global advancement.

During the late twentieth century, Chinese and Maoist revolutionary zeal which influenced Chinese foreign policy and largely defined its parameters within the pantheon of the communist states, considerably shifted from the left to the right largely due to the political and economic failure of the Cultural Revolution, the CCP, and the Maoist government. This shift to the right was carried on by modern pragmatic, professional, and intellectual elites rather than by orthodox and populist sympathizers of the masses and inexperienced, untrained and visionless agents of the Red Guard movement. The elites who formed the enlightened bureaucracy cherished Mao's revolutionary unification of China but disliked his culturally archaic and mass orchestrated autocratic insecurity, preindustrial, traditional, and unscientific religious and philosophical systems of thought and Marxist, Leninist, and Stalinist proletarian totalitarianism. Such an ideologically revolutionary and isolationist foreign policy was replaced with Deng's pragmatic, internationalist and activist approach to international relations. Mao's foreign policy rejected the norms and values of the international system which he wanted to overturn using revolutionary zeal. His foreign language's linguistic expressions were bombastic, undiplomatic and antisuperpower (U.S. and U.S.S.R). He was friendly to Third World nations but hostile to the Bretton Woods system of international organizations (Medeiros and Fravel 2003). Such form of isolationism was replaced with the less confrontational and modern foreign policy optimism of the multilateral, neoliberal, neorealist and constructivist schools of thought and political enlightenment (Kegley 2002; Sagini 2004).

## CONTEMPORARY CHINESE FOREIGN POLICY

The authors of modern Chinese foreign policy were inspired by a long historical tradition that is rooted in the Qing Dynasty whose imperial legal tradition made the Chinese empire strong, prosperous, assertive, and respected at home and abroad. This tradition enabled Chinese foreign policy analysts to construct foreign policy that is rooted in Chinese history, culture, philosophy, and that erases the victimhood centuries-old mentality created by twentieth century Western and Japanese colonialism. The tradition also enables the nation to psychologically and diplomatically use power to eliminate historic and colonial humiliations. The goal of the PRC is to optimistically construct a strong, independent, powerful, and united China that is a great power within the world without…"Persuing any hegemonic or warlike ambitions." These ideas are "part of the new security concept which is China's vision for the post-Cold War era in which nations interact economically and diplomatically for mutual benefit and in which they avoid forming exclusive alliances and or blocs" (p. 2)

The foundation of China's new diplomatic history of the last 60 years was laid down by CCP leaders at the Common Program of the Chinese People's Political Consultative Conference (CPPCC). In September 1949 this document became the provisional constitution of China. The basic principle of the document's foreign policy agenda was to "guarantee independence, freedom, and territorial integrity of the state, support protracted world peace and friendly cooperation among peoples of all countries in the world, oppose imperialist policies of aggression and war." The architects of this type of foreign policy under which the nation has attained relative super power status were Mao Zedong, Zhou Enlai, and Deng Xiaoping (Huaqiu 2007). The first two leaders were intellectual and bureaucratic ideologues of the Marxist, Lenist, Stalinist and Maoist intellectual tradition. That tradition believed in the zealous use of revolutionary power to bring change in the world. As explained above, their communist ideology which glorifies the masses rather than scientific rationality, freedom, democracy, justice, and human rights contributed not only to the economic and political collapse of China but, also to its chronic and global isolationism. On the contrary, Deng Xiaoping, like his younger successors, was a pragmatic intellectual leader, who, in spite of the challenges from the "Gang of Four, or in spite of the fact that he did not rise to the Pinnacle of Power (as Chairman or General Secretary of the CCP, Prime Minister or president) he possessed "idiom table power like Mao's (Sodaro 2008, 678). His formative years of learning in France when he edited a student pager, in Moscow where he learned how to work with workers, unions, and the masses, and where Stalin encouraged Chinese Communist and nationalist students to unite and lay a foundation for a one China policy during the 1920's and as a member of the People's Liberation Army, he fought against KMT and Japan. In 1945, he was promoted to party membership in the Central Committee. When Mao died in 1976, two years later, Deng Xiaoping became China's leader for 13 years before he died in 1997. He grew up, studied, and worked in three countries; was able to analyze and compare diplomatic structure and life with that of other Eastern and Western countries and decided to try what works rather than what doesn't. In 1972, the late "Chairman Mao Zedong, motivated by Nixonian and Kissingerian U.S. influence, decided to open the door to Sino-American relations and put forth the ' one line' strategy that extended from Japan to the U.S. and to Europe, in order to counter the Soviet Challenge" (Huaqiz 2007, 2). Before the 1972 Sino-American breakthrough, China had opened up diplomatic relations with France eight years earlier (1964). This strategy which ended in the late 1980s was instrumental to relaxing tensions in Chinese security because it did not only curb soviet expansionary and hegemonic influence, but, the "China Card" strategy effectively contributed to the containment and isolation of the U.S.S.R. and its eventual and peaceful collapse in 1991 (Huaqiu 2007; Sagini 2001; Brzezinski, 1989).

Chinese foreign policy was constructed from the 1949 (CPPCC) during the First Plenary Session of the Eighth National People's Congress. The constitutional theme from which the foreign policy goal are rooted states that:

> China adheres to an independent foreign policy as well as to the five principles of mutual respect for sovereignty and territorial integrity, mutual non-aggression, non-interference in each other's internal affairs, equality and mutual benefit, and peaceful coexistence in developing diplomatic relations and economic and cultural exchanges with other countries; China consistently opposes imperialism, hegemonies, and colonialism, works to strengthen unity with the people of other countries, supports the oppressed nations, and the developing countries in their just struggle to win and preserve national economies, and strives to safeguard world peace and promote the cause of human progress (http://english.people.com.cn/china/19990914A128.html).

In matters affecting Chinese People and the interest of the nation, China maintains decisive independence, does not yield to pressure or threats from within and from without. China respects the independence of other countries and "any country, big or small, rich or poor, and strong or weak, should be equal" (p. 1). The government of the People's Republic" opposes arms races, regional domination, and nuclear proliferation, destruction of nuclear weapons and reduction of conventional and military troops" (p. 2). In 1985, China eliminated one million troops in two years and signed the Treaty on the Non-proliferation of Nuclear Weapons in 1992. These actions positively enhanced Chinese global diplomacy. The five principles of political equality and mutual gain complement each other's needs. The principle of peaceful coexistence advocates the search for common interests, reservation of differences, respect for each other and living harmoniously regardless of systemic and ideological distinctions.

The PRC's government believes in the promotion of peace, stability, justice, and rationality of the world order by conforming to the purposive principles of the U N Charter. China supports the legitimate demands of the Third World Countries particularly in Asia, Africa and Latin America where in most of the world population lives. These countries identify themselves with China because they know that throughout its history, it has gone through difficult and good times that make them feel that the latter is a "tested ... and reliable friend" (p. 3). As a formal observer of the 77 Group of nonalignment movement, she has been ratified for genuine membership.

China does not respect or condone any form of unnecessary external interference in its internal affairs. In the light of this philosophical position, the PRC does everything, both in short-range and in long-term strategic focus in order to promote the reunification of China in respect to the status of Hong Kong, Macao, and Taiwan. Taiwan's historical separation from China was effected by Western, imperialist, and colonial masters. For the purpose of accomplishing China's reunification, Deng Xiaoping developed and reinforced the theory of "one Country, two systems" (p. 3) policy. By that he meant that China and Hong Kong (British colony), Macao (ex-Portuguese colony), Communist China, and Taiwan (nationalist China) will all be part of the greater "ancient" China as they were before Europeans contributed to their "Political and cultural estrangement from greater China. Both the first two Chinas were reunited with China in 1997 and 1999 respectively. The reunification took place peacefully because the values of these relics of colonialism had become irrelevant, outmoded, and competitively inferior. Taiwan has not been reunited largely due to its geostrategic importance to the West. As historical events that help to resolve the conflict between communist and nationalist China evolve, such evolution will create new diplomatic and historico-political dynamics that will propel Taiwan to cultivate new economic and cultural synergistics for her eventual reunification with the motherland.

Are there institutions responsible for the formulation of Chinese foreign policy? Formal policy analysis, reconstruction, and implementation of Chinese foreign policy is managed by the ministry of Foreign Affairs of the PRC. Although, in practice, this ministry is responsible overall, for the foreign policy agenda, in reality, it is subordinate to the Foreign Affairs Leading Small Group of the Communist party of China. Unlike many countries around the world, "much of Chinese foreign policy is formulated in think tanks sponsored and supervised by, interlocuters .... outside of the government. One distinctive aspect of Sino-American relations is that much of the foreign policy discussion takes place between interlocutors who form the think tanks. Because these discussions are unofficial, they are generally more free and less restricted than the discussions between government officials." Distinctively, China has a specific body of people specialized in Chinese strategic thought and theory of international relations which is different from that of its Western counterparts. The implications of this aspect of single country (China's) foreign policy versus multi-country/multi-regions (U.S., E.U., France, etc.) foreign policies of Western nations could have serious implications on each nation's/region's effectiveness in terms of addressing their respective interests in the global arena. The unilateral and preemptive U.S. attack on Iraq is a case in point. The attack weakened and marginalized the U.S. government in respect to its role in the global community.

Chiang Zemin developed a comprehensive and independent Chinese foreign policy intended to promote peaceful diplomatic relationships with all countries in the world. He advanced and defined the ten most important foreign policy principles as follows:

> safe guard independence; opposing hegemonies and safe guarding world peace; developing good neighborly relations; strengthening unity and cooperation amongst Third World nations; establishing and developing friendly cooperative ties with all nations-the basis of the Five Principles of Peaceful Coexistence; maintaining a positive attitude toward international cooperation; making energetic efforts to promote the establishment of a new international order; opposing arms race and promoting the disarmament process; Practising comprehensive opening to the outside world; and actively enhancing the friendly people-to-people contacts throughout the world (Huaqiu 2007).

Chinese scholars and policy analysts argue that the theory that supports China's peaceful and gradual rather than dramatic and aggressive rise to superpower status is, apparently valid (Vice President Zzheng Bisian). The nation is not interested in policies that replicate Japanese or America imperialist policies of hegemonic conquest and colonization of the world. Instead, the buying consensus is interested in a different foreign policy that is motivated by a fierce defense of national borders and interest, and an increasing commitment to multilateral institutions such as the U.N (Heston 2000). Its policies are independent of the multilateral institutions such as the World Bank and the IMF. The country's development is driven by the desire to escape historical trauma reminiscent of its masses of the people and the Maoist struggle for national integration and reunification. In the light of historical past, its political establishment values peace and stability greatly. It places great emphasis on the marriage between evolutionary economics and politics for the purpose of advancing cultural development.

In foreign policy affairs, China is interested in strengthening the role of the UN and international rule of law. It is also preoccupied with the development of an integrated, regional, and Asianist federation. The peaceful rise theory is designed to promote positive and responsible relations with its domestic and regional neighbors and the international community. Such a policy will conveniently serve the nation's interest in enhancing massive domestic consumption and foreign investment that are essential for contributing to the rise of living standards and Chinese global economic competitiveness. China's passion for regional integration is likely to result in the formation of the Asian Economic Community whose Asian currency; the Yuan (renminbi) will challenge both the dollar and the Euro in global and international markets. China has resolved all land disputes with its neighbors. It has signed non-aggression treaty with ASEAN. It is also one of the ten nations that make up the ASEAN after joining the group in 2003. It has successfully helped the U.S. and together with Japan, Russia, and South Korea to influence the archaic communist North Korea to sign a treaty of nuclear deescalation and disarmament in Asia. In this agreement, North Korea will receive oil and gas from China and rice and other consumables products from South Korea and Japan. This form of Clintonian Bushificition is a form of pacification that helps to appease a potential aggressor that is well armed and that is potentially detrimental to the US interests in south East Asia. The latest aggression in which the North attacked the South's islanders in the Pacific has provoked the issuance of strong international condemnation of the North and pressured China to rhetorically advocate the immediate dismemberment of the North, reunification of the Korean Pensula and the South's domination of the entire Korean political, socioeconomic, and cultural terrain. Though China's rhetoric may have been a quick and brilliant reification of its foreign policy stand, future actions and political behavior by the North will reveal more concerning "the dreams of Northern antiquity" and those who assist in its sustenance in the global age of regionalism, multilateralism and multipolarity. Also, the North's attempt to threaten S. Korea and Japan in 2013 never materialized because the two nations and their allies may have planned for its demise.

The Chinese give aid to ASEAN countries and receive imports from them. They have carried out joint and neighborly military exercises with Russia, Kyrgyzstan, India and Pakistan. Chinese supported the UN resolution on Iraq but kept allowing foreign reserves a float. They have more than $2.65 trillion of foreign reserves they use for buying dollars and government bonds in the US market. The nation has benefited greatly from globalization and membership in WTO system due to Xiao Ping's support. China does not like to intervene in any other country's internal affairs except for humanitarian reasons. It respects all nations and their role in the international system. For instance, Li Zhaoxing, Foreign Minister, argued that countries, big or small and strong or week, are equal before international law and, in basic norms governing international relations. The existing international, multilateral institutions, and the U.N. at the core, are the best venues for all countries to participate in the international affairs on an equal footing. The institutions guarantee for democratic and law based international relations. We "have every reason to strengthen it and no excuse to weaken it" (p. 116).

The Chinese political establishment has carried out one of the most important foreign policy moves. In the wake of the peaceful, dramatic, and historically ironic dissolution of the USSR, China, Kazakhstan, Kyrgyzstan, Russia and Tajikistan-the Shanghai five (p. 117) tend to negotiate treaties that made their 4,300 miles border demilitarized and have started to cooperate in security and trade affairs. When "Uzbekistan joined the shanghai five in 2001, they changed their name to Shanghai Cooperation Organization (S.C.O.) which created a regional anti-terrorism structure that regulate economic, border and law enforcement matters as well as two combinations of military exercise" (p.117).

The apparently new Shanghai spirit for regionalism whose principles are "mutual trust, mutual benefit and equality" (p. 117) is likely to bring not only "stability and optimism to the region, but it will also use these and other resources to help stabilize failed states, protect people from genocide, tackle global warming and prevent the proliferation of WMD" (p. 118).

Although it's nationalistic sentiments over Taiwan, closeness to the center of world energy supply (Middle East) and support for Iranian and Sudanese regime oddities tend to frighten Western observers and political regimes, its ultimate contributions to global and regional security and community will largely depend on how the US and the E.U. treat it. An attempt to "contain China and thwart its development could drive its nationalism" (p. 119) in order to annex and reintegrate Taiwan. Also, if the West treats China as a partner that is responsibly bound into global interests and institutions, it will remain wrapped up in its own multilateral logic (p. 119). This also may be a form of Western wishful thinking that comforts its Americocentric and Eurocentric interests, security, and power due to lack of knowledge about the future.

Though China's peaceful rise theory tends to politically and psychologically calm the hot political temperature in the affairs of men, the U.S.'s realization of the possibilities of China's misuse of its power and influence in Asia has continued to make the U.S. to retain its military contigents in the Philippines and other places. The US/Japanese political, economic and military alliance strengthens each other's industrial and technological edge that enables them to futuristically perfect their nuclear missile defense systems whose capability will enhance China's peaceful rise theory. The theory will enable the country to strengthen its global network of mining petroleum firms and gas pipelines from Russia through Thailand. The same theory will diplomatically enhance the support by others, of its global and shipping sea lanes that need to be respected without conflagration and unilateralist or preemptive attacks on its territory and on the state and its diplomatic, security, and economic instruments. The economic muscle of China will continue to be a hybrid of private companies and large government owned firms in key industries such as power generation, resource mining exploration, transportation, truck and car manufacturing, as well as large private-sector firms with inextricable links to government agencies and officials (Fishermen 2005). Its economic openness in terms of allowing more than one million Western and Japanese companies to invest and do business with the Chinese people is a form modern economic and diplomatic nationalism that undercuts the economically retrogressive Maoist policies of the Cultural Revolution Era of the 1960s and 1970s. Such a form of openness, which relies on connections and relationships, makes China to be an effective, strategically important, and positive rather than negative promoter of global and Western diplomatic interests that serve to reach other security needs that reinforces the peaceful rise theory (Beinstein and Munro 1999).

Above all, China has considerably invested in more than 48 African countries and in many Asian and Latin American countries. If China's peaceful rise theory is going to contribute to its long term superpower status, then China must not replicate exploitative, colonial, and imperialist policies of its former colonizers. China should foster scientifically, empirically, and technologically rooted elements of development that will create and promote a new legacy for liberating people from poverty, disease, and ignorance. China should chart a new trajectory of global and international development. It should use a new development paradigm that is relatively democratic, philosophically attractive in its emotional appeal, and materialistically harmonious with nature, the environment, and the human race. That is one of the meanings of peaceful rise theory. Other meanings could be several and relevant or irrelevant in our time. Only time will prove the nature and character of the theory in question. But, it is a good beginning.

## REFERENCES

1967. *The Soviet bloc: Unity and conflict*. Cambridge, MA: Harvard University Press.

Abbott, Carl, et al. 2007. *The American journey: A history of the United States*. Upper Saddle River, NJ: Pearson Education.

Abramowitz, Morton I. 1997. *China: Can we have a policy?* Washington: Carnegie Endowment for International Peace.

Allen, Kenneth W., Glenn Krumel, and Jonathan D. Pollack. 1995. *China's air force enters the twenty-first century*. Santa Monica, CA: Rand.

Arnett, Eric, ed. 1997. *Military capacity and the risk of war: China, India, Pakistan and Iran*. Oxford: Oxford University Press.

Bennett, Andrew, and John G. Ikenberry. (2006). The review involving relevance for U.S. foreign policy 1906-2006. *American Political Science Review* 100, 4: 65-8.

Berger, Thomas U. 1998. *Culture of antimilitary tourism: National security in Germany and Japan*. Baltimore, MD: Johns Hopkins University Press.

Bernstern, Richard, and Ross H. Munro. 1999. The new China lobby. In Eugene R. Wittkopf and James, eds., *The domestic sources of American foreign policy: Insight and evidence*.

Brzezinski, Zbigniew. 1998. *The grand failure: The British and death of communism in the twentieth century*. New York: Charles Scribner's Sons.

Cohn, Theodore H. 2008. *Global political economy: Theory and practice*. New York: Pearson Longman.

Feste, Karea. 1990. *American and Soviet intervention: Effects on world stability*. New York: Crime Russak.

Fishman, Ted C. 2005. *China inc: How the rise of the next superpower challenges America and the world*. New York: Scribner.

Geiss, Imanuel. 1968. *The Pan Africa Movement. A history of Pan-Africanism in America, Europe, Africa, and* New York.

Gill, Bates, and Taeho Kim. 1995. *China's arms acquisitions from abroad: A quest for 'superb and secret weapons.'* Oxford: Oxford University Press.

Gregory, Robert. 1971. *India and East Africa: A history of race relation with in the British Empire 1890-1939*. London: Oxford University Press.

Haas, Peter. 1992. Introduction: Epistemic communities and international policy coordination. *International Organization* 46: 1-35.

Hall, Peter. 1989. *The political economy of ideas: Keynesianism across nations.* Princeton, NJ: Princeton University Press.

Heston, Alan W. 2000. *The Annals of the American Academy of Political and Social Science* 70: 1-24.

Huaqiu, Liu. 2007. *Qiushi Magazine* 23.

Jacob, Lawrence R., and Benjamin I. Page. 2005. Who influence foreign policy? *American Political Science Review* 99, 1: 107-23.

Jeffries, Charles. 1948. *The colonial empire.* London: The Colonial Office.

Kegley, C. W. 2007. *World politics: Trends and transformation.* Manuscript.

Larkin, Bruce D. 1996. *Nuclear designs: Great Britain, France, and China in the global governance of nuclear arms.* New Brunswick: Transaction.

Leonard, Mark. 2005. *Why Europe will run the 21st century.* New York: Public Affairs.

Lugard, Frederick. 1922. *The dual mandate in the tropical Africa.* London: London University Press.

Wittkopf, Eugene R., and James M. McCormick, eds. 1999. *The domestic sources of American foreign policy: Insights and evidence.* Lanham, MD: Rowman and Little Field Publisher, Inc.

Markovits, Andrei S. 2007. Western Europe's American problem. The chronicles review: *The Chronicle of Higher Education* 19: b6-b9.

Martin, Christopher. 2007. Crafting a U.S. response to the emerging east Asia free trade area. *The Whitehead Journal of Diplomacy and International Relations* VIII, 2:73-84.

Mayers, David. 1998. *Dialogues in Arab political: Negotiation in regional order.* New York: Columbia University Press.

Medeiros, Evan S., and Fravel M. Taylor. 2003. *Foreign Affairs* November/December.

Moller, Bjorn. 1997. A common security and NOD regime for the Asia-Pacific? *Pacifica Review* May-June.

Murray, Douglas. 2006. *Neo-conservatism: Why we need it.* Encounter Books.

Nathan, Andrew J., and Robert S. Ross. 1997. *The Great Wall and the empty fortress: China's search for security.* New York: W.W. Norton.

Nelkin, Dorothy. 1979. *Scientific knowledge, public policy and democracy. Knowledge, Creation, Diffusion, Utilization* September: 106-22.

*New Webster's Dictionary and Thesaurus of the English Language.* 1992. Danbury, CT: Lexican Publications, Inc.

Robinson, et al. African and the Victorian: The official mind of British imperialism.

Rosenau, J.N. 1968. The Concept of Intervention *Journal of International Affairs*, 22: 165-176.

Sagini, Meshack M. 2004. International diplomacy and the U.S.–Iraq conflict: The failure of unilateralism in a multilateral context. *Journal of Scholarly and Scientific Perspectives: An International Journal of Scholarly and Scientific Research* I.

__________. 2001 *Organizational behavior: The challenges of the new millennium.* Lanham, MD: University Press of America, Inc.

Shinn, James, ed. 1996. *Weaving the net: Conditional engagement with China.* New York: Council in Foreign Relations.

Sodaro, Michael J., et al. 2008. *Comparative politics: A global introduction.* Boston: McGraw Hill.

Staar, Richard F. 1991. *Foreign policies of the Soviet Union.* Stanford, CA: However Institution Presses.

Tang, Wenfang, and Parish William. 2000. *Chinese urban life under reform: The changing social contract.* Cambridge, UK: Cambridge University Press.

*United States Security Strategy for the East Asia-Pacific Region.* 1995. Washington: Department of Defense.

Vogel, Ezra F., ed. 1997. *Living with China: U.S./China relations in the twenty-first century.* New York: W.W. Norton.

Wan, Ming. 2008. *The political economy of east Asia: Striving for wealth and power.* Washington, DC.: CQ Press.

Williams, Walter. 2006. Should we copy Europe? *The Oklahoman* Saturday November 25: 13A

Williamson, J. W. 1949. *A short history of the British Empire.* London: Oxford University Press.

Wittkopf, Eugene R., and James M. McCormick, eds. 1999. *The domestic sources of American foreign policy: Insights and evidence.* Lanham, MD: Rowman and Little Field Publisher, Inc.

Woodby, Slyvia. 1989. *Gorbachev and the decline of ideology in Soviet foreign policy.* Boulder: Western Press.

Yahuda, Michael. 1996. *The international politics of the Asia-Pacific,* 1945-1995. New York: Routledge.

Zimmerman, William. 2002. *The Russian people and foreign policy.* Princeton, NJ: Princeton University Press.

# Chapter VIII
# E.U. Foreign Policy

## E.U. Foreign Policy: Evolution

Professor Christopher Hill and Lecturer Karen E. Smith have been instructors of Political Science at the London School of Economics and Political Science. They wrote *The European foreign policy: Key documents,* that was published in 2000. Currently, Professor Hill teaches at Cambridge University. Their book is the first and original scholarly analysis of the official documents which trace the evolution of the European foreign policy, that is "the collective diplomacy of the European Union" that has evolved from scratch during the last 60 years. The book contains major historical material that has fundamentally become the historical, political, constitutional, and theoretical foundation upon which the principles of E.U. foreign policy are rooted. In general, the materials, contained in the text are an important original source for ideas and insights on European politics, international relations and public and collective diplomacy.

The post World War II political climate in which the United States, the dominant pacifier and the USSR, the leftist occupier were emerging as the rival superpowers that were not only interested in the fate of Europe, but were also heavily armed with nuclear weapons. Their mighty power psychologically dictated some Europeans to form a forum for survival and cooperation in foreign policy matters. Although initially this vision was shallow and less specific, it evolved with the gradual involvement of more nations and the enlargement of the E U. In spite of the alleged fears concerning the intentions of the "sick man of Europe", France's vulnerability to her German rival, Nazi occupation, and Britain's wartime and postwar time exhaustion with victory in the wake American cessation of lend-lease and nuclear cooperation in 1946" (Hill and Smith 2000), caused the pound to fluctuate disastrously and lessened Britain's diplomatic and economic power in the world. The strong pre-war and influential European foreign policy was eclipsed by post-war American and Soviet rivalry in the global arena. Absence of a Western European superpower dictated the necessity for the gradual evolution of the E.U. foreign policy. The E.U.'s zonal foreign policy is a "weak patchwork of the European Union's federal and national Institutions."

Table VIII.1. Major Sources for E.U. Foreign Policy

1. Treaty of Economic, Social and Cultural Collaboration and Collective Self- Defense between the United Kingdom of Great Britain and Northern Ireland, Belgium, France, Luxembourg and the Netherlands (The Brussels Treaty). Brussels, 17 March 1948
2. The North Atlantic Treaty, Washington D.C, 4 April 1949
3. The Statue of the Council of Europe, 5 May 1949
4. The Schuman Declaration, 9 May 1950
5. Treaty Establishing the European Coal and Steel Community (Preamble), Paris, 18 April1951
6. The European Defense Community Treaty, Pairs. 27 May 1952
7. Draft Treaty embodying the Statute of the European community. Adopted by the AD Hor Assembly in Strasbourg (European Political Community Treaty), 10 March 1953
8. Protocol Modifying and Completing the Brussels Treaty, (Western European Union), Paris, 23 October 1954
9. Treaty Establishing the European Economic Community (Treaty of Rome), Rome, 25 March 1957
10. Draft Treaty for the Establishment of a European Political Union (Fouchet Plan I), 2 November 1961
11. Second Draft of the Treaty for the Establishment of a European Union (Fouchet Plan II).18 January 1962
12. Treaty between French Republic and Federal Republic of Germany Concerning Franco-German Cooperation (The Elysee Treaty), Pairs, 22 January 1963
13. Report on the Future Tasks of the Alliance (Harmel Report). Brussels, December 1967
14. The Maastricht Treaty which became the Second Pillar of E U in 1992
15. The Amsterdam Treaty of 1999
16. The Nice Treaty which amended the CFSP provisions.
17. The Treaty of Lisbon, December 2009

## European Union Institution

In 1957, France, West Germany, Italy, Belgium, Netherlands, and Luxembourg agreed to cooperate economically. The Treaty of Rome, the first pillar, effectively established the European Economic Community (EEC) for the purpose of promoting economic growth and eliminating tariffs and trade barriers within nations. These nations also jointly concluded commercial arrangements with non-member states. During the 1960's the EEC set up a Common Agriculture Policy (CAP) for enabling farmers to be competitive (using subsidies) regionally, internationally and globally (Sodaro 2008).

Gradually, the EEC was expanded to include Britain, Ireland, and Demark in 1973. Greece joined in 1981, Spain and Portugal attained membership in 1986. The EEC became known as the European Union (E.U.) in 1993, under the second pillar- the Maastricht Treaty. The Treaty was instrumental to the E.U.'s establishment of "Common Foreign and Security Policy" (CFSP) for the E.U. member states. In 1995, three nations- Austria, Sweden, and Finland joined the E.U. E.U. Membership was raised from 15 to 25 in 2004 when the Czech Republic, Estonia, Hungary, Latvia, Lithuania, Poland, Slovakia, Slovania, Cyprus and Malta joined. With the exception of the last two, the rest were formerly Communist and Vassal states of the U.S.S.R. In 2007, Bulgaria and Romania joined. To date, 10 of the 28 E.U. member states were formerly ruled by the USSR. Negotiations for accepting Croatia, Turkey, and Macedonia into the E.U. were in the pipeline and have been ratified.

In the light of the circumstances and, from the outset, Europeans have been divided between those who have wanted to accelerate the process of economic and political integration and those who have wished to keep integration within stricter limits in order to preserve greater freedom of action for their own national governments. Proponents of greater supranationalism have continuously sparred, and with advocates of state sovereignty, these debates still take place today, but there has always been a general consensus that varying degrees of both tendencies should coexist. As

> a consequence, the organizations' institutions were set up to permit significant levels of supranational activity while simultaneously preserving the member governments' rights to make important E.U. decisions and even to opt out of E.U. activities that they do not like ... in 2004 the E.U. completed the drafting of a constitution designed to reform its institutions and clarify their powers ... the document was put on hold after French and Dutch voters rejected it in the referendums held in 2006 (Sodaro 2008, 166).

The E.U.'s constitutional provisions that allow any member of the organization's supranational proceedings and constitutional mandate which do not meet the needs of member states did not only indicate that the member states are culturally and politically important and influential, but they are also more powerful than the federal patchwork of the "supranational state" whose raison detre depends on the states themselves. The constitutional convention of the E.U. has resurrected the old rift between those who fear the existence of a strong union that will trample on the rights of member states and those who think that the supranational state is weak in a variety of ways comparable to the Articles of Confederation system of government in the American experience. In spite of "the E.U.'s constitutional flaws, the constitution significantly advances E.U.'s central project whose trajectory creates a federal union of states that celebrate the pluralist, elitist, and majoritarian views of governance for the people of Europe" (Nicolaidis 2004, 97-110). In 2006, the E.U.'s organizational structure was the same as its original one, the 1957 Treaty of Rome that had the necessary key institutional components of which the European Commission, the Council of the European Union, the European Parliament, the European Council, the European Court of Justice, and the Central European Bank are of paramount importance.

## THE EUROPEAN COMMISSION (EC)

Each European country appoints a president to represent each member state. The major function of the E.U. is to propose and enforce common E.U. laws and policies in the field of CFSP. Although the EC is not an elected body, it may negotiate certain international treaties. Their power to make final E.U. laws is limited by state governments which appoint them. Once they have been appointed, their tenure depends on approval by the European parliament. Their 'actions are independent of national governments but dependent on their promotion of the general interest of the community' (Sodaro 2008, 167) rather than that of member states. The commission can ask the presidency to convene an emergency council meeting and give suggestions or recommendations for action to the policy unit. The EC implements the CFSP budget using appropriate and specific financial channels. Based on its competencies, the European commission is externally responsible for trade...humanitarian intervention, development assistance, rehabilitation and reconstruction, and sanctions regulations.

## THE COUNCIL OF THE EUROPEAN UNION

The council of the E.U. is the main decision making body which consists of elected cabinet ministers from member states. They participate in nine major functional committees. These heads of state and government and the commission president meet at least once every six months. They set priorities and give guidelines for E.U. policies and common strategies on CFSP. Under the Amsterdam Treaty, there are five fundamental objectives of CFSP: "To safeguard the common values, fundamental interests, independence and integrity of the Union in conformity with the principles of the United Nations charter; to strengthen the security of the union in all ways, to preserve peace and strengthen international security, in accordance with the principles of the U.N. Charter, as well as the principle of the Helsinki final Act and objectives of the Paris Charter, including those on external borders; to promote international co-operation; to develop and consolidate democracy and the rule of law, and respect for human rights and fundamental freedoms" (http://ec.europa.eu./external_relations/cfsp/intro/index/htm). The council of E.U., like the European commission, decides on common strategies and adopts joint actions and common positions because each member state makes laws and policies by voting. It also unanimously exercises the principle (process) of intergovernmental functionalism.

## THE EUROPEAN PARLIAMENT (EP)

The (EP) has 743 members from 28 member states, who are elected by the people. Although they make the E.U. law, their legislative power is not decisive in the area of foreign affairs and agricultural policy. Also, the EP has no right or power to raise revenue either. It sounds like the historical *Articles of Confederation* of the United States in which states had more power than the national government. This makes the EP a rubber stamp of member state legislatures. The EP is constantly kept informed and broadly consulted by insiders and outsiders of the European Union.

### The European Council

The council and commission are jointly responsible for ensuring consistency of E.U. external tasks holistically. It addresses external relations, security, economic and development matters. The European council is composed of heads of state and government. Together with the Commission President, they meet once every six months (per presidency). The council sets up priorities and gives broad guidelines for the CFSP. It employs common strategic goals and objectives. Their plans and decisions chart the Unions future directions. Each member country represented guards its territorial integrity and independence when faced with crisis. The 2002-2009 U.S. war in Iraq divided the council into two; one section led by Tony Blair supported America while the other one led by France and German abstained.

### The Community: External Representation and Troika

The European community which lives in the European Union is externally represented by the commission's delegations. Within the CFSP area, it is represented by the presidency of the Council which operates through the "local ambassador of the country holding the presidency" (p. 3). "Commission delegations, together with representatives of the future presidency, are fully associated with the presidency as part of a local troika, carrying out demands to third countries and establishing joint Heads of Mission report on political developments"(p. 3). All E.U. countries have a network of commission delegations in every foreign embassy representing each member state. They also represent the E.U. as a whole. Based on the Treaty of Rome and by extension, Amsterdam, community external powers which express its interests are in the areas of "trade, policy, associate countries and overseas territories, relations with other international organizations, research and technical development, environment policy, education, vocational training and youth, culture, public health, trans-European networks, economic and monetary union and …development cooperation" (p. 3).

## The European Court of Justice (ECJ)

The European Court of Justice consists of federal judges that are appointed by their member states. It is not clear how they are chosen, how long their tenure is and which supranational institution ratifies their appointment to the federal bench. The court is authorized to issue ruling and legal interpretations that concern "E.U. institutions, member governments, private businesses, associations"…. labor unions" and individuals in matters concerning European law" (Sodaro 2008, 167). They work in the context of the principle of judicial independence textured and philosophically interpreted in the light of Euro-American and Western legal jurisprudence.

## European Central Bank (ECB)

The European Central Bank coordinates the monetary policies of the 17 E.U. countries which have adopted the Euro as their local, national, and supranational currency. The other 11 member states have not eurorized -yet. Of the 11, Britain, Sweden, and Denmark are among the 10 new Countries that still retain the usage of their national currencies. The E.U. and the Euro zone have become a single common market, which "promotes the free movement of goods, services, money, and people throughout" (p.167) the Euro zone region. About 85% of the businesses of the member countries are regulated by the E.U. business law. In addition, the E.U. is engaged in coordinating immigration policies, anti-crime and anti-terrorism activities, …. environmental standards" (p.167) etc. that fall within the supranational rather than the domestic localism of individual member states. The gross domestic product of the region which the bank coordinates is $17 trillion compared to the $15 trillion for the U.S. The E.U., China, Russia, Canada and Japan are the U.S.'s major trading partners. "The per capita income of the U.S. is about $49,965 while that of the Euro zone is $32,842" respectively (U.S. Department of Commerce 2009; and 2013).

# STRUCTURE OF E.U. POLITICS AND GOVERNMENT

Without defining each and every facet of the E.U., its political structure in terms of institutional and functional components have been summarized and paraphrased with the use of http://wikipedia.org/wiki/common_Foreign_and_security:

Table VIII.2. The Political Structure of E.U.

1. Three Pillars
    - I: European Community (EC, Euratom) = European Atomic Energy Community
    - II: Common Foreign and Security Policy (CFSP)
    - III: Police and Judicial Cooperation in criminal matters (PJCC)
2. Political Institutions
    - Commission
        - President
        - Council of Ministers
        - European Council-Presidency
        - Parliament
            - President
            - MEP's
            - Constituencies
            - Elections
    - Political groups
    - Committees
3. Judiciary
    - Court of Justice- List of members
    - Court of First Instance
    - Civil Service Tribunal-Bureaucracy
4. Finance Auditing
    - European Court of Auditors
5. Financial bodies
    - European Central Bank
    - European Investment Bank
    - European Investment Fund
6. Advisory bodies
    - Economic and Social Committee
    - Committee of the Regions
7. Decentralized bodies
    - Agencies of the E.U.
8. Law
    - Acquis Communitarian
    - Procedure
    - Treaties
    - Recommendations Opinions
9. E.U. related topics
    - Economic and monetary union
    - E.U. Enlargement (issues)
    - Foreign relations
    - Pan-European Political Parties
        - Parties by country
        - Party affiliations on the Council
10. Foreign and Security
    - Security and Defense
    - Defense Initiative
    - Petersburg tasks
    - Foreign relations
11. Defense bodies
    - Defense Agency
    - E.U.ISS
    - Satellite Center
    - Military Committee
    - Military Staff
    - Defense Procurement

12. Military Forces
    - Rapid Reaction Force
    - E.U.FOR
    - Battle groups
    - Gendarmerie
    - Euro Corps
    - Deployment

## RELATED ORGANIZATIONS-WEU AND NATO

The Treaty of Paris, Treaty of Rome, Treaty of Maastricht, Treaty of Amsterdam, Treaty of Nice and the Europeans Union constitution are the historically fundamental and documentary philosophical foundations upon which the apparent integration of the European Union depends. In particular, the U.S. Bretton Woods System of using the dollar, which was strengthened by gold, a global reserve currency, creation of the World Bank and IMF for helping certain countries to get out of debt due to deficits in their balance of payments, and GATT (WTO) which promotes free trade, animated Europeans to regionally start to emulate this kind of American Political and economic supranationalism. Second, during the 1940's, the American Marshall Plan for the reconstruction of Post World War II Europe and the subsequent global geostrategic containment of the U.S.S.R. created necessary conditions for the gradual U.S.S.R demobilization, disarmament and de-escalation of conflict in Europe. These measures contributed to the gradual disintegration and total collapse of the U.S.S.R. The gradual formation and enlargement of NATO and the E.U. and the relative economic, political, and military marginalization of the USSR relied on those solid foundations. One logical Philosopher of antiquity has said that "to every action there is an equal and opposite reaction." In other words, the collapse of the USSR has been replaced by the emergence of new competitive, multipolar, and global powers discussed elsewhere in the text.

Third, In 1950's the Schuman Plan resulted in the European Coal and Steel Community (ECSC); German was constitutionally reformed and globally reintegrated during the Cold War that drove transAtlantic and the global climate for almost 50 years. With the emergence of the European Defense Community, Paul-Henry Spaak, a Belgian, produced the Monnet Plan which became the base for creating, the European Common market in 1956. In 1957, the Treaty of Rome founded the European Economic Community (EEC) and the European Atomic Energy Authority (Euratom). Above all, the Treaty of Rome founded the contemporary third fashion of "globalization, the transnational diffusion of an American model of consumerism and mass production" (Krieger 2006, 168).

Although globalization has more than 6000 year history, its modern component, which Marxists characterize as having "heavy tendencies" (p 180), began "with the voyages of exploration, discovery and continuing with colonization and mercantilism, progressing through imperialism and neocolonialism to the present period when financial globalization is a fact, when transnational corporations do see large areas of the plant as their territory, when advanced capitalism has spread well beyond the North American and European regions where it began and when new regions of the world have been integrated into its labor and product markets" (p. 180).

Over all, though the E.U.'s purpose for integrative existence is largely rooted in its attempt to respond to global challenges of social and economic interdependence, or a system that will ensure the provision of "social insurance, income redistribution... public provision of health care, university education and generous pensions" (p. 166), this oversimplified notation of its rasion detre should not be interpreted in the context of the Treaty of Rome alone. Instead, the regional Europeanization of the global heritage should be understood to be Europe's power's social and economic interests and those of its trans-Atlantic ally which they want to emulate. Though the two regions have had radical differences largely based on the use of force versus the ones of diplomacy, unilateralism versus multilateralism, and their implications on international law, and although they don't see eye to eye in their global policies toward China and Taiwan, Iran, North Korea, and the Middle East (Iraq), differences largely caused by "power a symmetry" (p. 184)...the U.S. has the preponderance of power and is prepared to use it, while the Europeans, lacking hard power, have succumbed to a psychology of weakness masked as international idealism"(p. 184). This division between Europeans and Americans concerning the role of their foreign affairs and collective security continues to be the new reality that they both tolerate. Since these conflicts are not civilizationally or culturally faultline based (Huntington 1996), they are "fraternal debates" whose cleavages and diplomatic burial tend to revitalize their "trans- Atlantic routes for the promotion of peace and alliance unity that are essential for reconfiguring a new and more prosperous trans-Atlantic trajectory" (Calleo 2006). That is the meaning of globalization - "the integration of economy through trade, direct foreign investment by corporations and multinationals, short term capital flows, international flows work of workers and humanity generally, and flows of technology" (Oatley 2005, 3). In other words, globalization is both the process of "growth of cross-border activities" as well as an outcome in terms of nationally based global economic interdependence. The center of world globalization is in the West and the term West, a part from its "economic, diplomatic, military and philosophical" orientation (Abramsky 2007, B8) may portray vague and imprecise elements of intellectualism, scientific and philosophical enlightenment, reactive anti- Westernism that is governed by elements of "terrorist organizations and failed nation- states ... that are on the fringes of Western civilization (p. B6) empire, Japan and the Third World and neo-Westernism (Abramsky 2007, B6-B8).

## Challenges to the E.U. and Global Integration

The E.U. does not exist on an island or in a vacuum. As a result, it faces some challenges among which the following are paramount: first, economic performance in Asia and U.S.A. is stronger than that of the Euro-zone due to Asian financial overflows. Second, Europeans, unlike Americans, have not accepted the notions of robust and diverse elements of multiculturalism that is being promoted by immense immigration and globalization policies of various countries in Western society. The society's public policies such as welfare, education, housing, health care, security (terrorism) and unemployment threaten people who fear union choices. In other words, immigrants and their potential contributions are more highly marginalized in the E.U. than in the U.S.

Third, the E.U. Constitution has not been fully ratified by all the E.U. member states. Fourth, individual states' sovereignty is stronger than the supranational principle. Fifth, the E.U. enlargement for economic and political integration, which America supports and finances, tends to work against state sovereignty and parochial independence as opposed to supranational interdependence. Sixth, Turkey's accession debates over (religion, culture and politics), viewed as civilizationally different, tend to threaten prospects for E.U. enlargement and prospects for economic and political integration. Seventh, evidence based on Euro barometer shows that European integration will not replace national identities because these multiple identities are stronger than supranational elements of the E.U.'s struggle with Euroromanticism (Sodaro 2008).

Despite the existence of E.U.'s chronic challenges, and contrary to the positive intentions for the foundation of E.U., Kalypso Nicolaidis, an Oxford Scholar, asserts that the draft constitution does much to advance the E.U.'s core objectives which include the promotion of peace and social justice as well as full employment within the context of the social market economy that describes Europe's distinctive economic and social model, which blends an efficient and competitive economy with generous welfare state benefits. He presents an intriguing vision of the E.U. as a new kind of political community, based on the mutual recognition of diverse European identities and institutional arrangements, principles of multi-level governance, and the prospect that transnational projects can become the glue that will bind the Union" (Krieger 2006, 194-195) together.

Multi-level governance (MLG) is employed to identify the growing complex relationships in organizational policy making, implementation, and accountability at the supranational, national, regional or state and local levels. Multi-level governance structures include the numerical growth of diverse political actors of which, "formal governmental bodies (non-elected bodies outside of government that have significant influence over public policy such as Judicial Ethics Commission or Amtrack in the U.S.) as well as many private actors" (Carmichael 2006, 103) complicate matters. Some of these organizations "manage, regulate finance, trade, expedite communications etc. (Held 2006, 94) in large areas that are no longer within the narrow territorial control of specific national jurisdictions.

Because countries are continuously involved in inexorable, global, and regional interconnectedness, they hardly control the results of interconnectivity by themselves. The outcome is "a distinctive new form of political activity and decision making, which muddies the distinctions between domestic political and geopolitical affairs and blurs the line between state power and influence wielded by international non-governmental organizations (NGO) and a variety of hybrid organizations like the E.U." (Held 2006, 94). Consequently, the international order cannot be understood fully as a system of interstate relations. Instead, it is a system of multilevel actors, multi-governance authorities that use a variety of political processes, diverse levels of coordination, supervision, regulation, and operation. In other words, as Held argues, politics is conducted by multi-governance authorities that use a variety of political processes, diverse levels of coordination, supervision, regulation, and operation. In other words, as Held argues, politics is conducted in a multilevel form that employs various networks and power centers through which the actors, governmental and non-governmental organizations, are involved in Charting new directions and outcomes without regard to institutional, cultural, and normative contradictions. In doing this, the traditionally well established Westphalia model of sovereignty in terms of national autonomy and territorial independence has been compromised because authority in multilevel, multidimensional, and diverse elements has become multicentrically centralized and decentralized, making it difficult or impossible for traditionally established local and national authorities to be legitimate, viable and decisively solvent-sovereignty (Krasner 2006, 77) without causing confusing, disruptive and delinked fragmentation (Sagini 2001) particularly at the periphery.

The current E.U.'s position and global challenge to American ascendance defy the wisdom of strategic and geopolitical genius and thereby neutralizes the mission of the national interest on global affairs "where it is stuck in the mud." Though the U.S., in general terms still has a huge economy, powerful popular culture, greater military capacity, it does not appear to be the driving force for influencing the affairs of post World War II democracies. Regionalism and emerging economies have taken the lead to plan, restructure and positively rationalize the emerging global agenda (Leonard 2005).

The reason why America does not lead these democracies is because of its unilateral and preemptive employment of hard instead of soft power (Nye 2006). Joseph Nye, Dean of Kennedy School of Government at Harvard and Chairman of the National Intelligence Council and former Assistant Secretary of Defense in the Clinton Administration argues that "Soft power determines the capacity of the United States to set the geopolitical agenda, influence the behavior of individuals, nations, and states across the world, and lead by example. Soft power inspires others to emulate America because they admire its values" (p. 132). However hard power, particularly the one applied in the process or outcome of globalization tends to ... "weaken the capacity of states to control outcomes and makes them vulnerable to transnational issues- from the spread of AIDS to financial transactions, to the threat of terrorism .... the form of soft power grows commensurately" (p.133). Nye concludes that the U.S. should use hard power without undermining the effectiveness of soft power, in an emerging multi-polar world, when dealing with other countries in the Middle East and Asia. Since international order is a public good, for all nations, no nation can survive by relying on hard power only or preponderantly. Even small nations like Afghanistan, can be very powerful in the global age. That is why the state department should be given more money for diplomacy and development of the global community. Each country can assist the United States in the "proliferation of the WMD, terrorism, drugs, trade, resources and ecological damage" (p. 136).

European GDP is slightly greater than that of the U.S., except in the military and diplomatic landscape. In this arena, the U.S. is viewed as being shallow and narrow because its political behavior, in some ways, makes it a lonely superpower that can bride, bully, and impose its will on the world (Leonard 2005). Unlike the United States, Europe has a sphere of influence that controls two billion people and a single large internal market of more than 501 million people. Europe is constructed as a loose federal state, slightly based on the U.S.-model called the European Union (E.U.). The E.U. has an invisible hand and political system that will Europeanize power. Ideologically, one-third of its population is foreign and marginalized compared with the well paid Eurocratic elite who largely represent their national rather that the federal interests. The large E.U. market has kept a low profile but managed to spread wings without much hostility from a quarter of the global arena. The E.U.'s economy is slightly larger than the U.S.'s whose anti-global or anti-American backlash has become rampant. European investment in Europe is larger than that of Japan. The former's (European) global invisibility is caused by its dark reminder of colonial history. This episode makes Europe reluctant to adopt, unlike America, imperial trappings. European Union institutions include the diversity of the council of ministers, European commission and European parliament which has (743 members), European court of justice whose members come from the states, is the Supreme Court of the E.U. Europe is an economic rather than a political superpower and is the largest economy in the world. The European countries share four common goals as follows:

(a) To preserve the Atlantic alliance.
(b) To restore the authority at the UN which the Bush administration tried to marginalize in the wake of the U.S.- Iraq war.
(c) To preview unilateral preventive war from being an established norm and to strengthen itself (E.U.).
(d) Federal constitution modeled on the U.S.

Europe uses surveillance to maintain law and order. The law is used as a foreign policy instrument to enhance diplomacy in order to legitimize its transformative power. European weapons of strength are the laws as opposed to spectacle. Power as spectacle is essentially destructive because it is not a good way for governance and security. In Iraq, after the defeat of Sadam Hussein, foreign fighters especially from Syria and Iran, countries the U.S. threatened to attack, fueled the insurgency with their own power which neutralized the American occupation and made it unpopular to govern a complex society. In Afghanistan, for the U.S. the allied forces had no problem to control the Taliban regime. However, the allies failed to rebuild the Afghan society from below the roots up. They introduced a cosmetic form of democracy which left the reality to be ruled by the warlords, corruption, and nepotism (p. 38). Drug lords and kingpins roam all over the country. The northern alliance is not reliable. When the U.S. lost its strategic objectives by going to Iraq, its power to transform Afghanistan was marginalized. Changing societies by imposing power from outside rather than from inside does not work and such inefficient occupation is economically, militarily, and geostrategically insolvent.

Foucault argues that using the Spectacle (military might and technology) to control society does not work. His metaphor of surveillance (p. 40) or what Jeremy Bentham called panolicon (a large circular prison with many cells each with a small window through which prisoners can see the only one guard watching over them from his exterior compartment, makes all prisoners to behave. In a modern sense, this prison is symbolic of using identity cards, photographs, finger stamps, timetables, medical records and law and order to control society effectively. Europeans have passively and aggressively changed their world role from that of pacifism to one of peace- making. Humanitarian intervention such as that conducted in eastern Congo and preventive engagement that is contrary to American preventive measures are what eliminates the essence of spectacle.

The U.S. military uses between $500 to 800 billion annually and applies a dysfunctional military doctrine (based on cold-war issues) that is used to fight against big threats when most of the wars are small and unconventional. For instance, in the Balkans, Somalia, Afghanistan, Iraq or Chechnya, war was not against national armies with battleships, planes and tanks. Instead it was fighting street by street, alley by alley, and house by house, against insurgents (Leonard 2005, 67). Many of them were armed with guns, pistols, religion, culture, small bombs, and Arab nationalism. Though Europeans have the best of the new and largest internal market, Americans argue that Europe needs to emulate U.S. in lower taxes, less social protection,... smaller state, and narrow focus on shareholders values (p. 70). Most of the largest corporations in the world are European: 61 of the 140 biggest companies on the global fortune 500 ranking come from Europe; these compare to 50 from the U.S.A and 29 from Asia (p. 74). In 2000, 35% of Europeans were over 60 years old. Based on current demographic projections, this number will be 47% in the year 2020 and 70% in 2050 if the E.U. government does not intervene either by creating national and by federal policies which raise the natural increase or modify that number via a new and reliable immigration policy. The size of the E.U. economy is $17.5 trillion, for the U.S. it is $16.4 trillion, and the world it is $70 trillion. The global GDP for E.U. is 28.19%, for the U.S. it is 24.52% for the population of 501 million and 315 million respectively. The population of E.U. is 7.3%, that of the U.S. is 4.51% and both have a global GDP of 52.71% (U.S. Department of Commerce 2010).

The secret associated with the U.S. economic miracle is that this lonely superpower finances its own balance of payments deficit by selling its depreciating currency to foreigners. This tactic may be challenged by the fact that China, since January 2007, Japan, Russia, and later India will be making their payments in Euro rather than dollar values in the global economy. Also, while US has a current account deficit of 5% of the GDP, the Euro has a surplus. In addition, and overall, U.S. households save less than 2%. The total household debt stands at 84% of GDP compared to 50% in the Euro zone (p. 77). Currently, the Euro's global exchange reserve is 18.7% while the apparently decreasing American counterpart is 64.5%. Within two decades, it is expected that the Euro zone population of 500 million or more will have a larger GDP than that of the U.S. Also, since 2003, OPEC countries had been influenced to switch the pricing of oil into Euros. Russia, China, Japan, India etc. are paying in Euro rather than dollar values.

The Euro zone is a continent of energy independence while the U.S. is a nation that dependents on energy supplies from the Middle East, Africa, Russia and South and Central America. U.S. uses one-quarter of the world production of energy (gas, oil, coal and electricity). The continuous integration and enlargement of E.U. relies on the overall size of its economy and the quality of higher living standards of Europeans. According to Professor Robert Gordon of Northwestern University, much of U.S.'s GDP goes into unproductive things such as cars rather than public transport, social costs of inequality e.g. 91% of inmates who are costly to maintain while expanding new prisons, and air-conditioning and heating in both summer and winter respectively.

European countries have become economically interdependent and their development dynamic is driven by the Stockholm consensuses and an innovative, open knowledge economy. This economy provides recourses for education of its citizens, treating their illnesses, providing child care so that adults can work, and integrate themselves (Leonard 2005). Contrary to the values of Stockholm consensus, the Washington consensus places emphasis on extreme forms of individualism that leads to economic marginalization of many who become inmates due to petty crimes, extortionate heating and cooling policies, and less forms of economic liberalism (welfare) and democratic socialism. Unlike these singular and collective elements of nationhood, American nationalism is different from European nationalism which the Euro ironically nationalizes.

Scholars such as De Tocqueville and others argue that countries which have powerful military force, fortresses, and wealth cannot govern others with different religions, laws, and languages. If they do, they will be forced to occupy the country and anarchy will be the result. This is the Iraq parallel. America should avoid using the plan civilizing mission which Europeans learned about in the hard way. The European commission has a list of 15 incentives ranging from more effective dialogue to perspectives of internationalism into transport, energy, and communication networks and enlarged and improved financial assistance (p. 106). People from 15 countries of the E.U. travel passport free and others from 10 countries have formed a military alliance. Although the military alliance reminds of Europeans of their twentieth century historical and Political realities, the nature of the new twenty-first century reality will be handled in the light of previous and current meaning of military preparedness.

Russia has built an empire of energy that is dependent on her European neighbors. This post-Soviet and post-Cold-War reality has caused the United States to plant military bases to the south and east of the Eurozone. There are US military forces in Iraq, Kuwait, Bahrain, Oman, Israel, United Arab Emirates, Uzbekistan, Tajkistan, and Kyrgyzstan. The U.S. plans to build more bases in Rumania, Poland, Bulgaria, Morocco, Tunisia, and Algeria in order to contain Russia and China, the rising and strongest challengers of NATO alliance. In his authorship of the *Culture of antimilitarism national security in Japan and Germany*, Thomas Berger uses cultural beliefs in both countries to comparatively explain the role of culture, other things being equal, and therefore not as an absolute determinant, formulating foreign policy without considering history, geopolitical dynamics, and post-World War II climate of global multilateralism. Thomas Berger's analysis about belief systems and ideological inclinations were involved with the crucible of crushing military defeat in the war and the tough experience the elite and the masses learned from this turbulent and cataclysmic past. This experience influenced the making of German and Japan defense and security policy in the context of strategic goals and norms that political actors, shaping elite and mass perceptions of both the domestic and international political environment, and influencing the capacity of political actors to mobilize national resources for military ends (Heston 2000).

Throughout this comparative analysis of the role of culture in military foreign policy decision making arena, Berger indicated that political cultures did not spring from the heat but emerged fitfully and conflictually within debated and among established political grouping or subculture that were bound by common ideological interpretations of history and definitions of reality. Once established through pluralist contestation, each political-military culture was subject to change, albeit on the margin as shifting domestic and international realities intruded. In such a situation, any war between nations is reflection of failure in diplomacy, leadership, and vision.

The author meticulously traces his observation of the difference between the true nation's strategies to military power and variation informed by their participation in the Second World War. He also tried to link the difference in their political- military culture to variation in behavior and outcome along several key dimensions of policy, such as political alliance, military and force structure, and civil-military relations. By conclusively employing a counterfactual analysis for comparison, he assertively and plausibly affirms that "German or Japan chose to act in a manner consistent with the political military culture, usually because the governing elite feared an antimilitarist public backlash" (p. 188). As evidence has shown, it is not easy to disentangle and isolate the influence of cultural beliefs from those of material interest and institutional structure whose struggles over foreign policy are driven by election politics and anti-military belief. This shows that culture does not only matter, but all other things being equal, it has a dominant influence, as a particularizer in the sea of Western and global democratic universalism.

## CONCLUSION

The E.U. and other institutions of the Eurozone have evolved amidst a complex variety of the theoretical, political, cultural and diplomatic millieux largely during the latter half of the twentieth century. Warleigh's idea of Europe of the Regions' might not be flexibly integrated as a federal system largely due to its "a La Carte variant" (p. 49) and the difficulty created in search for its feasibility, durability, and desirability. The la carte model of European integration is more functionalistic rather than federalist in essence. It seeks to produce a Europe whose integration has multiple governance of regimes rather than a European federal state that has a single constitution and currency and whose powers are based on several levels of governance that end to make governance even more problematic. Though the political evolution of the E.U. lacks a rasion detre for its legitimacy, its regional, economic, and supranational entity is the foundation for its existence whose democratic pragmatism helps to problematize its existential viability. Its criticism is directed at the other institutions of the international economic governance particularly the IMF, the WTO, the G8 and the World Bank – is more real than fictional. "Paradoxically, the E.U. is also a tool against globalization, a bulwark against deregulation and lower standards" (Meunier 2003, 86). Over all, and based on how the Union's feasibility is envisioned, and regardless of the current public mood concerning its viability as demonstrated by European voter's preferences (about 40%), individuals need to become constantly made to participate, to trust institutions, organizations, and agents of change and integrity. Such behavior might reinforce the internal regime(s) to rediscover, reinvent, and reformulate itself in order to become a coherent system with a unified common foreign policy that comes from a single and unified European nation as opposed to the current European nations. Why does Europe think it will be the leader of the twenty-first century?

Mark Leonard (2005) argues that although the U.S. was dominant in the twentieth century, it is less effective despite the vastness of its economic resources, popularity of its cultural institutions and way of life, and superior military power. Because it is less effective to lead the twenty-first century, American-lead and "sponsored project of pooled democracies in a previously war-torn territory…is commanding the global agenda". Europe has 501 million people and over 1.3 billion more in 80 countries that depend on the E.U. The E.U. employs soft power rather than hard power and spectacle, which American uses, to influence the world. The latter's foreign policy has suffered from severe retrenchment. Raymond Aron, a French author, has argued that American foreign policy is "a series of swings between the crusading spirit and a withdrawal into isolation far from a corrupt world that refused to heed the American Gospel"

(Leonard 2005, 121).

The American economy and security depend on globalization which is a new world order the U.S. created. Within its globalized armpit, it created political mechanisms for the destruction of Kyoto, the international Criminal Court, the ABM and Biological weapons treaties and started wars and military occupations that reflect the worst forms of modern colonialism. The triadicism in Iraq, global warming, illegal immigrations and drugs smuggling, and HIV/AIDS are problems America has failed to solve. A new template for reinventing a new world order that is more compassionate, multilateral, internationalist, and synergistically dynamic is in demand. For about 60 years now, the U.S. world leadership has been rooted in "a rule-bound system of international law and global governance that limited the prerogatives of the powerful as well as the weak. American strength and global influence was enhanced by its willingness to accept limits on the exercise of its hegemonic privileges" (Dadder and Lindsay 2006, 152). However, after 9/11/2001, the U.S. rules of "engagement" and involvement with the rest of the world radically changed. This change involved the "abrogation... the terms of postwar settlements... that ended the 50 years of strategic restraint" (p. 152). It also abandoned the principles which have guided and governed the manner in which it engages itself with the rest of the world.

In the wake of the 9/11 attack, the nation's reasonableness to itself felt that it could not rely on other nations to defend itself. This feeling was rationally natural and legitimate but geopolitically and strategically irrelevant in post Cold-War and multipolar world of competitive Euro-Russian, Sino-American and trans-Atlantic dialectical regionalism. These regions' dynamics hegemonically drive the global agenda. The post 9/11 world has evolved from Bush's political doctrine. The doctrine's influence positively contributed to the initial elimination of the terrorist talabanization of Afghanistan, systematic elimination and decapitation of the Baathist and Saddamist regime in Iraq. However, President Bush's doctrinal influence naturally failed to establish a permanent Indo-Pakistan rapprochement and a viable Israel- Palestinian rapprochement as well. Though humanity gained from his short term policies, the policies have collectively been marginalized by powerful political, anti-Imperialist, and anti-Zionist Syro-Iranian Shiism that is marked by disruptive and violent Hezbollahrization of Lebanon and Bin-Laden's Islamist regional, global, and anti-globalization radicalism, violence, and destruction. In the light of this scenario, the "Bush foreign policy doctrine that America unconstrained by the preferences of allies, or the conventions of multilateralism, should use its power to change the status quo and reshape the world to advance American interests and values" (p.152) is absolutely untenable. That is why Barack Obama's foreign policy model of engagement is more globally dynamic and appealing than George Bush's unilateralism and subsequent isolationism.

## REFERENCES


Abbott, Carl, et al. 2007. *The American journey: A history of the United States.* Upper Saddle River, NJ: Pearson Education.

Abramsky, Sasha. 2007. Defining the indefinable west. *The Chronicle of Higher Education* March: B6-B8.

Barnet, Michael N. 1998. *Dialogues in Arab politics: Negotiation in regional order.* New York: St. Martins Press.

Berger, Thomas U. 1988. *Cultures of antimilitarism: National security in Germany and Japan.* Baltimore, MD: John Hopkins University Press.

Bernstern, Richard, and Ross H. Munro. 1999. The new China Lobby. In *The domestic Sources of American Foreign Policy: Insight and* Evidence.

Brzezinski, Zbigniew. 1989. *The grand failure: The birth and death of communism In the twentieth century.* New York: Charles Scribner's Sons.

Calhoun, Craig. 2003. European studies: Always already there and still in formation. *Comparative European Politics* 1, 1: 5-20.

Callo, David P. 2006. Europe in the new world order. In Joel Krieger, ed. *Globalization and state power: A reader.* New York: Pearson Longman.

Carmichael, Paul. 2006. Briefing paper: Multi-level governance. In Joel Krieger, ed. *Globalization and state power: A reader.* New York: Pearson Longman.

Cohen-Tanugi, Laurent. 2005. The end of Europe*? Foreign Affairs* November/ December: 55-67.

Daaldar-Ivo, H., and James M. Lindsay. 2006. The Bush revolution. In Joel Krieger, ed. *Globalization and state power: A reader.* New York: Pearson Longman.

Feste, Karea. 1990. *American and Soviet intervention: Effects on world adaptability.* New York: Crime Russia.

Fishman, Ted C. 2005. China Inc: *How the rise of the next superpower challenges American and the world.* New York: Scribner.

Fukuyama, Francis. 2006. *American at the crossroads: Democracy, power, and the neoconservative legacy.* New Haven, CT: Yale University Press.

Geiss, Imanuel. 1968. The pan African movement. *A history of Pan-Africans in American, Europe, African, and New York.* Gregory, Robert. 1971. *India and east African: A history of Race Relation with in the British Empire 1890-1939.* London: Oxford University Press.

Haas, Peter. 1992. Introduction: Epistemic communities international policy coordination. *International Organization* 46: 1-35.

Hall, Peter. 1989. *The political economy of ideas: Keynesianism across national.* Princeton, NJ: Princeton University Press.

Held, David. 2006. Political globalization inc. In Joel Krieger, ed. *Globalization and state power: A reader.* New York: Pearson Longman.

Heston, Alan W. 2000. *The Annals of the American Academy of Political and Social Science* 70: 1-224.

Huntington, Samuel P. 1996. *The clash of civilizations and the remaking of world order.*

Jacob, Lawrence R., and Benjamin I. Page. 2005. *Who influences foreign policy?*

Jeffries, Charles. 1948. *The colonial empire.* London: The Colonial Office.

Krasner, Stephen D. 2006. Sovereignty it's discontents. In Joel Krieger, ed. *Globalization and state power: A reader.* New York: Pearson Longman.

Krieger, Joel. 2006. *Globalization and state power: A reader.* New York: Pearson Longman.

Lang, Peter. 2004. *European foreign policy*: From Rhetoric to Reality.
Leonard, Mark. 2005. *Why Europe will run the 21st century*. New York: Public Affairs.
Lugard, Frederick. 1922. *The dual mandate in the tropical African*. London: London University Press.
Markovits, Andrei S. 2007. Western Europe's American problem. *The Chronicles Review: the Chronicle of Higher Education* 19: B6-B9.
Mayers, David. 1998. *Wars and peace: the future American envisioned*. 1961-1991. New York: St. Martins Press
Meunier, Sophie. 2003. Trade policy and political legitimacy in the European Union. *Comparative European Politics* 1, 1: 67-90.
Multilateral Context. *Journal of Scholar and Scientific Perspectives*: An International.
Murray, Douglas. 2006. *Neo-conservatism: Why we need it*. Encounter Books.
Nelkin, Dorothy. 1979. Scientific knowledge, public policy and democracy. *Knowledge, creation, diffusion, utilization* September:106-122.
Nicolaodis, Kalypso. 2004. We the people of Europe. *Foreign Affairs* November/December: 97-110
Nye, Joseph P. 2006. Redefining the national interest. In Joel Krieger, ed. *Globalization and state power: A reader*. New York: Pearson Longman.
Oatley, Thomas. 2005. *The global economy: Contemporary debates*. New York: Pearson Longman.
Olsen, Johan P. 2003. What is a legitimate role for Euro-citizens? *Comparative European Politics* 1, 1: 91-110.
Robinson, et al. *African and the Victorian: The official mind of British imperialism*. London: Oxford University Press.
Rosenau, J.N. 1968. The concept of intervention. *Journal of International Affairs* 22: 165-76.
Ross, George. 2006. European Integration and Globalization and State Power. In Joel Krieger, ed. *Globalization and state power: A reader*. New York: Pearson Longman.
Sagini, Meshack M. 2004. International diplomacy and the U.S.-Iraq conflict: The failure of unilateralism in a multilateral context. *Journal of Scholarly and Scientific Perspectives*: *An International Journal of Scholarly and Scientific Research* 1:23-43.
__________. 2001. *Organizational behavior: The challenges of the new millennium*. Lanham, MD: University Press of American Press.
Sodaro, Michael J. 2008. *Comparative politics: A global introduction*. Boston: McGraw-Hill.
Starr, Richard F. 1991. *Foreign policies of the Soviet Union*. Stanford, CA: Hover Institution Press.
U.S.. Department of Commerce. 2009. *European Commission Directorate-General, and Trade Eurostat*.
Warleigh, Alex. 2003. *Spinning Around: Rethinking a Europe of the Regions' in the e Light of Flexibility*.
William, Walter. 2006. Should we copy Europe? *The Oklahoman* Saturday Nov. 25: 13A.
Williamson, J.W. 1949. *A short history of the British empire*. London. Oxford University Press.
Wittkopf, Eugene R. and James M. McCormick, eds. 1999. *The domestic sources of American foreign policy: Insight and Evidence*. Lanham, MD: Rowman and Little Publisher, Inc.
Woody, Sylvia. 1989. *Gorbachev and the decline of ideology in Soviet foreign policy*. Western Press.

Zimmerman, William. 2002. *The Russian people and foreign policy*. Princeton, NJ: Princeton University Press.

# Chapter IX
# Comparative Foreign Policies of Great Powers

## CHINESE FINANCIAL FOREIGN POLICY

China's financial foreign policy by Ken Miller (2010) and Garret FitzGerlad's paraphrased speech has largely been reflectively employed in this comparative essay on the great powers.With the 1979 Deng Xiaoping's economic reform and their persistent 30 year history of positive growth, their cheap labor and capital, China's investment has increasingly made its productivity to be incrementally astounding. China subsidizes exports heavily via favorable loans and good exchange rates to foreign buyers of Chinese goods. China employs "financial repression"(Miller 2010, 96) as measures through which the bureaucracy "imposes controls on the investment of Chinese citizens that allow it to funnel capital into Chinese businesses" (p. 96). In 2010, the Peoples Bank of China had $ 2.65 trillion foreign exchange reserve – the largest in the world. China's major goals are to reintegrate Taiwan, stimulate economic growth, and domestic job creation. Although the Chinese communist party's government is challenged with corruption, inequality, restricted freedoms, and environmental pollution, the country intends to internationalize the renminbi regionally and globally. Compared to USA $14.3 trillion economy and per capita income of $46,437, China's economy is second to that of the USA and has a per capita income of $8000. China's goal is to accumulate foreign currency reserves, invest in overseas in terms of direct investment aid, provide assistance and loans for raw materials, new technologies, managerial expertise; and foreign securities. Its banks preserve capital, liquid money, and profits. China has a save-and-export model and heavily deals in gold. Although its per capita income is low, it gives it control over financial power that gives it great influence in the global economy where it has threatened Americans and Europeans with a trade surplus of $298 billion and $196 billion for 2008 and 2009 respectively while these competitors have huge deficits.

Since the Chinese economic climate attracts offshoring activities that cause unemployment in other countries, Chinese global activities tend to experience resistance. Its annual growth in the last 30 years fluctuated between 9 and 15 (highest in the world). The US' fluctuates between 0% and 6%. Currently, it is between 2.4% and 3%. Also, Chinese investments are resisted in Europe, USA, and Australia despite the use of English as the global lingua-franca. Though China gives grants, aid, and concessional loans to Asian, African, and Latin American countries, this behavior tends to reproduce traditional Eurocentric repatriation of currency (capital); practices that are inherently imperialistic and mercantilist but also exploitative in nature. Though most economic issues between the US and China concern currency policy, jobs and related financial imbalances, the latter's foreign policy tends to stabilize world markets into which the Obama administration has encouraged the proliferation of more US exports.

Both the US and China and perhaps the E.U. have become transoceanic empires that display varying degrees of autocratic, humanitarian, and imperialistic political behavior. Throughout history, empires have established methods for imperial control. For instance, since most of them tend to have multicultural populations that are diverse, empires enforce "unity over difference" in order to preserve the harmony of those yoked together without creating unnecessary fractures on overall systems. By so doing, major imperial structures are maintained despite the underlying existing tension that reasonably becomes the driving synergistic dynamic for balancing power among diverse groups and rationalizing change when such change is imperative.

Each successful imperial system employed specific and major theories or ideas for rationalizing authority and enforcing power. For example, various Chinese dynasties employed cultural unity, the Romans used citizenship, the British depended on the law, Americans and Russians excelled in popularizing the importance of economic development particularly during the Cold War (Maier 2010). In addition, although empires also are organized around monotheistic religions especially Christianity and Islam, both of which provided religious, theological and ideological resumes for unity, these religions remained vulnerable to schismatic and dissenting influences of the age (Metzeger and Coogan 1993).

Professor Charles S. Maier of Harvard University has argued that the Han dynasty employed a scholar-class of bureaucratic officials who lacked localism for defying the center, a phenomenon comparable to the American bureaucratic state. The Romans did not have a scholar-class of bureaucrats. Instead they had the princes and governors some of whom could ambitiously challenge the imperial center. In the case of the Chinese, "palace factionalism, war lordism, and defection to neighboring imperial powers were constant problems that worried Chinese dynastic rulers. Well organized and considerably powerful empires deployed their solders at the frontiers, long distances from the capital in order to depoliticize and professionalize them. Such distances made it easy and possible to control the ambitious ones. To avoid rebellion, disunion, and imperial dismemberment, empires regularly conducted distant military exertions for the extraction of agricultural, mineral, commercial resources." In doing this, centralized states with huge fiscal and military institutions regularized the internal pressures that challenged them. Even though empires tend to frequently experience tremendous pressure arising from antagonistic dynamics between the center and internal and external peripheries.

In Asia, the Mongul Empire was wealthy and multireligious. It covered the area of Northern India, Pakistan, and Afghanistan. It existed between 1526 and 1857. Its liabilities included unruly provinces, aggressive neighboring peoples, financial shortages and a tenuous confederal structure – similar to that of the Holy Roman Empire. Like the seventeenth century Ottomans, empires suffer from boundary-based conflicts, revenue scarcity, rebellion, and territorial shortage. All these problems weaken imperial structures because conflict and bad imperial politics tend to make borders not only unfixed but also unstable and turbulent. The Roman, Chinese, and Berlin walls were symbols of ideological, political, and imperial turbulence. Though most tend to be exploitative, their viability is enhanced by the way in which they manage cultural differences that obtain within their territorial and ethnic zones. Though most empires fall due the fiscal crises, Ferguson demonstrates that collapsing swiftness of the Harsburg, Ottoman, Roman, and German empires was caused by war.

Empires use ideologies to justify their existential legitimacy. The ideologies may be reflections of grand civilizational supremacy, cultural disparity, transitory technological and military genius that serve as the hypocritical hierarchy for governance and domination. Others, according to Parsons, are masks for bear "self-interest masqueraded as virtue," some are "cartels of multiethnic elites in which local leaders hold on to their regional power by deferring to the overriding authority of the center" (Maier 2010, 157). Others "stabilize their rule horizontally across space by reinforcing vertical hierarchies within their diverse geographic holdings" (p. 157). An excellent example is US's role in Afghanistan today. Empires function well when they hire or recruit intermediaries by making reasonable arrangements with local elites. The intermediaries were creative political entrepreneurs who functioned as preeminent political interpreters among many others. The strategies for recruitment included intermarriage, linguistic talent, and potential for promoting essential economic innovations. Unlike Burbank and Cooper (2010) who believe that empires exist as wonderful structural systems for large scale governance that accommodates diversity without being influenced into forces of localism or competing empires, Parsons (2010) argues that empires are "sophisticated structures of conquest, domination, and exploitation" (Maier 2010 158) that are doomed to collapse.

In other words, whereas Parsons understands the demise to be the predetermined result of dialectical resistance, Burbank and Cooper view the situation to be associated with intermediary ambition, autonomy, and defection to other colonizers or conquerors. Although Immerman (2010) sees US foreign policy as a product of Enlightenment philosophy of the US nationalist phase, the manifest destiny of the agrarian and republican society, he views its dominant genre to be couched in political, legal, and racial ideas rather than in its capitalist quest for markets. In other words, politics, law and racism, according to Immerman, were the dominant motivating factors for US imperialism. J. Foster Dulles and Paul Wolfowitz were ambitious and ideological absolutists. The dominant have an enlightened purpose and natural mission. The intellectuals of the empire rationalize its goals in the light of justified and justifiable progress. At times, empires are sustained by violence or associations of interest.

Militarily, China's armed forces are the largest in the world. The People's Liberation Army (PLA) has 1.7 million soldiers since 2005. In 1985, they were 2.2 million compared to the US 1.4 million active service officers and enlistees, China's military, though slow, conservative and relatively backward, has enlistees and officers whose professional and technical skills are far more advanced than those of the USSR's military during the 1950's and 1960's. In spite of the fact that every PLA unit does not have cutting edge military equipment, these forces are regularly integrating new weapons, doctrine, training, and command and control systems (Thompson 2010, 88). The Chinese dictum of "peaceful rise" does not mean that the country's leaders are a sleep. They want to develop a military strategy whose capability will enable them to establish bases, air and sea assets networks and together with ballistic and antiballistic weaponry, use them to conquer and reintegrate Taiwan (Formosa), project power in the Pacific, and catch up with the West.

The US, in addition to its 1.4 million military personnel, has 250,000 contractors and 180,000 soldiers who carry out the reconstruction process in Iraq and Afghanistan. The Chinese military does the reconstruction itself. In 2009, the US military spent $738 billion on defense and homeland security. The Chinese spent $150 billion. Currently, the US has 285, 773 active duty personnel deployed at bases around the world. China does not have the luxury to deploy such a force although a few of its PLA personnel are stationed at Chinese embassies abroad and on fellowships and in UN. Peace keeping missions (Thompson 2010). Even though,

> China's Military today, if not a near rival to the United States, at least a fast-learning organization, in the view of many close foreign observers. It is deploying weapons that neutralize key US advantages, such as ballistic missiles and supersonic sea-skimming missiles that can target US aircraft carriers in the region, an enlarged super marine fleet, homegrown satellite reconnaissance and communication capabilities, and recently, the demonstrated capability to eliminate satellites and intercept ballistic missiles (p. 88).

Notwithstanding the fact that the PLA's competitiveness is challenged by its inferior technology, its lack of enlightenment and the nation's one–child policy, corruption, and domestic unrest, fragile Infrastructure, the military is not without aspirations for global ambitions. For example,

> China's war plans are all about invading Taiwan .... Chinese military leaders in the recent past did place intense focus on preparing their armed forces to fight a "limited war" over Taiwan, fully expecting that the United States would enter the conflict. Many weapons systems the PLA acquired or developed, as well as the exercises it trained for, were largely aimed at fighting a technologically superior enemy-with particular emphasis on developing tactics to keep the United States from bringing naval assets to China's shores, a strategy known as "access denial" in the past, massive annual amphibious-assaults, known derisively as the "million-man swim", defined the military experiences of hundreds and thousands of conscripts. Although stimulating a Chinese D-Day on Taiwan might be tidy demonstration of the PLA's core mission, the armed forces today are developing capabilities and doctrine that will eventually enable them to protect China's expanding global interests. The PLA's Second artillery Corps and science-and-technology units are increasingly capable in space and cyberspace operations, and they have honed the ability to launch and operate satellites to improve communications and intelligence collection. New air and naval platforms and capabilities, such as aerial refueling and new classes of ships, also increase PLA's ability to deploy abroad. Official Chinese military writings now pay increasingly more attention to greater range of military missions, focusing not only on China's territorial integrity, but on its global interests, from oil rigs in Nigeria to a crude-oil pipeline under construction that will connect Yunnan's capital city to Burma's port Sittwe on the bay Bengal, Beijing thinks it must be able to defend its people, infrastructure and investments in some of the world's most volatile-much as the British did in the 1800s" (Thompson 2010, 90).

Evidently, there is a great element of deep strategic mistrust between the US and China. The mistrust is probably rooted in the psychological clash over their global interests. China's rapid and continuous economic growth, steady military advancement and profound domestic military propaganda help to shape perceptions, raise expectations and lessen the chances for compromise with other nations. Obviously, Chinese war planners see a future in which China will be able to defend itself offshore and its navy will operate beyond what is sometimes referred to as the first island chain (an imaginary line stretching from Japan, through Okinawa and Taiwan, and south to the Philippines and the South China Sea), eventually, encompassing much of the Western pacific up to the "second island chain" (p. 90) that runs from Japan to Australia via Guam.

Joel Andreas has written a classic named *the Rise of the red engineers: The cultural revolution and the origins of China's new class* (2009). In this book, Professor Andreas argues that the current 8 out of 9 engineers who rule China through the Politburo Standing Committee are the most powerful elites in the country. Comparatively, the top ruling elite class of the USSR particularly during the era of Brezhnev administration were engineers. In both the USSR and Chinese cases, these ruling elites were selected through the use of convoluted, protracted, and conflictual processes. The processes also were manipulative strategies that were employed via a series of trial and error tactics and ideologically purist measures for painfully but successfully reinforcing politically, culturally, and philosophically established elitist credentials of the ruling class. Overall, the main reason for allowing engineers to become dominant in largely agrarian, industrializing, and emerging powers was rooted in the belief that leftist national and scientifically managed industrialization and technological superiority were attainable through the use of ideologically embedded political, cultural and "red" elitist standards, the latter of which, was the cause for disaster often times. In essence, whenever and wherever great empires attempt to rise, they face many developmentally based dialectical struggles, disappointing challenges, crushing failures, and spasmodic successes before they set their feet on "the sun." Regardless of how they do it as they climb the stiff and crevice-laden escalator of progress, they frequently tend to repeat history as they travel through the narrow and binding prism of their unclearly defined national and cultural goals and perceptions.

## THE E.U./U.S. AND THEIR CHALLENGES: POTENTIAL FOR CRISIS FOR E.U.

The Eurozone has about 500 million people whose Gross National Product of $17 trillion, slightly larger than that of the USA but slightly lower in per capita income. The E.U.'s military budget is a half of that of the USA. European history is replete with civil and continental wars that became the synergistic dynamic for rivalry and national unification, political, cultural, economic, and military expansion called globalization or colonization of the Americas, Africa and Asia during the past 500 years. In the wake of USSR's collapse and the subsequent evolution of the E.U., China and India as the potential rivals of the United States, Europe's potential to survive and compete does not only rely on "twinning" but also on "circular discourse and circular interaction" (Radzvilas 2009, 1). This form of behaviors, among many others, shows weakness in the suprasystem. One hundred years ago, a new source of weakness within the European system had also started to appear in some countries. Demographic changes, through which eventually Europe's population, even at that time a small proportion of that of the globe, was going at first to stabilize and then, a century or so later, actually to start falling.

The process by which Western Europe whose economic strength and power was already in 1900, coming under long-term threat, moved almost overnight in the immediate aftermath of World War II, from world dominance in the second half of the twentieth century, exercised selfishly, to a far more constructive and positive role in the world, has been quite extraordinary one. Unfortunately ,it had required two destructive and lethal intra-European wars-the second of which brought the continent to the point of near self-destruction - to force military its western part to pull itself together and to set out consciously to reverse the dangerous tide of its history, in a way that has since come to re-shape radically, Europe's global role and ambitions.

The key issue today is whether the New Europe thus created still has the time, the commitment, and the energy to develop the kind of dynamic collective leadership that would be needed to deploy its emerging value system in such a manner as to influence the great powers of the future: Russia, China and India, as well as United States, to join in the creation of a world free from violence, injustice, and corruption. European contributions in the last 50 years have enhanced the prospects for European integration irrespective of the existing anti-federation challenges. Among many others, the following seven points are remarkably paraphrased by Garret FitzGerald, the former Irish Prime Minister.

1. International law: Contrast Europe's commitment to international law with that of the US, for example over the mining of Nicaraguan ports and the refusal of even Margaret Thatcher to support Israel bombing of the PLO in Tunis in the 1980s. This was contrary to international law. The obvious reluctance with which she agreed to support the US bombing of Libya as a quid pro quo for the support of the US in the Falklands War, and latest, US unilateral and preemptive attack on Iraq although Iraq did not have WMD and was its ally for many years is paradoxically self-explanatory.
2. Supra-national supervision of human rights: Contrast Europe's acceptance of Supra-national supervision of human rights through the Strasbourg Court, given the unwillingness of the US even to accept the Geneva Convention is very revealing.
3. The creation of European Zone of Peace: The increasing dedication of European national armies to peace-keeping, and peace-making missions- admittedly, have experienced failures, such as Srebrenica and Rwanda massacres. After 1989 the E.U. zone of peace spread to Eastern Europe, except for a period in the Western Balkans. Europe's zone of peace has also had an indirect influence on Russian policy with Georgia and Ukraine although not yet in Chechnya. This is contrarily comparable to the US invasion of Iraq without the UN authority.
4. Substitution of aid: Concerns transfers from rich to poor that are concerned with assistance even admittedly, with a neo-colonial element in the form of tied aid and military equipment sales. Europe's civil aid program far exceeds that of the US by being three to four times greater than that of the richer United States.
5. Abolition of capital punishment: rejection for E.U. membership of any country which keeps this penalty, contrast this with the retention of death penalty in many US states
6. European initiative on global ecologic action: Contrast Europe's key role in this area with US rejection of Kyoto, and the United States' subsequent slow movement towards a more enlightened approach. However, recent Obama leadership may have enhanced the policy.

7. International Criminal Court: US rejected it, and its attempt to sabotage the International Criminal Court was real. The potential future impact of this policy on war, e.g., the British CIGS refusal to initiate military action in Iraq without an assurance from Attorney General. This required the Attorney General to change his mind at the last minute, this was dubious about its legality.

The result of these challenges is that Europe is now an extraordinary positive force in the world. It has the potential of influencing the US eventually towards a similar approach-regardless of opposition from within the US itself concerning American abuses of power. Europe has potential influence also on Russia and China. Alternatively, all these depends on whether upon Europe will act cohesively in order to maintain its moral leadership. This is currently at risk for several reasons. First, although Britain shares the above seven values, its linguistic and social relationship with the US, and its desire to maintain its "special relationship" with the country, greatly weakens Europe's capacity to influence the US positively and the Iraq war showed that Britain on its own could not influence the US significantly.

Second, the attempt by some European Governments to cozy up to the US, and the continuing East European hang-up on security vis-à-vis Russia, and the potential consequences of over-reliance on US for their security, have had similar negative effects in the past.

In the long run, only a cohesive European effort to "sell" its new value system offers it hope for influencing the US to develop similar values. Over a longer time-scale the same could be true about Europe and Russia and, eventually, Europe and China.

But time is now running out against Europe. Within 40 years, demography will have reduced Europe's work-force by one-quarter and economic growth will be sustained without a reasonably stable workforce. Immigration cannot easily solve this problem either: the temporary influx from Eastern Europe to Ireland and Britain was a one-time phenomenon, for the demography of those countries is even more skewed towards older people than that of Western Europe. And, beyond a certain point, immigration from outside Europe can prove disruptive, and could weaken Europe's potential to play a positive role. In other words, issues such as terrorism, drug trafficking, and anxiety to compete with "outsiders" make it harder for Europeans to be a strong superpower.

For Europeans to exert the kind of positive moral leadership that the world needs at this juncture, Europe needs to act coherently in future. Its capacity to do so has clearly been weakened in recent times by poor political leadership, by persistent economic failure in five major continental economies, reflecting inability to tackle structural weaknesses in labor market policy in particular, and above all, by the inadequacy of Stability and Growth Pact-which has totally failed to prevent the present economic crisis. It is self-evident that this crisis could even threaten the Euro itself which has proved unexpectedly vulnerable to policy failures in small countries like Ireland, Greece, Italy, Spain and Austria and Portugal.

Inadvertently, such negativism for European economic insecurity impacts on the American dollar whose negative performance also tends of create financial instability in world markets. Disturbingly, the democratic authority of European representative democracy has been weakened by a clever populist campaign to denigrate the authority of elected governments: the widespread use of the word "elite" to describe such governments is potentially dangerous, for this rhetoric is open to abuse of the kind we saw three-quarters of a century ago in Germany. There has never been a more difficult moment at which leaders seek to discern Europe's future. The European Union is currently faced with three interconnected crises, the resolution of each of which will require exceptional political courage and leadership that is clearly absent at this time.

First of all, there is the longer-term demographic problem. The next twenty years will see the start of fundamental shift in Europe's population. The population of working age is likely to drop by 7%, whilst the proportion aged 60 and above will rise by about 30%. At present, rates of human reproduction, even to maintain Europe's population and labor force at a static level would require a large inflow of people from outside Europe, and already a relatively small inflow of such immigrants is seen to be causing social tensions. The alternatives facing Europe are thus economic decline because of a falling population, or high immigration from outside the European continent-unless, of course, Europeans can boost their birth rate, a matter to which no serious thought is currently being given, except in France, which with Ireland, are the only European countries with a stable population, enjoying a reproduction rate in excess of two. After 1985, Denmark and Sweden showed that the birth rates could be increased, at least for a period, by up to 25% through the provision of generous maternity and paternity leave. Although this kind of policy is arguably needed throughout, Europe, it does not focus on most E.U. national states' policies.

This low birth rate problem is even more acute in eastern than in Western Europe. Ireland's recent high immigrant inflow from Eastern Europe was a purely temporary phenomenon, a one-time short-term consequence of E.U. enlargement. In the medium-term, these eastern and central European countries will themselves need net immigration to increase or even to maintain a younger population large enough to support their own rapidly growing number of pensioners. Second, there is also the economic crisis, which requires drastic reforms in many E.U. states. A restoration of confidence is needed to get people spending again. Key reforms are required in labor laws as well as cut backs on some of the more extravagant aspects of social welfare-whilst maintaining the basic elements of continental market uniqueness. Third, there is the now urgent problem of the Stability and Growth Pact, which has proved ineffective in the face of the present economic crisis. The truth is that a fiscal disciplinary system that ignores debt levels and takes no account of cyclical factors is an inherent absurdity. All these problems test solidarity of the E.U. The truth is that the European Commission, as it has developed in recent years, does not have the authority to run an economic union, which needs a central fiscal authority, with power to prevent national budgetary excesses that risk destabilizing Euro currency zone.

In the fifteen years following the presidency of Jacques Delors-whose appointment FitzGerald succeeded in organizing 1984 presidency of the European Council, despite Margaret Thatcher's opposition, successive European Commissions have become weaker and the power of the three leading states stronger. The Single Market that Delors created, (despite initial Greek, British, and Danish opposition), on the basis of the report of Representativeness of Heads of Government that was established in 1984 under Irish Chairmanship, was the last major E.U. break-through except for the Lisbon Treaty which raised some doubts about E.U. viability. Larger states have different interests.

Most small countries such as Ireland have rightly seen their interests at best protected by strong European Commissions, whose exclusive right of legislative initiative was, from the outset, designed to prevent larger states from successfully pursuing their own interests at the expense of smaller members. There is an element of parallelism with the US under the Articles of Confederation (1776-1786). That is why Garret FitzGerald, former Irish Prime Minister fought to protect the Commission's role from erosion by one or other of the Big Three, or sometimes by all three of them, as was the case in 1974, when the Big Three, led by a new French President, Giscard d'Estaing, attempted to create a Directoire by seeking to exclude the commission from the G8 meetings, and by creating a European Council of Heads of State and Government that they hoped would bypass the Commission's exclusive power of legislative initiative. It was easier to block such moves as some of the smaller states like Ireland and Benelux countries succeeded in doing, when the Union involved a smaller number of states. It is much more difficult to organize twenty or smaller states to block efforts by the larger ones in order to influence the union to meet their purpose since some of the new states could be more easily intimidated by larger ones.

In this analysis, emphasis has been placed on the key role of the commission in blocking large power bullying and protecting small states' interests because we know that at a moment when Greece is under pressure from European Commission, over its financial situation and over the inadequacy of its statistics, there must be a danger of populist anti-commission rhetoric that could obscure the longer-term interest of smaller states and the Commission's supportive role in the Union. The Union's role in the world has not been advanced in recent years by the tendency of the larger states to pursue their individual national interests at the expense of interests of the Union as a whole. For example, the E.U.'s relations with Russia and energy policy remains to be the issue of the colonizer versus the colonized.This is all the more unfortunate because it has become increasingly evident that the world has an urgent need for "soft power" that has grown out of the development of Europe's international value systems.

> If Europe could pull itself out of its present political and economic difficulties, with its states working coherently together, in what may turn out to be the last historical period when it has the capacity to exercise global influence, it might

> both be able to help the United States to complete the re-thinking of its recent unilateral approach to global problems, and to assist countries like Russia, China, and India to evolve gradually towards democracies playing a constructive and peace–oriented role in world affairs (FitzGerald 1984).

It is hugely believed that if Europe recovers quickly from the ills that at present afflict its economy and politics, both Europe and the rest of the world will be stronger. A strong and self-confident Europe, demonstrating how much more can be achieved by its "soft powers" than by "hard power", could assist in creating the emergence, during the twenty-first century, of a world order of peace, stability, and justice.

Many analysts and political commentators have pessimistically and persistently talked about the historical and potential crisis inherent in the Eurozone and NATO in general. While the source of the crisis in question may have historically been both internal and external, the North Atlantic Treaty Organization is , has been, and will continue to be the "most successful security institution in human history" (Thies 2009, 553). Having written *Why NATO endures*, Thies argues counterintuitively and confidently that this regenerative institution has outlived its doomsayers for three reasons: "the distribution of capabilities, the scope of pace of warfare, and the presence or absence of divisive ideologies" (p. 554) of this democratic, mechanized, and strategically rationalized trans-Atlantic alliance. The alliance is also a cultural, political, and military enterprise that organizationally relies on scientific analysis, technological innovations, creative industrial inventions, and global market-driven economic competitiveness.

## U.S. Interests in Asia

Currently, the US is a weak superpower in both military and economic competitiveness. Even though, it is still the only strongest superpower alive. China has the capacity to rival the US in its quest for a place in "the sun". China's "peaceful rise" dictum, which means peaceful development, will be judged with empirical rather than – rhetorical evidence. The U.S. and its allies should ensure that a hostile coalition of great powers does not materialize to encircle it. The U.S. should read history in context of Cold War compound containment and its effects on global civilizations' economic and military power. The superpower should be conversant with the concept of mutually assured and destructive economic relationship and its coercive economic warfare implications. Professor Nye rightly argues that an enemy should be treated as an enemy. In essence, the U.S.'s chief interests in East Asia include but are not limited to the following: the policy of Sino-American mutual and assured destruction, stability in East Asia and peaceful resolution of Taiwan's situation, peaceful denuclearization and gradual unification of the Korean Peninsula, strategic preservation of U.S.-Japan alliance and Japan's nun-nuclear condition, peaceful negotiation of China's maritime disputes, and protection of free navigation in the South China Sea (Art 2010).

Both China and the U.S. need to adhere to certain general specific principles that will enable them to chart new directions in strategic and geostrategic equilibria of international relations. Among the most important of those include but are not limited to:

1. not undermining Sino-American mutual assured destruction,
2. avoiding methods which produce adverse and self-fulfilling prophecies,
3. maintaining transparent positions on the Taiwan Issue,
4. cohesively maintaining U.S.'s East Asian alliances and security structures,
5. preserving U.S. maritime supremacy in East Asia and
6. institutionalizing security multilateralism in Asia (Art 2010).

In the light of this analysis, China's interests and ambitions will increase relative to its power. "What a state does in international relations is determined by both purpose-the values it holds and the political choices it makes-and power-the capabilities it wields" (p. 390). Although it has started to act as a responsible stakeholder by helping to pay the costs of maintaining the security, stability, and prosperity of the international system, its assertive and irrational nationalism might inadvertently come into conflict with Americas' optimistically unintentional and judicious credibility. Given this scenario, the top policy makers from both camps must realize that the globe is larger than themselves and no single nation can dominate the world without the support of the rest. The rest cannot respect unilateral decisions taken by either of the two powers. Both nations must base the construction of their relationship on the commonality rather than the particular uniqueness of their interests. They should establish a hotline channel of communication which will enable them to diffuse serious bilateral relations before they become the escalators for the war momentum. They should openly establish and discuss their strategic cooperation and geostrategic rivalry for the purpose of controlling potentially conflictual and disastrous political behavior reinforced by irrational and ungovernable nationalistic sentiments.

## REFERENCES

Acharya, Amitau. 2009. *Whose ideas matter? Agency and power in Asian regionalism.* Ithaca, NY: Cornell University Press.

Andreas, Joel. 2009. Rise of the red engineers: The cultural revolution and the origins of China's new class. Palo Alto, CA: Stanford University Press.

Art, Robert. 2010. The United States and the rise of China. *Political Science Quarterly* 55, 3: 359-91.

Burbank, Jane and Cooper Frederick. 2010. *Empires in world history: Power and the politics of difference.* Princeton, NJ: Princeton University Press

Immerman, H. Richard. 2010. *Empire for liberty: A history of American imperialism from Benjamin Franklin to Paul Wolfowitz.* Princeton, NJ: Princeton University Press.

Lynch, Marc. 2010. Veiled truths. The rise of political Islam in the West. *Foreign Affairs* July/August: 138-47.

Maier, S. Charles. 2010. Empire without end: Imperial achievements and ideologies. *Foreign Affairs* July/August: 153-9

Metzger, M. Bruce, and Coogan D. Michael. 1993. *The Oxford companion to the Bible.* New York: Oxford University Press.

Miller, Ken. 2010. Coping with china's financial power: Beijing's financial foreign policy: *Foreign Affairs* July/August: 96-109.

Parsons, Timothy. 2010. *The rule of empires: Those who built them, those who endured them, and why they always fall.* New York: Oxford University Press.

Radzvilas, Vytautas. 2009. On the issue of relations between the E.U. and Eastern European Countries. *World Political Science Review* 5, 1: 1-15.

Thies, Wallace. 2009. *Why NATO endures.* New York: Cambridge University Press.

Thompson, Drew. 2010. Think again China's military: It's not time to panic yet. *Foreign Policy: Global Politics, Economics and Ideas* March/April: 86-95.

# Chapter X
# The Global Political Economy and the NGOs

The world's economic system is stratified (Nemeth and Smith 1985; Schott 1986) in terms of core, semi-periphery, and periphery. It also makes the strata to be seen as discrete clusters (Wallerstein 1974) or structural continuum (Chase-Dunn 1989). Some of the strata within the world-system play certain roles which serve hegemonic, regional, and spatial interests of these clusters and trade partners (Bollen 1983; Evans 1979a; Snyder and Kick 1979; Steiber 1979). In other words, the role of each country or cluster within the stratified world's economic system is either different or unique to each country or mutually reciprocal. The positions of the continual strata members have unequal trade exchange relationships whose theoretical and philosophical underpinnings exacerbate dependency (Bunker 1984; Mandel 1975; Firebaugh and Bullock 1987). In recent history, traditional hegemonic powers have been relatively neutralized by the emergence of a multicentric core stratum whose network, block or sub-blocks has not only produced a new international division of labor, but the new division of labor has been reinforced by the character of "currency flight" to Third World areas where the cost of production of goods, services, and labor are comparatively lower than those in the core countries (Caporaso 1981; Arrighi 1982). The dramatic and historic collapse of the ex-Soviet Empire and the current financial mismanagement and fiscal stability in Southeast Asia may have threatened investors to return their currency back to the United States and Western Europe. In the wake of Western decline, this behavioral phenomenon may not only help to explain the apparent resurgence of these Asian economies, but the previous use of these currencies for the geo-strategic containment of the empire in question, may have helped the East to formidably eclipse the rival empire while hegemonically reasserting itself anew on the global plane of international relations and political economy. That reassertion is accomplished through international economic cooperation, mobility of capital, and imposition of fixed rather than flexible exchange rates (Webb 1995). Cooperative mobility of capital may cause regional or global economic turbulence.

In the light of the structure of international political economy, 15 major trade variables have been selected to represent the structure (in terms of blocks and sub-blocks) of the major types of global commodity exchange goods. These blocks and their respective sub-blocks, as Smith and White (1992, 886) have noted, include variables identified in Table X.1.

Table X.1. Major Global Trade Variables

1. High technology heavy manufacture
   - machinery
   - nonelectrical
   - artificial resins, plastics, cellulose, esters, and ethers
   - manufactures of metal, not elsewhere specified
2. Sophisticated extractive
   - paper, paperboard, and articles of paper pulp
   - pulp and waste paper
   - gas, natural and manufactured
3. Simple extractive
   - oil seeds and oleaginous fruit
   - animal oils and fats
   - cereals and cereal preparations
4. Low wage/light manufacture
   - articles of apparel and clothing accessories
   - footwear
   - travel goods, handbags, and similar containers
5. Food products and byproducts
   - meat and meat preparations
   - dairy products and birds' eggs
   - crude animal and vegetable material, not elsewhere specified.

The structure of the global economic system is hierarchical, competitive, hegemonic, and reciprocal. Countries in the core strata are richer and more economically and geostrategically competitive than those in the semi-periphery. Likewise, countries in the semi-periphery are wealthier and more economically and geostrategically competitive than those in the periphery of marginalization. Both the semi-periphery and the periphery are the middle and lower socioeconomic and global strata of blocks, each of which is further subdivided into two sub-blocks. The sub-block is the fifth stratum which has been more recently described as the Fourth World or the "underclass." For instance, Table X.2 shows five countries that represent each of the five strata into which the global economic system (calculated in terms of GNP per capita income) is categorized (Smith and White 1992).

Table X.2. Selected Countries Representing Five Strata: Core to Periphery

| GNP (1979 | Core | Semi-Periphery 1 | Semi-Periphery 2 | Periphery 1 | Periphery 2 |
|---|---|---|---|---|---|
| $10,610 | USA | | | | |
| $8,870 | | Australia | | | |
| $1,380 | | | Turkey | | |
| $1,200 | | | | Morocco | |
| $300 | | | | | Niger |

Table X.1 further illustrates the simplified and tabular construction mentioned above. Theoretically, network analysis which explains and validates the morphological hierarchy and structural stratification of the global economic system has been used to demonstrate that "massive intracore trade is one of the defining features of this strata's global dominance" (Smith and White 1992, 886). These global trade patterns are asymmetrical. They tend to promote unequal exchange which continually reproduces, perpetuates, and rationalizes the expressed inequality and hierarchy. Given this understanding:

> results support world-system and dependency arguments about asymmetrical flows of raw materials versus processed goods. Exports of high-technology heavy manufacturing goods flow primarily within the core and from the core to the lower blocks. While the lion's share of these commodities circulates within the core, the interblock exchanges follow a cascade pattern: all through the international system it is more likely to move from higher to lower strata. The standard image of core advantage in high levels of processing and capital intensiveness implies precisely this pattern ... The reciprocal pattern of exporting agricultural goods (crude animal and vegetable material, meat products) also fits this model: while intracore exchange is still very large, we find that interstrata exchange is more likely to move from the periphery to higher blocks, including the core. Highly industrialized capital-intensive agriculture is the exception in that it is mostly exported from higher to lower blocks (p. 886).

Some countries in the core stratum are dependent on others. Canada is a classic example of a core country which depends on the U.S. Other countries such as Libya which enjoys core and semi-periphery economic status is not treated so by economists largely because of its geopolitical, technological, and ideological uniqueness. Though some semi-periphery countries like Brazil and South Korea tend to triangulate in the core areas very aggressively, their progressive ascendance toward the core area tends to be arrested by their own technological and socioeconomic relativity. In other words, with the use of specific trade nets, all blocks and subblocks display the tendency to move toward the core rather than moving away from it. Since the global economic system is structurally stratified and hierarchically arranged, and since intrastrata mobility is more easily facilitated than interstrata mobility, lower case mobility of the periphery and semi-periphery to the core is not only difficult, but such difficulty is associated with the forces of global and geostrategic rationality which tend to thwart such a form of mobility. By thwarting rapid or frequent attempts to ascend toward the core, which is the center of world civilization, the core area countries protect themselves against such forceful and carefully calculated "penetrating projectiles" from the outer periphery and "alien" lands. In other words, the dynamics of global centripetal forces (which undermine autonomy) and centrifugal (disruptive) economic and geostrategic forces of the world economic system tend to reproduce its antagonistic equilibrium. The dichotomy of these negative and positive forces tends to gravitate around issues which equilibrate and rationalize global stability and interinstitutional and interorganizational coexistence and reciprocity. Whether reciprocity is reached at through coercive diplomacy, the use of the stick and the carrot, or through design or accident could be a matter of theoretical controversy rather than conjecture (Etzioni 1996).

Evidently, quantitative analysis of global exchange is a powerful tool to analyze the stricture, structure, and dynamics of the world's system and its constituent countries. Regardless of its dialectical components, global and state politics stimulate block, intra and interblock politico-economic strategies for development that reproduce international economic dependency. Explicit and implicit state policies are constructed by economically and politically pressured elites. Such exerted and external pressure influences the development of industrial and export strategies (Gereffi and Wyman 1990). The development strategies and the extent of their implementation helps to influence changes in the composition and structure of exports and each country's structural level within the international political economy. Therefore, in order to understand how national mobility in the world system takes place, it requires the linkage of the global external analysis similar to this one, in order to articulate, rationalize, and reconstruct research agenda that focuses on internal, regional, national and historico-political economies. According to a critique of the neoliberal institutionalist thesis (Mansfield and Milner 1997) regionalism is rationalized as the solution to the collective dilemmas and high transaction costs associated with multilateral institutions which are more highly institutionalized in the Americas than in Asia. These institutions serve functionalist and hegemonic values of the countries in question. These countries are dominated by self-interested actors who initiate the formation of the institutions.

## Domestic and Foreign Corporate Political Activity

In the United States, the elites and their corporations have tremendous influence on the culture, politics and economics of the country at large. They massively contribute large sums of money through PACs in order to support the electoral campaigns of Senators, members of Congress and even the president.

Other elites become trustees in university and college boards where they help to formulate institutional and organizational policy. Some of these corporate elites have multiple directorships in business and industry (Burris 1991).

Most of these capitalistic and profit minded corporate elites are politically conservative rather than liberal. These capitalists are highly connected and have control at the pinnacle of the elite kinship of intercorporate networks. The influence of their corporations and their political behavior is interlocked. This influence varies with the "level of government regulation, defense contracts, and geographic location" (Burris 1991, 543). In other words, the attempt to control the political system is purposefully grounded on electing political "officials whose ideological position is sympathetic to the general interests of their class" (p. 547). In addition to the "partisan interest in electing candidates sympathetic to business, corporations have a pragmatic interest in maintaining access to and influence over elected officials of both parties" (p. 547). Practically, this tends to translate into a "strong temptation to support incumbents, regardless of party ideology" (p. 547). In the wake of specific legislative and administrative action, there is no doubt that lobbying, director interlock networks, and political behavior become the payoffs of the system derived from such actions. Corporations that are marginalized into the periphery by the interlockage of the "over-class," tend to behave like most individual capitalists. Since they are ideologically conservative, the only way available to them for reaching the incumbents is that of making large donations to conservative, liberal and moderate incumbents. This behavioral attitude helps to explain why most incumbents are elected more often times than nonincumbents. By making contributions for the election of public officials, lobbyists or individual capitalists indirectly become conservative elements of the elite class which is represented at the highest level of policy planning arena. For instance, PACs have become an extended arm of the corporate sector for "government regulation and defense contracts" (p. 548). As far as this is concerned, there is no

> need to hypothesize a tendency toward ideological liberalism within the inner circle of the business community. As individual citizens, members of the inner circle exhibit political behavior that is more consistently conservative than other capitalists. As corporate decision makers, they are involved in interorganizational networks that allow and encourage efforts to co-opt potential political opponents. The reduced support they give to right-wing candidates in this context is not a sign of ideological liberalism, but of a conservatism that assumes a more pragmatic stance when confronted with a different structure of political opportunities (p. 548).

Both Smith and White (1992) and Burris (1991) used the methodology of social network analysis to conduct research on two different types of problems, namely, the structure of international political economy and the cohesive mechanisms for regulating its geopolitical and strategic dynamics; and the political behavior of U.S. corporations and corporate elites whose intercorporate strategic networks form interlocking directorships that are class networks and structures for political cohesion and bases of political action in the capitalist society. Since all capitalist elites in capitalist societies have the same psychology, lifestyle and socioeconomic entrenchment, it is not surprising that the internal needs for social cohesion, decision-making (policy planning and formulation) and survival (both as individuals and as a nation) extend beyond their national frontiers in the structuration, regulation and control of the "international other" particularly those in the semi-periphery and the periphery of marginalization. In a sense, they can profitably use their domestic (U.S.) experience to replicate the behavior of the political and economic elites in the global strata in order to dispel political instability and help create favorable economic markets for the supply of raw materials and demand of corecentric manufactured products, investments and repatriation of capital. In general, such behavior of class networks and corporate networks or inter and intrastrata networks may be viewed as structures of cohesion and bases for internal and external political control and action. Viewed from a corecentric perspective, these intercorporate, intraclass and intracore multinationals which radiate from metropoles and megalopolises have used, through dependency, suckling tentacles (*milija ya unyonyanji*) to control, impoverish and marginalize the Third and Fourth Worlds.

Eichner (1991) has used a post-Keynesian perspective to comment on the macrodynamics (money, finance, inflation, income distribution and the labor market) of advanced market economies most of which are the core countries of the global economic system. At the center of these market economies is the megacorp which is the archetypical oligopolistic industrial sector that is dominant in modern economic investment, production and pricing. While post-Keynesianism rejected neoclassical orthodoxy for its "idealized, timeless, institutionless, nonmonetary and barter framework" (Eichner 1991, 416), of the neo-Walrasian model, the former argued that post-Keynesian macroeconomic model is relevant because it is methodologically empirical and predictive rather than descriptive. As a subset of human activity post-Keynesianism is both institutionalist and cybernetic rather than dialectical and an unspecific historical explanation.

The megacorp is the dominant form of the modern corporation that strives for growth and survival. Its investment decisions are strategic (long-term) while its pricing ones are tactical (short-term). The neoclassical profit maximizing firm's pricing decision is made independent of its fixed costs or its investment decisions. When pricing and investment decisions are incorporated, the megacorp makes short-term profit (Eichner 1976). The megacorp makes profits because it acquires and maintains market share which it controls because of its investment expenditures. Intertwined with its market power, production structure, and pricing mechanism, the megacorp operates productively. In the light of classical thinking, prices are determined by the reproduction requirements of the economy in the face of factors of scarcity.

In the private enterprise economy, the three basic types of cyclical effects around the long-term trend include "(1) the multiplier effect, (2) the accelerator effect, and (3) the cash-flow feedback effect" (Eichner 1991, 422). The first two effects are common to many macroeconomic models. However, the cash-flow feedback effect comprises "the actions of different economic sectors (megacorp, nonmegacorp firm, household, government, and foreign) and their component units to imbalances between their income and expenditure flows" (Eichner 1987, 98-106; Eichner 1991, 422). In the megacorp sector, higher profits generate higher investment returns and cause booms. Lower profits lead to lower investment which causes recessions. The megacorp generates demand and enhances capacity.

In a neoclassical way money that is saved by households and firms make profits that are spent in future. The modern economy is based on credit rather than on commodity or fiat money. Money is put outside the scarcity realm of neoclassical economics. It is regulated by the central banks or Federal Reserve Bank which determines the discount rate (interest rate) for the banks.

While inflation may be caused by increases in wage rate and markup above technological progress (increase in productivity), income is distributed mechanistically due to its determination by technical production and innate intelligence. This is a neoclassical position, on the contrary, post-Keynesianism humanistically argues that income is socially distributed in segmented labor markets that are stratified and substratified along class lines. Competitive firms within the industry evolve with changes in structure. The changes influence the "development of new technologies, new products, and new industries and the elimination of old technologies, products and industries" (Eichner 1991, 427).

Studies done by political scientists, economists, and sociologists have demonstrated that corporate political action committees (PACs) are financially heavily subsidized by corporations, industries, and Japan at state and national levels. The 270/500 Fortune and other 1,000 companies were analyzed. The purpose of making such financial contributions to electoral candidates was to gunner legislative support for securing sales and avoiding regulation costs. Evidence indicates that corporate officials are extremely sensitive to press releases on their connections. They become nervous about negative aggressive and potentially prosecutorial news reporting. Such involvement of the corporate sector in political affairs indicates that the corporation is a political as well as an economic institution which tends to capitalize on "free-rider incentives" which are used as models for "organizationally constrained profit-maximizing behavior" (Mitchell, Hansen, and Jepsen 1997, 1018). Foreign political activity, especially the Japanese corporations, has been observed to be disproportionately active in American political system (Choate 1990; Prestowitz 1988; Tolchin and Tolchin 1988). In doing that, the corporate sector, which influences the regulation of industries, government procurement, social connections, corporate culture, secures its place in the "sun." Consequently, "elected" government learns and understands how, when and where to facilitate government regulation, corporate visibility, legitimacy and counter mobilization. In doing that this businessantibusiness dynamic is politically and legally rationalized in the face of political complexity, economic interests, and social and legal expediency.

## INTERNATIONAL PERSPECTIVES ON CORPORATE POLITICAL BEHAVIOR

Unlike in their home countries, international business corporations behave differently in order to maximize their own business interests. The corporations advance different "assumptions concerning the political nature of international business and the role of government as a factor of production, which firms manage ... (Boddewyn and Brewer 1994, 119) through a chain-nexus of contingencies. These corporations use business principles to interact with firms, industry, and nonmarket factors to influence political behavior for the successful implementation of their resource-based strategic objectives. The corporations view government as a variable rather than constant that has to deal with international firms particularly the "exporters, importers, licensors, and foreign direct investors" (p. 119) that need to politically negotiate the terms for their "entry, operation and exit" (p. 119).

According to Fayerweather (1969), international business deals with policy-oriented research that stresses 'the accumulation of interests and resolution of conflict' "between international firms and political actors at home and abroad" (Boddewyn and Brewer 1994, 119).

Based on resource dependence, institutionalization, and interorganization theories, business-government relations tend to be conflictual, isomorphic and relational (Pfeffer and Salancik 1978; DiMaggio and Powell 1983; Benson 1975). In addition, resource-based theory of strategic advantage (Barney 1986; Collis 1991; Conner 1991; Grant 1991; Peteraf 1993) shows that international firms have competence to deploy economic and organizational rather than political capabilities. Under normal circumstances, political factors act as constraints (Conner 1991). Even though, in respect to the tradeability of resources, economic rather than political markets are important. These economic markets are "means acquired and used to gain rents ... aim of strategic behavior ... purely" 'economic' (Boddewyn and Brewer 1994, 120; Etzioni 1988, 218-220).

In a business environment, business political behavior is a required component. Political behavior is the "acquisition, development, securing and use of power ... where power is viewed as the capacity of social actors to overcome the resistance of other actors" (Boddewyn and Brewer 1994, 120). These social actors exist in nonmarket settings. The actors include governments, interest groups, the intelligentsia, media and public opinion. The interaction between business corporations and the nonmarket sector involves various actions such as "compliance, evasion, negotiation, cooperation, coalition building, and co-optation" (pp. 120-121).

Political behavior creates winners and losers in the marketplace (Leone, 1986). Although political behavior does not necessarily require wealth, it may be the product of other resources such as used "time, organizing ability, legitimacy, privileged information and access" (Boddewyn and Brewer 1994, 121). Political behavior may be a form of collusion (collective action) that is legally sanctionable. Political power may be retained longer than economic power for the purpose of sustaining competitive advantage (Hayes, 1981). Although actors may not benefit from their actions, they may gain through "political externalities" (Perrow 1986, 234) such as protectionism which benefits a few at the expense of millions of people. In other words, there are more losers than winners in the marketplace of competition.

An integrated model of business political behavior may be triangularized to show its interactive, strategic, and dynamic infrastructure as in Figure X.1. In the light of the essence of corporate political behavior, the political behavior of international firms can be affected simultaneously by differences in the task-based nature in which the firms operate. These firms comply when government actions have a low level of strategic salience and are favorable to them. Moreover, due to their narrow political base, the firms suffer from inadequacy of resources for challenging governmental actions. The firms tend to evade or circumvent government policies as long as the gains of such behavior exceed their legitimacy costs. At times, conflictual political behavior prevails under three conditions: (a) when actions of international firms and governments have high strategic salience for the other party, (b) when both sides perceive the situation as zero-sum game, and (c) when they have enough power to influence, through bargaining, the uncertain outcomes concerning winners and losers.

In other situations, political partnership between international business firms and governments may prevail if three conditions are met: (a) when states are willing to correct for natural market failures or to generate unnatural market imperfections, (b) when both parties to the conflict (deal) perceive the situation to be strategically beneficial to them—parties, and (c) when both parties have enough power to influence uncertain outcomes of their bargaining processes that may result in mutual gains. The intensity of political behavior on the part of the international business firms is greater when the stakes are not only higher, but also when opportunities to leverage and arbitrate governmental policies are plentiful. In addition, intense political behavior is displayed when the international businesses' political competencies are advanced and enhanceable.

Since international business firms are strategic thinkers and operators, they make choices on resources, competitive methods and geographic zones and areas (Morrison and Roth 1989). Strategic planning literature emphasizes profitability, population ecology, resource dependence, transaction cost analysis (emphasizes survival), various strands or resource dependence, industrial organization and political economy theory. These strategic elements are collectively viewed as aspects of international dominance, monopoly, and hegemony (Perrow 1981). The sources of profits are efficiency and are congruent with the values that are dominant in the nonmarket environment, legitimacy becomes a political resource firms want to secure. This behavior helps firms to have access to policy makers, influence public policy making, and reduce opposition from other competitors and stakeholders. Both governments (at home and abroad) expect these firms to treat local political imperatives as goals and private economic imperatives, e.g., flexibility and profitability as constraints (Doz 1986). The firms' legitimacy is enhanced when they contribute to national goals of development such as employment, technological development, and balance of payments surplus. Further still, firms enhance their legitimacy when they abide by local laws, customs, symbols, and loyalty during interstate conflicts (Kindleberger 1969).

Figure X.1. Model of Business and Political Behavior

*Forms*

- nonbargaining
- compliance
- avoidance
- circumvention
- bargaining
- conflict
- partnership
- intensity

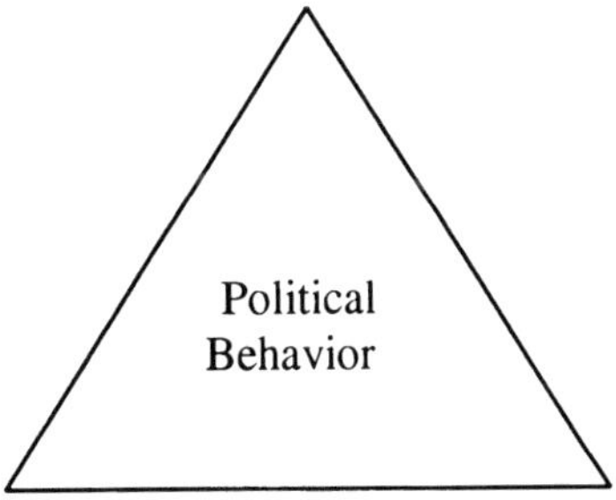


***Interactive Conditioning Factors***

- in the firm
- in the industry
- in the nonmarket environment

***Business Strategic Objectives***

- efficiency
- market power
- legitimacy
- access

Consistent with conceptions of efficiency, firms can act politically to reduce their own production and transaction costs for the purpose of providing cheaper, better, or unique products to their customers. They can do this while raising the costs of production for their rivals at home and abroad. This is called protectionism or 'sheltering' (Rugman and Verbeke 1990, 8; 1992, 206). This is a resource-based model of strategic management. These same firms have market power. The struggle to obtain market power is based on a dialectic of ideological and empirical beliefs regarding whether profits are more readily secured through efficiency and competitiveness as opposed to through anticompetitive market power. In a sense, a firm's "ability to raise prices, eliminate competitors or collude with them, to obtain favorable regulations, and to deny such benefits to others by raising barriers of entry and mobility is a real source of competitive advantage in the domestic and international markets" (Boddewyn and Brewer 1994, 134).

To meet their strategic objectives, international corporations and firms use resource strategy, competitive methods, and political markets to strike deals for profit maximization. Politically, the international businesses have to use better intelligence and cognitive maps in order to penetrate nonmarket climates and environments. These nonmarket areas have better access to decision makers and opinion leaders and secure better bargaining or nonbargaining influence. To be effective in generating sustainable rents, their bargaining and nonbargaining skills should be competencies that are nonimitatible and nonsubstitutable. For instance, their strongest "weapons" should be "reason, argument, persuasion, and diplomacy" (p. 136) rather than bribery, evasion, and circumvention. However, they must be aware that since they have a lot of power, they should use it carefully and wisely, lest it "corrupts people, organizations and society" (p. 136) in general.

## POLITICAL ECONOMY IN THE THIRD WORLD

With the recent decline and total collapse of the communist economic and political system, most countries, especially those in the Third World, view reformatory economic transitions to be associated with democratization of their political systems. In some cases, inconclusive evidence seems to suggest that economic growth tends to be conducted better and faster in authoritarian rather then in democratic countries. In other words, democracies are less capable of imposing economic reforms than authoritarian regimes. On the other hand, it is easier for democracies to implement legitimate economic reforms if their policy processes are more transparent, and accountable than when decision making is conducted secretively and corruptly. Successful economic reforms largely depend not only on the policy design, but they also depend on the state's implementation machinery. Given these arguments, it may be argued that regime type may not necessarily be an objective indicator or determinant of economic performance (Diamond and Plattner 1995). Of importance, it is observationally important to say that the politics of authoritarian structures and democratic consolidation cannot be understood in isolation from the economic choices and constraints associated with the transition.

What are the proper governmental strategies for operationalizing economic reforms? In a political, competitive, and global or open environment, this question's answer could have a lot of dialectics. However, in accordance with the wisdom of eminent and scholarly analysts, several, may be mentioned. First, based on the shock-therapy school of thought, rapid and radical reforms are essential for forestalling countermobilization by previous elites who might be attempting to build popular confidence which indicates that economic changes do last. In addition, economic development gradualists argue that shock-therapy is invalid in many democratizing societies where the president lacks political insulation and predominance for imposing economic policy by decree.

Second, different political strategies are more effective than one that is used for various economic development reforms. The involvement of relatively simple and straightforward administratively guided economic reforms in which liberalization and stabilization measures can be accomplished through presidential leadership is a possibility. Third, complex and all drawn-out structural and institutional transformations require different political approaches that involve broad mobilization of social support from constituencies. Social support for economic reforms should be conducted wisely because, politically, the winners are fewer than the losers. These short-term winners of economic reforms are fewer and difficult to organize politically. The losers, who are the majority, are members of the "ancient regime." To strike a compromise in this dichotomous conundrum, it might be wise "to co-opt critical segments of the electorate by providing government benefits to compensate for the effects of economic austerity" (Henderson 1996, 448). Fourth, reductions in government revenues in addition to spending cuts can collectively be reconciled with compensatory schemes in order to placate politically relevant losers who could become potential and socially disruptive malcontents. One of the problems of this strategy is that most Third World political regimes are too poor to afford buying off both the middle and lower income voters. This difficulty makes it almost impossible to build broad-based coalition support and reform the movement. Even neocorporatist solutions are not more solvent than social coalitions. In a large number of new democracies "corporatism (which depends on the state-mediated cooperation of organized business and labor interests) is rendered infeasible by fragmentation and differences of interest within the labor movement and employer's groups. Given the difficulties of mobilizing new social coalitions, many democratizing states may be tempted to seek support among the beneficiaries of the old regime—with possible negative consequences for democratic consolidation and economic reform.

Haggard and Kaufman (1995) have attempted to construct a comprehensive theory of democratic transition. In this attempt, they have tried to identify critical factors whose propensity destroys authoritarian regimes. They have also tried to identify reasons that enable the newly elected governments to strengthen democracy and pursue economic reforms. They indicate that most political actors "overlook the socioeconomic and institutional factors that shape" these "actors' preferences" (Henderson 1996, 449). While this argument sounds convincing, it becomes more contradictory and less convincing when the authors try to tabulate specific socioeconomic and institutional factors accountable for democratic transition.

Haggard and Kaufman have strongly proposed a simple model of authoritarian structure based on economic performance and elite cohesion. They argue that authoritarian regimes tend to collapse "when poor economic performance undermines their ability to purchase social compliance and when elite fragmentation weakens their ability to manage economic and political problems" (p. 449). Recent examples include Indonesia, Marcos Philippines, Thailand and Mobutu's Zaire. On the contrary, cohesive elites can effectively prevent economic crises and withstand political pressures. When cohesive elites operate under noncrisis economic conditions, even when they come under pressure to democratize, they positively impose and enforce a political solution which protects their future access to power by limiting the options of their potential successors. Gradually and subsequently, bargains worked out during the transition are revised later in order to balance power at different intervals. Consequently, predictions based on the terms of pacts of the exercise of power lose their significance over time. To use political consolidation for the improvement of economic performance in the new democracies, Haggard and Kaufman (1995) have prescribed a theoretical model of institutional structure. First, "the organization of executive authority and the structure of the party system—are important in determining the success of economic reform and political transition" (Henderson 1996, 449). A centralized executive authority is essential for initiating economic reforms. That forum of consolidation of economic reform and political democracy requires creative assemblage of coalition of interests—supporters and beneficiaries. The most effective machinery for effecting such support base is the utilization of a cohesive nonpolarized political system. In the era of democratization, technology and ethnicism, it is difficult to realize such a uniform structure on a grand scale. Democratization and ethnicism in themselves are dialectically problematic because they are the sources of polarization and fragmentation particularly when they are not well managed. In other words, the ultimate causes of political outcomes may not lie in the characteristics of particular party systems, but in the "social and economic forces which gave rise to them" (p. 449).

Haggard and Kaufman have used a minimalist rather than maximalist explanatory model by using examples from South America and Asia and by avoiding to include European and African cases in their study. Doing so does make the study less generalizable and less international (global). It should be made clear that economic and political reforms for democratic consolidation requires a strategic institutional shift. Democratizing states need to move from reliance on broad discretionary powers to reformist executives and be invested in newly constructed institutional mechanisms for governmental consultation with the interests of society. In a world that has a diversity of presidential versus parliamentary structures, two versus multiparty systems, and a variety of electoral systems and mechanisms for representation, the political economy of democratic consolidation can hardly be regulated by the perceptually visualized perfect and reformist state which Haggard and Kaufman have proposed.

Moreover, paradigmatically speaking, the political ideologies upon which the economic foundation of these nations is based have profound Western theoretical and empirical underpinnings that make them difficult if not impossible to productively implement in the Third World. These political ideologies are conservative, liberal and radical (Gondwe 1992). The hegemonic character of their use in the market does not only ignore the "balance between individual rights and social obligations and responsibilities, as well as the role of culture and traditions in human behavior" (pp. 8-9), but these paradigms place emphasis on the employment of capital investment that mimics the path of historical development structure of more advanced and well established capitalist nations. Because this is ill-advised and destructive, many poor nations suffer from regressive development. Use of appropriate technology, well trained and well placed human capital should complement existing or reformed power structures in a 'people-centered theory of value' (Chapter 7) to enhance development.

Given the fact that most state-driven economic programs have failed in many countries, the World Bank has confirmed that more than 3,000 private firms and transactions have been established in the Third World since 1980. The reasons for privatization include attempts to solve "macroeconomic problems, particularly in reducing budget deficits and public debt" (Ramamurti 1996, 10). Further still, privatization was driven by structural conditions in each Latin American country particularly the cost of government ownership and management and external pressure from international organizations (DeCastro 1997). Ramamurti (1996) has made a compelling argument that privatization results in important improvements in the "quality of services, capital expenditures, labor productivity, and financial performance of the firms involved" (p. 998). Other types of mergers/acquisitions, and privatization transactions invariably require paramount changes in systems, structure, and culture.

Privatization introduces competition which lowers prices for customers, consumers and government. The firms that were privatized in Latin America included those in telecommunications, transportation industries, roads, airports, ports, prisons, educational systems, tax collection, and duty assessment. Also, telephone companies and airlines were privatized.

Though privatization has its merits, it is not without profound demerits which also are constraints on the effective functioning of the state's autonomy. Privatization diminishes the power of the state because the global financial markets enforce the dictates of the IMF particularly in Africa, Asia, Latin America and even in Britain and France. Indeed, the power to overrule majority governments that is wielded by international capital markets and by the IMF constitutes the greatest contemporary threat to substantive democracy in this era, when, paradoxically," liberal democratic political systems have flourished" (Pauly 1997, 427). For example, majority governments in Poland, South Africa, Philippines, Haiti and Bosnia control their political systems without the capacity to determine their nations' economic destiny or rule over most of the things that matter. International financial markets and multilateral institutions have considerably narrowed state power. In doing that the states, particularly the ones in Third World countries, have become "toothless extensions" of the institutions (IMF, World Bank) which have become the regulators of the unregulated economies. Since the need and interests of these financial institutions are inconsistent with those of the people and nations of the Third World, international institutions may be addressing the needs of these nations exploitatively and criminologically. In other words, "the bankers, both the private ones operating in the global financial markets and the public ones—the international public servants, central bankers, and finance ministers who operate the IMF" (Pauly 1997, 427) as well as those who operated its predecessor agencies of the League of Nations should reexamine their policies which constrain governments, isolate them from their peoples and marginalize them in matters of decision making, policy initiative, implementation and nonmarket influence of the iron triangles (Volkomer 1998). Paradoxically, the national governments suffering from the constraints of the global markets and intergovernmental obligations were responsible for either strengthening or mismanaging the affairs of their state systems that have now become vassal elements of the international capitalist economy. This form of "casino capitalism" (Pauly 1997, 428) has been existing since the 1920s though it became more highly pronounced since the 1970s. Pauly makes a strong and persuasive argument by encouraging states to promote democratic decision making while demonstrating their accountability to their domestic and international obligations. Decisions should not be secretly carried out by central bankers, finance ministers and political executives. Instead governments should mobilize their citizens to make decisions that open global markets and provide viable and necessary coordination of national economic policies. If that happens, development and democratization will actively become legitimate and meaningful elements of the new world order.

Since the end of the Cold War, Western Europe's relations with Africa have contributed to the marginalization of the latter. For instance, during the 1960s, Black Africa's share of the world trade was 3.8 percent. In 1989, it had declined as low as 1.05 percent. Also, the whole continent's share had declined from 11 percent during the 1980s to 4 percent in 1994 (Olsen 1997). Marginalization is a dependency theory of development because African nations view foreign aid as the only main external source of funding for development projects and foreign exchange for most African regimes. These former colonial masters buy nearly 50 percent of the continent's exports (raw materials and minerals) while importing 60 percent of what the continent consumes—resulting in an imbalanced balance of payments. In spite of the trade concessions contained in the Lome Convention, the African, Caribbean and Pacific countries have failed to increase and maintain their market share in the E.U.

African countries are dealt with as a "collective clientelism" (Ravenhill 1985, 22-23). This interdependent relationship is asymmetrical, has emotional ties, is noncomparable and paternalistic form of neocolonialism which has transformed Lome's decolonization principles into aspects of stagnation. Democracy, as a capitalist ideology, has replaced development. This is comparable to when the communist ideology and its long awaited results, became comparable to development too. The outcome of ideologically rather than rationally and realistically guided socioeconomic system is chaos, bankruptcies, political repression, and worst forms of statecentric authoritarianism.

The South American, Asian and Eastern European regions have received greater amount of assistance than Africa which used to get such comparable assistance from the Western World when it faced the threat of communism during the Cold War. The African, Caribbean and Pacific countries (ACPs), irrespective of the principles enunciated in Lome I and II, have not only been progressively denied the requests they demand, but compensation for the losses entailed by the General Agreement on Tariffs and Trade (GATT)—the equivalent of WTO, have heavily curtailed their protection of favored access to the European market. Further still, recent political crises in Somalia (1992-1996), Rwanda (1994-1996), and Eastern Zaire (1996-1998) have demonstrated E.U.'s lack of economic and political interest in the region. Moreover, France, may have conspired against the central African nations for their rejection of its neocolonial and paternalistic attitude. Without the formidable U.S. humanitarian intervention for the normalization of relations, a greater catastrophe in terms of loss of human life and farther political destabilization of the interlucastrine region could take place. The task would have been impossible without U.S. supplies and transport planes which delivered food, medicine and shelter to the refugees.

After the Second World War, especially during the last 20 years, the global economy has been characterized by increasing global interdependence among states. During the 1980s and afterwards, trade liberalization significantly contributed to globalization. However, in recent times, foreign domestic investment (FDI) has become more important than trade as a force that underpins growth in terms of interdependence. Technologically, developments in communications and transportation "enabled firms to extend their operations abroad, and multinational corporations (MNCs) increased their FDI to gain access to foreign markets, benefit from economies of scale, and gain control over all states of the production process" (Cohn, 2008: 314). Recently, "developed countries accounted for 88.5% of the outward FDI stock and 72% of inward stock in 2004" (p. 314). The E.U., North America and East Asia are the main sources of FDI, which practice intercore and intracore investment regimens. Though the US dominated the FDI between the 1950s and 1970s, Japanese and Western European competitiveness have neutralized American global FDI. Though this form of assertive competitiveness has caused the US to be sensitive, the latter is making adjustments to continually regularize its performance. Such a situation has made the DCs, which are the bases for the MNCs try to eliminate obstacles to incoming FDI.

In contradistinction, the LDCs are host rather than home countries for foreign investment. That is largely why the LDCs have "lower per capita incomes, inadequate infrastructure ... and limited availability of modern technology. Poorer LDCs have widespread poverty and malnutrition ... have lower levels of social development such as limited educational facilities, low literacy rates, and inadequate health and sanitary facilities...have unstable and authoritarian governments. LDCs also have less influence in settling the agenda and making decisions regarding the global political economy" (p. 7). Although LDCs have liberalized their investment strategies since the 1980s global "debt crisis, the opposition to the negotiation of a multilateral agreement on investment in the OECD or WTO shows that this liberalization has" (p. 314) both limits and a variety of negative consequences that are subject to conflicting liberal, realist and historico-structuralist interpretations. Specifically:

> Liberals view MNCs as positive agents of global change that contribute to increased efficiency and stimulate innovation, economic growth and employment. Liberals also often argue that many MHCs are becoming 'stateless' or removed from close association with any single state. Thus, a chief executive officer of IBM has argued that large MNCs are becoming 'globally integrated enterprises' that are fundamentally changing the way in which they supply the global market (p. 314).

To illustrate this phenomenon, Japanese carmakers, Western European chemical multinational companies, and the US industrial giants have constructed huge manufacturing plants, firms and enterprises that supply both the Chinese domestic and global markets worldwide. Likewise, Western and Japanese insurance corporations and companies, service firms and information technology companies have established service and R and D centers in India to supply customers, employees, and production and distribution worldwide. Hence, comparatively speaking, "liberals advise states to upgrade the skills of their populations to attract investment, regardless of source. Realists ... believe that MNCs nationality does make a difference and that the competitiveness of a state is closely linked with the competitiveness of its MNCs.

> Realists also believe that host states should be able to impose performance requirements and other regulations on MNCs to promote industrial development and protect the national interest. Historical structuralists argue that MNCs overchange for their goods and services, crate dependency relationships with LDC host states, and pose a threat to labor groups in the home as well as host states... MNCs contribute to a deterioration of working conditions and a competitive race to the bottom by transferring operations to affiliates in states with lower wages and environmental standards (pp. 314 - 315).

In essence, liberals, realists and historical structuralists (neo-Marxists) differ radically concerning their views on regulation as related to the MNCs, the host state or the home state. In this conflicting and differential conjecture the UN, WTO and OECD have also all failed to design a comprehensive multinational agreement concerning investment options. In the absence of a dominant and legitimate domestic (individual nation) or multilateral regime, the North has employed bilaterally and regionally deviced governance strategies that limit host states on FDI. Classic examples of this form of exploitative regionalism include but are not limited to the bilateral investment treaty BIT and investment conditions in the ELI and NAFTA. In the absence of a multilateral regime regulating MNCs, NGOs have also pressured MNCs to alter their behavior through voluntary agreements and self-regulation. Although liberal NGOs have emphasized MNC reform, rejectionist NGOs have emphasized ideological confrontation. In general, FDI regulation is a patchwork quilt due to the fact that there is "no effective multilateral regime for foreign investment" (p. 315). However, based on historical structuralist development lenses "transnational capital is the main beneficiary of RTAs (regional trade agreements) such as NAFTA, and LDCs and the poorest in all member states are the main losers" (p. 270). Since "RTAs permit MNCs to locate production facilities in states with the lowest wages and environment standards, they have a negative effect on labor, environmental, health safety, public service, and consumer protection standards" (p. 270). In 2004, there were 70,000 MNCs, which controlled 690,000 foreign affiliates whose total sales accounted for $19 trillion (Cohn 2004, 4). These transnational corporations are multinational enterprises that "sit at the intersection of production, international trade, and cross-border investment" (Oatley 2005, 171).

## CONCLUSION

Political economy is greatly associated with globalism. The global idea is the electronic and telecommunication movement of the world community and its resources. The movement is futuristically realized in the global vision of the village. Some of the challenges of globalism in the next century will arise from the notion that technology will be the dominant force in human history that will influence society for good or for worse.

Castells (1992) argues that the global economy is different from the world economy. The global economy is an economy that works as a unit on real time on a planetary scale. It is an economy where capital flows, labor markets, commodity markets, information, raw materials, management and organization are internationalized and fully interdependent throughout the planet, although in an asymmetrical form, characterized by the uneven integration to the global system of different areas of the planet (p. 5).

This global economy is witnessing the emergence of global cities that coordinate the economy. The characteristics of the global cities are duality of life (economic restructuring characterized by "decline of manufacturing industry, loss of skilled manual middle-income jobs, growth of highly skilled and highly paid and managerial stratum which will manage the new global economy and financial system" (Dieleman and Hamnett 1994, 358). This global city will be paralleled by the emergence of "low-skilled and low-paid service jobs to 'service' the service sector, is said to be accompanied by a growing polarization or dualization in the occupational and income structure, which is paralleled by high levels of spatial and ethnic segregation" (p. 358).

The cities will be the hub for the control, coordination, and regulation of global finance (Thrift 1987; Sassen 1991), producers of business services (Daniels 1991), experiencing control and coordination of new international division of labor (Friedman 1986), key nodes of the international urban system (Mollenkopf 1993) and linking pins of global capitalism (Smith and Feagin 1987). These cities have been infrastructured with telecommunications which allows control and coordination to be managed from remote centers by phone, fax, cell phone, I phone and computer networks that utilize satellites and fiber optics. This technology is used by multinational corporations, companies, firms, financial markets and political executives and diplomats. Banks, accountants, lawyers, managers and consultants use the same telecommunication infrastructure.

Cities are polycentric, multimodal or monocentric. The monocentric city has high levels of congestion. Religious, ideological, economic, racial, housing and political issues divide cities into zones of quartered, nucleated, or spatial settlements. Connected to centrol functions and global functions, global cities are physically and socially rich in infrastructure. Their office buildings are distinctly and architecturally designed to symbolize an image of power and prestige (Zukin 1992). Main international airports, superfast trains, and telecommunications networks are global elements of a world city. Their social networks are strengthened by a rich variety of cultural and entertainment industry.

Viewed in this light then, the world city does not only coordinate the free flow of the global economy, but this new, dynamic, and high-income growth city seems to be coveted and highly valued in spite of its inherent hegemonic and segmented inequality (Dieleman and Hamnett 1994). Cities have grown with rapidity and spectacle during the twentieth century. Shanghai has 20 million people, Sao Paulo has 18 million, New Delhi has 12 million, Cairo has 15 million, Tokyo and Yokohama have 29 million, Mexico City has 28 million. There are more than 2,500 metropolises each of which has 1-4 million people. More than 40 cities are 'supercities' which have between 4 million and 10 million people. Twenty-four 'super giants' have more than 10 million each. Predictions indicate that by the year 2050, the world will have 80 super giants (Moyer 1998).

Historiographically, these developments, many of which are taking place in the Third World, have challenged mainstream academic scholars and researchers to change their analytical traditions in terms of their intellectual universe. Their loaded concepts of race, identity, nation, and tradition have been unbundled. They have theoretically and empirically lost their notions of colonized and colonizer or center and periphery or empire and its others. Academic disciplinarians are negotiating the relationship between local and global. Their academic debate and agenda particularly in the social sciences, focuses on problematics of displacement and relocation, national literatures, transnationality and the challenges of creating and preserving localisms in the context of modernization and globalization.

Politically, the territorial nation-state and its inhabitants are likely to be affected by the technological revolution's impact on the world's political economy and culture. Floods of money, goods and services (labor) and information will be relocated once or several times. Evidently, rational choice which will enable these happenings to take place need to be managed to avoid anarchy (Elkind, 1995). In other words, extraordinary effects of contemporary technological and economic processes are likely to overwhelm the traditional controls known by territorial states. If the newly globalized resources will have been decoupled from their territorial roots, then new forms of governance structures will be needed to foster and necessitate "new nonterritorrial political and social configurations throughout the globe" (Mendlovitz 1997, 229). Corporations, firms, religious institutions, professional organizations, parliamentary and congressional political institutions, NGOs, and other organizations will require new forms of governance structures, values and norms in order to formalize and rationalize their informal and new existence. Formalization of their existence will include but will not be limited to the regulation and control of nuclear proliferation, reduction of global differences that arise from economic inequality and market competition (trade wars); there should be rigorous processes for regulating information technology in order to enable competitors to practice fair competition in the market, such as the split decision issued by the courts to reduce Microsoft's monopoly. As usual, some noncompetitive, unreformed, and mechanistically dominated organizations will disappear because their humanistic and behavioral existence will be inconsistent with the technologically and organizationally reformed ways of managing things.

Unlike the unreformed decline and extinction of the medieval institutions and organizations (lords, knights, vassals, serfs, fiefdom, church, commerce, or the city and town), whose system undermined land commodification, commerce and scientific exploration, to survive and flourish, the modern society of the future should establish strong structures for self-reconceptualization, self-reconstruction, new citizenship, and collective global and moral rearmament all of which become the framework and springboard for production, recreation, self-realization, and self-actualization.

In the New Millennium, each individual will inherit a new sense of multiple identities, which will continue to transform him/her. They will not only be very multicultural, but they will also be reflective of a plurality of cultural elements of nation-state citizenship. This global society, to practice its civilian and vocational life, will select to participate by seeking membership among a wide variety of "electronic communication groups, international groupings, new political processes and organizations, citizenships" (Mendlovitz 1995, 229).

The new inhabitants will exercise individual choice more assertively in order to keep up with the electronically governed communication structure in order to reaffirm their new identities. Social arrangements and self-conceptions will be shaped exclusively by and through existing societal structures rather than the family, kinship group, or one's own culture. Current societal structures are radically preparing people for globalization. They have become consciously aware that new global interactions have enabled the evolution of these formally nonexistent interactional relations to exist. The "old citizen" is being "unbundled" (p. 229).

The socioeconomic evolution of the global and post-Cold War society has produced a global mind in terms of transnational corporations, global social movements, world religions, and the growth of regional and global supranational economic and political organizations. Elkind calls them 'anarchy.' These new social and economic organizations are an articulated, self-conscious transnational civil society that is being analyzed, socialized, and transformed to produce supranational global political institutions like UN, NAFTA, E.U., APEC, NATO, and the Third World which will function as centralizing rather than decentralizing forces. Since 1992, more than 30 UN global conferences including those of the NGOs have tried to agree on the construction of the global formative order. NAFTA in itself is a regional rather than multilateral instrument of U.S. economic and foreign policy (Bhagwati 1992/93).

For instance, the environmental movement is a stimulus for nonterritorial political organization which articulates it in the fashion of unbiblical and unspiritual way. With the impetus for their ideological spiritual union, environmentalists, feminists, and peace and human rights activists, and civil rights or social justice advocates are recognized elements of the new global society which has no territorial boundaries or cultural norms of a traditional type. These groups advocate the promotion of decentralized governance (small is beautiful). They are assertively contributing to the formulation and institutionalization of global political standards. In the era of global communications, economics, technology and culture, historically and culturally established notions of Western culture and civilization are being questioned. A new paradigm of global hegemony is arising in the East to which region power has significantly shifted. This power is being exercised by nongovernmental and nonprivate entities which Drucker calls the 'third force' (p. 230). This force, whose influence of cities and world religions are characterized by vibrant and revolutionary world spirituality which is galvanizingly unparalleled in world history.

What role should the state play in such a climate of economic and sociotechnical change? This question has been central to political economists since the time of Adam Smith's classical era of the *Wealth of nations.* Neoclassical economists see that perceived role to be both laissez-faire and neoliberal rather than radical. Neoliberal economists view the role of the state to be central in moving planned economies to a market orientation and in maintaining macroeconomic stability where prices are freely determined by competitive markets. As an agent of economic change, the state should play the dual role of entrepreneur and conflict manager (Chang and Rowthorn 1995). This has happened in European and East Asian countries in which industrial policy, entrepreneurial vision and bureaucratic involvement have used a gradualist and incremental perspective rather than the "big bang" or shock-therapy for growth through global, institutional, and organizational interdependence.

The methodology of the new political economy rejects the old dichotomy between agency and structure which fragmented classical political economy into separate disciplines that were based on ideological rather than rational reality. The new thinking in political economy seeks instead, to build on those approaches in social science, such as the structuration theory, institutional economics, new public choice theory and critical theory, which have tried to develop an integrated analysis, thereby combining parsimonious theories which analyze agency in terms of instrumental rationality with contextual theories which analyze structures institutionally and historically. The aim of the *New Political Economy Journal* is to create a forum for work which seeks to bridge past empirical and conceptual divides. The emphasis will be based upon explanatory and innovative work which draws from different disciplines and which addresses core issues in the emerging research agenda in the field of political economy which is a subparadigm of organizational theory. In totality, this paradigmatic discipline is a sound framework for interweaving social, political, and economic history.

## REFERENCES

Aggarwal, V.K. 1996. *Debt games: Strategic interaction in international debt rescheduling.* New York: Cambridge University Press.

Amin, S. 1974. *Accumulation on a world scale.* New York: Monthly Review.

Arrighi, G. 1982. A crisis of hegemony. In S. Amin, G. Arrighi, A.G. Frank, and I. Wallerstein, eds. *The dynamics of global crisis.* New York: Monthly Review: 55-108.

Benson, J.K. 1975 The interorganizational network as a political economy. *Administrative Science Quarterly* 20: 229-248.

Berger, S., and R. Dore, eds. 1980. *National diversity and global capitalism.* Ithaca: Cornell University Press.

Bhagwati, J. 1992/93. Beyond NAPHTHA: Clinton's trading choices. *Foreign Policy* 89: 155-62.

Blake, D.H. 1977. *Managing the external relations of multinational corporations.* New York: Fund for Multinational Management.

Boddewyn, J.J. 1986. *International political strategy: A fourth "generic" strategy?* Working Paper. New York: Baruch College.\

Boddewyn, J.J., and T.L. Brewer. 1994. International business political behavior: New theoretical directions. *Academy of Management Review* 19, 1: 119-43.

Boesche, R. 1996. *Theories of tyranny from Plato to Arendt.* University Park: Pennsylvania State University Press

Bollen, K.A. 1983. World system position, dependency and democracy. *American Sociological Review* 48: 468-97.

Brewer, T.L. 1993. Government policies, market imperfections, and foreign direct investment. *Journal of International Business Studies* 24: 101-20.

__________. 1992a. An issue-area approach to the analysis of MNC-government relations. *Journal of International Business Studies* 23: 295-309.

__________. 1992b. MNC-government relations: Strategic networks and foreign direct investment in the United States in the automotive industry. *The International Executive* 34: 113-29.

Bunker, S.C. 1984. Modes of extraction, unequal exchange, and progressive underdevelopment of an extreme periphery: The Brazilian Amazon, 1960-1980. *American Journal of Sociology.*

Burris, V. 1991. Director interlocks and political behavior of corporations and corporate elites. *Social Science Quarterly* 72, 3: 537-51.

Caporaso, J.A. 1981. Industrialization at the periphery: The evolving division of labor. *International Studies Quarterly* 25: 347-84.

Cardoso, F.H. 1973. Associated-dependent development. In A. Stephen, ed. *Authoritarian Brazil: Origins, policies and future.* Yale University Press, 142-76.

Castells, M. 1992. *European cities, the informational society, and the global economy.* Amsterdam: Centre for Metropolitan Research, Amsterdam University.

Chang, H.G., and R. Rowthorn. 1995. *The role of the state in economic change.* Oxford: Clarendon Press.

Chase-Dunn, C., and R. Rubinson. 1977. Toward a structural perspective on the world system. *Politics and Society.*

Chen, F. 1995. *Economic transition and political legitimacy in post-Mao China.* Albany: State University of New York Press.

Choate, P. 1990. *Agents of influence: How Japan's lobbyists in the United States manipulate America's political and economic system.* New York: Alfred A. Knopf.

Collis, D.J. 1991. A resource-based analysis of global competition: The case of the bearings industry. *Strategic Management Journal* 12: 49-68.

Conner, K.R. 1991. A historical comparison of resource-based theory and five schools of thought within industrial organization economics. *Journal of Management* 17: 121-54.

Croft, S. 1997. International relations and Africa: Review article. *African Affairs* 96, 385: 607-15.

Daniels, P.L.D. 1991. *Services and metropolitan development: International perspectives.* London: Routledge.

Deane, P. 1978. *The evolution of economic ideas: Modern economics.* Cambridge: Cambridge University Press.

DeCastro, J.O. ed. 1997. Privatizing monopolies: Lessons from the telecommunications and transport sectors in Latin America. *Academy of Management Review* 22, 4: 997-1010.

Deprez, J. 1991. The macrodynamics of advanced market economies: The post-keynesian perspective of Alfred Eichner. *Social Science Quarterly* 72, 3: 415-30.

Diamond, L., and M.F. Plattner., eds. 1995. *Economic reform and democracy.* Baltimore: Johns Hopkins University Press.

Dieleman, F.M., and C. Hamnett. 1994. Globalization, regulation and urban system: Editor's introduction to the special issue. *Urban Studies* 31, 3: 357-64.

DiMaggio, P.J., and W.W. Powell. 1983. The iron cage revisited: Institutional isomorphism and collective rationality in organizational fields. *American Sociological Review* 48: 147-60.

Doz, Y. 1986. *Strategic management in multinational companies.* New York: Pergamon Press.

Eichner, A. 1987. *The macrodynamics of advanced market economies.* Armonk, N.Y.: M.E. Sharpe.

__________. 1976. *The megacorp and oligopoly: Micro foundations of macro dynamics.* New York: Cambridge University Press.

Elkind, D. 1995. *Beyond sovereignty: Territory and political economy in the twenty-first century.* Toronto: Toronto University Press.

Etzioni, A. 1996. The responsive community: A communication perspective. *American Sociological Review* 61: 1-11.

__________. 1988. *The moral dimension: Toward a new economics.* New York: Free Press.

Evans, P. 1979a. Beyond center and periphery a comment on the world system approach to the study of development. *Sociological Inquiry* 49: 15-20.

__________. 1979b. *Dependent development.* Princeton: Princeton University Press.

Fayerweather, J. 1969. *International business management.* New York: McGraw-Hill.

Feagin, J.R. 1985. The social costs of Houston's growth. *International Journal of Urban and Regional Research* 9: 164-85.

Firebaugh, G., and B. Bullock. 1987. Level of processing of exports: Estimates for developing nations. *International Studies Quarterly* 30: 333-50.

Fox, A.B. 1995. Environment and trade: The NAFTA case. *Political Science Quarterly* 110, 1: 49-68.

Frank, A.G. 1969 *Latin America: Underdevelopment of revolution?* New York: Monthly Review.

Friedmann, J. 1986. The world city hypothesis. *Development and Change,* 17: 69-84.

Gamble, A. 1996. *The New Political Economy Journal.* File: ///CVIconovex/EchoSearch/Work/Views/5.html#ICVX8000C.

Gereffi, G., and D. Wyman. 1990. *Manufacturing miracles: Paths of industrialization in Latin America and East Asia.* Princeton: Princeton University Press.

Gondwe, D.K. 1992. *Political economy, ideology, and the impact of economics on the Third World.* New York: Praeger.

Grant, R.M. 1991. The resource-based theory of competitive advantage: Implications for strategy formulations. *California Management Review* 33, 3: 14-135.

Haggard, S., and R.R. Kaufman. 1995. *The political economy of democratic transitions.* Princeton: Princeton University Press.

Hayes, M.T. 1981. *Lobbyists and legislators: A theory of political market.* New Brunswick, N.J.: Rutgers University Press.

Henderson, A.E., ed. 1997. Afrocentrism and world politics: Towards a new paradigm. *American Political Science Review* 91: 448.

Jacoby, S. 1995. *The workers of nations: Industrial relations in a global economy.* New York: Oxford University Press.

Keohane, R. 1984. *After hegemony: Cooperation and discord in world political economy.* Princeton: Princeton University Press.

Kindleberger, C.P. 1970. *Power and money.* New York: Basic Books.

__________. 1969. *American business abroad.* New Haven, CT.: Yale University Press.

Klein, L.R., R. Pauly, and P. Voisin. 1982. The world economy—a global model. *Perspectives in Computing* 2: 4-17.

Korzeniewicz, R.P., and T.P. Moran. 1997. World economic trends in the distribution of income, 1965-1992. *American Journal of Sociology* 102, 4: 1000-39.

Leone, R.A. 1986. *Who profits: Winners, losers and government regulations.* New York: Basic Books.

Linnemann, H. 1966. *An econometric study of world trade flows.* Amsterdam: North Holland.

Mandel, E. 1975. *Late capitalism.* London: Mew Left Review.

Mansfield, E.A., and H.V. Milner, eds. 1997. *The political economy of regionalism.* New York: Columbia University Press.

Marklew, V. 1995. *Cash, crisis, and corporate governance: The role of national financial systems in industrial restructuring.* Ann Arbor, MI: University of Michigan Press.

Mendlovitz, S.H. ed. 1997. Beyond sovereignty: Territory and political economy in the twenty-first century. *American Political Science Review* March: 229-30.

Mitchell, N., W.L. Hansen, and E.M. Jepsen. 1997. The determinants of domestic and foreign corporate political activity. *The Journal of Politics* 59, 4: 1096-1113.

Mollenkopf, J.E. 1993. *Key urban nodes in the global system.* New York: Social Science Research Council.

Morrison, A.J., and K. Roth. 1989. International business-level strategy: The development of holistic model. In A.R. Negandi, and A. Savara, eds. *International Strategic Management.* Lexington, MA. Lexington Books: 29-49.

Moyer, B.C. 1998. Surrounded? Thank God! The urban paradox. *Adventist Review* June: 12-5.

Nemeth, R., and D. A. Smith. 1985. International trade and world system structure: A multiple network analysis. *Review,* by Ferdinand Braudel Center, 8: 517-60.

Naughton, B. 1995. *Growing out of the plan: Chinese economic reform, 1978-1993.* Cambridge: Cambridge University Press.

Olsen, G.R. 1997. Western Europe's relation with Africa since the end of the cold war. *The Journal of Modern African Studies* 35, 2: 299-319.

Pauly, L.W. 1997. *Who elected the bankers? Surveillance and control in the world economy.* Ithaca: Cornell University Press.

Perrow, C. 1986. *Complex organizations.* New York: McGraw-Hill.

__________. 1981. Markets, hierarchies and hegemony. In A.H. Van de Ven and W. Joyce, eds. *Perspectives on Organization Design and Behavior.* New York: Wiley: 317-86.

Peteraf, M.A. 1990. The cornerstones of competitive advantage: A resource-based view. *Strategic Management Journal* 14: 179-91.

Pfeffer, J., and G.R. Salancik. 1978. *The external control of organizations: A resource dependent perspective.* New York: Harper and Row.

Prestowitz, C. 1988. *Trading places.* New York: Basic Books.

Ramamurti, R., ed. 1996. *Privatizing monopolies: Lessons from the telecommunications and transport sectors in Latin America.* Baltimore: The Johns Hopkins University Press.

Ravenhill, J. 1985. *Collective clientelism: The Lome Conventions and the North-South relations.* New York.

Rugman, A.M., and A. Verbeke. 1992. Multinational enterprise and national economic policy. In P.J. Buckley and M. Casson, eds. *Multinational Enterprise in the World Economy.* Aldershot, England: Elgar: 194-211.

Sassen, S. 1991. *The global city.* Princeton: Princeton University Press.

Schott, T. 1986. Models of dyadic and individual components of a social relation: Applications to international trade. *Journal of Mathematical Sociology* 12: 225-49.

Sethi, S.P. 1994. *Multinational corporations and the impact of public advocacy on corporate strategy: Nestle and the infant formula controversy.* Boston: Kluwer Academic.

Smith, D.A., and D.R. White. 1992. Structure and dynamics of the global economy: Network analysis of international trade 1965-1980. *Social Forces* 70, 4: 857-93.

Smith, M.P., and J.R. Feagin, eds. 1987. *The Capitalist City*. Oxford: Blackwell.

Snyder, D., and E. Kick. 1970. Structural position in the world system and economic growth: A multiple network analysis of transnational interactions. *American Journal of Sociology* 84: 1096-1126.

Steiber, S. 1979. The world system and world trade: An empirical explanation of conceptual conflicts. *The Sociological Quarterly* 20: 23-36.

Thompson, W.R. 1983. Uneven economic growth, system challenges, and global wars. *International Studies Quarterly* 27: 341-55.

Thrift, N. 1987. The fixers: The urban geography of international commercial capital. In J. Henderson and M. Castells, eds. *Global Restructuring and Territorial Development*. Newbury Park: Sage.

Tolchin, M. and S. Tolchin. 1988. *Buying into America: How foreign money is changing the face of our nation*. New York: Times Books.

Wallerstein, I. 1980. *The modern world system*. New York: Academic Press.

__________. 1979. *The capitalist world economy*. New York: Academic Press.

__________. 1974. *The model of world system*. New York: Academic Press.

Webb, M.C. 1995. *The political economy of policy: International adjustment since 1945*. Ithaca: Cornell University Press.

Yan, S. 1995. *The Chinese reassessment of socialism, 1979-1992*. Princeton: Princeton University Press.

Zukin, S. 1992. The city as a landscape of power: London and New York as global financial capitals. In L. Budd and S. Whimster, eds. *Global Finance and Urban Living: A Study of Metropolitan Change*. London: Routledge: 195-223.

# Section Three: Effects of Globalization

Section three comprises chapters eleven to fifteen that collectively discuss the causes and effects of globalization by focusing on how the drivers of globalization come into conflict with it in the areas of foreign and economic policy. Also, the political economy of HIV/AIDS, the origin, development, and maturation of terrorism and its concomitant risks make globalization more complex. Evidently, the eruptive provocation of Islamist fundamentalism and its attendant effects on the global society, and the subsequent challenges associated with global enery security in a dangerous, transnationally globalized, and ideologically emdedded fundamentalist age complicate and weaken the frameworks for effective, putative, and rationalized globalization. The current crisis in the Middle East speaks volumes in this regard.

# Chapter XI
# Globalization and the Challenges of the New World Order

In antiquity, Medieval era, and Modernity, the forces which propelled i ividual nations to cross the seas searching for wealth and national prestige varied from civilization to civilization. However, during the last 500 years, Sir Walter Raleigh's principles of political economy have been used to successfully globalize the Anglo-American led World civilization. Raleigh singled them out by saying that "whoever commands the sea commands the trade; whosoever commands the trade of the world commands the riches of the world, and consequently the world itself"(Boydston, et al 2004, 26). During the last five centuries, European expansion and contact with the New World and the Old has helped the European nations to plant and transplant new values to the new "outposts in the global economy" (p. 26). Historically speaking, the manner in which the globalization project has evolved and acquired Spencerian individualistic tenets of competition, which functionally destabilizes the traditionally established homeostatic assemblage of social institutions, by creating more disequilbrial social segments of conflicted Marxist and neofascist nature, challenges itself with groups and communities that have, within it, strong ties to religious, historical, and civilizational traditions whose resistance contributes to destroying world empires.

Globalization, which is a form of modernization, is a technologically, politically, economically, psychologically and culturally integrated historical and contemporary movement whose neocolonial depth, breadth and complexity produces winers and losers. The movement civilizationally and in some aspects, spontaneously, transforms both the willing and unwilling human collectivities in order to refashion them for change. The processes through which globalization is animated, rationalized and assessed for change are inherently dialectical. Some of these processes have been viewed with disdain for destroying, in some cases, the sovereignty and evolutionary development of the Third World countries' institutions and their values. Though the use of technology for the international exchange, interconnectedness, and fusion of cultural, economic, and political universality benefits our wealthy northern neighbors, this system of capitalistic globalization intensifies closeness by eliminating distance and by encouraging exploitative interdependence (Ayeni 2003; Giddens 1996) and controlling local contextualties. Through this process, our experience over time and space is compressed and changed (Babari e 2001). To this end , globalization comes to dominate the totality of its processes, components, communities, individuals, and imperialistic contradictions.

Globalization is an historically chameleon-like paradigm that has partially caused the disintegration of the traditional global order of states. Twentieth century decolonization produced nation states or pseudostates that lacked solid institutions, internal cohesion, and national consciousness (Stanley Hoffman 2002). For instance, in the wake of the collapse of the USSR, Yugoslavia disintegrated into eight smaller territorial units whose historic animosity against each other exploded into the Balkan War during the 1990s. In Iraq, Sudan, Afghanistan, and Haiti, autocratic tyrants oppressed their peoples so much so that by design or accident, fighting broke out and demanded international intervention particularly from the U.S. Sometimes such expected humanitarian overtures run against the principle of national sovereignty, territorial integrity, and nonintervention. The intervention contributed to the fragmentation of states at the periphery of their internal, economic, cultural, political, and social integration-hence globalization.

On 9/11/2001, an "ill-defined, illusive and ... persuasive" (Teeple 2005) and poorly armed but determined transnational terrorist group effectively challenged, surprised, and wounded the only remaining and dominant World Superpower-the United States. This incident showed that the globalization project, regardless of its merits, has its own demerits in the sense that fanatics can create forms of violence because their terrorist influence tries to exacerbate war and thereby making interstate relations of the global society more risky. Therefore as many people and groups become global actors along with states, insecurity and vulnerability tend to rise. Francis Fukuyama's thesis about the "End of History" (ideology) and the triumph of economic and political liberalism of the twentieth century, in which secular religion fought bloody wars against each other, overlooked Samuel Huntington's (1997) narrow but accurate theoretical prediction that violence, emanating from international terrorism, anarchy, and islamo-fascism (Bush) originates in a fault-line climate of lack of common values and institutions of different civilizations rather than among liberal states and their ideologies.

In his book *From empire to community*, Amitai Etzioni argues that the "clash of civilizations" about which we do not have enough resources for waging it conclusively, should be avoided by cultivating a new world order that resembles the United States where Eastern and Western values of spirituality and moderate Islam can evolve to become competitive and globally accepted public philosophies. He adds by stating that transnational issues can be too overwhelming to the extent of side tracking our development. To avoid such a trapping route, nations should collectively establish building blocks in the new world order by fighting against terrorism, encouraging multilateral attempts for the deproliferation of WMD, strengthening humanitarian interventions, and supporting new supranational institutions including those that focus on internet governance. Cooperation is needed to validate basic safety and security, human rights and protection of the environment. Etzioni encourages moving away from the empire to establishing communitarian values which enhance the potentially prosperous futurity of human civilization. The progressive evolution of global governance, which is not only interesting but also original in its fundamentals, should place emphasis on the celebration of power oriented realism and law guided liberalism which wisely and thoughtfully help to constructively chart new directions in international relations. In the light of the current fragile social ecology, the values of shared humanity which Etzioni discuses are a new, visionary, and pragmatic synthesis which positively enhances global hope, optimism, and sustainability. Unlike Etzioni's optimistic intellectualization of globalization, Bhagwati, who is a professor of economics at Columbia, argues that those who are antiglobalization see no virtues except the vices and vincibilities of globalization. The trilogy of its discontents is composed of "the idea of capitalism, the process of globalization, and the behavior of corporations" (Bhagwati 2002). In other worlds, capitalism's triumphalism over twentieth century trilogy of fascism, communism, and socialism is no model for emulation particularly when it is deconstructed. Its destructiveness may have led to nihilistic and anarchical overtones evidenced in Iraq, Palestine, Sudan, and Lebanon.

Anne-Marie Slaughter of Princeton University has produced the book, *A New World order* (2004). As the Dean of Princeton's Woodrow Wilson School of Public and International Affairs, she firmly discusses that in the global age, governments work together through transcontinental networks. By so doing, they respond to the challenges of interdependence rather than through unilateral unipolarity. Interdependence connotes the self-evident universal realization of the emergence of a multi-polar world as opposed to the unipolar one. In their interdependence, these governments deal with a variety of issues such as organized crime, human rights, the environment, finance, and trade. To address these challenges, officials exchange information, coordinate policies, enforce laws, and regulate markets through increasingly elaborate intergovernmental channels as these states pursue their national interests. They do so in an anarchically and globally decentralized and less transparent environment. For instance, they use well mapped out networks for dealing with the activities of judges, regulators, and legislators of foreign counterparts and NGOS. Interestingly enough, the cooperation between national judicial powers and international and regional courts serve to globalize jurisprudence. In other words, the globalization project is not only a political and economic endeavor, but it is also a legal, educational, and cultural proposition that has become systematically and universally institutionalized. Groups, governments, and institutions have been "unbundled" because "things have fallen apart" (Achebe) and in place. Professor Slaughter concludes that the challenge of the global new world order lies in making the networks transparent, accountable "without ceding authority to potentially coercive centralized multinational organizations" (Ikenberry 2004).

In his book *Politics and passion: Toward a more egalitarian liberalism*, Micheal Walzer (2004) vehemently asserts that standard liberalism in which self-governing people deliberate and move freely in society tends to fail to come to grips with the pre-existing cultural, religious, and social associations that shape identities and choices by missing to detect or understa nd the deeper role of passion in democratic political order. In the light of this context, Walzer's concern is that "liberal theory's neglect of collective powerlessness, the problems posed by cultural marginality, the hierarchies of civil society, the politics of social conflict, and the force of passionate engagement renders the struggle against inequality more difficult" (Ikenberry 2005). In such a situation, social structures and political orders which sustain inequality can be effectively opposed only through political struggle that is driven by passionate intensity which liberals fear. In this case, Walzer has made one point clear; the social and cultural forces that sustain inequality in a justless polity are hidden in its hierarchically established institutional structures that are risky to unbundle, reprogram, and restructure even in modern democratic society in which the complex issues of diversity and multiculturalism equally compete with those of globalization and hegemonization.

Within such a global terrain, some states have become either too weak or have become failed social systems. The West does nothing to strengthen them. At times, the West engages them as humanitarian crises. With the increasing boundaryless globalization of terrorism, crime, and disease, the intensity of these problems, particularly when associated with the weak or failed states, tend to become first-order international issues and crises (Fukuyama 2004). Pessimistically, the weak state lacks strength or capacity for maintaining law and order and for protecting property rights. Often times, external actors pursue policies that weaken rather than strengthen the weak Third World political, social, and cultural institutions. Alternatively, developed nations tend to use neocolonial or mandate systems that come into conflict with the established global norms and values concerning sovereignty. In addition, though the West (U.S.. in particular) behaves as a global imperial power whose progressive historical force provides laws, order, and materialistic prosperity, the governance style of this last surviving empire is indirect and informal. The indirectness and informality of its governance system does not only protect people trapped in conflict and anarchy, but it creates an open and materialistic economy that it has globalized. This form of imperial capitalist modernization is sustainable. However, whenever the empire spreads its influence by using capitalist modernization and western religious and secular beliefs, it generates global conflicts. The twenty-first century Iraq war is a classic example. In other words, twentieth century British indirect rule in tropical Africa and the French assimilatory system of the same era were more effective colonial governance systems than the style which the U.S. had imposed in Iraq. That is the main reason for pessimism. In other words, U.S. development in Iraq seemed to generate more negative than positive reactions everywhere.

James Harding has described capitalistic globalization in the following terms: "It is wide in its tactics and ambition, violent and revolutionary on the edges, peaceful and reformist in the main. It rushes in often contradictory directions, anti-corporate and entrepreneurial, anarchist and nostalgic, technophobe and futuristic, revolutionary and conservative all at the same time" (Green and Griffith 2005, 319).

In *The global future: A brief introduction to world politics* (2005), Charles W. Kegley and Gregory A. Raymo have quoted Thomas Friedman (journalist) while defining globalization. They said that "globalization is the integration of everything with everything else. A more complete definition is that globalization is the integration of markets, finance and technology in a way that shrinks the world from a size medium to a size small. Globalization enables each of us, wherever we live, to reach around the world farther, faster, deeper and cheaper than ever before and at the same time allows the world to reach into each of us farther, faster, deeper and cheaper than ever before" (p. 254; Spiegel, et al. 2005, 313). These views of the global village stem from the notion that the world has become integrated and interdependent in spite of the digital divide through which the communications revolution is rationalized in terms of the technological "halves" of the Global North and the technological "have-nots" of the Global South (Kegley and Raymo 2007).

The integration of the world market place-WTO has 147 countries and 33 of them are under the observer list. Its regulative integration determines the states sovereign independence. As an intergovernmental organization, WTO lacks supranational powers (IGO) for consensual governance. Because each member state has veto power over rules, the organization is 'hyperdemocratic' rather than antidemocratic. It has a staff of 530 and a $78 million budget (p. 262). Global trade has outpaced the rate of world output.

There are four levels of globalization which measure the extent to which states are integrated into the globalized world. First, political engagement is the number of memberships in international organizations, foreign embassies hosted, and the United Nations Security Council missions in which each country participates. Second, technologically, how many internet users, internet hosts, and secure servers does the country have? Third, personally how many contacts, in terms of international travel, tourism, international telephone traffic, and cross border transfers does each person make in a particular nation? Fourth, economically, how is the nation globally integrated in trade and foreign investment, portfolio capital flows, and income payments and receipts (Kegley and Raymo 2007)?

"Capital flows internationally through loans by commercial banks and private creditors and through foreign direct investments (FDI) in businesses located in countries different from those of the investors" (p. 268). This kind of movement of capital across borders has been going on since 1860 but has accelerated since 1950. In the global political economy more money circulates in the Global North than in the 49 poorest countries of the Global South which only receive 0.5% to 1% of the total.

The question which scholars and policy makers ask is whether this is the ideal of the nation state. Most experts, particularly from the Third World argue that "nation states give their people identity, raise taxes, provide social safety nets, protect the environment and guarantee internal security" (p. 272). For these reasons and many others more, the nation state will be a weak but viable survivor that rationalizes its existence. The nation state will exist though multinational corporations, assemble goods, and heavily move them across the borders and provide legal accounting, advertising and computer consulting in a borderless world. Financial markets are dominated by private traders who control currency flows that are worth $1.3 trillion a day. Supranational institutions such as the UN, WTO, World Bank, and IMF have eclipsed the power of nation states because the former have a global bureaucracy accountable to none. The globalization movement has marginalized the poor countries and alienated them-hence delinkage (Sagini 2001).

Such a gloomy picture for Third World countries (LDC) also shows that over 300,000 children participate in wars as soldiers. Since 1400, about 2566 wars take place every 10 years with the exception of the period called the Thirty Years War of the 1600s. Most of these conflicts are in the South in which 38 of them were going on in 2002. Most of these conflicts are in a form of civil wars that exacerbate failed, splinter, and new states. If this trend continues unabated, the world will have about 500 states by 2025 (Keglay and Raymo 2007). Some of these conflicts are terrorist related and their incidence fluctuates periodically. For instance, in 1968 there were 174 terrorist incidents while in 1987 there were 666. The U.S. homicides in 2001 were 11,000 (*Office of the Coordinator for Counterterrorism, U.S. Department of State, 2002).*

Martin Wolf (2004) authored *Why globalization works*. He advocates outward oriented rather than protectionist policies of anti-globalizers for global development. For example, he supports outsourcing and offshoring as constructive elements of good economic growth policies because markets are open for foreign investment, international trade, and a variety of other financial transactions. Wolf dismisses contemporary critiques of free trade, the role of global multinational corporations (MNCs), and capital mobility. He argues that globalization policies help to raise standards of living particularly in China, India, and Mexico. However, he also shows that the ability of trade and investment to improve growth may be determined by poor governance. Poor governance performers have corrupt, predatory, or brutal governments that create civil wars resulting from competing war lords. In the Third World, particularly South America, neoliberal reforms including trade liberalization are disappointing because of the results of the globalization movement. Since the continent has overborrowed and since that overborrowing is accompanied by dolarization and structural adjustment policies of the past, these policies have caused the Latinos and Africans to experience vulnerable financial crises. Wolf also shows that rich countries such as the United States practice 'hypocrisy' and 'double standards' by setting trade barriers against poor countries while extremely lowering tariffs for the wealthy ones. This happens when the imposition of WTO rules and regulations are operationalized.

Largely due to the fact that developing countries do not participate in early negotiations in order to make arrangements on liberalizing subjects; they are burdened with higher tariff barriers imposed on industrial products that are produced by established capitalist competitors that are agents of globalization and its menu. In addition, developed countries massively subsidize their agricultural exports while developing countries do not. These subsidies, particularly those given by E.U., reduce the prices of exports of the Third World, particularly those from African countries and also reduce grants and loan concessions given to these countries by the metropolitan governments. Worst of all, these countries (33-45) import food and other agricultural products. The renewal of tariffs and subsides would hurt instead of helping the countries to raise the prices they pay for the imports. This lowers their export earnings and raises import purchases (Sagini 2001), contributing to their lowest standards of living in the world.

## WHY GLOBALIZATION WORKS: THE ECONOMIC PERSPECTIVE

Globalization can be understood through integrative analysis of the disciplines of anthropology, history, political science, religion, economics, sociology, and military science. According to political sociologist Charles Tilly, "globalization is and increases in the geographic range of locally consequential social interaction especially when that increase stretches a significant proportion of all interactions across international or intercontinental limits" (Tilly 1995, 1-2). No place is untouched, unfamiliar, and completely unknown to the rest of the modern or contemporary world. Globalization is the sale of currencies and government bonds in the world market; it is the outsourcing of computer manufacturing to China, India, and Mexico; the transnational terrorist conflict, the global diffusion of human rights, and the global production, distribution, and consumption practices (Kesselman 2007).

To define it, economists study the activities of transnational corporations, changes in technology, international trade and investment, and the flow of finance through permeable borders. Unlike economists, political scientists define globalization by "focusing on the role of states in facilitating or hindering transnational activities, as well as the role of international organizations such as the United Nations or International Monetary Fund" (p. 4) or the World Bank. Contrary to the professional definitions of globalization by political scientists, who largely reflect on how power is exercised by states, major international organizations, socialists and anthropologists define globalization by analyzing the "diffusion of culture as forms of globalization" (p. 4). Historians see globalization, contrary to other social scientists, as the ingredients of the rise and fall of great empires and other civilizations of historical antiquity, medievalism and the modern world. Obviously, and largely due to the increase in human population, advancement, and sophistication in modern technology and the evolution of the capitalist system, the past was less globalized in comparison with nineteenth and twentieth century's density of the globalization regimen. Major world wars, pandemics, economic depressions, and failures in technological advance tend to slow or eliminate the nature and character of particular forms of globalization. The globalization processes help to expand global capitalism. According to Polanyi, the main features of capitalistic globalization are as follows:

- Production is not carried on for immediate consumption by the producer but is intended for exchange ... in the market.
- Markets are arenas in which buyers and sellers voluntarily meet to exchange money for commodities on the basis of a mutually agreed-upon price.
- Goods are exchanged through sales in the market by producers to consumers. A sale involves a voluntary contract or agreement between producers and consumers/purchasers to exchange a commodity at a selling price... specified by the producer. Producers seek to reap the maximum possible gain/profit; consumers seek to purchase goods at the lowest possible price.
- Production is organized privately, rather than by public authorities...a decentralized among producers, organized in firms, which compete with each other in the market.
- The firm is divided between those who own and manage it, and those who receive wage or salary to perform productive work.
- The core elements of capitalism therefore are compromised, decentralized, privately organized, market-based production for profit, with production occurring by wage labor (Kesselman 2007, 5).

The Washington Consensus exemplifies neoliberal policies that expand functional global capitalism which tends to relatively support Third World political economies but spirally continues to animate globalization. The Washington policies which animate it include but are not limited to:

- Dismantling regulations passed in the postwar years that restricted business activity in the name of social and environmental goals.
- Reducing spending on social welfare, both to reduce government expenditures and to encourage citizens forcibly to seek private employment rather than relying on public support.
- Reducing corporate and personal income taxes.
- Privatizing a host of services, products, and functions that were formerly provided by government, in the area of telecommunications, water, education, prisons, transportation, and so on.

- Reducing tariff and nontariff barriers to international trade, investment, and other forms of capital mobility (e.g. currency exchanges) and
- Liberalizing international capital mobility, that is reducing restrictions on inward and outward flows of capital (p. 7).

The functional nature of global capitalism has extended social life markets in 'leisure' industry particularly the "restaurants, tourism, entertainment, computer and video games and dating services" (p. 8) all of which have become the second largest economic sector in the U.S.

## WHAT DRIVES THE INFLUENCE OF GLOBALIZATION?

Globalization is driven by or caused by the capitalist production processes, practices, and aspirations; public policies and collective identities and processes in the realm of industrial and information technology, international and internal migration, currency movements, ideas, communication, and culture (Kesselman 2007). In this case, globalization has been made "possible by transnational cooperation and coordination among scientists, engineers, and support staff and production workers throughout the world" (p. 8). Several clusters of organized actors tend to drive or propel globalization to higher levels of sophistication; these actors include but are not limited to:

- Powerful transnational corporations that serve as the engines of global economic integration.
- The United States and the International Institutions such as The World Bank (WB), International Monetary Fund (IMF), The World Trade Organization (WTO), The United Nations Organization (UNO), USA Foundations and Businessmen (USAFB), USA Communication Industry, Agents (USACIA), Americans Dominated International Companies (multinationals).
- The Western European Governments (WEG) or E.U.
- The Organization for European Cooperation and Development (OECD)
- The World Business Community for Sustainable Development (WBCSD)
- Capitalist Political Parties (CPP)
- Nongovernmental Organizations (NGO)
- States, organizations and associations (of citizens) and
- Powerful regions particularly Western Europe, North America and East Asia. All these are agents of globalization.

In the twentieth century, Lenin argued that imperialism was the last stage of capitalist development. However, he was wrong. In the twenty-first century it might be argued that globalization is the highest and last stage of capitalist and imperialistic development. Although it is regarded as the highest phase of humankinds development, its degree of development is asymmetrical rather than symmetrical, partial rather than impartial, unbalanced rather than balanced and uniquely, mercilessly, and wantonly exploitative. Globalization uses long, global, and sleeky tentacles which suck the life, blood, and sweat of the livelihood of peoples of the Third World. It has tendencies that economically impoverish, emotionally desensitize, culturally destroys, kill, and educationally retard and strangle, psychologically supplant and paralyze, politically fragment and disempower, developmentally satirize and psycho-spiritually and socially alienate - delinking. It also causes homelessness and cultural genocide.

Globalization contributes to global warming, droughts, irregular downpours, hurricanes, tornados, and depletion of vital resources such as petroleum, drinking water and forests for the benefit of a global minority of individuals, groups and nations. In particular, globalization contributes to the spread of HIV/AIDS, terrorism, poverty, new forms of slavery, outsourcing and offshoring, and affects women badly. It contributes to the stagnation of wages and salaries of lower income wage workers in the industrialized countries where top corporate executives, particularly in the United States are "paid $10.9 million a year or 262-500 times the average worker's earnings of 41,861, the Economic Policy Institute said" (*The Daily Oklahoman* June 25, 2006, 8c). While globalization from above is the process by which powerful people in "transnational corporations, governments and international organizations shape globalization," globalization from below is "the ways that people organized collectively in an attempt to influence the character of globalization" (Kesselman 2007, 11). The former originates globalization ideas, strategies, ways and means and ends, the latter is reactive, emotionally and politically rhetorical, and universally relatively powerless. The former is transcendant and visionary, the letter is constrained.

Despite the negative and challenging influences of globalization, New World Order thinkers feel that the movement "uploads stability, avoiding large scale war and discouraging the use of force in international relations. Other New World Order thinkers evaluate world order by a reference to certain widely shared values, such as "Wilsonian" ideals of peace, equity, rule of law, human rights, degrees of democratization and environmental protection"(Falk 2005, 307). The shapers of the NWO are powerful states, market forces and popular transnational movements. In other words, the new world order is globalization itself.

The global new world order advocates the global spirit of humane political governance. However, its inherent market forces, population explosion, a rising levels of consumption tend to push humankind toward the direction of unsustainable development. It is not easy to influence political leaders everywhere to create and implement policies that restrain consumption in order to reduce environmental degradation and climate change or greenhouse effect. Thomas Friedman and Robert Kaplan (2002), using a journalistic perspective, have argued that success in globalization is getting the fundamentals right. "It is not about the wires or about the bandwidth or about modems, it's about reading, writing and arithmetic. It's about churches, synagogues, temples, and mosques. It's about the rule of law, good governance, institution building, free press and a process of democratization. If you get these fundamentals right, then the wires will find you and the wires will basically work. But if you get them wrong, nothing will save you" (Spiegel, et al. 2005, 315).

Globalization, in the Third World, is the state in crisis situation in which states particularly the USSR became disoriented, discouraged, decayed from within, and failed by collapsing largely due to lack of creativity, ineffective technology, global alienation, containment and bureaucratic aloofness. The three major categories of globalization are those of (1) statists who understand the pros and cons of globalization and who are rooted in nation-state and international role of states within globalization, (2) alternatives who are 'anarchists' (p. 324) or deconstructionists who oppose market forces that encroach into their cultural and political niches, and (3) reformists who try to eliminate injustice and inequality by pacifically using gradual and peaceful means. They accept the role of the market which should be regulated to bring effective change. Top world leaders in government, industry, and the corporate sector belong to this third elitist group.

## Globalization – US Foreign Economic Policy after September the 11th

Barry Eichengreen is a Professor of Economics a Political Science at the University of California, Berkley. His thesis concerning global terrorism is interesting and paraphraseable. Unquestionably, the events of September 11th helped to shape the debate about globalization. A trend that many economists characterize as irresistible suddenly appears less so. Foreign assembly operations have become less attractive to US corporations now that there is the fact, or even the danger, that their trucks will be stuck in mile long queues at the US-Canada or US-Mexico border. Companies like McDonalds and Starbucks, whose main opportunities for market growth, are outside the US, now must factor in extra costs of security when contemplating opening another outlet abroad. Computer programmers from India and graduate students from the Middle East will face additional hurdles when attempting to obtain temporary residency in the US. American companies, in the wake of Western anti-islamofascism, will think twice about posting their executives abroad. Foreign trade, foreign direct investment, and international migration all will grow less quickly than they did before the terrorists' attacks in 9/11/2001.

All this is common sense. But it is also common sense not to push the argument too far. For one thing, there will be a strong incentive to invest in new technologies that will minimize disruptions to domestic and international business. We already use infrared scanners on certain trucks coming from Mexico and CAT scans on selected luggage at airports. More investments in such equipment will allow international traffic to move faster whether that traffic takes the form of trucks, container ships, or passenger airliners. Technologies that are hard to imagine now, precisely because they have not been invented yet, will help to move these lines even faster. The 60 percent rise in the prices of the stocks of security related companies in the four weeks following September 11th confirms that the incentive for their development is there.

International cooperation will work in the same direction. Vicente Fox, Mexico's President and Felipe Calderon have already proposed major investments in immigration control on Mexico's southern border, which will limit the burden on U.S. immigration officials, along the United States' own southern border (The Associated Press 2006). A survey of 250 Canadian CEOs, taken at the end of October 2001, similarly yielded an overwhelming consensus that the two neighbors should urgently agree on a common set of rules of immigration in order to protect Canadian access to the U.S. market. The three NAFTA partners have the largest investments in globalization of virtually any other country in the world. They have a strong incentive to make us see the relevant security zone, North America and not simply the United States.

The terrorists targeted the World Trade Center because it was a magnificent symbol of American capitalism and one of the most visible manifestations of American financial markets. Among the victims were large numbers of persons who worked for companies, foreign as well as domestic, whose business was international finance. This brings up the question of how international capital flows will be affected by these events. Clearly, bonds issued by countries that are on the front lines of the so called war against terrorism, Pakistan for example, can be regarded as even riskier than before. But there are plausible reasons for thinking that disembodied portfolio investment, as opposed to direct investment, will be stimulated rather than depressed by the attacks. Buying a bond of a foreign government or opening an American factory abroad or checking into the Intercontinental Hotel in the capital city of a country whose government is not a member of the Bush Administration's coalition against terrorism is less risky. There is still a big world economy out there. Investors still want "foreign exposure" in their internationally diversified portfolios. Arguably, portfolio investment will be even more attractive than before as a way of getting it.

The main impact on capital flows thus will not be on their level but on their composition and direction. Investors will have an even stronger incentive to differentiate among countries according to the strength of their economic, financial, and political institutions. One of the problems of the 1900s was that investors, in their enthusiasm for emerging markets, failed to differentiate adequately among destinations for their funds. Any new tendency for capital to flow more disproportionately to countries that have built relatively strong financial systems, political institutions and international alliances can only be a good thing from the point of view of financial stability. This will also sharpen the rewards for countries that build strong democratic institutions that deal with minorities in ways that minimize ethic strife, and that build bridges to their neighbors, since these will be the places where Americans will seek to invest. Of course, this also means that the gap between the haves and the have-nots will widen largely due to competitive globalization. More foreign investments have been flown to the first-tier countries of Eastern Europe, attracted by their democratic institutions and entry into the E.U. Investments in Sub-Saharan Africa, in contrast, have remained to be less attractive than before largely due to historical and traditional Western attitudes and perceptions about Africa and the Africans. However, recent massive and expansive Chinese investment in Africa may have drastically changed Western perceptions on the issue.

This new emphasis on politics, democratization, international politics in particular, means that investors will be paying special attention to the implications of recent events for International Monetary Fund assistance for emerging markets. The Obama Administration has continued to make it clear that it will use every weapon at its disposal in the fight against terrorism. The IMF is on such an instrument, like it or not, since the United States is the fund's largest single shareholder. This clearly enhances the prospects for multilateral assistance for frontline countries such as Turkey, which are now, due to the war on terror, too geopolitically important to be allowed to default on their debts. Geopolitically and geostrategically, Turkey is the West's gateway to the Middle East and vice versa.

Just as the Asian crisis ultimately forced Congress to acknowledge the need for an IMF quota increase, the current crisis highlights the need for the international financial equivalent of the FDNY. Thus, the extreme view on Capitol Hill that the IMF should be abolished is likely to be extinguished once and for all. On the other hand, the legitimacy of the IMF and its economic advice will not be enhanced if it is viewed by other countries, even more than before, as an instrument of U.S. foreign policy. Calls for reform of the institution's voting formulas and procedures to enhance the representation of developing countries are likely to be met in Washington by the response "possibly now." If the IMF becomes less of a politically enlightning pole here, the opposite is sure to be true in the developing world. The appointment of Paul Wolfowitz, former Assistant Secretary of Defense under George Bush Jr., as the Chairman of IMF and the architect of the U.S. Iraq War calls for reform even more.

The new enthusiasm for IMF programs will be only one manifestation of more outward looking for U.S. foreign economic policy. Clearly, it will be easier for the Obama Administration to make the case for Fast Track Authority to reward friendly countries with enhanced access to the U.S. market. It will push harder for debt relief for highly indebted poor countries in the hope that less debt will mean more growth and more growth will mean fewer disaffected religious fundamentalists. Progress in granting debt relief has been slowed by the perception, note entirely accurate, that it has budgetary costs for the OECD governments that are the principal creditors, and that blanket relief would penalize countries that had made serious efforts to reform while protecting spendthrift governments. These objections are likely to be shelved as a result of the new urgency attached to enhancing stability and restarting growth in the poorest countries.

What of foreign aid? Talk of a "Marshall Plan for Afghanistan" was examined. It was followed by arguments that the U.S. could not continue giving only pitiful amounts of aid to countries where young men seek refuge from grinding poverty and lack of opportunity in political and religious fanaticism which the President George Bush called Islamo-fascism. Some increase in U.S. foreign aid was viewed to be consequential. The Marshall Plan was most directly motivated by the eruption of the Cold War; some kind of "New Marshall Plan," could be confidently predicted and be proposed by the Administration in response to the war on terrorism. Although whether the U.S. would be prepared to devote two percent of its GNP over many years to such an initiative, as it did between 1948 and 1951, was another question.

The answer lied, in part, on what return we could expect on our investment. The Marshall Plan may have been a great economic and political success, but a reading of its history and the history of foreign aid generally cent ers on pessimism that its success can be replicated in many of the poorest countries today. Foreign aid has worked only where there has existed a domestic constituency for reform and where multilateral assistance tipped the balance in its direction. This was recognized by the IMF's early managing directors, per Jacobson, as early as 1959, when he observed that foreign assistance "can only succeed if there is the will in the countries themselves." Why, then, did Marshall Plan funds work after World War II to help bring about inflation stabilization, fiscal consolidation, a market friendly reform? The answer is that European governments were strongly predisposed to adopt these policies and the Marshall Plan tipped the balance by limiting the short run pain and sacrifices that had to be imposed on their constituents. Europe already had long experience with the market, which inclined toward the adoption of market friendly reforms. It had democratic governments with checks and balances that prevented aid from being diverted into the pockets of elites. Many European countries had single party governments or strong coalitions capable of credibly committing to the relevant reforms. Finally, given the geopolitical and economic conditions of Europe at the time, the Marshall Plan was the only hope for Europe. No wonder it worked.

Where, on the other hand, has foreign aid not worked? It has not worked where there did not already exist a strong domestic constituency for reform, where the government was weak and where democracy was absent or the government otherwise lacked the capacity to commit to the relevant reforms. Thus, scholars like Andrew Macintyre ascribe the failure of IMF assistance to produce quick results in Thailand in 1997-1998 to a flawed constitutional design that generated weak coalition governments and uncohesive political parties unable to commit to reform. They attribute the severity of Indonesia's crisis to the weakness of democratic institutions, which vested arbitrary decision making power in the hands of one person, Suharto, who could as easily change his mind to stay the reformist course.

These historical observations caution against exaggerated hopes that foreign aid conditioned on a laundry list of reforms and policies can play a major role in getting a postwar Afghanistan back into economic feet. They suggest relatively pessimistic conclusions about whether providing sustained U.S. aid as opposed to dropping dehydrated meals from the skies and hiring U.S. construction companies to rebuild bridges and airstrips, will do much to alleviate the problems of countries that have not yet succeeded in putting the relevant political and economic infrastructure in place.

It is known that much more needs to done about how to help developing countries that have already begun to take these steps. Abolishing restrictions on the scales of bananas to Europe and apparel to the U.S. can invigorate their exports, raise their rates of economic growth and help to create improved living standards for their masses. The Multifiber Agreement, an historical anachronism dating from 1974, continues to limit imports of textiles and apparel into the U.S. markets. If Congress is serious about addressing the problems of developing countries as a way of bringing them into the fold, it could start by abolishing the Multifiber Agreement. U.S. foreign economic policy cannot solve the problems of the entire world. Some parts will have to first begin to help themselves. But where they have done so, and where we have instruments that can usefully push the process along, it would be a crime not to do so.

As a transitive imperial and eclipsing system, globalization can be defined as a technologically, politically, economically, psychologically, and culturally integrated historical and contemporary movement whose global depth, breadth, and complexity produces winners and losers as it civilizationally transforms both the willing and the unwilling human collectivities in order to refashion them for the strategic needs and interests of contemporary civilizations.

## CONCLUSION

In this chapter, leading scholars have explained what globally happened and what needs to be done to chart new directions in solving global problems before they become too unbearable and unmanageable. The chapter has also defined globalization, shown why it works, what drives it, its inextricable relationship with U.S. foreign policy, and its domestic and global consequences.

The effects of globalization on global culture and development has been reviewed in order to establish the theoretical framework for logically, empirically, and theoretically rationalizing the naturalistic and analytic observations on how Western and largely American values in art, music, dance, culture, education, economics, and politics have penetrated arid, rural and urban cultures of the world, which they have relatively supplanted. As an ardent advocate of the preservation of global cultural stability, the author argues that cultural diffusion should be indigenized and strengthened in order to "buffer" the Foundations of global cultural heritage. Their dynamism and stability have been compromised by constantly being " attacked" by an intense, persistent and humongous nexus of international organizations such as the World Bank, U.N.O., I.M.F., WTO and other organizations that constantly serve the imperialistic and neocolonial interests of the globalization project. Third World Peoples are at "war" and they do not know how to win it particularly as they rely on "blunt" rural, village and urban tools and resources which are not sophisticated enough to withstand the challenges of globalization.

The author employs an interdisciplinary perspective to articulate, with an interdisciplinary bent, the challenges of the globalization project on global cultural, economic, political, and legal Foundations and society's institutions. It clearly shows that globalization is the realist, liberal and conservative Americanization(Westernization) of the world and Third World in particular. The globalization project is destructive because it causes fragmentation of society by exacerbating conflict, disunity and disbelief for material gain. It exacerbates the spread of HIV/AIDS, crime, slavery, and conflict. By so doing, the Third World has been rapidly marginalized and peripheralized in the predominantly multipolar world of capitalists. The globalization rhetoric of democratization is a functionalist and exogenous rather than an internally evolved and immanently articulated developmental strategy. Globalization and democratization are strategies the West uses to change the world; these strategies have been weakened by other cultures for changing their educational, artistic, aesthetic, and moral Foundations. Other continent's primordial values of privacy, respect for the elderly, obedience, honesty, and other tabooed customs and traditions which once protected the desert, village and the rural countryside, have lost their purity and innocence because the people's lives have been unbundled and left naked for the world to see.

Globalization is the fragmentary integration of everything with all other things through which "markets, finance, and technology" have been used to "compress" the world into the "interconnectedness" of its individuals, groups, companies, and countries" (Spiegel 2005, 2-3) that form the global village. Globalization is Westernization, secularization, democratization and capitalistic consumerism that organismically and distributively undermines the village, rural and urban societies of the Third World.

In the light of the human rights perspective, the fundamental and ethical rationality and ideology of capitalism and globalization do not honor humanity's rights. Global "capitalism" has outgrown human rights as the ethical and ideological precepts of an earlier stage in capitalist development...in this shift to global accumulation of capital the rights that once had a certain practical and theoretical validity for some are being more or less rapidly eclipsed, undermined, usurped and persuasively violated as a consequence of the expansion of the very system that gave rise to them" (Teeple 2005, XI).

Particularly, globalization has increased poverty in the Hispanic community in America. Poverty among blacks, though still high, declined and has come back. Among non-Hispanic whites, it held roughly steady. Health insurance coverage has also been affected. Since 1995, Hispanics account for about 78 percent of the increase in the uninsured. The bottom line: productivity gains and improvements in efficiency are going disproportionately to those at the top. We do not really understand why globalization has produced weaker unions, increasingly skilled jobs, frozen the minimum wage and the "winner-take-all society"; (CEOs, sports stars and movie celebrities getting big payouts) have been all cited as reasons. Costly employer-provided health insurance also squeezes take-home pay in the middle. What might the government do? The Bush administration's enthusiasm for tax cuts for the rich could be tempered to reduce the budget deficit. The taxes could be raised without dulling economic incentives. Equally, liberals and others who support lax immigration policies across our Southern border should understa that these policies deepen U.S. inequality. But many familiar proposals would be mostly symbolic or hurtful. Raising the minimum wage might directly affect only about 5 percent of workers and might destroy some jobs. Protectionism might save a few well-paid jobs but would inflict higher prices on those least able to afford them. Still, no one should be happy with today's growing economic inequality. It threatens America's social compact, which depends on a shared sense of wellbeing.

Though, to some globalists, the phenomenon "Globalization" means the emergence of supranational institutions whose decisions shape and constrain the policy options of any particular nation-state. For others, it is the overwhelming or superseding impact of global economic processes, including processes of production, consumption, trade, capital flows and monetary interdependence (Nicholas and Carlos 2000). To others, it is the removal of barriers to trade and integration of national economies and its potential as a force for reducing poverty levels in the world (Carlos and Roberto 2004). To some other scholars, it implies the emergence of new global cultural forms, media and technologies of communication, which assist to reshape the relations as well as interactions of identity and interaction within and across local cultural settings (Derrick 2004). Others look at it as the linkage among nations as well as the social system; for others, the phenomenon is primarily a perceived set of changes, a construction used by state policy makers in accordance with rules, regulations, and procedures establishing the international order or system and for which global institutions (IMF/ World Bank) were established to ensure the smooth and orderly functioning of the system (Adam 2004; Vinayak 2004).

Some social scientists, however, perceive globalization as a process. For example, Castells (1998) pointed out that three of such processes are essentials, independents, that coincide. These are information technology revolution, the restructuring arising from the economic crises of capitalism and statism and finally, the upsurge of social movements like feminism, human rights etc. Aina (2002) buttresses this view by describing what constitutes the key components of the globalization process as follows:

- The emergence of time-space compressed interdependent world,
- The emergence of a new world order, i.e. a shift from bi-polar to unipolar, and ultimately, multipolar world,
- The emergence of a new international division of labor in the context of the polarized global economy seeking to integrate all local economies through trade liberalization and deregulation etc.,

- The emergence of a new flow of persons, cultures, ideas, and funds (finances),
- The emergence and spread of new technologies particularly IT and their transnationalization and integrative capacities on markets etc.
- The increasing significance of knowledge and information for production, culture, and economy (pp.14), and
- The spread and emergence of new diseases such as HIV/AIDS.

The point therefore is that some see globalization as a new era with greater advantages that promise interconnections in terms of cultures, education, politics, economy, trade, health and so on while others see it as a process of transformation or remaking of our world (a constructionist notion) at various levels: political, economic, military, labor etc. through the flows that enhance interdependence. In this sense, globalization may be seen as flows (cultural, linguistic, social, economic etc.) in the form of penetrations (usually from stronger to weaker nations) and counter-penetrations from equi-influential as weaker nations and countries to strong ones. It may therefore be unidirectional (where there is no counter-penetration or there is a weak response) or bi-directional.

Globalization is a "declaration of war" upon all other cultures. In culture wars, there is no exemption for civilians; there are no innocent bystanders. Why should it be expected that ancient and rooted civilizations are going to accept this peripheralization without a struggle? The answer to that is that globalization carries an implicit promise that will relieve poverty as global capitalism will create wealth; it is assumed that this priority must sweep aside all other human preoccupations, including all existing institutions, interpretations, and searches for meaning in the world. Globalization has therefore introduced a sub-cultural transfusion, such cultural imperialism could be described as Americanization of other cultures and vice versa.

## REFERENCES


Adewale, S.A. 2005. Culture and Socialization. In Ajiboye, J.O. and Omolade, Z.A., eds. *Fu ndmental themes in social studies and education*. Nigeria. Lucky Odoni Enterprises.

Aina, Tade. 1997. *Globalization and social policy in Africa: Issues and research directions*. Working Paper Series 6/96, Dakar: Codesria.

Ajayi, S.I. 2003. Globalization and African's dilemma: The myth and the reality. *Nigerian Tribune*: 23-26.

Alexara, M., and H.T. Jonathan. 2000. Functionalism and structuralism. In Borgatta, E.F. and R.J.V. Montgomery, eds. *Encyclopedia of sociology*, 2 ed., vol. 2. New York. Macmillan.

Ake, Claude. 1995. The new world order: The view from Africa. In Holm HansHerick a G. Sorense, eds. *Whose world order: Uneven globalization and the end of the cold war*. London: Westview Press.

Ayaale, E.A. 1998. *African renaissance: The cultural dimension.* A paper presented at the symposium on the African Renaissance to celebrate the 80th birthday of President Nelson Mandela.

__________. 1974. *The educated elite in the Nigerian society.* Nigeria. Ibadan University Press.

Ayeni, M.A. 2003. Moral education and globalization. *Nigerian Journal of Educational Philosophy* 10, 1: 28-35.

Awoniyi, T.A. 1978. *Yoruba language in education: An historical survey 1800-1974.* Nigeria. Ibadan. OUP.

Awonusi, Segun. 2004. Globalization and hegemonic English in Nigeria: Identity conflicts and linguistic pluralism. In Duro Oni, Susan Gupta, Tope Omoniyi, Efurosibina Adegbija, and Segun Awonusi, eds. *Nigeria and globalization.* Centre for Black and African American Arts and Civilization (CBAAC): 85-102.

Babarie, Kola. 2001. Globalization and its challenges for educational theorizing in Africa. *Nigerian Journal of Educational Philosophy* VIII, 1: 103-10.

Bagudo, A.A. 2003. Technologies for global educationandthe challenges of enhanced educational delivery in Nigeria. *Nigeria Journal of Educational Philosophy* 10, 1: 79-87.

Byrne, Richard. 2006. At annual meeting, political scientists explore mechanisms of powers. *The Chronicle of Higher Education* LIII, 4, September 15: A16.

Bhagwati, J.N. 2002. Coping with antiglobalization: A trilogy of discontents. *Foreign Affairs* January/February.

Boydston, J., et al. 2004. *Making a nation: The United States and its people.* Upper Saddle River, NJ: Prentice Hall.

Carlos, T., and H. Roberto. 2004. Rock art, education and identity. In Los Andes province of Chile File: //A:/Ar% 20 Rock, 5 20 Education, % 20 Identity, % 20 Chilie. November 2, 2005.

Castells, Manuel. 1998. *The information age, economy, society, and culture: E of the millennium,* Vol. III. Blackwell Publishers.

Crutsinger, Martin. 2006. U.S. trade gap hits record high: Exports near 4th peak, but imports climb more. *The Oklahoman* Wednesday September 13: 6B.

Derrick, L.C. 2004. Globalization, knowledge, education, and training in the information age. File://A:/ Globalization Knowledge, Education and Training htm. November 2, 2005.

Enemuo, P.C. 2002. An analysis of globalization, privatization and commercialization and the challenges to Nigeria Education system. *Nigerian Journal of Educational Philosophy* 9, 1.

Etzioni, A. 2004. *From empire to community: A new approach to international relations.* Palgrave Macmillan.

Fidelix, O. 2001. Globalization as imperialism: The Nigerian experience. In Odion-Akhaine, ed. *Globalization, United Nations and the fringe players.* Lagos, Nigeria: Centre for Constitutionalism and Demilitarization.

Finjal, N. 2001. Globalization, social development and United Nations. In Odion-Akhaine, ed. *Globalization, United Nations and the fringe players.* Lagos, Nigeria: Centre for Constitutionalism and Demilitarization.

Friedman, T.L. 1999. *The lexus and the olive tree: Understanding globalization.* New York: Farrar, Straus and Giroux.

Fukuyama. F. 2004. *State-building: Governance and world order in the twenty-first century.* Ithaca: Cornell University Press.

Gibbons, M. 1998. *Higher education relevance in the twenty-first century*. Paris: UNESCO World Conference on Higher Education.

Good, W.H. 1964. World cultural anthropology and linguistics. In L. Dellvine, ed. *Languages in culture and society*. New York. Harper Row.

Hoffman, S. 2002. Clash of civilizations. *Foreign Affairs* July/August.

Huntington, S.P. 1997. *The clash of civilizations: A the remaking of world order*. New York: Simon and Schuster.

Ikenberry, G.J. 2005. In praise of empires: Globalization and order. *Foreign Affairs* January/February.

__________. 2004. A new world order. *Foreign Affairs* May/June.

Kanagy, C.L., and D.B. Kraybill. 1999. *The riddles of human society*. Thousand Oaks, C.A.: Pine Forge Press.

Kegley, C.W., and G.A. Raymo . 2005. *The global future: A brief introduction to world politics*. Thomas Wadsworth.

Kesselman, M. 2007. *The politics of globalization: A reader*. Boston: Houghton Mifflin Company.

Kiplagat, B.A. 2006. Speech for the inauguration ceremony of the chancellor, James K. Tuitoek. *Egerton University* January, 31.

Kivuva, L.A. Secondary education reform in Kenya: The question of access quality and equity.

Lal, D. 2004. *In praise of empire: Globalization and order*. New York: Palgrave Mcmillian.

Love, M.C., ed. 2007. *Beyo sovereignty: Issues for global agenda*. Thomson Wadsworth.

Maduagwu, M.O. 2003. The phenomenon of globalization and African response: A cultural perspective. In M.O. Maduagwu and V.C. Onu, eds. Fulbright Alumni (Nigeria) Book of Readings. No. 1: *Globalization and national development in Nigeria.*

Maritian, J. 1943. *Education at the crossroads*. New Haven: Yale University Press.

McGurk, H. 1975. *Growing and changing*. Lo on: Methuen & Co.

Mestenhauser, J. 2006. *Rethinking campus internationalization. International: Michigan State University* 7, Spring: 10-11.

Momoh, A., and D. Seteolu. 2001. Economic globalization and the African economies: Development, depe ency, or marginalization. In Odion-Akahine, ed. *Globalization, United Nations and the fringe players*. Lagos, Nigeria: Centre for Constitutionalism and Demilitarization.

Nations of the World. 2002. *A political, economic and business handbook*. Grey-House Publishing.

Nicholas, G.B., and A.T. Carlos. 2000. *Globalization and education: An introduction*. London: Routledge. November 2, 2005.

Odor, P.C.P. 2002. *Understanding globalization and opposing its evils form "globalism" to "globalization"*. Lagos: Gal Publisher.

Ogunteade, Olufemi. 2003. African renaissance in global trap. *Africa Insight* 33, 3: 20-7.

Otakpor, N. 2003. Education and organization. *Nigerian Journal of Educational Philosophy* 10, 1: 6-13.

Oni, A. Adesoji. 2003. Globalization: A menace to African values and education. *Zimbabwe Journal of Educational Research* 15, 1.

Panagariya, A. 2004. The miracles of globalization. *Foreign Affairs* September/October.

Risser, P. 2006. Not your granddad's university. *The Daily Oklahoman* Friday July 28: 13A.

Ritzer, G. 2000. *Sociology theory*. Singapore. The McGraw-Hills Companies.

Rodney, W. 1972. *How Europe underdeveloped Africa.* Lo on: Bogle-L Ouverture Publications.

Sagini, M.M. 2006. *Strategic planning and management in public organizations.* Lanham, MD: University Press of America, Inc.

_________. 2006. HIV/AIDS: The Triadic Triplets. *Journal of Scholarly and Scientific Perspectives* 2.

_________, ed. 2004. Sustainable development. *Journal of Scholarly and Scientific Perspectives* 1.

_________. 2001. *Organizational behavior: The challenges of the new millennium.* Lanham, MD: University Press of America, Inc.

_________. 1996. *The African and the African American University: A historical and sociological analysis.* Lanham, MD: University Press of America, Inc.

_________. 1983. *A study to analyze Kenya's higher education goals between 1962 and 1982, and their implications for the University of Eastern Africa.* Berrien Springs: Andrews University of Graduate Studies.

Saitoti, E.G.H. 2005. *The release of 2004 KCSE examination results. Republic of Kenya: Ministry of Education, Science and Technology.* Nairobi: Jagoo House.

Salami, N. 2001. *Sociology of education.* Lagos & Ibadan: Olu Akin Publishers.

Samuelson, R. 2006. Rising economic inequality. *The Oklahoman* Wednesday September 27:10A.

Sanda, A.O. 1992. *Lectures on the sociology of development.* Ibadan and Lagos: Facts Fi ers International.

Schotler, J.H. 2000. *Political reaction to globalization.* Lo on: Sage.

Scott, J.C. 2006. The mission of the university: Medieval to postmodern transformations. *The Journal of Higher Education* 77, 1:1-39.

Seabrook, J. 2004. *Localizing cultures.*

Slaughter, A.M. 2004. *A new world order.* Princeton: Princeton University Press.

South Centre. 1996. *Liberalization and globalization. Drawing conclusions for development.* Geneva: South Centre.

Spiegel, S.L., et al. 2005. *Readings in world politics: A new era.* Thomas Wadsworth.

Teeple, G. 2005. *The riddle of human rights.* Ontario, Canada: Garamo Press Ltd.

The Associated Press. 2006. Mexico declares president elect. *The Oklahoman* September 6: 11A.

Tilly, C. 1995. Globalization threatens labor's rights. *International Labor and Working Class History* Spring:1-2

Tuitoek, J. K. 2006. Becoming Egerton University: An eternal journey: *Inauguration Ceremony* Tuesday, January 31.

Vagos, S. 1996. *Social change. United States of America.* Prentice-Hall, Inc.

Vinayak, S.D. 2004. *Globalization and cultural dimensions.*

Walzer, M. 2004. *Politics and passion: Toward a more egalitarian liberalism.* New Haven: Yale University Press.

Waters, M. 1995. *Globalization.* London: Routledge, Key Ideas series.

Williams, Robin. M. Jr. 1965. *American society: A sociological interpretation.* 2nd ed. New York: Knopf.

Wolf, M. 2004. *Why globalization works.* New Haven: Yale University Press.

# Chapter XII
# The Political Economy of HIV/AIDS

This theoretical and interdisciplinary chapter is an historical, political, economic and sociological analysis concerning the origin, development, and effects of HIV/AIDS in Africa and elsewhere. Though an etiological and phylogenetic analysis would have been more appropriate for this approach, the culturally, sociologically and economically emphasized interpretive conclusion is an honest admission of the ignorance that imperial creators of knowledge impose on researchers, scientists, policy makers, thinkers, and society in order to rationalize, control, predict, and theorize about laboratory experiments which need not to have existed in the first place and whose results ratify the mission and motives of the drugs industry and scientific and political establishment.

## HIV/AIDS Related Theories of Political Economy

Currently, "only two structures of approximately 20 or 30 proteins of HIV-1 have been determined and none from the related viruses HIV-2, HTLV-1, HTLV-11 and SIV?" (Duesberg 1996). The atomic structures of HIV and SIV related retroviruses may provide new knowledge on the functions of many virus components that are necessary for the development of new vaccines, therapies and diagnostics. Although some scientists such as Carter and McKenzie believe that structural biology is the biotechnological linchpin for research in HIV/AIDS, other scientific disciplines such as chemistry, advanced x-ray crystallography and physics should be used to search for the cure of the modern plague which is also extremely pandemic. This introductory note advocates the use of interdisciplinary scientific disciplines to search for the permanent cure and elimination of "death." The implications of such scientific inability to provide viable results for human survival and longevity are being discussed pessimistically in the context of modern and contemporary discourses of history, sociology, and political economy.

The term "political economy" is derived from politics and economics. Economics is acting in certain ways. Politics is a platform from which action takes place. Economics rationalizes what is done and why. Politics is a context for doing and acting. Sometimes economics is about an existing activity excluding market institutions, though such exclusion may not fully define the term without the latter. Economically, market institutions tend to satisfy human wants better than any others that are known and thereby making them more dominant than politics, which is subordinate to them – economics. Politics means "who gets, what, when, and how" (Lasswell 1936). It is "the struggle for power" (Morgenthau 1948). Politics is "the art and science of government" and "the socialization of conflict" (Schattschneider 1960). Politics is "the authoritative allocation of values" (Easton 1953). Evidently, it is "pure conflict" (Schmitt, 1976) and "the conciliation of conflicting interests through public policy" (Crick 1962; Caporaso and Levine 1997, 8). For instance, after the 2004 presidential elections in the USA, we witnessed how morality, i.e., values, militarism and ideas about economic rationality, were explained to defeat intellectual elitism and the afflicted voices of hope and humility. Through the struggle for power, in which conflict was socialized, the winning regime was authoritatively authorized to allocate values or resources through the conciliation of a variety of interests in the realm of political economy.

In real life there are many major theoretical approaches to the study and application of political economy whose diverse views influence organization theory and political practice and vice versa. The theoretical approaches have a variety of assumptions, stage actors, and different explanatory, interpretive and inferential issues. Political economy is a structure of national and international dependence in terms of division of labor. The system is held together by exchange contracts among legally independent property owners (the market economy). These property owners have property rights, which the political system legally protects (Sagini 2001). Specifically, seven theories of political economy are highlighted.

First, classical economists associate the term "political economy" with the unlimited but satisfied wants that exist in a world of scarcity and competition. To satisfy people's wants, society is depoliticized because politics is eroded with the rising dominance of the autonomous and self-interested primitive capitalists who dominate Third World economic and political markets. The state defines how production and distribution of the wealth among classes is to be conducted. The economy is mercantilist in character. Second, Marxists argue that politics and economics can be connected by using revolutionary activity to transform political and economic structure, social democratic politics and the Marxian state model, whose radicalism is anti-competitive market, anti-democracy and anti-free enterprise. Their production goals are based on satisfying needs rather than wants. Planning is centralized and production and distribution are collectivized. The theory emphasizes partial rather than holistic inclusion of the state. The state coercively emerges to resolve the irreconcilable contradictions in society, which the pre-capitalist and capitalist classes fail to deal with. This theory contributed to the collapse of the Soviet Union largely due to the latter's lack of creativity and destruction of competitive genius. Marxism is a living intellectual reservoir that exists only as a radical school of thought and critique of the organizing principle of the capitalist system and its liberal, sociological, conservative and competitive values including those of the market. Evidently there is inevitable and considerable tension between economics and politics in both classical Marxism and modern capitalism. In Marxism, the tension is contradictory, irreconcilable and eventually destructive of itself and its political economy.

Third, the end of the classical period was epitomized by the classical and Marxian models, which were replaced by the neoclassical economic theory of marginalism during the 1870s. Neoclassical economic theory of laissez faire was a shift from the fascination with class categories to the concern with individualism through which the individual selfishly sought productive utility in the areas of consumption and profit maximization. The individual's self-seeking behavior is manifested in both perfect and imperfect competitive settings of the market. In itself, individualism has been viewed as a form of liberal political philosophy where the individual has "a commitment to personal initiative, self-sufficiency, and material accumulation. This principle upholds the superiority of private-enterprise economic system and includes the idea of the individual as the foundation of society" (Petterson 2000, 4). Within neoclassical political economy, politics becomes deterministic when market failure prevails. In other words, in such an arena self-seeking, particularly that of the state, can enter non-market institutional and organizational domains in order to "provide public goods, correct externalities, and solve collective action problems through coercion" (Caporaso and Levine 1997, 219). Within the neoclassical economic realm, market economics lacks the full potential for productive exploitation. As a result, economics fails to reconcile the relationships between wants and means. Such failure caused the Great Depression of the 1930s when FDR used New Deal and Keynesianism to involve political leadership in the circular flow including the securing of incomes and investment to challenge the failed creativity of specialization and capital markets. In other words, human needs and wants cannot be satisfied under neoclassical economic theory unless creative and bold transformational leadership introduces regulatory measures that become the checks which balance the viability of neoclassical economic theory of the market-driven society.

Fourth, neoclassical economic ideas, in the form of rational self-interest, have been extended into the political arena. Rational self-interest is used to analyze politics. "Neoclassical political economy, with its focus on the state's role in market failure, offers a way to complete the liberal project in one direction" (p. 220). In other words, rationality is used to analyze the market in order to enhance the political economy and uplift the state's interest and stake in it. For instance, currently the Clinton Foundation has been working with the governments of South Africa, Mozambique, Tanzania and Rwanda. These countries are likely to possess one-third of all Africa's AIDS cases. The same foundation has worked with the Caribbean nations of Haiti, the Dominican Republic, the Bahamas, Jamaica and Eastern Caribbean states. These nations account for 95% of the AIDS cases in this region, which is also second highest infected region in the world. Lately, the Clinton Foundation also has begun work in China. Other organizations that are members of the Clinton Foundation include Columbia University Institute, Harvard Medical School Division of AIDS, Health Alliance International at the University of Washington, Medecins Sans Frontieres, Pangaea Global AIDS Alliance, Partners in Health, PharmAccess International, University Research Corporation (Magaziner 2004) and Brown University Medical School. These organizations share the experiences and results concerning the HIV/AIDS scourge. The Presidents' Foundation has donated ten million dollars.

The suppliers with which the Clinton HIV/AIDS Initiative and Care Consortium deals with are Aspen Pharmacare Holdings Ltd., Cipla, Ranbaxy Laboratories Ltd., Hetero, and Matrix Laboratories Ltd. The Pharmaceutical companies involved include Bayer Diagnostics, Beckman Coulter, Inc., Becton, Dickinson and Company, BioMerieux and Roche Diagnostics. The donor governments, which give money directly to the recipient nations are those of Canada, Ireland, Norway, Sweden, and the U.K. Later, the Clinton Consortium plans to get support from more countries. In consonance with the theories of political economy, some of the strongest pharmaceutical industries, which are dominated by the conservative economic and political elite, are rationally opposed to President Clinton's effort for economic, globalization and exploitative reasons.

In his book *Disease and democracy: The industrialized world faces AIDS*, Peter Baldwin uses a comparative approach to discuss the politics of public health issues in advanced Western countries. He paradoxically argues that while nations such as the U.S., Sweden and others undertook a variety of interventionist strategies to combat the disease both at home and abroad, France and Germany employed a laissez faire attitude about the suffering and dying millions. Although the two European nations were largely less involved for ideological reasons, the reality of their behavior is better explained in the light of historical and colonial experience in which the "path dependence" model was reinforced. The author vividly demonstrates that public debates on the pandemic were highly politicized. In France, Switzerland and the United Kingdom, policy on AIDS was removed from public opinion and political discourse. Surprisingly enough, knowledge about the economic, psychological, social and medical costs of the disease was utilized to galvanize society to willingly and legitimately integrate the Western gay community into its social and cultural institutions.

The last three theories of political economy are power-centered, state-centered and justice-centered. The power centered theory sees relations of power and domination in the market to be existing between the market and the state and within the state itself. Economic agents who include firms and pressure groups may challenge the state by voting and lobbying over the political process, economic agencies and consumers. Since power is almost everywhere within the political and nonpolitical spheres of the state, to address the state's interest and the interest of citizens, policy analysis, including the one on HIV/AIDS, should be more focused rather than being broad and generalized. In the metropoles, since HIV/AIDS largely resides within the province of marginalized groups, HIV/AIDS policy can be brief and highly generalized. That is why the problem is not a major issue in Western political campaigns. State-centered theories of central political institutions can define politics decisively. Since politics is what the state does in and with society, this may involve the "regulation of the economy and economic actors, the effect of the economic actors on the state policy, distributional effects of policy on economic resources, and traditional macroeconomic policy along Keynesian lines" (p.220). Finally, the justice-centered approach concentrates on fairness and rights instead of concentrating on individualistic efficiency. Justice is not an historical accident; it is a politically, legally, and morally definitive state policy for reconstructive economic and political practice. In the light of such an understanding of political economy, including the HIV/AIDS policy, the problem may or may not be rationalized through a political process for sound economic planning and distribution (Grosh 1999). All these theories, or most of them, place emphasis in market and state domination over the individual, who is also self-centered and rational enough to maximize certain choices for personal rather than societal gain. Globalization, which is a form of neocolonialism, means capital crossover, raw materials, brain drain and currency flows tend to weaken the economic, social and cultural social fabric of Third World peoples more than that of the systems of the people of Japan, Western Europe and the Anglo-American world where the HIV/AIDS pandemic is less highly pronounced (see Table XII:1).

Tables XII.1 and XII.2 show that HIV/AIDS significantly increased in all the nine or ten regions of the world during the last three years. Currently, the Sub-Saharan African region leads the world with the highest cases of HIV/AIDS seroprevalence. The region has over 10 % of the world's population. Of nearly 40 million infected, 60% are Sub-Saharan inhabitants while 40% live in other regions of the world. In 2006, more than 65 million were infected with HIV and more than 25 million have died while 15 million children are orphans. Some regions have higher concentrations of HIV infection than others. In East Africa, Uganda reduced its HIV/AIDS prevalence because it used technologically-advocated prevention measures that were financed by the United States. However, U.S. strategies that encourage abstinence are neither popular nor effective in the region. In Southern Africa, 10-12.6 million people are infected and most of them are women. All over Africa, the 15-24 year- olds show that for every 36 women living with the disease, 10 young men remain to be their counterparts as both groups struggle for survival. Transmission is largely through heterosexuality.

Table XII.1. AIDS/Living and Dying with AIDS

| Region | Living with HIV/AIDS | Newly Infected in 2000 | Deaths in 2000 |
|---|---|---|---|
| Sub-Saharan Africa | 25,300,000 | 3,800,000 | 2,400,000 |
| South and Southeast Asia | 5,800,000 | 780,000 | 470,000 |
| Latin America | 1,400,000 | 150,000 | 50,000 |
| North America | 920,000 | 45,000 | 20,000 |
| Eastern Europe and Central Asia | 700,000 | 250,000 | 14,000 |
| East Asia and Pacific | 640,000 | 130,000 | 25,000 |
| Western Europe | 540,000 | 30,000 | 7,000 |
| North Africa and Middle East | 400,000 | 80,000 | 24,000 |
| Caribbean | 390,000 | 60,000 | 32,000 |
| Australia and New Zealand | 15,000 | 500 | 500 |
| Total | 36.1 million | 5.3 million | 3.0 million |

*Source:* Rachel Zimmerman and Michael Waldholz, *The Wall Street Journal*, The U.N. Plots a War on AIDS, 2001.

Table XII.2.HIV/AID World Statistics, 2004

| Region | People Living with HIV | New Infections | AIDS Deaths | Adult Prevalence % |
|---|---|---|---|---|
| Sub-Saharan Africa | 25.4 million | 3.1 million | 2.3 million | 7.40 |
| Asia | 8.2 million | 1.2 million | 540,000 | 0.40 |
| Latin America | 1.7 million | 240,000 | 95,000 | 0.60 |
| North America and Western and Central Europe | 1.6 million | 64,000 | 23,000 | 0.40 |
| Eastern Europe and Central Asia | 1.4 million | 210,000 | 60,000 | 0.80 |
| Middle East and North Africa | 540,000 | 92,000 | 28,000 | 0.30 |
| Caribbean | 440,000 | 53,000 | 36,000 | 2.30 |
| Oceania | 35,000 | 5,000 | 700 | 0.20 |
| Total | 39.4 million | 4.9 million | 3.1 million | 1.10 |

*Source:* www.unaids.org Joint United Nations Programme on HIV/AIDS (UnAids) 2005.

In populous Southeast Asia, national HIV infection cases are small compared to those of the Sub-Saharan African region. The disease has spread to all the 31 provinces of China where selling blood plasma, paid sexual favors and injecting drug use are common. In Japan, men who have sex with other men tend to transmit the virus to female sex partners. The empowerment of leadership and the forging of partnerships can be scaled up to target injecting drug users and sex workers in order to prevent the escalation of the disease. In Oceania, the Caribbean and Western Europe, the HIV/AIDS concentrations are found in people of African descent. While transmission in New Zealand continues to be associated with sexual intercourse between men, and unlike Latin America, transmission is largely heterosexual in the Caribbean, particularly in Haiti, Jamaica, and the Dominican Republic. In Cuba, the communist government's policy of quarantining and the universal free access to antiretroviral therapy have made infection rates almost non-existent. In terms of care and treatment, the Caribbean region places emphasis on strong and better governance that utilizes resources cost-effectively to strengthen health care systems. Monitoring and evaluation systems that use strategic information to enhance cooperation are encouraged. Leadership should be empowered by using the strategic planning tactics, information sharing, involvement and partnership building. The money from Global Fund and the World Bank is used to promote care, treatment and prevention strategies.

In North America, AIDS is found among the three highest causes of death in the African American community in which 25-54 year old men and 35-44 year old women are mainly the victims. Of the U.S. women affected, 72 % are African Americans. The medium of transmission comprises injecting drug use, sex between men, and the practice of heterosexuality that is characterized by undisclosed risk behaviors. However, in Canada unsafe sex between men, injecting drug use, and unsafe heterosexuality are not uncommon. Between one-quarter and one-third of African Americans in America are poor people. Most HIV/AIDS victims are poor. Such kind of victimization of African-Americans is exacerbated by "their low incomes, high incarceration rates, particularly for men; injecting drug use, and unprotected sex in prison institutions" (http://www.unaids.org 2005).

In North Africa and the Middle East, the medium of transmission includes paid sex, sex between men, and injecting drug use. Sudan has the highest HIV/AIDS infection rate that is predominantly transmitted via heterosexuality. In Eastern Europe and Central Asia, the number of HIV/AIDS cases has increased nine times in ten years. Ukraine and the Russian Federation are the leaders in this pandemic in which 80% of the infections are found among people who are less than 30 years old. The strategies employed to confront the pandemic include "fostering partnership forums, supporting emerging organizations of people living with HIV, facilitating access to financial resources, generating and for harmonized monitoring-and-evaluation systems." Though antiretroviral medication is rather expensive, the strategies of better treatment and perestroika-openness (Sagini 2001) are in demand to eradicate taboos and denials that challenge prevention efforts.

The Southeast Asian region has a variety of AIDS comparable to the pandemic experience of the Sub-Saharan African continent. In Latin America, the HIV/AIDS pandemic is most prevalent in large cities, particularly in Brazil, Argentina, Mexico, Guatemala, and Honduras. In this region, one-third of the AIDS cases are in Brazil. Cities are centers of localized epidemics. Preventive measures include the "empowerment of leadership, strategic planning, information sharing, and partnership involvement of people living with HIV, and mobilizing of resources" (http://www.unaids.org/en/geographical+area/by+ region/latin+america.asp 2005).

## HISTORY OF HIV/AIDS PANDEMIC

The way in which governments (states) react in terms of making policy decisions regarding HIV/AIDS depends on which political and economic policy in planning for local, national, regional or international development is dominant. In addition, technology advancement, the cultural terrain of the society and how each country is affected by the structure and architecture of international political economy that is hierarchically stratified and universally hegemonic (Smith and White 1992; Wallerstein 1980) become the building blocks for decision making about such policy- related issues.

Historically, the HIV/AIDS disease may have existed in the U.S. particularly in laboratories where it was used in experiments that were managed by Eugenic and racist thinkers and scientists such as Betrand Russell, Earl Traub and Joseph J. Kinyoun. Between 1878 and 1950, the HIV virus, which is a man-made "syndrome" rather than a natural disease (Duesberg 1996), was used to perform experiments on goats, cats, monkeys, sheep, horses, birds and humans including gays and African Americans. During the last 30 years, the disease has explosively and progressively become a pandemic, particularly in societies that are relatively closed, technologically challenged, economically poverty ridden, and characterized by sensitively high birth rates and cultural traditions that disregard common sense and preventive scientific methods. Over the years, the United States government has made it its policy to eliminate the "undesirable, the unsuspecting and nonessentials." During the 1970s, U.S. and Russian governments may have secretly conspired to use the HIV virus as a form of biological germ-warfare to control world population particularly in Africa and, subsequently, elsewhere (http://content.sciencewise.com/res...47-11DA-A71F-004F4E05317F}_215.htm). The long political history of covert and unethical medical experimentation on humans, particularly African Americans and Manhattan gays, is both interesting and questionable (p. 2). The use of the "super germ or synthetic biological agents that is refractory to the immunological and therapeutic processes" (p. 5) upon which the medical and scientific professions depend on to prevent infectious disease could be developed in the future and be militarily employed to reinforce potential military technological superiority. In light of this argument,

> It is difficult if not impossible, to determine the truth about global biological warfare capabilities and their possible effects on world health. The American taxpayer is kept ignorant about U.S. chemical and bio-warfare programs. Scientists involved in bio-warfare research are sworn to secrecy and silence. Thus, "classified" and "top secret" medical experimentation continues to be promoted by powerful government agencies, such as the CIA, the CDC, the Department of Defense, the military, and other institutions. (Cantwell, http:content.scincewise.com/res...47-11D4-A71F-004F4E05317F}_215.htm).

Evidently, the long history of government policy on Los Alamos laboratory and other experiments and the progressively evolutionary and explosive consequences of those experiments in terms of their pandemic effects should bring to rest the shallow, uninformed and distorting debates concerning the green-monkey, the gay-plague and the African-origin theories that are largely elements of media propaganda that cover up for "our evil and myopic genius." Dr. Wolf Szmuness, Polish Jew and Soviet-trained world expert in Hepatitis-B who is now a U.S. citizen, Dr. Robert Gallo, foremost expert on AIDS at the CDC, Dr. Donald M. MacArthur, spokesman for the U.S. Department of Defense, and a large number of experts in HIV/AIDS and AIDS-related disease experts agree that there is an "ominous link between cancer and AIDS, between animal experimentation and the genetic engineering of viruses, between biological warfare technology and drug companies, between genetic experiments and AIDS, and between vaccine programs and the contamination of the nation's blood" (http://content.sciencewise.com/res...s/ Reporter/HIVorigin/ wfdigest.htm).

If scientists maintain a flow chart, which informs them about the results and effects of the experiments and if these experiments have accidentally backfired due to the fact that they have caused what is truly bio-warfare terrorism, which started with MK-NAOMI to Manhattan experiments and now the worldwide pandemic, don't we have the freedom and rights to question the role of bad science? Shouldn't political, scientific, medical, and legal leaders everywhere unite to use forensic science and sue individuals, firms, institutions and governments for this shocking news? Wasn't President Mbeki of South Africa right when he raised this issue at the beginning of the twenty-first century?

The disease spreads through "unprotected sex, needle sharing, donating blood or other tissues and infected mothers" at delivery (http://healthmba.com/hiv-test.html). All HIVS are parasitic and virulent retroviruses characterized by rapid, toxic and poisonous severity. They are malignant because they cause the disease AIDS. SIVS are benign. HIVS are retroviruses, while AIDS is the disease they cause in their hosts, humans or animals. Phylogenetically, in other words, based on their origins, a variety of theories that explain their origin and development display dubious scientific validity because the theorists ignore laboratory experiments that have been carried out for over 100 years and put emphasis on the current symptoms, effects, similarities, and regency of the disease which has evolved as a result of the globalization project and its geostrategic and structural interests. The man-made theory, the out-of- Africa theory, the chimpanzee to man theory, the vaccines theory, the hepatitis theory, the polio theory and the germ warfare theory (http://content.sceincew...er/HIV_origin/wftoc.htm) have been used to advance new knowledge, introduce controversial distortions, and compare results, all of which are largely man made and prescribe culturally biased conclusions regarding the origin and development of HIV/AIDS.

Three scientists from the Universities of Michigan, Maryland and Massachusetts (Mindell, Shultz and Ewald) respectively wrote an article on the phylogenetic evolution of the HIV/AIDS pandemic. The thesis and conclusions of this phylogenetic tree are paraphrased and discussed. The AIDS pandemic is a new problem for humans, but it is not clear whether the human immunodeficiency virus (HIV) giving rise to AIDS is also new to humans. Either (1) HIV has recently infected humans, in which case we have a new virus and a new disease, or (2) HIV infected humans long ago (being mild and/or restricted in range until recently), in which case we have an old virus and a new disease. There are precedents for each scenario among known viruses causing diseases (Shope and Evans 1993). The new virus and old virus scenarios have profoundly different implications for understanding the mechanisms of HIV propagation and the etiology of AIDS, for combining AIDS, and, potentially, for efforts to prevent future epidemics. The terms "new" and "old" are ambiguous beyond denoting relative age so for purposes of this chapter we consider a new virus one that has infected its host species within the past 50 years or so.

The first view, that HIV has only recently contacted humans, entails recent cross-species transmission of a simian immunodeficiency virus (SIV) from one or more nonhuman primates, and represents the current conventional wisdom (Dietrich, et al. 1989; Doolittle 1989; Allan, et al. 1991; Fox 1992; Myers, et al. 1992, 1993; Hirsch, et al. 1993; Temin 1993; Myers and Korber 1994). However, some have suggested that certain rural African populations of humans may have been infected with an immunodeficiency virus for many decades, centuries, or even millennia (Montagnier 1985; Hahn 1990; McClure 1990); Ewald (1991, 1994) and have described an evolutionary model in which virulent strains are placed at a selective advantage by higher rates of sexual partner change.

Understanding HIV origins is of general interest to systematists as well. Viruses evolve by descent with modification like any other group of organisms, and systematizers will become increasingly involved in attempts to understand their complex histories as more of their DNA sequences become available. Systematists working on viruses need to consider distinctive features of viral evolution, including extremely high rates of molecular sequence evolution, subsequent high levels of within-population sequence variability (variously described as yielding species swarms or quasispecies), evolutionary rates that vary depending on the species of host and type of cell infected, potential for recombination when representatives of different viral lineages infect the same host cell, and potential biases in the sampling of host species (Ewald, et al. 1991).

The objectives of these scientists were to (1) assess the evidence used in support of the "new virus" hypothesis, (2) present their own phylogenetic analyses of representative viral taxa, (3) estimate the most-parsimonious evolution of the character "virus host" in the study taxa, and (4) comment on methodological issues in the systematics of viruses. Although it is not possible to reject either hypothesis, they concluded that any consensus favoring the "new virus" hypothesis was not justified on the basis of current evidence and that the "old virus" hypothesis remained a viable but scientifically dubious alternative (Ewald, et al. 1991).

Evidence currently available does not support the popular view (the "new virus" hypothesis) that HIVs have recently colonized humans and that PIVs in humans are recent descendants from one or another of the PIV lineages known from nonhumans. "Phylogenetic trees show only sister relationships for extant taxa, not ancestor-descendant relationships for extant taxa." Use of the phylogenetic hypothesis and a parsimony criterion to estimate the smallest number of host species shifts (that is, to diagnose changes in the character "viral host") indicates humans to be the ancestral host species for a clade including SIV cpz from chimpanzee and for a clade including SIV sms from sooty mangabeys. The three scientists specifically do not claim that the latter analysis resolves the issue of ancestral host, however, in light of potential sampling biases. Their point is to show that current evidence does not support the "new virus" hypothesis. Support for the "new virus" hypothesis then devolves to unjustified assumptions that pre-1959 human blood samples testing negative for PIV presence successfully represent all human populations potentially harboring PIVs, and that new viruses are virulent and old viruses are mild. Small human populations with dormant PIVs may readily have been missed by limited sampling, and the assumption that new viruses are virulent and old viruses are mild ignores the ability of natural selection to affect an increase, a decrease or stasis in virulence over time. Even if the latter assumption were valid, inferred newness of PIV infection of humans is contradicted by discovery of noncytopathic HIV2uc1 and relatively low virulence (longer latency and asymptomatic periods) of PIV2s in rural human populations having relatively low rates of sexual contact among individuals (Ewald, et al. 1991).

Retroviral evolution challenges systematists with a variety of distinctive and potentially confounding "features, including (1) extremely fast rates of molecular sequence evolution (due to short generation times, large numbers of progeny, and low fidelity replication), (2) evolutionary rate heterogeneity within and among virus sequences (due to potential host specific and cell-type specific rate differences and variable use of three different replication enzymes having variable error rates), and (3) potential for genetic recombination among different lineages infecting the same cell, complicating character homology determinations. Improved understanding of these features and greater sampling of primate host species will enhance future studies of immunodeficiency virus phylogeny and may entail revision of current hypotheses of relationship" (p. 12).

During the 1980s and 1990s, the major challenge for the HIV/AIDS establishment was to search for the cause(s) of AIDS disease. With the influence of governments, major organizations in the U.S., Europe and Japan, created bureaucratic structures and complex physical and scientific infrastructure for funding, R and D, treatment and prevention policies and procedures. Their political, scientific and economic strategies were largely guided by extrinsic rather than intrinsic motives. In the U.S., the race to study the cause(s) of AIDS became the focus of the National Institute of Health (NIH), the Center for Disease Control (CDC), the Food and Drug Administration (FDA), the National Institute on Drug Abuse (NIDA), all other divisions of the federal Department of Health and Human Services, and all researchers and scientists who secured federal grants and contracts. Because these strategies and efforts were and are guided by market-driven extrinsic factors protected and controlled by the policy elite and the drug industrial establishment, scientific and creative voices of dissent are tolerantly intolerable in terms of their contributions to the search for the cure. This could be the reason why more than "100,000 AIDS experts, particularly eminent medical doctors, virologists, immunologists, cancer researchers, pharmacologists...Nobel Laureates" (Duesberg 1996, 9) have been unable to find the cause and cure for AIDS. Although HIV virus appears to cause AIDS, the same scientific establishment which made that discovery has not succeeded in preventing deaths caused by AIDS. Given the scenario, and as the "research establishment becomes more centralized, bureaucratized, and fraught with commercial conflicts of interest, each episode achieves more monstrous proportions" (p. 10). Moreover, the same scientific community which is researching for the cause and cure of AIDS may be directed to the causes via "inappropriate experimental designs and very short follow-up times" (p. 334).

Scientific critics and dissenters of the AIDS establishment (bureaucrats, pro-AIDS scientific community, scientific AZT, DDC and DDI popularizers, organizations, drug manufacturers and distributors and journalists can mobilize their forces to censor dissidents' work in professional literature and silence or alienate the critics regardless of the validity of their discoveries and contributions. Since "a scientist's career depends heavily on peer-reviewed grant money, peer-reviewed opportunities to publish in scientific journals, and invitations to conferences" (p. 396) such vulnerabilities can "ostracize," alienate, and silence creative genius and dissent due largely to the group think of the AIDS and drug establishment.

During the 1960s, many people heard about the availability of psychedelic drugs, which nonconformists, rock stars, war protestors, sex gurus, and intellectuals preyed on. With the extrinsic motivation and commercialization-driven policies, those who use cocaine, nitrite inhalants, amphetamines, heroine, LSD, marijuana, PCP and a variety of psychoactive drugs have collectively generated new disease epidemics unparalleled in human history. Since AIDS is incurable but "host-tamable," it may be "caused by long-term consumption of the above mentioned recreational drugs and by AZT and its analogs. Hemophilia-AIDS, transfusion-AIDS, and the extremely rare AIDS cases of the general population reflect the normal incidence of AIDS – defining diseases in these groups plus AZT induced incidence of these diseases under a new name" (p. 411). If each of these recreational drugs is toxic, then AIDS may have many causes. Since scientists, for obvious reasons, have not and, under the current climate will not, examine a multicausal hypothesis, the cure for AIDS is made more illusive, obscure and distant. The AIDS establishment should disestablish its command science and explain why an agent is a plausible cause of one or all of the thirty fatal AIDS diseases that are AIDS-related.

Why is there no AIDS cure? There are three main reasons; first, the scientific AIDS establishment's enthusiastic acceptance that the "virus-AIDS hypothesis is not based on its scientific rigor or its fruits" (p. 595). Instead, it is based on the universal administration and respect for germ theory, which globally and psychologically enhances the geopolitical and imperial power of the state and its military industrial complex. Second, though funding for the AIDS establishment is humongous, there is limited scientific expertise on the subject in question. Third, world-wide ignorance of the poor masses who are vulnerable, or those who get sick and die or struggle for survival results in a lack of scientific information concerning the cause(s) of AIDS and how, when, where and why it is transmitted, how it can be prevented and why people are vulnerable.

Both in the U.S. and elsewhere in the developed world, "new medical treatments have turned AIDS from a death sentence into a chronic illness for most people infected with HIV virus. While no cure for AIDS yet exists, most HIV positive people can live productive lives, raising families and contributing to society" (Magaziner 2004, 28) even though "the future ... is not nearly so hopeful for the tens of millions of men, women, and children living with the disease in the developing world". AIDS "includes 25 previously known diseases and two clinically and epidemiologically very different AIDS epidemics, one in America and Europe, the other in Africa" (Duesberg 1996, 510) and elsewhere. The American European epidemic is characterized by the "male homosexual epidemic, the intravenous drug user epidemic, the hemophilia epidemic, and the transfusion recipient epidemic" (p. 510). The American and European AIDS can be sub-epidemically described as the homosexual Kaposi sarcoma (Selik, et al. 1987) drug-user induced tuberculosis; cocaine related pneumonia and tuberculosis; hemophiliacs who suffer from opportunistic fungal and viral pneumonia and Kaposi sarcoma (Evatt, 1984 and Koerper, 1989); transfusion cases with pneumonia; hemophiliac wives with pneumonia; babies with dementia (Center for Disease Control 1992b); and users of cytotoxic DNA chain terminator AZT who develop anemia, lewipenia and nausea. According to Greenfield, University of Oklahoma professor (2005), representatives from all American racial and ethnic groups have AIDS. These patients are middle class, urban, rural, elderly people and minority populations.

During the 1980s, and compared with American and European AIDS cases, only 0.3% of Americans out of 6 million worldwide HIV positive cases were identified as carriers. In other words, although very few Africans were AIDS-infected twenty years ago, now Africa leads the world in HIV/AIDS pandemic. Table 1 illustrates that phenomenon. African HIV/AIDS includes common diseases such as tuberculosis, diarrhea, chronic fever, weight loss, pneumonia and other neurological diseases (Hishida, et al. 1992). It is difficult but not impossible to provide a classic definition of African HIV/AIDS (Gilks 1991), particularly when serious cases of malnutrition, Ebola, parasitic infections and poor sanitary conditions are prevalent causes of death. Sixty percent of the HIV/AIDS infected persons in sub-Saharan Africa are women. Polygamy, sexual coercion and violence against women contribute to their distress. Girls are sexually exploited by old people who pressure them for sexual promiscuity in exchange for food, clothing and school tuition (Marton, 2004).

Volberding invented Zidovidine (AZT) an antiviral drug. "AZT blocks DNA production, not only in human T-cells or retroviruses, but also in any bacteria that might exist in the body...it can act as an indiscriminate antibiotic, killing opportunistic infections while destroying the immune system. Even Burroughs Welcome...billed the drug as an antibacterial" (Duesberg 1996, 321). The drug destroys the pancreas, bodily nerves, T-cells and bone marrow largely because of its extreme toxicity. It seriously contributes to collateral damage.

Jerome Horwitz developed Dideoxycytidine (ddc) in the 1960s. It is marketed by Hoffman-La Roche and is used in combination with AZT. It also terminates the production of DNA as AZT does. The effects of Nevirapine, (which prevents mother-to child transmission and is used in poor countries), is not clearly known yet. Didanosine (ddi) is manufactured by Thailand. After the Thai government prevented Bristol-Myers Squibb, a U.S.-based pharmaceutical company from Thailand, it expanded its treatment program by producing a single pill that contains the medicines stavudine, lamivudine, and nevirapine – a combination recommended by the WHO. These drugs appear to be effective. Third World countries should buy anti AIDS drugs from Thailand.

Robert Gallo, M.D., Director of the Institute of Human Virology and professor of microbiology and immunology at the University of Maryland, gave a presentation on *HIV/AIDS research: The light and the dark* at the Oklahoma Medical Research Foundation in Oklahoma City on March 8, 2006. During the 1980s and 1990s, his research helped physicians develop HIV therapies that prolong people's lives. In 1996, Dr. Gallo discovered "chemokine" a natural compound that blocks the HIV virus to stop the progress of AIDS. As an internationally known scientist and a decorated member of the National Academy of Sciences and the Institute of Medicine, he believes that HIV has become a chronically treatable illness rather than a death sentence. However, Dr. Gallo knows that "we must continue to make significant advances in developing new therapies because of drug resistance to some of the present therapies and drug toxicity" (The *Oklahoman* February 24, 2006, 3). He also asserts in *Lancet* (2005, 366:1894–98) that although most of the scientific community is pessimistic about the cure of AIDS, he is optimistic because the "rational pathways toward development of an effective vaccine" are available. Dr. Gallo concluded that the three major therapeutic advances that have been increasingly helpful in treatment and care for the HIV/AIDS victims have been the 1984 blood test, the 1986 anti-viral treatment which came with the AZT and the 1995 Highly Active Antiretroviral Therapy (HAART), which has made people live longer and have healthier lives.

On February 6, 2006, the 13th Conference on Retroviruses and Opportunistic Infections was held in Denver to discuss the prospects of new experimental drugs. First, Manufacturer Panacos reported that PA-457 prevents the virus from sending infectious materials into the blood stream. This drug is a maturation inhibitor. Second, Pfiser Global Research scientists have identified and designed UK-201844 to prevent the virus from fusing with other cells at the beginning of the infection process. As a result, Trimeris scientists have received positive results concerning the cell entry or fusion inhibition. Also, new drugs such as TRI-1144 and TRI-999 seem to "be 100 to 150 times more potent than Trimeris first generation fusion inhibitor, Fuzeon, in fighting HIV infection." The dosage lasts for one week.

## THE POLITICAL ECONOMY OF HIV/AIDS

We live in a world of 6.9 billion people, which grows by nearly 76 million annually. Nearly three billion (2 in 5) people struggle to survive on less than $2 a day. More than 1 billion people lack safe drinking water, and 2.4 billion are without basic sanitation. More than 800 million people are chronically undernourished, 2 billion lack food security, and the fertility rate (child bearing age) group is 78 million annually. Half of the world's original forest cover has been cleared, and another 30 percent is degraded. By 2030, 60 percent of the world's population will be urban. Currently 15-24 year olds competing for jobs are 1 billion and 137 million women want to delay their next birth or avoid another, yet more than 350 million couples lack access to a full range of family planning services. Three billion young people will enter their reproductive years within this generation. Today, about 65 million people have HIV/AIDS and most of these are in Africa (see Table XII.1). AIDS, like malaria and tuberculosis, kills 6 million people yearly in the Third World (*The Population Institute* 2004).

In the context of the structure of global political economy, Bratton, Mattes, and Boadi (2005) have written *Public opinion, democracy and market reform*. The authors concluded that support for democracy in Africa is wide but shallow. Africans find themselves trapped between the state and the market. Beyond multiparty elections, people want clean and accountable government. They like economic structural adjustment only if it is accompanied by an effective state, the availability and provision of jobs and an equitable society. These attitudes originate and are constrained and informed by social structure and cultural values that are a product of rational experience and contextual and collective cultural wisdom. How do these demographics and people's expectations about governance inform international organizations such as the World Bank?

Structural adjustment in Africa is national economic reform programs undertaken by countries in return for assistance from the World Bank and other international donor institutions. Numerous countries in Africa began to experience difficulty meeting their financial obligations during the 1970s. By the early 1980s, most African countries were receiving loans from international financial institutions that were subject to conditions on borrowers' national economic policies. The conditions that accompanied these loans were known collectively as structural adjustment policies (SAPs). The lending agencies responsible for devising SAPs included the World Bank, the International Monetary Fund (IMF) and bilateral agencies such as the United States Agency for International Development and European aid agencies.

The history of SAPs is more controversial in Africa, possibly than anywhere else. The results have been disappointing. Critics portray SAPs as a failure, foisted on Africa by heartless and exploitative outsiders. Other critics have complained that theorists unfamiliar with African problems designed policies that are poorly suited to African conditions. Defenders claim that incomplete and incoherent implementation of SAPs often accounted for their disappointing results. They emphasize the benefits of these policies, not the failings. If anything, the benefits are enjoyed by international organizations and NGOs rather than by the Third World peoples who have less competence to rationalize the incompleteness and incoherence of the SAPs.

The increase in oil prices of the mid-1970s caused problems for African oil importers in their balance of payments (in a given country, total money received in export earnings and financial assistance, less total money spent on imports and external debt). When oil prices increased, many countries found that the money they received in export earnings and aid funding was insufficient to cover the cost of oil imports. Many countries met their increased need for foreign exchange by borrowing funds rather than by curtailing other imports or increasing exports. As a result they were unable to adjust to the new scarcity of foreign exchange.

Meanwhile, they increased their foreign debts and worsened their long-term balance of payments problems. In the future, they would have to pay not only for oil imports but also for the interest on debt. Although Blair initiated G8 Prime Minister Conference, resulted in debt relief initiatives and funding programs, the historically practiced repatriation of capital strategies are likely to be imposed on these debt relief overtures in order to perpetuate the status-quo – the irony of African economic problematic. A number of commodity booms in the mid-1970s temporarily generated increased foreign exchange earnings for some African countries. Prices of coffee, cocoa, tea, and phosphates were all high, and the boom encouraged more borrowing and less saving. Banks were willing to loan to African countries because of the countries' high export earnings at the time and because the banks needed to find ways to invest the petrodollars on deposit from the oil exporters. However, the recession in the early 1980s caused commodity prices to collapse as global demand dropped. High interest rates imposed by the Federal Reserve Bank to fight inflation in the United States caused real interest rates to rise to highs that were unforeseen when African countries negotiated their external loans. By the early 1980s many African countries facing potential bankruptcy turned to the World Bank, IMF, and bilateral agencies for assistance. In addition, geopolitical and technological conditions that contributed to the collapse and dissolution of the U.S.S.R. encouraged Western nations to invest in Eastern Europe, Asia and Latin America to the detriment of the African region which became less "bankable."

Assistance included additional lending, some grants, and some debt forgiveness. Lenders required acceptance of conditions intended to promote short-term stabilization, generally combining devaluation of the local currency with government financial austerity. They also required policy changes aimed to increase growth over medium to long term periods. Currency devaluation was expected to improve the balance of payments because it would make imports more expensive and hence reduce demand for them, while it would make and hence increase the supply of foreign exchange. Financial austerity measures required governments to reduce expenditures or increase taxes or both. This was supposed to reduce monetary growth and, hence, inflation. Inflation contributed to currency overvaluation by making domestic prices rise faster than international prices. Inflation increased demand for imports and reduced supply of exports. Reducing inflation was essential to regaining balance of payments equilibrium. Since devaluation itself spurred inflation by increasing the prices of imported goods, it needed to be combined with austerity measures to keep overvaluation from recurring. Such an economic climate could not and does not enable these countries to buy expensive drugs which the pharmaceutical industry and the drug establishment controls.

## Politico-Economic and Cultural Interpretation

AIDS poses a threat to the survival of millions, especially in the Third World where health and social infrastructures weakened by prolonged economic crises cannot bear the heavy burden of this new disease. Ninety percent of the more than 40 million people who had contracted HIV/AIDS by 1998 lived in less developed countries; more than two-thirds of the total, some 35 million, were Africans. Nearly half of those infected were female.

Sexual transmission of HIV/AIDS between heterosexual partners predominates in Africa. Adolescent girls are especially biologically and socially vulnerable to sexual infection by older men, and up to six times more girls are infected than boys of the same age. As in poverty-stricken United States, both urban and rural areas, AIDS is the leading cause of death in youth and young adults in Africa. Because of lack of funding in Africa, effective screening of the blood supply, transfusions for victims of acute malaria, hemorrhage in childbirth, or traffic accidents carry a significant risk of HIV infection. Since over half of infected Africans are females of childbearing age, many children – about 10 percent of the total number of those infected – acquire HIV in the womb, at birth, or during breast feeding. Countries with intravenous drug use can expect that shared syringes will become an additional source of HIV infection.

The period between infection with HIV and the onset of disease of symptoms is lengthy and varies among individuals, apparently depending on their genetic makeup and the makeup of the virus. The viral strain predominant in high-prevalence areas of eastern and southern Africa, HIV-1 type E, is readily transmissible in heterosexual intercourse and accounts for an estimated 80 to 90 percent of infections. In addition, an untreated sexually transmitted disease (STD) such as syphilis or gonorrhea increases the likelihood of sexual transmission of HIV. Most Africans do not have access to effective antibiotic treatment for STDs. Together, these facts help to explain high rates of HIV transmission. The so-called opportunistic infections that characterize AIDS include tuberculosis, pneumonia, and severe diarrhea, forms of cancer, blindness, and brain disorders. Effective treatment is costly and inaccessible to the poor majority in Africa.

Since people who carry the virus appear to be, and feel healthy for some years, and since HIV testing is not widely available in Africa, most people who are infected do not know it. Therefore, most do not protect sexual partners from infection. A major challenge for prevention is to encourage people to accept the possibility that they may have been infected and, in that case, use condoms regularly except when conception is desired to decrease the risk of transmission. Another major challenge is to persuade or empower youth to delay sexual activity, use condoms, and avoid sexual promiscuity.

The prolonged disease process is extremely painful in its later stages, and the sick require extensive care. Much of the burden of care falls upon women, who may be sick themselves and without resources. Ninety percent of deaths occur among adults aged 20 to 49 years, the prime working years, more than half of those infected are 15 to 24 years old. HIV and AIDS exacerbate tuberculosis, a leading cause of death for young African women. More African children now die from AIDS than from malaria or measles, formerly the major killers.

In the United States, before new disease-delaying drugs became available in 1985, about half of those infected with HIV developed AIDS symptoms within ten years. Expensive new drug combinations can suppress viral replication and delay disease onset, but the rapidly mutating virus develops drug resistance. To date, no person with HIV has recovered a healthy immune system.

Most may be expected to progress to AIDS eventually. In Africa, where sophisticated drugs and medical monitoring are not widely available, death generally occurs within two years following the onset of AIDS. Neither a cure nor effective vaccines are likely to emerge in the near future, and if they do become available, most people's access will be blocked by inability to pay, especially in poor regions such as Africa. Despite price reductions offered by pharmaceutical companies seeking African subjects for vaccine and drug testing, the poor or middle classes will not generally be able to afford these drugs.

Because public health authorities largely perceived AIDS as an urban phenomenon, they believed that the majority of Africans lived in "traditional" rural areas and hence would be spared. Many social scientists, however, saw the coming catastrophe: first, few people anywhere have only a single lifetime sex partner, and rural areas are neither isolated nor unchanging. Second, even if condoms can be made available, very cheap and on a regular basis, a variety of stigmatized political, social, and cultural obstacles discourage their use. Third, harsh economic conditions have divided families, increased disparities in wealth and power and changed behavioral standards in both rural and urban areas. These economic hardships have fueled the epidemic by increasing the number of vulnerable youths and young adults.

Since the mid-1970s, increasing millions of Africans have lived in abject poverty, their survival precarious, deprived of hope for the future. The deepening economic crisis and structural adjustment programs of the 1980s fell hardest on the poor. Peasant incomes and wages declined sharply and governments were forced to greatly reduce funding for public services, including education and health care. Dwindling government jobs and deindustrialization raised unemployment levels. Wars and military occupation brought civilian deaths, rapes and mass population displacements. These conditions set the stage for sex with multiple partners and led to ever more widespread dissemination of HIV.

Poor people's survival strategies include migration in search of paid work, carrying goods long distances to urban markets, smuggling and trading sex for food and shelter. Mines, plantations, trading towns, fishing camps and ports attract job seekers in large numbers. Most are youths and men who come without their families; girls, divorced women, and widows also provide low-cost migrant labor and are vulnerable to sexual exploitation. Workers' camps are visited by girls and women who arrive on paydays, often traveling long distances. Poor women have few income-earning opportunities that pay as well as sex. Often they must support dependants and provide for themselves. Poverty and pervasive gender inequality make it especially difficult for girls and women to avoid unsafe sex – even within marriage. Sexual violence – on the rise with deteriorating social conditions – further increases the risk of contracting HIV.

Some cultures stigmatize diseases associated with AIDS such as tuberculosis, dementia, sexually transmitted diseases (STDs), and skin rashes. Because it is sexually transmitted and incurable, some may blame AIDS on moral transgressions and unseen forces; a woman is often blamed for a man's infection.

AIDS often provokes fear and hostility toward the afflicted. Husbands may abandon wives. Families unable to hide the nature of the illness may find themselves isolated. AIDS orphans may be shunned and left to roam the streets, where they are particularly vulnerable to HIV infection. With many people falling sick and others overworked and demoralized by so much death around them, the impact on all economic activities in the affected areas is severe. AIDS particularly disrupts seasonally labor-intensive agriculture, food processing and family life. Blaming others allows people to deny risk and avoid taking realistic steps to protect themselves and others. Where people believe that AIDS is caused by women or by unseen forces, scape-goating, witch hunts, and social unrest compound socioeconomic disruption and the misery of the poor.

Effective prevention involves enabling large numbers of people to change sexual practices that are widely considered to be natural and essential to health. Children are highly valued, and they may allow a woman to hold a steady partner and gain community respect. Condoms are not popular among men, many of whom employ a double standards to rationalize their relations with numerous, often younger, sex partners, while they strictly control their wives' sexuality. Condoms have been widely stigmatized by being associated with prostitutes and STDs.

In many countries, powerful interest groups have treated AIDS, like other STDs, as a moral issue rather than a health issue. This makes it difficult for some governments to conduct rational prevention campaigns. Many adults believe that sex education and condoms will increase sexual activity (seen as immorality) among youth, although research carried out in numerous settings shows that access to condoms will lead wives to become unfaithful. Most of the wives, however, are infected by their husbands. In Uganda, Tanzania, and Senegal strong resistance to effective prevention by religious leaders and community elders continued into the early 1990s.

In sum, an epidemic such as AIDS is an essentially social process, shaped by political economy and culture. Today, several economic processes fuel the spread of the epidemic. These include a global economy that relegates Africa to production of a few agricultural and mineral exports and distorted domestic economies inherited from colonialism. These circumstances result in unfavorable terms of trade, massive foreign debt, landlessness, unemployment and widening disparities in wealth that are exacerbated by repressive politicians who siphon wealth from public funds. All of these processes, combined with the continued subordination of women, lead Africans to act out of desperation in ways that promote the spread of AIDS, while persistent poverty leaves most Africans without access to effective treatment.

A major new center of HIV infection lies in South and Southeast Asia, home to well over 2.5 billion people. Despite its rapid industrial development, economic crises in Southeast and East Asia can be expected to increase the spread of the AIDS pandemic, which is already rampant in the sex "industry," and among the military and intravenous drug users. Within the United States, new infections are disproportionately concentrated among poor, especially the people of color, women, youth, and the elderly regardless of age, class, race and status, both in the rural and urban sectors, and homosexual environments.

## Conclusion and Discussion

The monolithic HIV/AIDS hypothesis limits the opportunity for more rigorous, scrupulous and penetrating scientific inquiry into the cause(s) of the AIDS disease. HIV causes the AIDS disease. AIDS is not caused by the AIDS virus. Of the new diseases which have been discovered such as hantavirus, Ebola virus, legionnaires disease, lyme disease, chronic fatigue syndrome and toxic shock syndrome, HIV/AIDS has by comparison attained pandemic notoriety due largely to its resistance against the politico-economically orchestrated production of pharmaceutical and medical drugs. In other words, scientific utility is intimately related to economics, politics and policy making. In this arena, policy makers call on scientific experts to measure health problems as a basis for political negotiation that is in line with response strategies. Scientists acknowledge that their wisdom needs to be depended on in determining the nature and quality of policy. However, evidence shows that, if anything, the influence of science on politics and policymaking is quite "varied and sporadic." In other words, instead of being the guardian and "eye" of politics, science is subordinated to political whims as it becomes the handmaid of politics. For instance, because science funding is limited and always insufficient, policy makers and their appointees choose between research proposals, indirectly selecting what knowledge is to be pursued and how. Most "science...is instituted and thus, designed, to answer questions of interest to policy makers that may not be of interest to pure science. Sometimes the political environment may demand conclusions from scientists ahead of sufficient science understanding of the relevant process" (Harrison and Brynes 2004, 327). Such a situation creates a climate in which neither the scientists nor the policy elite have the grip on what they are really supposed to do by using pure science objectively in order to solve societal and civilizational problems of which the HIV/AIDS pandemic is a classic example.

Due largely to economics and politics in the developed world, HIV, which was invented in U.S. laboratories for eliminating the Manhattan gays and other unwanted, unsuspecting and nonessential victims, it accidentally backfired to spread into the heterosexual population which has been terrorized by it, particularly in the poorer communities of our global economy. The African, Eurasian, and Asian continents have become targets for the ill-intentioned pandemic. Although uninformed media experts and journalists have used many theories to explain the origin of the disease, the HIV/AIDS establishment related individuals are handmaidens of the policy makers who have apparently controlled the HIV/AIDS establishment for political and economic rather than of scientific and health gains for the human race.

The focus of local, national, and global strategic approaches to the monitoring, treatment and evaluation of HIV/AIDS should encourage participation by all stakeholders. The approaches should be conducted comprehensively and realistically. The plans should be given adequate resources. The resources should be coordinated, implemented, monitored and evaluated by adequately trained scientific manpower, which relies on sustainable technical help. Monitoring and evaluating programs should strike a balance between the generation of valued and reliable tactical information for program managers. Managers should ensure that the use of public data banks does not create avenues for discrimination and stigmatization of people who are positive in human immunodeficiency virus.

Managers (coordinators) and strategic planners should ensure that national HIV/AIDS programs are monitored and evaluated to generate information, not only for use by donor agencies, but also for improving their implementation and treatment programs. Although the 2001 Declaration of Commitment on HIV/AIDS by 189 countries served as a benchmark for universal action, definite and specific deadlines should be used to put pressure on the countries to quicken diagnostic implementation and treatment programs. However, progress reports show a low response rate for certain indicators including concern for data quality. To minimize the prospects for the concern over data quality, local, national, and global implementation and treatment agencies should identify incentives and opportunities for collaboration rather than isolation and the provision of counseling, medical, and therapeutic services.

National strategic planners and program managers should secure data from different geographical areas within each country in order to plan for and monitor the adequacy of service delivery for the HIV/AIDS patients. They should ensure that patients have access to the services which exist. "An operational plan for monitoring and evaluation with a detailed budget is an essential step moving from an indicator set to a functioning, monitoring and evaluation system" (Wilson 2000, 101). Based on Uganda's, Thailand's, and Ghana's experiences in monitoring and evaluation programs, data should be used to adjust national and local priorities, policies, and practices in order to improve the program. In particular, the Ghanaian model of treatment, monitoring and evaluation as illustrated by Wilson, is simple, strategically well-coordinated and synergistically participatory.

Evidence based on a variety of sources has demonstrated that ineffective public health intervention can cost substantial amounts of money that could be used to advance more effective treatment, monitoring, curative and evaluation programs. All in all, it is necessary to proceed with the best available evidence in order to eliminate or minimize the suffering associated with the HIV/AIDS scourge. Ineffective national monitoring and evaluation systems geared toward generating data for the donor community can fail to gather basic information because the systems are exclusively unaccountable. In spite of the challenges associated with theoretical, methodological, economic, and political intricacies in the realm of the HIV/AIDS pandemic, effective monitoring or implementation and evaluation systems could turn things around for the better.

The African continent, according to Nicolas Van de Walle, has experienced "the third decade of economic crisis and state decay." Regardless of what global index is used to assess Africa's viability, political repression, armed conflicts, perennial corruption, the brain drain, poverty, and lately the HIV/AIDS pandemic, have all contributed to the continent's loss of its global competitiveness. It requires extraordinary ingenuity, in terms of the use of academic and policy relevant research and a wisely coordinated multiplicity or sectoral engagements, to turn things around. Unlike in the developed societies where the poor, particularly women, ethnic minorities, illicit drug users, the homeless, and the mentally ill are frequently HIV/AIDS positive, their Third World counterparts come from all classes, age groups and demographic groups. The disease kills them indiscriminately.

Based on the U.N. Conference on HIV/AIDS, in New York in 2001, seven out of ten people infected with HIV/AIDS are sub-Saharan Africans (Ayittey 2001). Twenty-five million Africans are infected, and 90% of them don't even know it. This year, the number of AIDS orphans will reach 15 million, a figure larger than the population of London. Africa has already lost 16 million people to AIDS –more than Africa has lost in all its wars. The World Bank estimates that $5 billion a year is needed to combat the HIV/AIDS epidemic in Africa. The G8 suggests 10 billion in five years. The economic toll is no less hard to imagine. AIDS is decimating Africa's labor force, killing the youngest, brightest and strongest at a disproportionate rate and further crippling its efforts at economic recovery and development.

In 2001, an impassioned appeal by U.N. Secretary General Kofi Annan called for the creation of a "global war chest" of $7 billion to $10 billion a year to battle AIDS. The Bush administration promised $200 million, the British a matching sum, and the Canadians about one-third of that. One can never be sure how much of this was actually being raised and how much was merely the expression of good intentions. But, after bickering over the inclusion of words like "homosexuals" and "prostitutes," the conference patched together an essentially rhetorical document calling on governments to reduce infection rates and protect those at risk. Two years later, the U.S. government promised to give $15 billion to the global HIV/AIDS fund.

Such gestures will not affect the spread of the disease in Africa. Nor will the constant clamor of AIDS activists who continue to target the pharmaceutical industry, accusing it of putting profits ahead of lives by refusing to lower the cost of drugs for poor African patients. Merck, Bristol-Myers, Squibb, Boehringer Ingelheim, GlaxoSmithKline, and Hoffmann-La Roche have offered to sell their AIDS drugs to poor nations at cost. Since "at cost" is still beyond the means of most Africans, activists are geared up to put more pressure on the industry for further price reductions, principally through a weakening of international intellectual property rights. This is the wrong approach for a disease which has no cure, or prevention.

Notwithstanding their noble intentions and concerns for AIDS sufferers in Africa, activists have pushed this campaign into dangerous territory. The exclusive focus on drug prices has left a number of major players off the hook and consequently has the potential of exacerbating the epidemic. It's also ironic, since it is the pharmaceutical industry that is spending billions of dollars in R&D to find better treatments and one day, hopefully, a cure.

Let's take African leaders for an example. It is incomprehensible that they should continue to spend scarce resources on the procurement of arms to oppress their people and to prosecute senseless civil wars. Each year African governments spend more than $8 billion on new weapons and the military. The South African government alone has just spent $5.5 billion on new arms purchases.

The 14 or so conflicts currently raging on the continent have created about 12 million refugees-more than half of the world's refugee population. The refugees, in turn, serve as easy targets for sexual predators and breeding grounds for the AIDS virus. West African peacekeeping soldiers fathered some 25,000 children in Liberia. According to Teniola Olufemi, coordinator of the Ecomog Children Project, the Nigerian contingent accounted for 50% of the cases. In addition, the healthcare systems required to deliver and administer AIDS medicines have collapsed in many African countries as has the infrastructure of roads, electricity, water, communications and other basic requirements for an effective response to the epidemic. Besides, cultural taboos and outdated myths in polygamous societies are a major obstacle to detection and treatment.

Even African public health experts have themselves warned that unless public health systems are strengthened, the benefits of cheaper AIDS drugs could be undone by ineffective distribution or misuse, leading to the development of new strains of drug-resistant viruses. The South African government, for example, now admits that the health system must be upgraded before the drugs – even at lower prices – can be safely distributed in public hospitals. Finally, at a recent meeting on AIDS in Abuja, the Nigerian capital, an expert warned that there was great opportunity for corruption in selling and distribution of AIDS drugs. Other Nigerian experts say that studies have found that pills sold over the counter to the poor are often counterfeit or substandard. This kind of exploitation of the poor by the wealthy discourages many for whom the sophisticated industry and AIDS establishment do not speak. No wonder the cure remains dubious at best and hopeless at most. Germ warfare is a silent form of terrorism which wealthy nations have unintentionally imposed on the poor. It is a new form of class warfare whose purposive roots are sociologically and scientifically deterministic.

During the last 10 years, HIV/AIDS infections have been reduced by 20% worldwide and 20% of the deaths have been reduced during the last 5 years. International donors and national governments raised $15.9 billion in 2009. This funding effort needed $10 billion more for the same period. Raising funds is a shared international responsibility. However 90% of the funds used to fight HIV/AIDS comes from high-income rather than low-income countries. In West and Central Africa, HIV reduction is 25% and 1.4 million pregnant women and 370,000 children have recovered. As the HIV/AIDS pandemic enters its 4$^{th}$ decade, its epidemic has left a stamp of "discrimination, inequality, and social exclusion based on health status, gender, sexual orientation, drug dependency, disability, and migrant and refugee status". In some cases, certain societal forces prevent people from accessing life-saving HIV prevention, treatment, care and support services. Treatment and care are now considered elements of "human rights and gender equality" impeded by bilateral and multilateral trade agreements. There are 33 million people living with HIV daily. In 2009, there were 2.6 million infections worldwide. Those who receive treatment are 5 million only (Sidibé 2010 www.unaids.org).

## REFERENCES


Allen, J.S., M.E. Short, S. Taylor, V.M. Su, P.R. Hirsch, G.M. Johnson, and B.H. Shaw Hahn. B.H. 1991. Species-specific diversity among simian immunodeficiency viruses from African Green Monkeys. *Journal of Virology* 65, 2816-28.

Appiah, K.A., and H.L. Gates. 1999. *Africa: The encyclopedia of the African and African-American experience.*

Associated Press. 2004. *The Edmond Evening Sun* July 14: 11.

Ayittey, G.B.N. 2001. AIDS conference avoids real issues. *The Wall Street Journal* June 28: A16.

Bhattacharyà, J., et al. 2003. The link between public and private insurance and HIV-related mortality. *Journal of Health Economics* 22, 1105-22.

Bozzette, S., et al. 1998. The care of HIV-infected adults in the United States: HIV costs and utilization study consortium. *New England Journal of Medicine* 33, 26: 1897-1904.

Bratton, M.; R. Mattes, and E. Gyimah-Boadi. 2005. *Public opinion, democracy and market reform in Africa.* New York: Cambridge University Press.

Caporaso, J.A., and D.P. Levine. 1997. *Theories of political economy.* London: Cambridge University Press.

Cook, J.A. 2002. Use of highly active antiretroviral therapy in a cohort of HIV-seropositive women. *American Journal of Public Health* 92, 1: 82-7.

Crick, B. 1962. *In defense of politics.* London: Penguin Books.

Dietrich, U.M., M. Adamski, R Kreutz, A. Seipp, H. Kuhnel, and H. Rubsamen-Waigmann. 1989. A highly divergent HIV-2 related isolate. *Nature* 342: 948-50.

Doolittle, R..F. 1989. Immunodeficiency viruses: The simian-human connection. *Nature* 339: 338-9

Doolittle, R.F., D.F. Feng, M.S. Johnson, and M.A. McClure. 1989. Origins and evolutionary relationships of retroviruses. *Quarterly Review of Biology* 64: 1-30

Duesberg, P. 1996 *Inventing AIDS virus.* Washington, D.C.: Regency Publishing, Inc.

Dwyer, G., S.A. Levin, and L. Buttel. 1990. A simulation model of the population dynamics and evolution of myxomatosis. *Ecology Monograph* 60: 423-47.

Easton, D. 1953. *The political system: An inquiry into the state of political science.* Chicago: University of Chicago Press.

Ewald, P.W. 1994. *The evolution of infectious disease.* New York: Oxford University Press.

__________. 1991. Transmission modes and the evolution of virulence with special reference to cholera, influenza and AIDS. *Human Nature* 2: 1-30.

Fox, C. 1992. Possible origins of AIDS. *Science* 256: 1259-60.

Gifford, A.L., et al. 2002. Participation in research and access to experimental treatment by HIV-infected patients: HIV Costs and Services Utilization Study Consortium. *New England Journal of Medicine* 346, 18: 1373-82.

Grosh, B. 1999. Structural adjustment in Africa. In *Africa: The Encyclopedia of the African and African American Experience.*

Hahn, B.H. 1994. Viral genes and their products. In S. Broder, T. Merigana, and D. Bolognesi, eds. *Textbook of AIDS medicine.* Baltimore, MD: Williams and Wilkins.

Harrison, M.E., and G.C. Bryner, eds. 2004. *Science and politics in the international environment.*_Lanham, MD: Rowman and Littlefield Publishers, Inc.

Institute of Medicine of the National Academies. 2005. *Public financing and delivery of HIV/AIDS care: Securing the legacy of Ryan White.* Washington, D.C.: The National Academies Press.

Joseph, R. 2005. News and events. *Program of African Studies - North-Western University* 15, 2: 2.

Lasswell, H.D. 1936. *Politics: Who gets what, when and how?* New York: Whittlesey House.

Magaziner, I. 2004. Scaling-up care and treatment for people living with HIV and AIDS in the developing world. *The Brown Journal of World Affairs* XI, 1: 27-34.

Marton, K. 2004. A worldwide gender gap. *Newsweek* May 10: 1.

McClure, M.M., M.S. Johnson, F. Feng, and R.F. Doolittle. 1988. Sequence comparisons of retroviral proteins: Relative rates of change and general phylogeny. *Proc. National Academy of Sciences, U.S.A.* 85: 2469-73.

Montagnier, L. 1985. Lymphadenopathy-associated virus: From molecular biology to pathogenicity. *Ann Internal Medicine* 103: 689-93

Morgenthau, H.J. 1948. *Politics among nations.* New York: Alfred Knopf.

Morin, S.F., et al. 2002. Responding to racial and ethnic disparities in the use of HIV drugs: Analysis of state policies. *Public Health Reports* 117, 3: 263-72.

Myers, G., and B. Korber. 1994. The future of human immunodeficiency virus. In S.S. Morse, ed. *The evolutionary biology of viruses.* New York: Raven Press, Ltd.

Myers, G., D. Macinnes, and B. Korber. 1992. The emergence of simian/human immunodeficiency viruses. In *AIDS research and human retroviruses.*

Myers, G., K. Macinnes, and L. Myers. 1993. Phylogenetic moments in the AIDS epidemic. In S.S. Morse, ed. *Emerging viruses.* New York: Oxford University Press: 120-37.

Myers, G., B. Korber, S. Wain-Hobson, R.F. Smith, and G.N. Palakis, eds. 1993. Human retroviruses and AIDS 1993. *Theoretical biology and biophysics.* Los Alamos National Laboratory: Los Alamos, New Mexico.

Patterson, T.E. 2000. *We the people: A concise introduction to American politics.* Boston: McGraw-Hill.

Phillips, M.M. 2001. The silver lining in Africa's AIDS pandemic. *The Wall Street Journal* June 20: A12.

Piot, P. 2004. A prescription for change: Using policy to win the battle against AIDS. *The Brown Journal of World Affairs* XI, I: 11-6.

Rugg, D., G. Peersman, and M. Carael. eds. 2004. *New directions for evaluation. Global Advances in HIV/AIDS Monitoring and Evaluation,* Number 103.

Sambamoorthi, U., et al. 2000. Antidepressant treatment and health services utilization among HIV infected Medicaid patients diagnosed with Depression. *Journal of General Internal Medicine* 15, 5: 311-20.

Schattschneider, E.E. 1960. *The Semi-sovereign people: A realistic view of democracy in America.* New York: Holt, Reinhart, and Winston.

Schmitt, C. 1976. *The concept of the political.* New Brunswick, N.J.: Rutgers University Press.

Schoeff, B.G. 1999. AIDS in Africa: An interpretation. *Africa: The Encyclopedia of the African and African-American Experience*: 55-7.

Turner, B.J. 2001. Effects of drug abuse and mental disorders on use and type of antiretroviral therapy in HIV infected persons. *Journal of General Internal Medicine* 16, 9: 625-33.

Wilson, D. 2004. World Bank contribution to building national HIV/AIDS monitoring and evaluation capacity in Africa: Going beyond indicator development and conceptual training. *Global Advances in HIV/AIDS Monitoring and Evaluation*, Number 103: 101.

Zimmerman, R., and M. Waldholz. 2001. The U.N. plots a war on AIDS. *The Wall Street Journal* June 28: A12.

# Chapter XIII
# Terrorism and Its Risks

Terrorist attacks on and since September 11th, 2001 have stimulated public soul-searching, military and diplomatic responses, and efforts to reform public policy. Both the attacks and responses to them have raised a host of questions about social organization, basic social institutions, how people mobilize amid crises, and how differences of culture and politics shape conflict and cooperation.

## RISK

Insurance and Safety After September 11: Has the World Become a "Riskier" Place? Following the devastating events of September 11, 2001, it has become commonplace to hear statements to the effect that the world has become a "*riskier*" place. However, what do people mean by this statement? And – if we accept that the statement is true – how will it affect the way people behave?

### What Is Risk?

When used in every day speech, the word risk is typically associated with an activity that involves some chance of incurring a loss or "negative outcome". Moreover, the mere fact of being alive can be thought of as being risky in the sense that there is always some chance that we could suddenly die for a variety of reasons.

From an analytical perspective, the risk of an activity can be thought of as having two components. One is the chance or probability that the negative outcome will occur; the second is the size of the outcome. Generally speaking, the larger the probability and potential loss, the greater the "risk". Risk can therefore be increased or decreased by taking actions that affect the sizes of the loss and the probability of its occurrence. Thus, for example, you may decrease the risk in driving an automobile by wearing a seatbelt (i.e., the potential loss is smaller than if no seatbelt worn); or you may increase the risk by driving recklessly (i.e., you increase the probability of an accident).

Conceptually then, it is easy to think about risk. Operationally, however, it is much more difficult. From an analytical perspective, you have to "know" the probability of the loss occurring and the amount of the potential loss. How do people do this?

## Risk and Insurance

One place to start thinking about how people handle risks is to examine the workings of the insurance industry. This exists because people are willing to pay sums of money – or incur sure losses – to avoid the chance of incurring larger losses. In other words, one person pays another to avoid having to face a risk.

In short, the insurance market provides a mechanism for quantifying risk that is expressed by the premiums paid to insure against specific risks. However, this mechanism depends heavily on two factors: one is the availability of past data that can be used to assess probabilities and losses; the second is competition between insurance companies that let customers have some confidence in the level at which premiums are priced.

Conceptually, you could arrange for an insurance contract for a wide variety of different activities and, in fact, this happens. For example, pop singers buy insurance to avoid losses that could if their voices were damaged protect them from pertinent risks. Similarly, pianists insure their hands; and so on. Indeed, Lloyd's of London has made a specialty out of insuring people against the occurrence of many bizarre events. However, if there are no data on which probabilities and losses can be assessed, and few or no companies interested in offering insurance, the assessment of risk is problematic. Moreover, whereas as much daily activity can – and is – covered by insurance (consider, e.g., life and medical insurance), there is much that is not. This therefore raises the more general issue of how people assess risks in life and particularly when they do not have access to and relly on statistical data.

## Handling Risk in Everyday Life

It is important to realize that risk is not a new phenomenon and that dealing with risk is something that humans have done ever since they evolved as a species. From an evolutionary perspective, therefore, one should expect that we would have developed innate mechanisms for handling risk and, in fact this is true-up to a point. The mechanism that we all possess is the emotion of fear and it is illuminating to consider how this works. Fear stimulates an action on your part that helps you remove yourself from the source of danger. In this sense, the emotion of fear-and the reaction that it provokes – is part of our natural endowment for handling risky situations.

The point I am making is that we naturally do have "automatic systems" for handling situations that we recognize as risky. Thus, it is important to investigate the origins of these systems and to recognize both their possibilities and limitations.

Our ability to recognize dangerous situations and to react in consequence can be thought of as having two sources. One is natural in the sense that it is inherited through evolution; the other is learned. Psychologists have made extensive studies of learning and experiences. Thus, individuals can differ significantly in how they react to different stimuli depending on their idiosyncratic experiences. One person, for example, may be quite afraid when flying in an airplane because of previous bad experiences; a second may feel little or no fear. The critical point about learning is that people have either experienced a negative outcome (or "loss") personally or they have been socialized by others (e.g., a parent) to associate potential losses with certain activities.

It can be safely said that our understanding of how evolutionary development has shaped us to experience fear in the face of specific stimuli is less complete than our understanding of learning. However, our ability to acquire the response of fear is a genetically inherited mechanism. In addition, there is evidence that it takes very little exposure to acquire fear reactions to some stimuli and yet not to others. For example, it takes only one or two exposures for people to acquire the fear of snakes, spiders, and heights and yet, these same people may experience far less fear when crossing a busy intersection in a city (which for them might be objectively more dangerous). It just seems that we are better "prepared" to learn fear reactions from some kinds of stimuli than others. "More recently, neuroscientific studies of the brain indicate that people process information concerning fear reactions in two distinct areas. First, automatic reactions in the amygdala, a small, peanut-sized organ that lies deep in the back of the brain. Second, the amygdala receives information directly from the sensory thalamus and uses it to initiate evasive action if danger is signaled. This level of processing, however, is approximate in the sense that it does not involve detailed analysis of the impending danger. Third, it acts as a kind of reflex to a class of stimuli. Fourth, the incoming information, however, will also be processed- albeit in a slower and more thorough manner-in the neo-cortex at the front of the brain and this appropriateness sparks off different reactions. Clearly, it is functional for the first system to act quickly even if it is mistaken on occasion. More generally, several researchers believe that our emotional decision making systems that work without our conscious awareness are tuned through experience to pick up "markers" or signals of potential danger and that they help us to avoid making the wrong decisions by eliminating dangerous alternatives from consideration.

Risk and past experience have enabled our learning evolutionary history to endow us with fear reactions that can stand us in good stead when we are confronted with potentially dangerous situations. In facing the dangers in today's world, however, both mechanisms suffer from the same disadvantage. They only provide reactions to situations that have been experienced in the past and cannot handle risks or dangers that are "new". Indeed, if we rely only on our emotions (whether inherited or learned) to guide our risky decision making, we are liable to suffer many losses.

Sociologist Charles Perrow has implicitly made an interesting analysis of this situation from a larger societal perspective. In a book entitled *Normal Accidents,* he makes the point that society typically learns to handle new technologies by responding to breakdowns or "accidents". For example, regulations for fire hazards that involve limiting the number of people who can be present in buildings at the same time were not the result of authorities planning what might happen when many people crowded into the same building. Instead, they are a result of what society learned from past accidents where reported forecasts were calculated in the light of past experiences; while traffic regulations were implemented incrementally as society gained experience with accidents. Thus, argues Perrow, if society continues to act in the same fashion, accidents will also occur when new technological advances are introduced-indeed, they are inevitable or "normal". Lacking past experience that could signal danger is human nature. To continue to push the frontier until something happens seems to be natural and unexpected at times. "As a recent example, consider the French Concorde, the supersonic jet that flew commercially without a fatal accident for some 25 years. Note that the fact that Concorde was (or is) a safe technology was reinforced on a daily basis for a quarter of a century. But when the Concorde accident happened, human reactions to Concorde related fear was the result of psychological awareness based on the recent and past happening.

In addition, when an unimagined and life-costing accident did occur after this long accident-free service, the airplane had to undergo substantial modifications of its undercarriage to avoid similar accidents in the future. And yet, for the first 25 years of its service, no fatal accidents had occurred and no one saw the need to introduce the modifications. It should be clear that, in an increasingly technological and complex society, we cannot rely only on our emotions of fear – whether these are determined genetically or environmentally (i.e., the result of experience). It is important to assess risk and find means to deal with it. Instead, people's assessments of the components of risk (i.e., the chances and the amounts of potential losses) must involve their subjective perceptions of what these are likely to be in the future. In turn, such assessments must depend on imaginary as opposed to "real" experience. And indeed, many studies of risk assessment over the last 30 years have highlighted the role played by imagination. Sometimes, people fail to imagine the possibility of certain risks occurring and so fail to take protective actions (e.g., the Concorde example, given above). On other occasions, people's imagination may lead them to believe that risks are greater than more objective analysis might show.

Let's start with risks that people don't imagine and which therefore do not represent risks from their point of view. There are many of these in everyday life. For example, and as noted earlier, each time you walk down a street you could have an accident. However, the possibility of accidents such as these rarely come to the attention of a fit and able person. In a sense, these accidents fall below the threshold of imagination and thus worry. Second, there are many activities where people feel "in control" and thus do not see the risks in the same way as others might. For example, when considering their ability in driving automobiles (and thus their propensity not to have accidents), most people consider themselves to be well "above average." Similarly, many business people do not consider that they are engaged in risky decision making because, not only are they in control of what they do, they are also experienced. "Finally, there are many made decisions where people do not experience any immediate negative feedback from taking risky actions and thus may fail to see the link between what they do now and what happens in the future. For example, the effects of eating foods with high levels of cholesterol or smoking are delayed in time. In both cases, the activities are pleasurable and negative consequences will not be experienced until much later. In fact, even if people "know" about the negative effects of tobacco and cholesterol, neither of these have much meaning to them if the consequences occur in a distant future with which they cannot identify.

A further example highlights how making the description of an event very specific can induce people to see it as much more risky. In an investigation of the effects of wording on people's intentions to buy insurance for air travel, researchers found that people were willing to pay more for a policy that would insure them against "terrorist acts" as opposed to death from "all possible causes." And yet, as must be obvious to the reader, death from terrorist acts is only one of many ways that could lead to death on an airplane. However, because this scenario was made explicit, it became more salient to people thereby increasing their perception of the risk as measured by their willingness to pay an insurance premium.

Following a series of extensive investigations over more than 20 years into how people perceive the risk associated with new technologies, psychologist Paul Slovic and his colleagues have determined two important dimensions. One, they call dread and the other risk of the unknown. The former includes feelings of fear, lack of control, and apprehension about catastrophic potential. The latter refers to lack of knowledge of the risk that could be unobservable, novel, and possibly have important delayed effects. Clearly, one could argue that with good information, people might be able to understand the risks better; however, this alone would not necessarily help people to overcome their fear.

A related issue is whether people's concerns about one source of risk affects their attitudes toward other sources. For example, imagine that you have been sensitized to risk in one area of your life, e.g., you are concerned about the outcome of a medical treatment. Will this affect how you view risks in other areas? The evidence suggests that it will. People's assessments of risk have been found to be affected by their general emotional state, e.g., if you are scared, you are likely to see risks as generally greater than if you are not. As a further example, the recent attacks involving anthrax were seen by the general public to signal far greater risk precisely because of their temporal proximity to September 11, 2001. However, there is now considerable doubt as to whether the same terrorist organization was responsible for both September 11 and the letters contaminated by anthrax".

To summarize, I have argued that risk involves some chance of a negative- or bad-outcome occurring. The extent of risk therefore depends on both the size of the probability of the event occurring and the size of the negative outcome. In dealing with many risks, however, people (and even insurance companies) do not have access to data that allows them to assess and calculate risks in a rational manner. They therefore rely on more tacit or intuitive ways of dealing with risk that involve feelings or emotions. In addition, imagination plays an important role. Tacit or intuitive knowledge, however, is limited by past experience about which imagination may be insufficient or unrealistic. In addition, both can be affected by the context of immediate experience that may or may not be relevant to the issues at hand.

## Implications on the Aftermath of September 11

Let me now return to the aftermath of September 11 and address some specific issues. How have the terrorist attacks affected the way we experience and assess risk? Second, how will such experience and assessments affect insurance markets? And third, should we believe that the world has become more risky and, if so, should we change our behavior?

> To answer the first question, it should be quite clear that the terrorist attacks have not affected the way we experience and assess risk. However, what the unforgettable television images have undoubtedly done is to increase our awareness of the possibility of terrorist attacks and the nightmarish quality of potential outcomes. At the same time, we-the general public-have become much more knowledgeable about the way terrorist's networks operate, the effects of religious fundamentalism, and the limit to which fanatics are prepared to go in order to achieve their goals. For example, although most Westerners were aware of suicide bombers, the idea of killing oneself for a religious cause is not part of our way of seeing the world. September 11 helped us understand that we have a very small worldview (Anonymous).

From the viewpoint of understanding risk, what September 11 highlights is the two-eyed nature of knowledge. On the one hand, if we are unaware of certain possibilities-i.e., we cannot even imagine them-we clearly cannot regard these events as risky. However, if we do gain some knowledge of their possibility, our awareness leads to feelings of risk even though, from an objective viewpoint, there may be no difference in the world except for our awareness. Moreover, if this knowledge is imperfect, and we know it is imperfect, then our assessment of the risk could well be biased by a number of different and unknown factors.

> At the individual level, one could argue that the fact that one person has become aware of a risk may not be of great importance. However-and this is one of the critical factors of September 11-when many people become aware of a risk, the implications are quite different. A classic illustration can be provided by what happens in certain kinds of bank failures. If one person senses a risk that a bank will fail and so withdraws his or her funds, this would typically have little effect on the bank. However, if that person communicates the feeling to others, and they to others, soon so many people will want to withdraw their funds that they will in fact bring about the failure of the bank. Panics can sometimes be instigated by totally erroneous information. People, it should be remembered, are social animals and much of what we know-including information about what is and what is not risky-comes from social interaction. Thus, a critical part of managing situations such as the aftermath of September 11 depends on whether people can trust what they are told by government officials. If we cannot believe what the government says, our general sense of risk is accentuated (Anonymous).

As to the insurance markets, there are a number of effects. First, the destruction of property and lives by the terrorists was huge. Moreover, it would be fair to state that all the property (or at least almost all) was insured against all kinds of calamities and many claims have also probably been made in terms of life insurance, medical claims, loss of earnings, and the ability of firms to operate, and so on. Thus in the short term, insurance companies paid out huge sums of money. In fact, it has been reported that the claims being submitted to Lloyd's of London represent the largest single loss in its venerable 300-year history and special facilities may have to be extended to Lloyd's in order for payments to be made on time. Second, despite the short-term difficulties of meeting the payments attributable to September 11, prospects for insurance as an industry now seem quite optimistic. "For example, two months after September 11, the stock price of large German insurance group Allianz had risen 31%; the price of its French competitor, Axa, had risen 44%. In other words, investors believe that, following September 11, insurance became a good business".

Why should investors believe that an industry that has just suffered huge losses is going to do exceptionally well in the future? The answer can be found in our previous discussion. First, the effect of September 11 is to increase people's perception of the level of general uncertainty in the world and their imagination of the kinds of negative events that could occur. This uncertainty, in turn, engenders a desire to take actions that can reduce the uncertainty. Many kinds of actions are possible. For example, one can avoid taking airplane flights and thereby reduce some obvious risks. (Indeed, in the month of October, major US air carriers reported reductions of between 25% and 33% in passenger traffic.) People can also take out insurance to protect themselves from any different kinds of potential losses, e.g., destruction of homes, the need for medical treatment, and so on. They may decide that, in light of recent events, their current insurance coverage is insufficient and that they need to protect themselves against larger potential losses. In other words, one major effect of September 11 has been to increase the demand for insurance. And, when demand for a product increases, suppliers (in this case insurance companies) can be more selective with their customers and also increase prices.

However, there is another reason why insurance companies are increasing prices and this also relates to increased uncertainty. Simply stated, before September 11 insurance companies had never faced such a devastating loss. Moreover, this one loss made an approach to assessing risk based on looking at past data somewhat anomalous. The past data approach works only when you are dealing with many relatively small losses over time that occur in a way that allows premiums to be calculated in a straightforward way. However, catastrophes-like September 11-send a signal that the world might have changed and that the kinds of losses that would occur in the future may be different from what happened in the past. In assessing thc chances of losses, therefore, insurance companies consider that the estimates they make are clouded by ambiguity. For the long term, they might believe that the pattern of losses will not really change; however, in the short to medium term, they will demand larger premiums to take on risks.

But, has the world really become a more risky place in which to live and should we change our behavior in consequence? As noted above, it is clear that we are now aware of more sources of risk than we were in the past. However, if it were possible to establish an objective measure of risk, I believe that an argument could be made that the world might even have become a less risky environment. The reason is that since September 11 society has started taking actions that reduce risk. For example, security at airports-although far from perfect-has been increased; emergency planning and procedures have been established in many public locations; there has been a heightened state of surveillance in many public services; and so on. Paradoxically, the mere existence of these measures could also accentuate the perception of risks of which we were previously unaware.

We can also ask whether the world is a more risky environment than it was, say 100 years ago. When we think of all the dangers of modern technology, most people's immediate reaction is to say that it is more risky or dangerous. Humans possess the means to impose massive destruction and we cannot necessarily control who has and does not have access to such weapons. On the other hand, life expectancy has increased dramatically over the last century and, on this basis alone, one could argue that the world has become a lot safer. What has changed, however, is the nature of the risks that we now face.

To conclude, I do not believe that people should curtail their normal activities because of the events of September 11. On the other hand, like any other risks that we have learned to deal with in the past, we should accept and adapt to public safety measures and exercise appropriate caution. This, in turn, implies listening to our feelings and emotions but also investing in imagination. However, to do the latter effectively, we need to become much better informed about social and economic conditions in different geographical regions as well as different world views. The greatest risks that we can all work to reduce are those induced by poverty, ignorance, and prejudice.

## RISKS IN ORGANIZATIONS

Risk breeds uncertainty, control, and destabilization. Public organizations will operate under "open arms theory", promote instability, power, and conflict that is associated with or promotes uncertainty, hostility, and risk. In the era of bureaucratic organizational turbulence, organizations may cope with risk rather than uncertainty.

In most cases leaders who are supposed to make solvent decisions, try to make decisions whose consequences will support their preferences. Instead of addressing risk (the real problem), or, acting accordingly, they invent a solution which is acted on in a good rather than the "best" way. They enjoy satisficing rather than optimizing. Leaders implement decisions (the only decisions) which promote their interests. Those which do not promote their interests are abandoned. The decisions are made and implemented in an open climate of politics, conflict, and partisan struggle. For instance, in 2003, our president (Bush) made the decision to attack Iraq not because Iraq had WMD, or was a terrorist state, but in order to get cheap oil and use its sale for reelection. Secondly, in 1986-87 the challenger disaster in which 7 astronauts were killed happened not because the scientists, engineers, and Thiokol (corporation) did not recommend a no launch decision (because they knew the problem of O-rings which could malfunction in cold temperatures), but, in spite of their knowledge about the potential catastrophe, political motive (Reagan) and NASA's bureaucratic pressure made the launch decision against the wisdom of engineers and scientists. The results were catastrophically appalling. Third, instead of using $10 billion in five years to train people in African countries how to become technologically self-reliant and economically productive, the G 8's decision to forgive Africa for its debts will still leave Africa perpetually dependent in order to avoid competition, strengthen the Liberal and Labor (LibLab) (alliance for Blair's political survival), particularly by influencing the support of Anglo-Africans and Anglo-West Indians who have significant influence in the LibLab Alliance. The Result was to perpetuate the "Vicious Circle" of dependence and poverty in Africa. When Africans accept such decisions which superficially look good, they risk being impoverished out of ignorance (in the long run). Fourth, also, many African leaders make decisions based on the politics of the stomach in which bribery, nepotism, tribalism, and patriarchal authoritarianism instead of using research, scientific objectivity, professional ethics, and issues of cultural diversity. Such stomach related decisions are risky because they do not solve problems comprehensively and effectively.

To What Extent is Risk a Problem? Risk is destructive and complex exposure to loss, injury, danger and uncertainty. The realm of social science disciplines has analyzed the concept of risk in a variety of ways. First, psychologists define risk in terms of perceptual and psychological loss that can be measured psychometrically (Slovic 1989). Second, economists view risk in terms of uncertainty because of the potential for economic gains and losses. Uncertainty can be measured with the use of models of statistical probability. Third, in a volatile climate of financial uncertainty, analysts view risk to be associated with "market risks, inflation risk, corporations, social movements and the public synergistically produce scientific interpretations that are reflective of their respective political interests. For instance, risk, knowledge or ability, and expertise are associated with great political power. Also, since risk politicizes scientific knowledge, it is capable of casting doubt on social and scientific rationalities (Nelkin 1979).

Risks are not accidents of historical periodicity. They characterize every era and civilization. They may be viewed as acts of God or nature (earthquakes, plagues, pestilence, diseases, famines, droughts, etc.). Attribution on these risks lay without the province of society. Contrary to such naturally and mythically induced risks, modern risks are attributed to a lack of internal mechanisms for controlling problems that are the inevitable products of their productive creativity. As a result of such a lack, people depend on "political, economic, social and organizational" decisions to resolve the risks. In other words, "risks are not caused by people's ignorance of solutions; they are caused by unintended and unforeseen effects of the solutions themselves" (Shrivastava 1995, 121). In other words, the source of danger is managerial or organizational ignorance (Beck 1992a). Contrary to ancient risks of societal antiquity, modern risks are pervasive, long-term, imperceptible, incalculable, and often unknown. Radio activity and chemical contamination are associated with risks emanating from Chernobyl nuclear accident that proved to be geographically pervasive, temporally transgenerational, crossed national boundaries, and remain incalculable. Ecological degradation contradicts the interests that advance industrialization, and it has differential social risk positions. Risks cross-economic class, gender, ethnic, generational and national boundaries. Risk positions exacerbate inequalities based on these variables, but wealth or power does not provide complete protection from modernization risks (Shrivasta 1995, 121). The risks adversely affect those who produce them without discrimination. In other words, since these risks transcend their traditional boundaries, their harmful effects are classless, raceless, nationless and genderless. The risks do not discriminate without merciless indiscrimination (Clarke 1989; Luhmann 1990).

The science of producing risk, spreading or diffusing risk, and commercializing it is inherent in capitalistic and socialistic modes of production through which human needs are not only articulated, but, the satisfaction of those needs is an element of societal self-edification and self-referencing. "Modernization, in seeking economic growth, inadvertently but systematically unleashes risks and hazards. Once created, such risks can expand and evolve independently of economic gains" (p. 121).

Risk has proliferated and its influence has become a global problem in terms of "population explosion, industrial pollution, environmental degradation, and lack of institutional capacity for risk management and terrorism" (p.121). For instance, the world population has increased from 2.8 billion to 6.89 billion during the last 500years (Getis, Getis, and Fellmann 1998). In the next 40 years, it will double and reach 12.6 billion. Such an uncontrollable expansion becomes a risky ecological burden on the earth's ecosystems particularly when their natural resources are depleted (Ehrlich and Ehrlich 1991). Furthermore, over 50% of the world's fish resources have been depleted in 50 years. Over 42,000 square miles of wildlife-tropical and rain forest are destroyed annually. Industrial agriculture contributes to soil degradation in terms of dehumusification, erosion, destruction of natural habitats and pollution and reduction of water table supply systems. Above all, the annual desertification of 26,000 square miles of productive land is a further risk in terms of human incapability to manage nature's bounty for his or her own long-term survival. To make matters worse, the rates of consumption growth in world reserve oil, natural gas, coal and minerals are likely to be depleted within a single century if these natural resources are not consumed with caution. The current population needs 3 to 15% annual increase in world production of goods and services in order to create a viable and balanced momentum for ecological sustainability (Clark 1989; Daly 1977; McNeill 1989; World Commission on Environment and Development 1987).

The risks of industrial pollution to human health have diffused to become "urban air pollution, smog, global warming, ozone depletion, acid rain, toxic waste sites, nuclear hazards, obsolete weapons arsenals, industrial accidents and hazardous products" (Shrivastava 1995, 122). For example, the United States alone has more than "30,000 documented uncontrolled toxic waste sites" which increase at the rate of 2,000 to 3,000" annually (p. 122; Carson 1962).

The pollution and mismanagement of the environment and organizations particularly in the "weapons policy" area seemed to have been built on "convoluted logic." For instance, Charles Bandy has argued in *The age of paradox* that both the two rival twentieth century superpowers manufactured more and more weapons of mass destruction but these missiles with multiple warheads did not only lead.

## DEMOCRATIC VIRTUES DEFEND POLITICS AGAINST TERRORISM

Peter Alexander Meyers (http://www.ssrc.org/Sept11essays/meyers. htm) argued from France, in this paraphrased soliloquay, that the world needs to defend democratic politics against terrorism. The latter has emerged and started to proliferate largely due to Western acceptance of "relativism, multiculturalism and social construction of societies". While such noble forms of liberalism are defensible, in the politics, sometimes they lead to situations in which good and evil cannot coexist largely due to the desire of both to either search for security or escape insecurity respectively. Nations should reevaluate their public policies as they utilize unimpeachable knowledge to examine with certainty, the role and purposes of certain liberal projects. It is only the human race which tolerates such social projects for living together because they use language, utter words that are

forms of speech and that can be read, written, and be reasoned about for communicative competence. The degree with which people understand such communication depends on their "ethos or character and the type of friends they surround themselves with. The inescapable truth of human implication in language concerns politics in the broadest sense, not merely the parts played by leaders or states or citizens. "Man is by nature a political animal," wrote Aristotle in the *Politics*, and we "alone of the animals possess speech." Dogs and chickens can howl or squawk with pain or pleasure; they have a *voice*. It is the miracle of human *speech* that only we can indicate to each other what is "advantageous and what is harmful, what is just and unjust." The people of Homer were convinced that to live without politics one would have to be less or more than human, either a beast or a god. What distinguishes beasts from gods is their tendency to "go it alone", to opt for unilateralism, with its inherent descent towards violence. Human beings have the alternative of politics, and we are often compelled by desire or constrained by circumstances to deploy it. People rely on violence when-for whatever reason-they are desperate or hubristic.

While politics in general is rooted in the fact that speech is essential for everyday life together, democracy is the regime which most thoroughly exploits that fact. You may ask, given what was just claimed about the alternative between speech and violence, why then do democracies produce so much violence? And although decidedly anti-democratic regimes like the Nazis or the Khmer Rouge were overwhelmingly violent, history also shows a special kind of entanglement of democracy with violence. This is not because democracy is based on violence, nor because it releases a violence already boiling within the mass of humanity. It is, rather, a secondary and unintended consequence of the extraordinary complexity of self-government, with its refusal to place everything in the hands of a small group of kings or commanders be they the rich, the virtuous, or the experts. An insistent reliance on speech over violence is as necessary for democrats as the web for the spider; it is likewise a construct of astonishing fragility. The frequency of violence points not to democracy's hidden essence, but to how easily and often it fails. Thus, even Aristotle's zoom *politikon* must constantly be on guard to spin out his history in accordance with his nature.

Of all that distinguishes the original democracy of the Athenians from our own, the American Founders rightly focused on differences of size and complexity: Athens was a city, America is a nation; Athenian citizens had Athenian progenitors, ours have come from every corner of the earth, bearing with them a bewildering plurality of persuasions. Whatever its form, the democratic *regime of speech* seems almost to require a commitment to equality. Everyone can talk, and surely, everyone has something to say. The Athenians institutionalized this equality in the principle that a citizen must rule and be ruled in turn. However, they tried to reduce the disorderly consequences of equality by strictly limiting the application of this principle. Women, slaves, foreign workers-the majority of *people*-were excluded from the number of citizens, and inequality prevailed in ancient times. Democracy was reborn in the nineteenth century when democrats began to take more seriously the principle of equality. They turned it against slavery in the fields and in the kitchen. Thus, distinctively modern versions of democracy have combined an enlarged understanding of equality with the attractions of freedom.

These developments help to explain contemporary common sense: asked why people are drawn to democracy, why they should lay down their lives for it, we think right away of the desire for freedom. Yet, the attraction to democracy may be even deeper, or it will be more visceral. Faced with the vicissitudes of life, our natural reaction is not to seek *freedom*, but to *speak out*. No one lives, and almost no one really expects to live, entirely unbound. "Ties to others are as often the solution to, as they are the cause of our problems. Democracy excites us because it offers practical possibilities for living as we must, using language to exploit our dependence on others and constantly negotiating boundaries rather than simply transgressing them. This is politics in the pursuit of freedom; in a democracy speech is not *mere words*, but the activity of politics. Freedom depends on politics which also depends on speech. The public conditions of speech, therefore, are the absolute center of democracy.

Recognize this, and you will understand why so many institutions and practices which characterize modern democratic life involve disposing citizens to speak, educating that capacity, and creating wherever possible circumstances for its exercise. The democratic citizen is apprenticed in schools, libraries, town meetings, museums, civic associations, talk shows, and the like. We are apprenticed to the public sphere. Love of country in a modern democracy has no higher form than defense of the present and future public sphere. This is ground gained with difficulty. Once had, it must be sustained. Not even noble rights of our Constitution can guarantee it. It is no "machine". It is a way of life.

"Anyone can see that terrorism is dangerous and terrorists murder people. Terrorism is morally inferior to an ethic of care – which aims to mend the suffering of others. It is even inferior to an ethic of retribution – which at least pretends to first determine the responsibility of those it kills. It is much more difficult, however, to ascertain the meaning of terrorism for the democratic citizen. This must be measured by its consequences for the public sphere." By this measure, terrorism produces two kinds of disorder. One is evident, the other hidden.

> The first is the spectacle itself. The chaos on the ground seems, paradoxically, to affirm the order of the public sphere. A terrorist act monopolizes in one instant all the means of communication. Images of death and destruction are everywhere, yet the public sphere itself explodes with life. It concentrates us. All

> faces turn to the news, all talk to the event. Suddenly, each citizen is animated by the tight sphere itself explodes with life. Out of curiosity is pointed in one direction. Two planes destroy the World Trade Center in Manhattan: the diffusion of this localized act into everyday life around the nation and around the globe seems to affirm – in some horribly inverted way – the vitality of the press, the media, and the nation. Exactly that same obsessive broadcast of the news which brings us to the terrorists' terror constitutes its apparent remedy: our newly pointed knowledge and angry unified resolve (http://www.ssrc.org/sept11essays/Meyers. htm).

This "new public order" hides a second and more enduring disorder of terrorism's making. It is hidden behind a mistaken equation of the commotion of commentators and self-inflated monologists with the real public sphere they are supposed to serve. *To speak* is not the game thing as *to be spoken to*, which is not the same as *listening*, which is in turn essential to *good speech*. The media – simply by "doing their job," whether in good faith or with the lust for profit – albeit the terrorists. They must bring us the news. But we *see* it first, and hear it only later, if at all. Terrorism, well-represented, perhaps on our astonishment, that first of all our passions. Astonishment is a suspension of time, of judgment, of action, and of words. With this weapon, terrorism takes the words from citizens' mouths. It reduces us to speechless shock. The bestial act imposes a consensus of brutes in which the animal *voice* of anguish and the god-like presumptuousness of unchecked power submerge the all too fragile democratic practices of political *speech*.

Not long after September 11, 2001 new and expansive Federal police powers were proposed in Congress. Practically, the only serious skeptic in a wave of affirmation, Senator Patrick Leahy sought to ensure that those powers would be properly checked. Former Attorney General, Ashcroft's response unwittingly showed how deeply terrorism can wound democracy. Ashcroft accused Leahy of stalling and declared that "talk won't prevent terrorism." Whether or not these powers offend constitutional rights. Ashcroft had it exactly wrong. Only talk can prevent terrorism, or prevent single localized acts of violence from producing widespread terrifying effects. Infectious terrorism, spreading out from one "Ground Zero" through millions of televisions and into every home and human spirit, kills authentically public talk.

The disease is transmitted through electrifying high drama and the self-evident urgency of self-defense. Normal, everyday differences between human beings which demand bridging, navigating, and negotiating words quickly seem to lose their importance. Yet, these differences – which are not a matter of "identities" but of contested choices and actions at every level – are the stuff of politics. The democrat, now as always, fights to forestall the moment of democracy's now as always, fights to forestall the moment of democracy's inevitable failure, the opening to violence. Our task is to make "unspeakable events" or feelings "no words can express" give way to dialogue. Seek out the hidden victim of terrorist attack, the public sphere, and set it right again. This is something no unilateral command, no executive administration, no police enforcement can do.

What, then, does the day after the day look for, is most important response to terrorism? If our project and purpose is democracy, we are called to defend politics, to defend democratic speech over violence. Only the moralist – the person who prefers the pretense of righteousness over all else – could insist that "this will be a monumental struggle of good versus evil." Democracy is a political regime not an ethical system; the rule of law in a pluralistic society depends mightily on the separation of the state from every form of church. Only the idiot – from the Greek word *idion*, or one who is concerned only with himself – could say that responding to terrorism excludes address to the national crisis in education. Schools belong in the defense budget of those who understand the democracy they love. Only the lawless believes that trampling on rights will help us now. The Constitution grants rights not only to protect individuals but to create a public sphere in which those who claim their rights may be judged and their claims redeemed by their fellow citizens.

I am talking about what happens in the long-run. In the short-run, it is perhaps inevitable that a violent reaction – bestial of god-like, depending on where you stand – will come on the heels of such an explosive act. But, here again, terrorism confuses. Is it a momentary event? Or is it the beginning of a "whole new world?" The least reflection will tell you it is neither, even if it seems like both. Violence arrests words. It snaps us into the present. Speech is concerned with life; in fact, it is the first sign of authentically human life. To say this is to say that speech is not just concerned with today, but with tomorrow as well. Thus, as the terrorist saps our words he attacks the future. The terrorist would reduce our dispositions in favor of speech and our capacities for it. He would corral us into a speechless unanimity. In such form of unanimity there is no future.

While pundits were checking the balance sheet of business after September11, 2001, an unaccounted cost for every citizen was rising. Each human being constantly encounters – in the large and small difficulties and irritations of everyday life – his own difference from others. He expresses these differences and navigates through them. When the way is blocked, he negotiates them in the only way he can: with speech. The terrorist act uses our own fears and desires to impose unanimity on us. This is an attack on politics at its core. It raises exponentially the stakes of even the most mundane negotiations. Thus, whereas a battle demands the courage of soldiers, and rescue demands the courage of civil service, the defense of politics demands the special courage of citizens. It takes courage to keep talking.

Do not mistake my words: this is not a call for talk with assassins. The situation of America or of any nation in history requires that we strike back if we can. The United States will do this within the framework of national or international law or without it. What I say here neither condemns nor condones the military actions presently underway in Afghanistan. It leaves the choice of the instrument of state policy – between bombs and diplomacy, assassination and trial – to those who will make that choice, regardless of what we think. The point is about the political life of democracy.

But we should insistently remind our leaders that, in the end, even war depends on politics. Any general will refer you to the motto of Clausewitz: "War is an extension of politics by other means and how democracies can make war. Even Mao Zetung used to say that war is the continuation of politics. We must struggle, however, not to make it against ourselves. The best way to do this is to defend politics."

## REFERENCES


Aktouf, O. 1992. Management and theories of organizations in the 1990's: Toward a critical radical humanism. *Academy of Management review* 17, 3: 432-64

Allenby, B.R. 1993. *Industrial ecology*. New York: Prentice Hall.

Archier, G., and H. Serieyx. 1994. L' enterprise du 3e Type (*The Corporation of the 3rd kind*). Paris: Seuil.

Brandy, C. 1994. *The age of paradox*. Boston: Harvard Business School Press.

Beck, U. 1992a. *Risk society: Towards a new modernity*. Newbury Park, CA: Sage.

Bell, D. 1975. *The coming of post- industrial society*. New York; Basic Books.

Bernstein, P.L. 1992. *Capital issues: The impossible origins of modern Wall Street*. New York: Free Press

Berquist, W. 1993. *The post- modern organization: Mastering the art of irreversible change*. San Francisco: Jossey-Bass.

Boje, D.M., and R. F. Dennehy. 1993. *Managing in the post-modern world: America's revolution against exploitation*. Dubuque, IA.: Kendall Hunt.

Brown, L.R. 1990. *State of the world 1990*. Washington, D.C.: Worldwatch Institute.

Caille, A. 1989. *Critique de la rasion Utilitaire, Manifeste du MAUSS (A critical Look at Utilitarian Intelligence- The MAUSS Manifesto)*. Paris: La Decouverte

Calvez, J. Y. 1970. *La Pensee de Karl Marx (The Thinking of Karl Marx)*. Paris: Seuil

Cannella, A.A., and R.L. Paetzold. 1994. Pfeffer's barriers to the advance of organizational science: A rejoinder. *Academy of Management Review 19: 331-41.*

Clarke, L. 1989. *Acceptable risk. Making decisions in a toxic environment*. Berkeley: University of California Press.

Commoner, B. 1990. *Making peace with the planet*. New York: Pantheon Books.

Couch, S., and S. Kroll-Smith. 1991. *Communities at risk*. New York: Peter Lang.

Dacin, M.T., et al. 1997. Selecting partners for successful international alliances: Examination of U.S. and Korean firms. *Journal of Worlds Business 32: 3-16*

David, F. 1989. How companies define their mission. *Long-Range Planning 22: 15-24*

Douglas, M., and A. Wildavsky. 1982. *Risk and culture*. Berkley: University of California Press.

Ehrlich, P., and A. Ehrlich. 1991. *The population explosion*. New York: Touchstone.

Etzioni, A. 1989. *The moral dimension: Toward a new economics*. New York: Free press.

__________. 1988. *The moral dimension*. New York: Free Press.

Evans-Pritchard, E.E. 1950. *Social anthropology*. London: Cohen and West.

Fagenson, E.A., ed. 1993. *Women in management: Trends, issues, and challenges in managerial diversity*. Newbury Park, CA: Sage.

Fay, B. 1987. *Critical social science*. Cambridge, England: Polity Press.

Fletcher, B.R. 1990. *Organization transformation theorists and practitioners: Profiles and themes.* New York: Praeger.

Giddens, A. 1990. *The consequences of modernity.* Stanford, CA: Stanford University Press.

Goldstein, R.L., and J.K. Shorr. 1991. *Demanding democracy after Three Mile Island.* Gainsville; University of Florida Press.

Gramsci, A. 1979. *Selections from the prison notebooks.* New York: International Publishers.

Habermas, J. 1989. *A theory of communicative action. vol. 1.* Boston: Beacon Press.

Harris, D.H. 1998. *Organization linkages: Understanding the productivity paradox.* Washington, DC: National Academy Press.

Heibroner, R. 1980. *Marxism for and against.* New York: Grove Press.

Katzestein, P.J., and T. Shiraishi. 1997. *Network power: Japan and Asia.* Ithaca, N.Y.: Cornell University Press.

Krimsky, S., and Golding. 1992. *Social theories risk.* Westport, CT: Praeger.

Luhmann, N. 1990. Technology, environment, and social risk: A systems perspective. *Industrial Crisis Quarterly* 4, 3: 223-32.

Mintzberg, H. 1994. *The rise and fall of strategic planning: Reconceiving role for planning, plans, planners.* New York: The Free Press.

________. 1989. *Inside of our strange world of organizations.* New York: Free Press.

Morgan, G. 1986. *Images of organizations.* Beverly Hills, CA: Sage. Naess, A. 1987. Ecology, *Community and lifestyle: Ecosophy.* Cambridge, England: Cambridge University Press.

Nelkin, D. 1979. *Controversy: Politics of technical decisions.* Newbury Park, CA: Sage.

Nelson, J.I., and D. Cooperman. 1998. Out of utopia: The paradox of postindustrialization. *The Sociological Quarterly* 39, 4: 583.

Perrow, C. 1984. *Normal accidents: Living with high risk technologies.* New York: Basic Books.

Peters, T. 1987. *Thriving on chaos.* San Francisco: Knopf.

Roy, W.G. 1997. *Socialization capital. The rise of the large industrial corporation in America.* Princeton, N. J.: Princeton University Press.

Short, J.F., and L. Clarke. 1992. *Organizations, uncertainties and risk.* Boulder, CO: Westview.

Shrivastava, P. 1995. Ecocentric management for a risk society. *Academy of Management Review* 20, 1: 118-37.

Sievers, B. 1993. *Work, death and life itself: Essays on management and organization.* Berlin- New York: de Gruyter.

Slovic, P. 1987. Perception of risk. *Science* 236: 280-5.

Young, O.R. 1997. *Global governance: Drawing insights from the environmental experience.* Cambridge, MA: MIT Press.

Zhao, S. 1997. *Power competition in East Asia.* New York: St. Martin's Press.

# Chapter XIV
# Effects of Terrorism in America: Challenges to National Security

## INTRODUCTION

Cathedral. The president spoke at the nation.

> War has been waged against us by stealth and deceit and murder. This nation is peaceful, but fierce when stirred to anger. The conflict was begun on the timing and terms of others. It will end in a way at an hour, of our choosing" (President G. W. Bush 9-14-2001).

September 11$^{th}$, 2001 was one of the most significant days in American history. For the first time since Pearl Harbor, America was attacked on its own soil. However, the attacks were not conventional bombings. Terrorists hijacked four of our domestic airliners and crashed them into critical infrastructure targets of America. This was a brutal and suicidal act that some would say was provoked by America's involvement in the Israeli- Palestinian conflict. Whatever reason the terrorists chose to attack us for is irrelevant now because the life of every American has changed forever. In the aftermath of September 11th, American's economy faced hardships, its citizens have developed a notable amount of Psychological problems and empirical sociological changes

In addition to damaging the economy and people of America, the events of September 11th, 2001 led to the creation of the Department of Homeland Security. Although the Department of Homeland Security promises to protect the homeland, it does not promise to protect the individual rights of all citizens. As a result of September 11th, the USA Patriot Act was passed. These act, and the original Homeland Security Agency, contain provisions that violate citizens' fourth amendment rights. This chapter will address all the issues mentioned in the paragraph above. The goal is to enlighten those who may not understand how September the 11th catastrophe changed many aspects of American life.

## THE PSYCHOLOGICAL EFFECTS OF TERRORISM IN AMERICA

Terrorism not only takes life and destroys property, but it also tries to alter the psychological health of groups of people. Those who survive a terrorist attack are not as mentally stable as they were before they experienced the attack. For example, after the events of September 11, 2001, a significant decrease in travel occurred in America. This decrease in travel was directly related to the psychological impact of the tragedy before the events of September 11, 2001. The psychological effects of terrorism in America are much deeper than just a fear of traveling. Now, because of the current threats associated with 9/11 of terrorism in America, people have developed many new phobias that unnecessarily affect their everyday life.

Terence T. Gorski suggested that "One goal of terrorism is to disrupt a society by causing wide spread psychological damage and social disruption." Apparently, the recent terrorist attacks on America are no different. Not only have these attacks dealt a severe blow to our once flourishing economy, but they have also introduced a multitude of interpersonal, social and personal problems among the groups of citizens of America. Some of these problems include stress related mental health disorders, substance abuse, and stress related to medical problems. This influx of interpersonal problems is a direct result of the psychological damage caused by terrorism in America.

Although terrorist acts affected the psyche of all Americans, there are certain Americans who are higher risks than others. Those Americans affected the most by terrorism are those who were physically injured or, experienced life-threatening danger or injury. These people have a high risk of developing post-traumatic stress syndrome (PTSD), as well as anxiety and panic disorders. "Experts estimate that somewhere between 70,000 to 100,000 people in New York City alone had the kind of exposure to the terrorist attacks that put them at risk for developing PTSD." Furthermore, many other Americans have experienced chronically high stress levels since the events of September 11, 2001. No wonder Congress and the president were able to pass a policy, in December 2010, which authorized the usage of public funds for their treatment and compensation.

Scientists classify dramatic events, which cause traumatic stress responses in two categories. The first of these two categories are the "Single Incident Traumatic Stress Experiences." This event is characterized by "a single time limited episode of traumatic violence that occurs and ends with no serious threats of recurring episodes of traumatic violence." For example, witnessing an F5 tornado tear apart your own town would be a single incident traumatic stress experience. Although the event is quite traumatic, it occurs in a limited amount of time and it is very unlikely that you would ever experience such a tragedy again. The second type of traumatic event is classified as a "Multi-incident Traumatic Stress Experience." This type of traumatic event is characterized by "Prolonged ongoing experience marked by continuous threat of or actual recurrence of episodes of traumatic violence." One example of this situation is the current dilemma between Israel and Palestine. The Israeli people live in constant fear of a violent event occurring (Horgan 2006).

America's War on Terrorism is an on going Multiple Incident Traumatic Stress Experience." The events of September 11, 2001 marked the beginning of a new lifestyle for all Americans. Since September 11, 2001, the American psyche has become vulnerable to multiple incidents of traumatic stress experiences. The media constantly reminds us that we are in a state of war. Everything from anthrax to car bombs threatens the American people. We are in the constant state of high alert. This state of high alert is damaging to the wellbeing of some Americans. Americans know that this is an ongoing war against terrorism, and that we can be attacked at any time. As a result, many phobias and stress related conditions have increased in America. Some of the immediate psychological problems that are caused by war are:

1. Chronic states of high stress resulting in stress-related health problems,
2. Chronic states of low-grade suspicion, paranoia, and hyper vigilance,
3. Persistent feelings of anxiety, fear, and dread,
4. Confusion and uncertainty, and
5. Reduced resiliency, increased depression, and demoralization resulting from continuous exposure to the threat of recurrent trauma.

Terrorism reaches deep into the psyche of adults as well as their children. Many children witnessed the events of September 11, 2001 on television. Although younger children may not understand the concept of terrorism, and finally of death, they can red behavior such as emotions. As expected, children can tell when something terrible has happened. This can affect them in a number of ways. Today's children are the future of America, which is why it is important for us to understand the psychological impact terrorism has on them. Unfortunately, terrorism has affected the psyche of America's children. Children of all ages may develop some of these characteristics after experiencing a traumatic event:

- Increased anxiety when separated from family members or re-experience the exposure through intrusive thoughts.
- Increased sensitivity to sound such as sirens, planes flying above, thunder, and loud noises.
- Sleep disturbance or fear of the dark and
- Increase in minor aches and pains due to constant worrying and poor concentration that influences decreased school performance, increased thoughts about death and dying, irritability, and worrying.

It is the parents' responsibility, as well as teachers, to make kids feel that they are safe. Parents and teachers must also reiterate the fact that America is still one of the best and safest places in the world in which to live and raise a family. Terrorism does affect that psyche of everyone in America. America's war on terror, which is, essentially, a Multiple Incident Traumatic Stress Experience, brings about this situation. Furthermore, the cost of medical treatment for these mental illnesses is staggering. For example, before the events of September 11, 2001, Americans spent $42 billion dollars on mental health issues alone. One could only imagine how much we spent on people with mental illnesses now that terrorism has provoked many more mental illnesses among Americans. As we can see, terrorism affects everything including the economy.

## THE ECONOMIC EFFECTS OF TERRORISM IN AMERICA

The events of September 11, 2001 had a tremendous effect on our nation's economy. Wall Street closed down for four days, thousands of lower Manhattan's employees were displaced, and the Pentagon also closed for a number of days. In addition to the loss of property, all airlines were grounded, which resulted in billions of dollars lost in the travel industry. However, the insurance companies stood to lose the most as a result of the terrorist attacks of September 11, 2001. Losses were expected to reach or exceed $50 billion dollars. Of the $50 billion dollar September 11 price tag, insurance companies were expected to pick up most of tab. "Reinsures were expected to pay the most-and gain the most-from this catastrophe." Insurance industry analysts said that reinsures, which insure the insurance companies, were to bear the brunt of the liability. As a result, these companies did most likely raise their premiums, which ended up giving the insurance industry a boost. Although reinsures stood to benefit from the events of September 11, the was going to exclude terrorism from future insurance policies. The main reason causing them to consider excluding terrorism from future policies was based on the idea that no one could truly estimate how much standard terrorist attack would cost. These same insurance companies had been lobbying for a House resolution, or a Senate bill that would require the federal government to intervene in the case of a terrorist attack. As indicated above, Congress ratified the bill that was signed by President G.W. Bush.Immediately after September 11th, the House introduced a resolution H.R. 3210 that would only require insurers to pay for the first $10 billion dollars in damages, and the government would be expected to cover the rest of the claims. Federal House Resolution 3210, which is called the Terrorist Risk Insurance Act of 2002, was released by the conference committee and enacted as Public Law107297. November 26, 2002 was the effective date for the law. Highlights of the law are as follows:

1. A terrorism insurance program was established within the U.S. Department of Treasury.
2. Participation in the program is mandatory for most insurers that offer property and casualty insurance.
3. The federal share of compensation paid for the insurance losses of an insurer will be 90%.
4. An insurer will in turn charge a policy holder a surcharge not to exceed three percent of the annual property and casualty insurance premiums.
5. Unless extended by a future Congress, this program was intended to sunset on December 1, 2005.

The Terrorism Risk Insurance Act of 2002 prevents insurance companies from raising premiums to unreasonable levels by requiring the government to pick up most of the cost insurance companies face after a major terrorist attack.

Although the aforementioned resolution will protect insurance companies from enormous losses in future terrorist attacks, major insurance companies still had to pay for property loss and casualties in New York that were the result of September 11th. The ripple effects of September 11$^{th}$ were felt all across the country. However, New York was the hardest hit by the attacks. In addition to the loss of one of New York's most famous buildings, many of lower Manhattans' big financial companies relocated to New Jersey. New York's flourishing tourist industry was also devastated by the attacks. Shortly after the attacks, analysts estimated that $20 billion dollars of real estate damage occurred. Brokerage Grubb & Ellis estimated that 15.5 million square feet of lower Manhattan office space was lost. "Of this, 15.5 million square feet, 11 million square feet was the world trade Center area. In addition, 10 million square feet of office space was so badly damaged that tenants stopped using it for almost a year after the attacks. Overall, a total of 36 million square feet of office space was destroyed in Lower Manhattan on September 11, 2001.

A direct loss of all the office space lost in New York was displacement of thousands of employees; many other employees were laid off as well. Both of these facts contributed to a decrease in consumer spending, the consumer preferences index tend to, essentially, drive America's economy. When consumer confidence decreases, the state of the economy usually follows right behind it. Two of the main factors that affect consumer confidence are employment and income. Obviously, September 11$^{th}$ had a profound effect on these two areas. Furthermore, the Foreign Policy Association with the 9/11 incident contributed to the War in Iraq - also factor into a decrease in consumer confidence and the associated 2007-2010 recession.

Consumer confidence is a very important part of the American economy. When the average consumer is confident that he will have a job, the ability to pay the bills, and the extra money saved, he will spend more on high priced items. However, due to adversity,the associated state of the economy places uncertainty in the mind of consumers. This uncertainty causes consumers to stay at home, travel less, and buy fewer high priced items. As a result, big business suffers. Airlines do not fill their seats, factories do not have surplus goods, and the price of many homes decreases. These companies lose money; therefore they have to lay off more employees and thereby decrease consumer confidence, which negatively drives the American economy (Heilbruner 1989).

Perhaps the industry hardest hit by terrorism was the airline industry despite receiving a federal aid package of $15 billion dollars when the nation was attacked. The airline industry is still requesting more funding to help pay for increased security measures mandated by the federal aviation requirements. The terrorist attacks have virtually made the airline industry a relatively an unprofitable business. War in the Middle East, an orange level terrorist alert, and decrease in consumer confidence, all contributed to the airline industry's dependence on federal funding.

## THE SOCIOLOGICAL EFFECTS OF TERRORISM IN AMERICA

The events of September 11$^{th}$ 2001 have, unfortunately, placed many Arab Americans in the national spotlight. Many Americans do not know anything about people in our country that are of Middle Eastern descent. As a result, Americans tend to create broad stereotypes that place all of these citizens into one category. However, September the 11th has forced our nation to distinguish between the 'Good American Arab" and the terrorist living in America. The United States Census Bureau estimated that there were 2 million Arab immigrants and 7 million Muslims living in the U.S. Although many of these immigrants are legal, many of them emigrated here illegally. September 11$^{th}$ raised questions about how all Arab and Muslim Americans should be treated.

In the days immediately following September 11th, political leaders urged Americans not to take out their frustration on these people. However, angry Americans used these people as scapegoats. Discrimination against Arab-Americans, and acts of violence towards them were committed. Yes, all of the hijackers of September 11th were of Middle Eastern descent, but why should Americans take their frustration out on all Arab Americans? Furthermore, how do Arabs and Muslims living in the United States view the way they have been treated since September the 11th?

Polls taken by Arab and Muslim Americans since September 11th indicate that many of these people feel that Americans have been relatively tolerant and respectful of Arab and Muslim Americans. However, some of these people feel that in America, as a whole, the situation is rather intolerant and disrespectful of Arab and Muslim Americans. Surprisingly, Middle Eastern attitudes toward terrorism do not vary much from those of average American opinion. In a poll taken by the Arab American Institute, which was taken before the bombing of Afghanistan began, approximately 88 percent of Arab Americans agreed with the way in which our President had responded to the event of September the11$^{th}$.

In addition, other polls showed that nearly 70 percent of Arab Americans supported an all-out war against all countries that support terrorism.

Although Arab and Muslim Americans tend to feel the same about the War on Terrorism, tactics used by the Homeland Security Agency tend to molest them more than the average Caucasian or African American. This fact brings up many critical questions. Should the civil liberties of Arab and Muslim Americans be sacrificed in order to secure the homeland? Although many Arab and Muslim Americans feel that random searches of people who look suspicious are justified, every American has certain inalienable rights that they are born with, or that protect them as American citizens. The rights of Arab Americans are no different. However, our government has sought out to impose certain procedures that violate the fourth Amendment rights of these Americans, which is the right to their privacy.

September the11th, like many other events in American history, has placed the civil liberties of one group of people at jeopardy. For example, during World War II, nearly a hundred thousand Japanese Americans were placed in concentration camps because of their suspected involvement in Pearl Harbor. Even though most of the Japanese people were citizens, the government still found it necessary to put them in detention camps in order to protect national security. This event was clearly a violation of the civil liberties of Japanese Americans. In his response to September the11th, President Bush was forced to put more emphasis on the rights of society as a whole rather that the rights of the individual.

As a result, the administration drafted a new legislation that would give law enforcement agencies more law enforcement powers. This legislation was passed on October 26, 2001 and it is called the Uniting and Strengthening of America by providing Appropriate Tool Required to intercept and Obstruct Terrorism Acts (USA Patriot Act). This act created a new crime called "domestic terrorism." Domestic terrorism is defined as:

> acts dangerous to human life that are a violation of the criminal laws of the United States or of any States; appear to be intended to intimidate or coerce a civilian population; to influence the policy of a government by intimidation or coerce a civilian population; to influence the policy of a government by intimidation or coercion; or to affect the conduct of a government by mass destruction, assassination, or kidnapping; and occur primarily within the territorial jurisdiction of the United States (Rosenzweig 2006).

Although this definition sounds fair and just, civil libertarians feel that the definition adequately coves acts of terrorism, but it also places people who actively protest against the government in the category of terrorists. Aggressive protests such as antiwar protests or abortion protests could, under the definition of domestic terrorism "be intended to intimidate or coerce a civilian population." Another set of provision in the USA Patriot Act allows the government to "sneak and peak" without having as much probable cause as the law before September the11$^{th}$ required. Some would say, including myself, that this is a direct violation of the 4th amendment. Furthermore, the act makes it easier for government police agencies to share information. This sharing of information makes civil libertarians worry that the government will use the USA Patriot Act to do something that is banned by law, such as engaging in domestic spy operations.

The USA Patriot Act also violates Article I, section 9, clause 2 of the U.S. constitution, which states that "This Privilege of the Writ of Habeas Corpus shall not be suspended, unless when in Cases of Rebellion or Invasion the public Safety may require it." Provisions of the USA Patriot Act declare that non-citizens can be detained for up to seven days without being told why, or being brought before a judge. That provision certainly doesn't encourage tourists to visit America, which negatively impacted on a suffering tourist industry at the time. In addition to the USA Patriot Act, many other measures had been taken by the Bush administration to strip Arab and Muslim Americans of their rights, as well as other ethnic groups suspected of being involved in terrorist activities. These rights are their civil liberties. Racial profiling after September the11th is also another situation that stands to violate the fourth amendment rights of many citizens.

Racial profiling is defined as, "using considerations of race, ethnicity, and national origin to help law enforcement officers decide which people to investigate." In the aftermath of September the11th, racial profiling increased dramatically, and, as a direct result, the fourth amendment rights of more Americans were being violated. Racial profiling at airport security gates is deemed necessary by the government because Federal agents feel that stiffer dogs, metal detectors, and other electronic screening devices fail to detect dangerous materials way too often. Although racial profiling at airports is an effective way to focus on potential perpetrators of terrorist acts, it is also a very effective way to make one group of people feel alienated from the rest of society.

Many critics say that racial profiling has two major flaws. One of these flaws is the fact that racial profiling focuses too much on a people of a specific race; therefore, innocent people are stopped and harassed way too often. The second flaw of racial profiling is that "it targets people who are, not what they are doing." in a sense, racial profiling violates the fourteenth amendment, which guarantees citizens equal treatment under the law. Under any circumstances racial profiling is, and will continue to be, "A morally indefensible, deeply corrosive practice."

Racial profiling corrodes the rapport between law enforcement officers who are expected to uphold the law, and law-abiding citizens that are the victims of racial profiling. As airport officials continue to racially profile Arab Americans, which is nicknamed "flying while Arab," the relationship between these officials and Arab Americans will decrease. Instead of looking upon these officials as people who are there to protect them, Arab Americans will look at these officials as people who intend to harass them. In addition to altering the way Arab Americans view airline officials, racial profiling at airports also causes emotional damage to these citizens. As the war on terrorism continues, the civil liberties of many Americans may be jeopardized. The civil liberties of Arab and Muslim

Americans are infringed on much more in a post September 11th world. However, it is the responsibility of every American to decide where they draw the line when it comes to sacrificing civil liberties, and they should vote accordingly (Taipale 2006).

The Homeland Security Agency is an entire government department that was created as a result of terrorism in America. President Bush introduced the Homeland Security Agency Act to the public during his 2001 State of the Union address. This agency "is, overall, intended to make the American people feel secure on U.S. soil." However, the statement does not justify the broad scope of measurements taken by this agency to insure that the American people can, without fear of terrorists, enjoy life, liberty, and actively pursue their happiness. Despite our nation's optimistic attitude about rooting out these terrorists, the homeland security faces many challenges throughout the pursuit of this long-term goal. Some of these challenges will be overcome by the compilation of knowledge that is attained as a result of sectors within Homeland Security Agency. In any case, the Homeland Security Agency is an amazingly complex entity designed to be organized, accurate, and efficient at preventing terrorist attacks on American soil and interests.

In the development of a more secure Homeland, the first step has been to get more organized. The United States has many different districts, and many more jurisdictions. Therefore, the Homeland Security Agency's first priority has been to make sure that all pertinent information about terrorist attacks flows through the correct channels. The only way that the Homeland Security Agency can effectively prevent terrorist attacks is to organize the structure of local governments' information regarding possible terrorist activities.

Participation of all state and local government in a national effort, which is designed to prevent terrorist attacks, requires an elaborate organization. This organization comes from creating a pyramid structure of The Homeland Security Agency. Indeed, a national strategy, which requires a national effort. This national effort is synonymous with an informed and proactive citizenry. Organizing all information from state and local governments is the first step towards, preventing terrorist attacks. Therefore, the homeland security agency has been focused on, and is working towards, the sharing of knowledge between government agencies such as the CIA, FBI, and even the DEA. All of the sixteen law enforcement agencies combined work together to perform several critical missions that are the core of the Homeland Security Agency (Murphy 2006).

Six critical mission areas provide the basis for all of the Homeland Security Agencies functions. These missions are part of a National Homeland Security strategy that is designed to prevent terrorist attacks on America and its interests. The best way to understand the Homeland Security Agency is to think of it as an agency that focuses on the following six tasks: Intelligence and Warning, Border and Transportation Security, Domestic Counter Terrorism, Protecting Critical Infrastructure, Defending Against Catastrophic Terrorism, and Emergency Preparedness and Response. Intelligence and warning, border and transportation security, and domestic counter terrorism are all missions that focus on preventing attacks. Protecting critical infrastructure, and defending against catastrophic terrorism are mission areas that focus on reducing our nation's vulnerabilities. Finally, the last mission of the Homeland Security Agency, which is emergency preparedness, is to ensure that if all other departments fail we can react to a catastrophic event to the best of our nation's ability (Parrish 2006).

Due to the fact that terrorism is dependent upon the element of surprise, the intelligence and warning sector of the Homeland Security Agency is probably the most important. In fact, the only way terrorists can achieve their goal is to strike without the enemy, which is the U.S., having any knowledge of their terrorist plans. Without the element of surprise authorities would apprehend terrorist plans before they are executed. The critical mission of Intelligence and Warning has five goals, which are to: Enhance the analytic capabilities of the FBI; Build new capabilities through the Information Analysis and Infrastructure and Protection Division as proposed by the Department of Homeland Security; Implement the Homeland Security Advisory System: Utilize dual-use analysis to prevent attacks, and Employ "red team" techniques (Collins 2006).

Government agencies have an insufficient amount of human resources that provide intelligence to us about terrorist actions abroad. This information is needed to provide a tactical threat analysis about the enemy. Knowledge of the terrorist's movements, capabilities, and current activities is the only sure way of preventing another catastrophic attack. In addition to assessing the capabilities of terrorists, this mission focuses on more than just the activities of the terrorist groups. A key part of the intelligence and warning sector is its ability to identify the political organizations, benefactors, and other sources of financial support of terrorist groups. Another important factor is to understand the motivation, goals, and current vulnerabilities of terrorist organizations in order to control their actions and influence.

The gathering of information about the enemy is just as important as assessing our own weaknesses. Assessing our vulnerability to attack is another important job of the intelligence and Warning system of Homeland Security Agency. Analysis of our own weaknesses coupled with an analysis of terrorist intentions increases our chances of preventing a catastrophic event. As mentioned before, one of the major initiatives of the Intelligence and Warning mission is to enhance the analytic capabilities of the FBI. As a result of September 11th, the FBI has made its top priority to be preventing terrorist attacks. A network of domestic and investigative information has been created to aid in the prompt investigation of terrorist activities, thus increasing the FBI's ability to thwart terrorist plans.

However, such a change in policy was not achieved instantly. The FBI underwent several changes as it incorporated preventing terrorist attacks into its main agenda. One major step the FBI took to implement Homeland Security procedures was to increase the number of staff that gathers and analyzes intelligence. Certain analysts with special expertise in the area of terrorism were hired to help analyze information; furthermore, these specialists were advised to collect data about terrorist cells in the U.S. In addition to hiring specially trained investigators, the CIA sent 25 of its analysts to the FBI. This act increased the total amount of knowledge the nation had about terrorists. The strategy was used to insure that any information that either agency had could be used to assist the other agencies in the prevention of a potential terrorist attack. As the FBI continued to gather more information that will build new capabilities, the security system had been strengthened.

Information analysis and information protection involve data analysis, and as a result, the protection of our nation's vulnerability to terrorist attacks. Before September the11th, the U.S. government did not perform vulnerability assessment on its main assets. These assessments are a critical factor in preventing an attack. Before the Homeland Security Agency came to fruition, no government agency was responsible for analyzing terrorist threats, mapping our threats against our weaknesses, and taking preemptive action. The Homeland Security Agency has enhanced the focus in the FBI and the CIA on terrorist activities, and in analyzing our weaknesses in order to protect our nation and its assets. New capabilities, which are the result of increased cooperation between the FBI and the CIA, enable the agency to carry out these tasks.

Implementing the Homeland Security Advisory system is another initiative that the Intelligence and Warning mission is responsible for carrying out. This advisory system is designed to disseminate information regarding possible terrorist attacks. The information disseminated comes from federal, state, local authorities, the private sector, and the American people. This information is used to create a common vocabulary, context, and message to present to the people about the current state of terrorist activities in America. The Advisory System is also used to inform people about the immediate threats the homeland is facing, and the measures that they should be taking to ensure their safety. Several levels of warning are used by the Advisory System to increase the public's awareness of possible attack. For example, our terrorist alert level in the United States is currently on orange. Hopefully by utilizing a dual-use analysis to prevent attacks our terrorist alert level will not remain on orange for long.

Utilizing Dual-Use analysis to prevent attacks means that this initiative is focused on limiting the public's access to certain materials that can be used for everyday life, or that can be used for terrorist purposes. For instance, items such as aerosol generator, protective gear, antibiotics, and disease-causing agents can be considered dual-use items because of their useful, or destructive potential. Unfortunately, these items can be purchased at a convenient store, and can be used to take American lives in terrorist attacks. This initiative involves the cross-referencing of these types of dual use materials to known terrorists. By cross-referencing these purchasers with FBI, CIA and other agencies databases, the risk of a terrorist attack that utilizes dual-use items can be significantly decreased.

"Red Team" techniques are specifically designed to strengthen the nation's defenses against terrorism. Utilizing "Red Team" techniques would include employing people who are responsible for viewing the United States from the perspective of its enemy. The goal of this method is to discern and predict the methods, weapons, and targets of the terrorists. The "Red Team" tactics would allow the U.S. to essentially, analyze its weaknesses and determine what form of terrorist acts we look for in being most vulnerable to Intelligence and Warning systems. This is one critical mission of the Homeland Security Agency especially intended to prevent terrorist attacks. However, preventing a terrorist attack requires so much effort including other missions of the Agency designed to aid in the prevention of an attack.

Illegal immigration into the U.S. has always been a hot topic; however, it has never been an issue that concerned keeping terrorists out of the U.S. A 5,525-mile border with Canada, and 1,989-mile border with Mexico provides many opportunities for terrorists to sneak into our country. This is where the Homeland Security Agency seeks to intervene. Every city in America is connected to the global community via train, plane, ships, or automobiles. America must provide adequate transportation systems for goods as well as people, while preventing terrorists from acquiring these transportation systems to deliver weapons of mass destruction.

The Border and Transportation Security sector of the Homeland Security agency has six major initiatives, which are to: Ensure Accountability in Border, Transportation, and Security, create "Smart Borders" that increase the security of International Shipping Act of 2001, recapitalize the U.S. Coast Guard, and to reform Immigration Services. All of these missions are crucial factors in the fight against terrorism. As analysts have learned, terrorists are ruthless individuals that are willing to use whatever means necessary to attack their enemies. The last time we were attacked, they used whatever means necessary to attack their enemies. The last time we were attack they used aircraft; however, that does not mean that they will not try to improvise some other method of mass transportation and use it to attack America. The Border and Transportation Security sector of the Homeland Security Agency is, perhaps the most important sector of the agency (Parrish 2006).

The Immigration and Naturalization Service Agency, U.S. Customs Services, U.S. Coast Guard, Animal Plant Health Inspection Service, and the Transportation Security Agency were all transferred to the Homeland Security Agency in order to ensure accountability in border and transportation security arena. In addition, foreigners will have to receive their visas through the Homeland Security Agency. Furthermore, the Department of State would coordinate the border-control activities of all federal agencies that are not incorporated within the new Department. Basically, all forms of human traffic and international containers, will be routed through, and inspected by the Homeland Security Agency. However, this goal cannot be accomplished without more secure borders, an issue which will be discussed in the following paragraph.

Post September 11th border management system will be much more different than the border management systems of the past. Today's border management focuses on linear borders, however, the Homeland Security Agency has created " the border of the future" that will be a continuum framed by land, sea, and air dimensions, where layered management systems enable greater visibility of vehicles, people, better security through better intelligence, coordinated efforts, and international cooperation against terrorist threats. Also, the border of the future will not hinder the progress of American trade, tourism, or our diplomatic interests abroad. One strategy used to forge this border of the future will be preemptive measures taken on international soil to prevent any dangerous material from ever reaching our shores. This effort will require the cooperation of many different countries around the world, as well as an effectively organized effort on the American shores, airlines, and borders (Riley 2006).

More database and travel documentation that includes biometric identifiers will also be used to prevent terrorists from entering the country. One main goal of the "Smart borders" is to decrease the misuse of travel documentation by improving the quality of passports, and the quality of other nations travel documentation. In addition to improving our own methods, the U.S. will demand that other country's control systems try to replicate our own. In future, people will be processed much more thoroughly at our borders, and more goods will be screened in an attempt to make America as safe as possible.

Increasing the security of international shipping containers is a major initiative that the Border and Transportation Security sector of the Homeland Security Agency is responsible for. These containers are a necessity when it comes to global trade, but they are vulnerable to be used as bomb careers when it comes to national security. For example, if a cargo ship coming with suspicious shipping containers, our nation would be in grave danger. Increasing the security of international shipping containers involves establishing security criteria to identify high-risk containers. In addition to the aforementioned strategies, smart containers will be used along with inspectors at foreign seaports to inspect U.S. bound ship containers (Neil 2006).

As we all know, the vulnerability in our transportation system started all this mess in the airline industry. However, implementation of the Aviation and Transportation Security Act of 2001 is consistent with the elimination this vulnerability. The core of this act is made up of a mandatory set of procedures that all airlines are obligated to adhere to. This Act recognizes security in all forms of transportation especially air transportation. However, the goals of this act cannot be achieved without the participation of state and local governments working in accordance with very strict federal guidelines. This is a broad initiative that focuses on achieving the highest level of security throughout every critical transportation agency the nation has. The U.S. plans to achieve this level of security by coordination of efforts at home and abroad, prevent the transportation of terrorists, or any dangerous goods that they would like to transport into the U.S.

Another very important initiative of the Border and Transportation security mission is the recapitalization of the U.S. Coast Guard. We know that terrorists will attack in very unconventional ways; therefore, we must put special emphasis on the area where we are most vulnerable, which is the ocean. Since 9/11/2001, every fiscal year's budget requested more money for the coast guard than has ever happened in the history of the U.S. In the past, the United States has asked the coast guard to play a major role to make a lot out of a little; however, that time has come to an end. The coast guard plays a vital role in Homeland Security, and this initiative will give them the funding to do everything in their power to prevent terrorist attacks (Bantzel 2006).

Perhaps the most important initiative involved with the Border and Transportation Security mission is the reform of immigration services. The reform of the Immigration and Naturalized Serviced (INS) was completed by the Bush administration. The INS will be internally divided into two sections one of which will enforce regulations, and the other will provide services functions. Full enforcement of INS regulations is one goal of this initiative. Another goal of this initiative is to enhance border security by implementing the Enhanced Border Security and Visa Reform Act. This Act would include the requirement that foreign visitors possess travel documents with biometric information. The Reform of immigration service's initiative is necessary for many obvious reasons, one of which is to aid in the process of domestic counter terrorism (Riley 2006). As far as domestic counterterrorism is concerned, September 11th was truly a wake-up call for our nation's security agencies. It clearly showed us the importance of gaining in-depth knowledge concerning terrorist groups and their activities. Law enforcement agencies have an additional mission now, which is to prevent catastrophic terrorist attacks. By changing the internal operations of law enforcement throughout these agencies, one major effort that has already taken place is the sharing of information between different security agencies. This effort involves the sharing of information in a cooperative environment.

Federal government agencies communicate with state and local agencies to ensure that no pertinent information is overlooked. This sharing of information is crucial to domestic counterterrorism. In addition to better communication between local, state, and the federal government, Domestic Counterterrorism mission is responsible for several other missions, which include improving intergovernmental law enforcement coordination, facilitating apprehension of potential terrorists, continue ongoing investigations and prosecutions, completing FBI restructuring to emphasize the prevention of terrorist attacks terrorists financing, and the tracking of foreign terrorists, which includes bringing those foreign terrorists to justice (Pluchinsky 2006).

Improving intergovernmental law enforcement coordination can be described as an effort to make sure that all important information about terrorists, and their activities, is available to state government, and local law enforcement agencies. In order to accomplish this goal, the FBI is expanding joint terrorism task forces (JTTF). These task forces' main duties are to investigate terrorist activities, and inform other sectors if the main duties are to investigate terrorist activities, and inform other sectors of the Homeland Security Agency about their findings. This FBI's task force is, essentially, "One of the Best" meaning that they are in the domestic trenches of America's war against terror.

Facilitating the apprehension of potential terrorism is the most important aspect of domestic counterterrorism. However, we cannot apprehend these terrorists unless law enforcement agencies have the information required to identify these suspects. As a result, several initiatives are underway that will create fully accessible database that contain information about suspected terrorist. The Department of Justice (DOJ) has already expanded its database conducive to 65,000 State and local law enforcement officers. In addition to extending accessibility to their database, the DOJ has added the names of over 30,000 fugitive aliens who are in violation of their deportation orders. This effort intends to restrict the number of fugitive aliens running loose in our country. Although all of the fugitive aliens are not terrorists, the agency wants to apprehend all of these aliens for questioning and deportation (Duecy 2006).

Furthermore, the FBI is establishing a terrorist watch list that will be the "top 10" list of terrorists that the government wants to apprehend. This list will also be accessible to all law enforcement agencies. The attorney General has established certain procedures that the FBI will follow that will allow them to collect all the information needed about terrorist groups. The Attorney General has also changed certain rules so that the FBI has more authority to investigate activities that are essential to effective domestic counterterrorism.

Continuing ongoing investigations and prosecutions is a goal that is achieved by all branches of law enforcement working together to locate and prosecute terrorists. Currently, the FBI is engaged in the largest and most extensive investigation ever; this investigation is nicknamed "the Penttbom" which is an inquiry into the event of September 11th. This initiative has one purpose, to constantly investigate confirmed and suspected terrorist activity. Continuing these ongoing investigations aids in the process of domestic terrorism by providing useful information to the remaining initiatives, which include: Complete FBI restructuring to emphasize prevention of terrorist attacks, Targeting the Financial resources of terrorists, and in the process, bringing foreign terrorists to justice (Caspersen 2006).

As said before, terrorists are very weak soldiers that exploit the weakness of their enemies in the form of unconventional attacks. September 11th was a wakeup call. The attack showed our government that it needs to protect our most valuable assets. Protecting America's most valuable assets is not an easy task. America has to protect certain areas that are considered critical infrastructure areas. These areas are: agriculture, information and telecommunications, energy, transportation, banking and finance, chemical industry, postal and shipping (McDonald 2006).

The Federal government plans to apply consistent measures to protect all of our most vital assets. Although the transportation sector is vital, every bridge is not as important as the next one. However, the most important infrastructure must be protected at all times from the most unlikely form of terrorist attack. Protecting these assets and infrastructure requires more than just resources. We also need the cooperation of many other countries, and the cooperation of proactive American citizens. Some of the major initiatives of this critical mission are as follows: unifying American infrastructure protection effort in the Department of Homeland Security, securing cyberspace, harnessing the best analytic and modeling tools to develop effective protective solutions, guarding America's critical infrastructure which must be protected at all times from terrorist attack. Protecting these assets and infrastructure requires more than just resources. guarding America's critical infrastructure and key assets against 'inside threats', building and maintaining a complete and accurate assessment of Americas critical infrastructure and key assets, ensuring effective partnership with state and local governments and the private sector, developing a national infrastructure plan, and partnering with the international community in order to protect our transnational infrastructure (Zimmerman 2006).

The private sector of business controls 85 percent of America's infrastructure; therefore, it is crucial that local authorities work together with the private sector to secure America's infrastructure. The airline was seized in order to attack other pillars of American infrastructure. In order to ensure that this scenario will not play itself again, there must be tight partnerships, and open lines of communication between private sectors of business and the law enforcement agencies looking for terrorists. This initiative is, without a doubt, the most important aspect when it comes to protecting America's critical infrastructure (Cunningham 2006).

## When Defending Against Catastrophic Threats

American policy makers know that defending our nation against terrorist attacks is one of the most crucial missions of the Department of Homeland Security. In the twenty first century, America is not the only country capable of forging WMD. In fact many countries, which also hate the U.S., have weapons of mass destruction that can be sold to terrorist organizations. The amount of carnage that occurred on September 11$^{th}$ would not be compared to the outcome of a nuclear terrorist attack. Therefore, our nation's intelligence agencies must monitor the countries that have the biological, radiological, chemical, and nuclear weapons of mass destruction. This step is necessary in order to ensure that the U.S. has knowledge required to act preemptively when a weapon of mass destruction is obtained by a terrorist organization (Nicholson 2006).

Defending against catastrophic threats is not an easy task. There are several layers that must be confused when you are trying to defend the nation against catastrophic terrorist attacks, which are very unpredictable. In fact, one part of defending against catastrophic events is trying to predict them. One way of preventing terrorists from using weapons of mass destruction on our land is to develop better methods of detecting these weapons of mass destruction. The Department of Homeland Security will have a special division that specializes in research geared toward the development; of sensors and technologies designed to prevent the transport of chemical and biological weapons of mass destruction.

The Departments of State, Energy, and Defense will all be working with other nations, as well as vulnerable areas on our continent, to ensure that none of these weapons of mass destruction will be transported into America.

Developing a broad spectrum of vaccines to protect our people from chemical and biological agents is the main priority of the homeland security agency. If all else fails, the development of these vaccines may be America's best defense against the risk of chemical and biological terrorist attacks. The agency plans to utilize the resources of the Department of Health and Human Services and Homeland Security Agency to develop a new generation of vaccines that will be effective against chemical weapons because they will be much safer than previous vaccines. In cooperation with several private sectors of the medical industry, and government departments, this critical mission, which is to defend the nation against catastrophic events, will be completed successfully.

Another important initiative that is directly related to defending our nation against catastrophic threats is the select agent program. This program is designed to aid in the prevention of terrorist attacks by tracking and securing dangerous biological agents. The Department of Homeland Security will oversee the program to monitor the shipment of certain hazardous biological and chemical toxins. By registering laboratories, the Select Agent Program has significantly increased the amount of chemicals that could be used for bioterrorism. Defending the nation against catastrophic attacks is the critical mission that is very closely intertwined with another critical mission of the Homeland Security Agency, the emergency preparedness and response.

## Interns of Emergency Preparedness and Response

The United States may take every security measure possible and still be the very victim of a catastrophic terrorist event. Therefore, one critical mission of the Department of Homeland Security is the mission of emergency preparedness and response. The mission's main goal is to minimize the damage in the case of a catastrophic event. The framework for completing this mission is already in place. Local governments, which are the immediate source of aid to victims after a terrorist attack, must be prepared to respond quickly and effectively. The Homeland Security Agency will prepare local governments for these disasters by having specially trained hazardous material teams, collapse, search, and rescue units, bomb squads, and tactical units on site at all times in order to effectively respond to a disaster (Robertson 2006).

Being prepared to respond to a catastrophic situation takes the coordination of many government agencies. In addition, local and state governments must participate. When dealing with emergency preparedness and response, the Homeland Security Department has assigned this mission a number of initiatives. The initiatives are intended to bring the state, and local governments, disaster plans in accordance with new government emergency plans. Furthermore, the health care providers and vaccination centers required to effectively treat a large number of people have been put into place. We can be assured that if any area of our nation is attacked by use of chemical or biological weapons, our disaster plans should be good enough to minimize casualties.

## THE COST OF THE HOMELAND SECURITY DEPARTMENT

Protecting our homeland is a mission that must be successfully completed in order to ensure the survival of a democratic America. But, there are some questions to ask when it comes to financing such a tremendous agency. Who will bear the financial burden of such an agency? How will the funds be spent? The government has guaranteed to aid them in the allocation of homeland security cost. The balancing of benefits and cost is an area to be concerned about. Decisions on homeland security spending must achieve two goals. The first goal these decisions must achieve is the devotion of the right amount of resources to homeland security. This goal can be accomplished by making sure that we have sufficient amount of money to support such a task. The second goal is to spend these resources on right activities. The goal of homeland security spending is to prioritize the spending plan in order to optimize our chances of thwarting terrorist plans.

The government will play two roles in determining the cost of homeland security. The government will mandate companies to adhere to certain procedures that are necessary to secure the homeland. Many private sectors of business will bear the brunt of this financial burden. For example, a private shipping company may be forced to buy very expensive nuclear weapons sensors before being permitted to continue shipping containers into America. However, the government will pay for all homeland security costs related to military operations and increased border security. The federal government will play an important role in homeland security, but it will also focus on specifying outcomes rather than the methods they will be achieved by.

Homeland security is not an inexpensive project. Not only does the agency require money, it requires physical labor and an abundance of resources. Some of these resources include labor, capital, technology, and managerial expertise. In some cases the nation will be sacrificing cleaner water and safer roads for homeland security. However, most of us would rather drink water that will not give us small pox. That water is clean enough to meet regulations and improved health standards. Either way, funding homeland security will mean less funding for other programs.

In the fiscal year 2001, the federal government allocated \$17 billion dollars to homeland security. The amount was increased to \$29 billion dollars. This same year President Bush budgeted \$38 billion for the newly created Department of Homeland Security's activities. However, these allocations were viewed as "down payments" to secure our most immediate vulnerabilities. Long term effects of these allocations were balanced out by higher taxes or inflation. Both of these circumstances acted against desire to recover, in an economic sense, from the events of September 11th, 2001. Spending must be reprioritized in order to prevent the homeland security agency from further weakening the state of our nation's economy.

On the state and local level, it is evident that governments are spending money on homeland security that is not meant to be spent in this area. States have acquired cost related measures to protecting critical infrastructure, improving technologies for information sharing and communications, and building emergency response capability. The cost incurred by states as a result of September 11$^{th}$ added up to about $6 billion dollars a year, and the cost incurred by cities was estimated to be $2.6 billion.

The government has developed an economic recovery plan that will improve federal support to state and local governments for incidents that states and cities cannot handle. Restoration of financial markets in cities is another area where the government will step into to aid in recovery. National economic recovery contingencies will also be the responsibility of the homeland security agency. The agency will take responsibilities for mapping the cost, and developing an effective response to costly terrorist attacks. It will monitor and develop economic sectors as well as assess the direct economic impacts of the incident.

## NATIONAL SECURITY

Overall, this chapter argues that a fundamental change is taking place in how the U.S. and other countries view, approach, and implement strategies to protect their 'national security. In the past,

> strategies underlying national security narrowly focused on threats that could be addressed by military and/or diplomatic means. Now, however, 'national security' is viewed in a much broader context, with the focus on preserving that which makes a country unique, and that includes the intangibles of its culture as well as what physically lies within its borders. The result is that countries are revising existing national security strategies (including those covering homeland security or domestic security) or crafting entirely new ones to address this much broader view of that which is to be protected. Drawing on recent literature and documents addressing diverse national security strategies, this chapter farther discusses the following areas: (1) the definition of national security, (2) the purpose of a national security strategy, (3) how a national security strategy is evaluated, and (4) implications for The National Security Strategy of the United States and The Nationals Strategy for Homeland Security (Caudle 2009, Abstract).

Against this backdrop, certain factors have been identified as the drivers of changes to the concept(s) of security. As identified by Biscop (2004), Brown (2003), Edwards (2007a, 2007b), European Union (2003), Herd and Lofgren (2001), and Kearns and Gude (2008), a long list of drivers: that contribute to the threat concert and meaning of national security include but are not limited to the following:

1. The diffusion of power within and among nation-states, marked by the rise of population-rich China and India and the increased importance of energy-rich states and regions;
2. The growth in the power of non-state actors such as terrorist groups and organized, transnational crime networks;
3. The proliferation of weapons of mass destruction;
4. Catastrophic national disaster;
5. Espionage;
6. Population-caused stress arising from differences in the population growth rates of rich and poor societies, illegal immigration, migration that dilutes societal identities, and the spiraling growth of mega-cities in poor countries;
7. Energy-caused stress, most importantly the increasing scarcity of conventional oil;
8. The threat of pandemics;
9. Stress caused by environmental or ecological factors that worsen or damage land, water, forests, and fisheries;
10. Climate change that causes food and water shortages and pressure on plans for economic growth;
11. Economic stress resulting from instabilities in the global economic system or economic integration, such as membership in the European Union;
12. Weaknesses in democratic institutions and an international legal order that is perceived to be ineffective;
13. Weaknesses in respect to and protection of human rights;
14. Socio-economic vulnerability resulting from business practices, such as just-in-time delivery of goods and manufacturing components;
15. Increased reliance on critical infrastructures that are vulnerable and have little spare capacity, and
16. Global poverty and ever-widening income gaps between the rich and the poor (Caudle 2009, 7).

Each of these drivers translates into threats to security, whether individually or collectively. The trend is to slot them into categories to provide a more useful framework for policy-making. The Canada Privy Council Office (2006) and the Finland Government (2006) generally categorize individual drivers into threats to (1) the security of each individual person, (2) national security, or (3) global or international security, with some overlap. For example, personal security is undermined by problems with economic security and/or the safety of food or water. Weapons of mass destruction threaten national security as a whole. Both individual personal security and national security can be threatened by organized crime or natural and man-made disasters. Similarly, global poverty undermines global or international security. Organized, transnational entry of non-citizens and terrorism imperils international as well as national security.

These sources and others (Dale (2008), Edwards (2007b), Fitz-Gerald (2008), GAO (2001b), and Snider and Nagl (2001)), suggest purposes that a successful national security strategy might serve are as follows:

1. Communicate a detailed strategic vision of the current and future security environment to help inform public audiences both at home and abroad about national intent;
2. Communicate the nation's values in the twenty-first century;
3. Present a comprehensive national security threat and risk assessment to define and prioritize requirements for the full range of threats to the homeland;
4. Bring together the plethora of department white papers, policies, and strategies covering national security;
5. Offer explicit prioritized, quantitative and measurable goals- objectives with timelines;
6. Identify what domestic and international factors, such as comparative capabilities, issues, and trends, that will affect achieving security goals and objectives;
7. Develop a framework for collaboration across government on national security policy, roles and missions, and identify policy areas where departments and agencies can be more efficient and effective in working together;
8. Indicate which elements of national power (ways and means) are to be used to meet goals and to guide other government departments and agencies processes for budgeting, planning and executing, and organizing, training, and equipping personnel, and
9. Clearly link goals and the approaches designed to meet them to provide a tool for requesting resources (Caudle 2009, 10-11).

## Evaluating a National Strategy

How is a national security strategy to be evaluated? Certainly, a starting point for evaluating a national security strategy is simply its content - its words. The GAO has written extensively on national strategy content, particularly that directed at evaluating a National Strategy combating terrorism and achieving Homeland Security goals. For example, GAO (2001a; 2002) advised that a national security strategy should contain a clear vision statement that defines what the nation hopes to achieve through programs that combat terrorism. Content should include information on the roles and responsibilities of all levels of government, establish prioritized goals and objectives with milestones and performance measures, recognize partnerships such as grants, regulations, tax preferences, and partnership to implement the national strategy and achieve national goal. GAO expected that a national strategy should be one way to ensure the integration and focus on all national effort elements to combat terrorism will be viable.

In 2004, GAO identified and defined the characteristics of an Effective National Strategy. GAO believes that federal agencies and other stakeholders might use strategies with certain desirable characteristics to shape policies, programs, priorities, resource allocations, and standards. GAO's characteristics are: (1) a statement of purpose, scope, and methodology; (2) problem definition and risk assessment; (3) goals, subordinate objectives, activities, and performance measures, (4) resources, investments, and risk management; (5) organizational roles, responsibilities, and coordination; and (6) integration and implementation. Drawing on the GAO work and the discussion above on scope and purpose, Table X1V.1 identifies possible characteristics and examples of key elements for each characteristic (http://www.bepress.com/jhsem/vo16/iss7/22).

On paper, a nation might have developed a national strategy that is comprehensive and that reflects all of these characteristics. Now the attention should move to implementation, whether it is effective, or even great. Sauter and Carafano (2005) provided some thoughts on the most influential strategies - those that they say mobilize the country. In large part, they believe that such strategies are those that provide clear guidelines and make hard choices about allocating scarce resources, setting clear goals, or establishing priorities. Their evaluation criteria include sufficiency and capacity. Sufficiency asks if a national strategy contains adequate guidance for directing national policies and programs. Capacity asks if the strategies can meet threats identified in the strategy. Davis, Johnson, Long, and Gompert (2008) also recommend that comparative alternative strategies should integrate expectations about effectiveness, risks, and resource implications.

Evaluation of greatness also may consider periods in the life of a national strategy. Initially, greatness might be evaluated with the development and issuance of a national strategy. In this time period, evaluation might ask to what extent the strategy clearly identifies stakeholders and their interests, the strategy's breadth and depth, alternative outcome choices, selection criteria for what should or should not be included, and its levels of detail - from a statement of principles to detailed action plans. According to Doyle (2007), a nation might

Table XIV.1. National Security Strategy Desirable Characteristics

| Characteristics | Description/(Example Key Elements) |
|---|---|
| Purpose, Scope, and Methodology | Why the strategy was produced, the scope of its coverage, and the process by which it was developed.<br><br>(Broad or narrow purpose statement; comparison/contrast with other national and international strategies; major functions, mission areas, and activity coverage; process producing strategy; key term definitions) |
| Problem Definition and Threat Assessment | The particular national and international short-and long-term problems and threats to which the strategy is directed. |

| | |
|---|---|
| | (Discussion/definition of immediate and longer-term problems, their causes, strategic environment; threat assessment and scope) |
| Goals Subordinate Objectives, Activities, and Performance Measures | What the strategy is trying to achieve in terms of scope, capabilities and steps to achieve those results, as well as the priorities, milestones, and performance measures to gauge result.<br><br>(National values and interests, overall national and international outcomes and specific result desired; hierarchy of strategic goals and subordinate objectives; specific means and strategies to achieve results; priorities, milestones, and performance measures; process for monitoring and reporting on progress) |
| Resources, Investments, and Threat Management | What national and international resources and partnerships are needed to address threats and how they will be allocated to address goals and objectives.<br><br>(Resource sources and amounts, partnership identification and needs, sources of resources; resource allocation mechanisms) |
| Organizational Roles, Responsibilities and Coordination | Who will implement the strategy, what their roles will be compared to others, and mechanisms for them to collaborate and coordinate their efforts.<br><br>(Specific roles and responsibilities all actors; lend support, and partner roles and responsibilities, processes for coordination and collaboration) |
| Integration and Implementation | How a national strategy relates to other national and international strategies' goals, objectives, and activities, and to subordinate levels of government and their plans to implement the strategy.<br><br>(Vertical and horizontal integration; details on specific international, federal, - state, local, or private strategies and plans) |

*Source:* Derived from GAO, 2004, Table 4, pages 30-31

question if it has the "right" national security strategy by examining the process by which it was derived: if the process for producing the strategy is flawed, the national security strategy will be flawed.

Because implementation of a national strategy occurs over a period of time, evaluation may consider what means and strategies have been put in place and what goals and objectives have been achieved, in what time frame, and with what outcomes. Here, Doyle (2007) might ask if the financial resources needed to make a strategy work are requested and if the strategy meets its goals and objectives on a global basis. Liotta (2002) cautions that grand strategies should focus on the means and mechanisms of the strategy, such as the size of military forces, compliance with international rules, or membership in international institutions, that are best suited to achieve security. Finally, as the national strategy outcomes emerge, evaluation can consider the strength of learning and updating, the sustainability of proven means, and the flexibility to respond to new threats and their implications.

## CONCLUSION

Obviously, September 11 and its aftermath radically changed the way Americans conduct their economic, political, social, diplomatic, military and even private lives. Economically, the stock market was the first and hardest hit sector of the American way of life. Following the attack, consumer confidence decreased dramatically and affected the American economy. In addition to a hurting economy, the terrorist acts and the Middle Eastern conflicts that are the result of the terrorist attacks, drove oil prices up. The increase in oil prices caused many people to get out less and spend less money, which also hurt the economy. Sociologically, the events of September 11th have changed the meaning of privacy in the context of the Patriot Act. The USA Patriot Act allows the government to "sneak and peak" on citizens without a specific reason. Furthermore, the Civil Rights of Arab Americans are open for infringement according to provisions in the USA Patriot Act. The main civil rights of Arab Americans that are violated are those concerned with the fourth amendment right, which is their right to privacy. Even Arab Americans who are law-abiding citizens can find themselves being spied on, detained without knowing why, or randomly searched in homes and airports because of their skin color and the region to which they belong.

The government has taken steps toward a safer homeland security system by passing the USA Patriot Act, and by developing the Homeland Security Department. The Homeland Security Department is the largest government entity ever created. It employs more than 170,000 employees, and it will be a combination of America's 22 major government agencies. The Homeland Security Department has six critical missions that are designed to keep America safe. These critical missions are: *Intelligence and warning, border and transportation security, domestic counterterrorism, protecting critical infrastructure, defending against catastrophic terrorism, and emergency preparedness and response.* Although the government promises to use the Homeland Security Department to defend America from terrorist attacks, it may not do so without challenge. This chapter's primary assumption is that national security strategies are valuable and certainly can be improved in addressing security challenges from what, for whom, and by what means. It has been argued that national security should be viewed in a broader context considering a wide range of threats from those posed by nation-states with global poverty and the growing income gaps. These threats should not be compartmentalized and boxed into traditional and non-traditional perspectives and actions. Each country will need to consider these as it crafts its definition of national security and approaches to national security. It has argued that the "for whom" now includes the security of individuals to the security of the international community. The chapter also has posed the many purposes a national strategy might serve and goes on to provide an evaluative framework for both content and effectiveness. Lastly, the chapter provides several recommendations for the current United States security strategies for national security and homeland security. The strategies should be united into one strategy. It contains much more substance to provide direction for security actions, provide clarity regarding leadership and accountability, and addresses implementation, sustainability, implications and overviews.

Though the immediate aftermath of the effects of terrorism in America, the West and in general, their allies, have largely been negative, such terrorist and fundamentalist challenge to contemporary world civilizations has stimulated a wakeup call for moral reconstruction, political and economic rationality, and military adventure and assertiveness during the Bush and Obama administrations. However, the New Obama administration, which seems to be more interested in the universal restoration of American domestic and foreign policy values has assertively started to, both by precept and example, encourage and empower the evolution of a new doctrine, vision and spirit that is essential for and critical to global coexistence, engagement, security, and prosperity. In the light of the concept of strategic global rationality, public officials, corporate and security executives, first responders and academia should gather data, analyze it, and interpret it to understand the motivations, psychology, and methods employed by terrorist networks to threaten, disempower and subdue or injure their enemies, "we the people".

In such a climate, the role of local, state and national government should be to partner with business, professions and labor by using intelligence to gather information for the development of risk management concerns, focus on security investments, concentrate on reduction of psychological impact of terrorist incidents, start securing important infrastructure, and cyberspace and digital systems. Government should also focus on border and transportation security through which transnational terrorism could penetrate and cause harm. Issues of immigration and maritime and aviation security should be monitored with care. Public health and medical preparedness that can proactively address the culture of disaster should be put in place. Science, technology and information should be shared innovatively in order to combat the threat of terrorism. Such kind of strategic counter terrorism is imperative. Such kind of strategic preparedness should be crafted wisely without counterterrorist knowledge and without violating the domestic spirit of liberty and international and constitutional law.

## REFERENCES

Biscop, Sveb. 2004. The European security strategy implementing a distinctive approach to security. In *Securite & strategie*, Paper 82, March 2004. Brussels: Royal Defense College.

Bryson, John M. 2004. *Strategic planning for public and nonprofit organizations, 3rd ed.* San Francisco, CA: Jossey-Bass.

Canada Privy Council Office. 2006. *Security an open society: Canada's national security policy*. Ottawa, Canada: Privy Council Office.
Caudle, Sharon L. 2009. National security strategies: Security from what, for whom, and by what means. *Journal of Homeland Security and Emergency Management* 6,1: 1-26.
Dale, Catherine. 2008. *National security strategy: Legislative mandates, execution to date, and considerations for congress*, Updated July 28, 2008, RL34505, Washington, DC: Congressional Research Service.
Doyle,and Richard B. 2007. The U.S. national security strategy: Policy, process, problems. *Public Administration Review* 67, 4: 624-9.
Edwards, Charlie. 2007a. *National security for the twenty-first century*. London: Demos.
__________. 2007b. *The case for a national security strategy*. London: Demons.
European Union. 2003. *A secure Europe in a better world: European security strategy*. Brussels: European Union, December 12, 2003.
Finland Government. 2006. *The strategy for securing the functions vital to society. Government resolution* November 23, 2006. Helsinki, Finland: Finland.
Fitz-Gerald, Ann M. 2008. A UK national security strategy: Institutional and cultural challenges. *Defense Studies* 8, 1: 4-25.
General Accounting Office. 2004. *Combating terrorism: Evaluation of selected characteristics in national strategies related to terrorism, testimony before the Subcommittee on National Security, Emergency Threats, and International Relations, Committee on Government Reform, House of Representatives*, February 3, 2004, GAO-040408T, Washington, DC: General Accounting Office.
Herd, Graeme P., and Joan Lofgren. 2001. Societal security, the Baltic States and E.U. integration. *Cooperation and Conflict* 36, 3: 273-96.
Homeland Security Council. 2007. *The national strategy for homeland security*. Washington, DC: Homeland Security Council.
*http://Abcnew.go.com/section.living.healthology.psychologicaleffects.html*
*http://www.beppress.com/jhsem/vol6/iss/22*
Kamien, David G. 2006. *The McGraw-Hill homeland security handbook: The definitive guide for law enforcement, EMT, and all other security professionals*. New York: McGraw-Hill.
Kearns, Ian, and Ken Gude. 2008. *The new front line: Security in a changing world*. Working Paper No. 1, London: Institute for Public Policy Research.
Liotta, P. H. 2002. Boomerang effect: The convergence of national and human security. *Security Dialogue* 33, 4: 473-88.
Obama, Barack, and Joe Biden. 2008a. Blueprint for change: Obama and Biden's plan for America. http://www.barackobam.com/issues/homeland_security
__________. 2008b. Homeland security. http://www.barackobama.com/ issues/homeland_security/index.phm (accessed November 5, 2008).
Presidential Directive.1. 2009. *Organizing for homeland security and counterterrorism* February 23, 2009.
*The 9/11 Commission report: Final report of the National Commission on Terrorists Attacks Upon the United States*. 2003. New York: W. W. Norton and Company.
White House. 2002. *The national security strategy of the United States of America*. Washington, DC: White House.
*www.cnn.com/2001/COMMUNITY/09/25/glasner/index.html*
*www.house.gov/constitution.html*
*www.Money.cnn.com/2003/01/27/news/economy/consumer/index.htm*
*www.money.cnn.com/2003/04/02/news/economy/factoryorders.reut/index.htm*

*www.money.cnn.com/2002/09/24/news/companies/airlineshearing/index.htm*
*www.money.cnn.com/2001/11/09/companies/aftershockinsurance/index.html*
*www.money.cnn.com/2001/09/18/economy/wtcoffice/index.htm*
*www.money.cnn.com/2001/09/17/companies/wtcinsurance/index.htm*
*www.ravanalyse.nl/reports/200`09301752.html*
*www.tgorski.com/Terrorism/talkingpointbulletion01 psycheffectsofgerrorism.htm*
*www.whitehouse.gov/homeland/*
*www.whitehouse.gov/homeland/book/index.html3*. *www.washtiems.com/upi-Breaking/06062002-062623-5936r.htm*

Yarger, Harry R. 2008. *Strategy and national security professional: Strategic thinking and strategy formulation in the twenty-first century*. Praeger Security International: Westport, Ct.

# Chapter XV
# The Global Energy Security

This chapter examines the specific elements of energy policy-making community and the relationship between this group of people and the national or supranational energy producing organizations and nations within the global, neoliberal, and neorealist political environment. This environment is influenced by strategic, technological, industrial and historical variety and distinctiveness. In other words, the "external policy-making concerning security matters and the internal policy making concerning organizational and market-related issues...is characterized by particular policy sub-systems with its own actors, instruments, arenas, and dynamics" *(Prontera 2009, Abstract).

## Energy Security

The history of the global oil industry since its inception is a succession of booms, threats and busts that psychologically influence policy makers to make adjustments in their national and regional development strategies such as, geopolitical and geostrategic thinking. Over the years, that thinking has been employed to treat oil as a fungible commodity or as a scarce resource whose availability, production, distribution and consumption must be secured with the employment of passive, neutral and active diplomacy that is backed by assertive and systematically hegemonic policies of the Carter, Powell, Bush II and Obama doctrines.

For instance, the geostrategic relationship between the United States and the Middle Eastern countries, particularly, the United States and Saudi Arabian relationship is rationalized beyond equation. In reality, the relationship was based on the congruence of interests between the two countries during and after the Cold War. The Saudi Arabian Kingdom was adamantly anti-communist and with this knowledge the U.S. administrations successfully built on that fact, to develop joint projects that wed Saudi financial resources and, at times religious influence to a series of targeted covert operations (Bronson 2006). Some of the underlying ventures include those that took place in Angola, Nicaragua, South Yemen and Afghanistan. Because the kingdom did not want its role to be known in these matters, the American public was left uninformed about it as well.

At the apex of U.S. Saudi Arabia relationship were radical differences over Palestinian and other Arab matters. For example, the Saudi Arabians were severely frustrated over the 1973 war between Israel and the Arabs. The situation influenced King Faisal to impose an oil embargo on the U.S. in order to put pressure on Richard Nixon and Secretary of State, Henry Kissinger, to be actively involved in post-war diplomacy. Kissinger resented this kind of pressure which he viewed to be a form of Saudi blackmail which he neutralized by engaging in shuttle (ping pong) diplomacy.

Though, the U.S. Saudi relationship became less important in the post-Cold War era, it was reignited in the 1990's when Saddam invaded Kuwait and threatened to attack the Kingdom and its neighbors. The Kingdom's need for an external protector made it necessary for the U.S. to station American forces on the land of Islam, an action that desecrated the two holy sites of Islam and its religious tenets. This external element on the Kingdom's foreign and domestic policy is questionable in the Arab World and did inadvertently create momentum for the rise of Osama Bin Laden. Throughout the 1990's and after, King Fahds place in history was made more precarious.

The King's relationship with the Clinton administration was "in tatters." When Bush II was reelected President (2004-2008), it was reignited. Currently, though the relationship between the U.S. and Crown King Abdallah, who has greater control over Saudi public policy, contributed to the dramatic rise of oil from $80 per barrel to over $103 per barrel may have not only made the U.S. to reassess its role in the Middle East, it but also influenced the US to turn to Africa in search of new friends and oil markets in the wake of fossil fuel diversification, solarization, and ethanolization of energy.

## THE HISTORY OF ORGANIZATION OF PETROLEUM EXPORTING COUNTRIES (OPEC)

OPEC was originally the inspiration of Venezuela and Iran in an intergovernmental organization that was founded in 1960 in reaction to the pricing and production policies of the big oil companies in 1959 and 1960. OPEC made it possible for producer countries to attain higher prices by driving the Western companies into the defensive and ultimately taking control of most of their holdings in the region. Throughout most of the 1960s, a surplus in oil production contributed to a downward push in real oil prices. Under these conditions, the objective pursued by OPEC was to prevent a further decline in prices. By 1970, market conditions had begun to produce an upward trend in oil prices. With the October War in 1973, a revolutionary chance in the oil market occurred when

Arab oil producers of OPEC-the Organization of Arab Petroleum Exporting Countries (OAPEC)-imposed an oil embargo upon the United States and the Netherlands for their support for Israel, during the Arab-Israel conflict. This was followed by the quadrupling of the price of oil by OPEC to U.S. $10.84. These developments continued through to 1978 when many OPEC governments nationalized oil companies operating on their territory.

OPEC now had the ability to set oil prices and determine production and sales policies. This change in oil prices contributed to a watershed in world economic affairs. Arab oil monarchies were in receipt of vast petrodollar reserves which they invested mainly in Europe and the United States. This dramatic increase in incomes financed the great economic boom of the 1970s and early 1980s in the Middle East while contributing to a slower, more erratic economic growth in the industrialized world. But the second oil price rise of 1979-1980 to nearly US$40 a barrel resulted in falling world prices, particularly in commodity prices. Oil prices soon began to decline until the prices collapsed in 1986 to a low at one point of $8, rising to $18 in 1987. After the use of oil as a political weapon in 1973-4, the power of OPEC was its ability to set the price of oil that consumers would have to pay. OPEC itself had and has no internal unity except on the matter of setting the price of oil to their advantage-and even here unity is not always evident. Saudi Arabia is the only oil producer that can raise or lower its oil production by a million barrels per day without seriously affecting its own economy or policy. For a time, it would attempt to discipline members who did not adhere to their agreed quota by threatening to raise or lower its own production. This policy utterly failed between 1980 and 1982, when the market was flooded by oil. When in 1986, the year of the price collapse, an OPEC conference finally met to set a maximum level for output and agreed to a quota system for all members except Iraq in order to reverse the decline and stabilize the price at $18 per barrel by 1987. But, when the Iran-Iraq War ended in 1988, and both Iraq and Iran came back into the oil market, the agreed quotas were undermined. Between 1988 and 1990, the year Iraq invaded Kuwait, the quota system collapsed. During the Gulf War(1990-1991), Saudi Arabia increased its production from 3 million barrels per day to 8.5 mbd and after the war it refused to return to its prewar level. A decline in the price set in because of a virtual production free-for-all advocated by the members. As many of the OPEC members were in great revenues, there emerged the problem as to how they would share the burden of reducing production or arriving at prices that would keep oil attractive to an increasingly and environmentally conscious industrialized world which was preparing to further trim its use of oil by 1999. Saudi Arabia and Iran had been competing with each other for market share pending the return of Iraq to production. Both were in great need of revenues, did not feel obliged to reduce its production while it was recovering from war. Indonesia, Algeria, Nigeria, as medium–sized producers with great need of revenues, did not feel that they should be asked to restrain their production. Small producers had increasingly felt that it was not equitable for them to be asked to cut their production. OPEC has brought great changes in the world economy and great benefits to its members but has not yet developed a formula for co-operation amongst its members (McLean 1996). Oil made some of its members to be viewed as small superpowers.

## THE MISSION OF OPEC

The main purpose of OPEC is to determine "the best means for safeguarding their interests, individually and collectively; devising ways and means of ensuring the stabilization of prices in international oil markets with a view to eliminating harmful and unnecessary fluctuations; giving due regard at all times to the interests of the producing countries; an efficient economic and regular supply of petroleum to consuming nations, and a fair return on their capital to those investing in the petroleum industry." (http://www.en.wikipedia.org/wiki/Opec). This purpose is also not only the aim but also the "mission" of OPEC.

OPEC was founded in Baghdad in September 1960 for the unification and coordination of member country's petroleum policies in terms of OPEC production quotas, pricing and production capacity levels. The original OPEC members are Iran, Iraq, Kuwait, Saudi Arabia and Venezuela. Between 1960 and 1975, OPEC expanded to include Qatar (1961), Indonesia (1962), Libya (1962), the UAE (1967), Algeria (1969), Nigeria (1971), and Angola (2007). Although Equador and Gabon joined later, the former withdrew in December 1992 and the later, in January 1995. Largely due to the 1990/91 post-Gulf War containment of Iraq, its production stopped to be part of the OPEC quota production arrangement in March 1998 when the UN controlled its oil production largely for food and welfare needs only. Estimates by EIA show that eleven "OPEC members account for roughly 40% of the world's oil production, and about 2/3 of the world's proven oil reserves" (p. 1). In 2000, the price of oil was $27.60 per barrel. In 2005, it was $50.71 while in August 2006 the price increased to $72.12 per barrel. In November 2007 it was about $100 per barrel. Those prices are set by oil ministers who regularly meet at Vienna, Austria-the OPEC headquarters. Currently, the price is about $100.

In 2005, the OPEC cartel accounted for 41.7% of the world's oil production while OECD was responsible for 23.8%. At the same time, former USSRA countries accounted for 14.8%. Whenever there is war in the Middle East, OPEC tries to escalate the price of oil in order to punish Western nations for their support of Israel. For instance, the 1973 Yom-Kippur War, the war between Israel and Syro-Egyptain forces caused OPEC to increase oil prices against the West for supporting Israel. Oil prices were raised by 10% in January 1975.

OPEC countries convened a meeting in Algiers, Algeria and initiated "a stable and just commodity prices system, international food and agriculture program, and technology transfer from North to South, and the democratization of the economic system" (p. 4). Though Saddam Hussein advocated the increase in prices during the 1980s Iraq-Iran War and during the 1990/91 Iraq-Kuwait invasion, the end of these conflicts caused the price of oil to plummet below world standards but only to skyrocket to above $90.00 in 2007 largely due to the prolonged U.S.-Middle East War. In 2003/04, OPEC produced 60%-62% of the world's oil energy supplies. Production cuts (supply cuts) increased prices because the demand was higher and the supply was smaller. In 1998, the South East Asian economies suffered terribly partly due to dollarization and partly because of inflation. These economic downturns caused OPEC to collectively lower oil prices and extend loans to the SE Asian economies. This contributed to the decrease in oil demand that also became highly exacerbated after 2005 as discussed earlier.

## THE CHALLENGES AND PROSPECTS FOR WORLD ENERGY SECURITY

The rise of the new global powers (E.U., Japan, Russia, China, India) and the great demand for and dependence on the Middle East gas and oil market greatly influenced U.S. diplomacy and international relations (Brookhyser 2007). U.S. diplomacy and international relations are severely being tested and challenged by Venezuela's Hugo Chavez who is a socialist and has threatened to nationalize oil industry in the Orinoco Belt where production has declined from "3.7 million barrels a day to 2.4 million barrels a day" (Chen and Jeffe 2007, 11). Saudi Arabia's Aramco Oil has cut prices over 20 years irrespective of U.S. investment assets in the company.

On the European continent, "while using Russian energy resources, the E.U. countries are seeking diversified supplies through alliance with the Arab network and Iran. In the Middle East, the E.U. countries are competing with Russia and China at the expense of their (European) relationship with the United States" (Satanovsky 2007). European soldiers have been fighting in the Middle East within NATO and the U.S. led coalition in Iraq; they are, at the same time, external to these structures that are actively involved in the lives of their former colonies. For instance, European soldiers in Iraq and Afghanistan have tried to distance themselves from the American counterterrorist and counter-guerilla operations in order to attain nonconfrontational relations with the populace. No wonder, comparatively speaking, U.S. casualties have been alarmingly higher than those of their counterparts.

Though Chinese-Russian interests in the Middle East converge for their collective anti-American incongruence, later, if Chinese hegemony neutralizes their influence, Russia may seek the support of India and Pakistan in order to counteract Islamist fundamentalism. Neither Russia nor China may succeed in getting Indian support since the latter, largely due to its geopolitical, democratic, and excellent scientific intellectual traditions, has joined the Western camp. In other words, diplomatically speaking, whether or not the U.S. acts in a passive, neutral, or activist and confrontational way in order to protect its energy producing allies, national oil companies (NOCs), though not eminently threatening to the U.S. national security interests, the rise and influence of NOC's appear to vigorously challenge U.S.'s geopolitical goals. As a result, the challenge also undermines "U.S. economic power, and the efficacy of international standards concerning basic human rights, good corporate governance, and global investment and fair trading practices" (Lhen and Joffe 2007, 14). These "national oil producing and pricing NOCs, in the coming decades" (p. 10), will challenge the U.S. because they are superpowers.

In 2005, "the globally proven oil reserves were 1,148 billion barrels 77%, 886 billion barrels of which were controlled by NOCs. Russian oil companies control 6% (69 billion barrels) while. ... Western International Oil Companies (IOCs), which dominated the oil industry during the twentieth century, now control about 10% of the world's oil and gas resources base" (p. 15). The leading national oil companies include but are not limited to Gazprom-Russian Lukoil, Iran's NIOC, Pemex of Mexico, Algeria's Sonatrach, INOC of Iraq, PetroChina, Kuwait Petroleum Corp., Brazil's Petrobras, Rosneft of Russia, ADNOC of Abu Dhabi and Nigerian National Petroleum . For Iran, national oil companies have made it to become a rich nation in which 36 countries have concluded $160 billion in business particularly in the energy sector. This kind of global economic involvement has made it difficult for the U.S. to isolate Iran for its hostile and fundamentalist rhetoric against Israel and the West. In addition, Chinese and Russian companies have heavily invested there. In Nigeria, Western Oil Corporations dominate the Nigerian oil industry particularly at the Niger Delta. Their environmental destruction and reluctance to invest in the local production by 25% (p. 15) cause friction. In future, if this situation is not "handled more deftly, the entry of NOCs into foreign exploration and production in areas marked by governance failures and humanitarian crisis, let alone hostility to the U.S., could fuel more internecine violence and international disputes, while ... destabilizing oil-rich areas needed for increasing global supply" (p. 15). The Current 6+1 deal may solve the "Iranian card."

In relation to energy security issues facing the NATO countries, Senator Richard Lugar (2007) has correctly argued that although oil rich Third World nations do not have technology, the geological structure and texture of these nations and the regional, global and political conditions in their countries have made them super powers because they have oil and natural gas companies. These governments set prices through their investment and production decisions and they have wide latitude to shut off the taps for reasons of politics and power" (p. 23). Lugar feels that NATO countries might be victimized by the fact that the countries have not only lacked investment opportunities in the oil industry but the "oil superpowers" might politically manipulate the West, which is also potentially under the cloud of Islamicist terrorist attack. In other words, "in today's geostrategic environment, fear threats are more perilous than the potential cut off of energy supplies. The use of energy as a weapon is not a theoretical threat of the future; it is current reality" (p. 25).

This challenge to trans-Atlantic alliance demands the two regions to militarily, economically, and geostrategically work together to create an International Energy Agency which can help them to secure and maintain reliable power for regulating and ensuring that world energy supplies will not be affected by manipulative and politically motivated oil new "superpowers". This is necessary because "jobs, health, and security of modern economies and societies depend on the sufficiency and organization of diverse energy resources" (p. 26).

NATO countries are highly challenged by global and geostrategic forces in the area of energy security. Energy security is a term that can be defined in terms of NATO's global energy dependency and its potential vulnerability in the light of energy cuts and supply disruptions caused by a variety of forces. In other words, these forces include "risks such as underinvestment in infrastructure, which can lead to massive power outages, and poorly designed markets, as well as disruption to energy supplies due to natural disasters, accidents, and international terrorism" (Legendre 2007, 29). If such conditions continue to threaten NATO's energy security as they have done in the past, NATO needs to counteract the possibility of such vulnerability by establishing a strategic and comprehensive mechanism that provides intelligence data, information, and decision making for political guidance, economic and military planning, defense planning, surveillance and protection of energy infrastructure, industrial planning, emergency planning, and the monitoring of terrorist activities particularly around the bottlenecks and centers and sites of origination. In addition, since the OECD countries "imports 44% of their natural gas; 50% of which comes from Russia (p. 30), this kind of mathematical dependence is not consistent with Western inability to diversify their energy independence requirements in terms of experimentation with ethanol varieties and industrial liquefaction of fossil fuel for hydrocarbon consumption.

Their potential diversification of the energy supplies will minimize such risks as:

> lines of communication and transportation. More oil and gas are either being transported over long distances through continental and even intercontinental pipeline systems, or increasingly, carried in tankers over vast oceans. Production of Liquified Natural Gas (LNG) will grow further and will be transported on supertankers over long distances as well. With 40% global oil supplies produced in the Middle East, transit through the Strait of Hormuz, the Persian Gulf represents a substantial choke point. The Hormuz Strait, as well as other choke points is not only vulnerable to international terrorism, but also to disruption by piracy or belligerent states. Furthermore, terrorists could attack infrastructure bottlenecks such as refineries, loading terminals, or offshore platforms, as well as pumping and pipelining infrastructure in member and partner territories. Finally, the potential for international conflict as a result of regional political upheavals as well as for increased instability in oil and gas producing countries; also threatens energy security (pp. 30-31).

To overcome or contain the source of the problems that are threats to energy security for the Western alliance, NATO has developed a variety of partnerships with Russia, the Middle Eastern countries, Ukraine, South Caucasus, Central Asia, North Africa, the Gulf countries, Korea, Japan, Australia and New Zealand. Consistent strategic planning, political consultation, and dialogue between partner states and partners are essential for maintaining readiness for strategic vulnerability of NATO. In other words, "responding to market-linked economic challenges, political friction, and military threats to energy supplies requires a broad combination of robust and multifaceted policies, which embrace all key global players" (p. 33). Any threats to energy security for NATO should be interdicted and attacked by NATO's air, maritime, and ground forces.

As a member of OPEC, Nigeria is one of the top ten countries that supply the U.S. with oil. In the wake of war, Muslim-Christian conflict, radical ethnic divisions and the differences between the federal government and states concerning the exercise of power over oil and gas, could threaten the security of the United States. In the light of all this, the U.S. has no options but to continue "boosting supplies from non-Middle East producers" (Coffey 2007, 28). In spite of the legitimate concerns that the new energy wealth in the Caspian region might cause conflict, potential conflict needs to be controlled. The conflict may lead "Southern Caucasus down the path followed by Chechnya, mimicking the territory's endemic conflict, criminality, corruption, thievery and strife" (p. 40).

Peter Droege views issues related to energy security to be controlled by the networked, global, megacities of the urban systems that also control the networked economy, the fossil fuels are its lifeblood" (Droege 2007, 56). The fossil fuel global revolution has powered an unprecedented level of prosperity across the world particularly in industrialized and technologically advanced countries. However, the capacity of fossil fuel and uranium sources threatens not only the long-term viability of the markets in question, but also the security of the global system. For instance, forty percent of the global oil fields supply six percent consumption, with seventy five percent of these in risk, contested, or war torn regions. More than three-quarters of the world's proven oil reserves are in the hands of national oil companies, capable of being used as foreign policy tools or weapons (p. 56). The U.S. produces forty percent of the domestic consumption of oil, gas and coal but is dependent on the world for sixty percent of its consumption of hydrocarbons.

Also, eight-five of the global energy supplies consists of fossil fuels. OECD countries use seventy-five percent of this energy output for stationary and transportation purposes. For instance, global transport is essentially fossil fuel based, with almost commercial transport in the air, on sea, road, or rail petroleum driven... The global dependence on urban systems in itself constitutes a massive energy risk, but the present energy crisis is looming due to an opportunistic and misguided call for an atomic renaissance in global water depletion crisis exacerbated by the primary thermal power generation systems; a global health crisis brought about by fossil based air, water, and soil pollution; an agricultural crisis brought about by the global dependence on petrochemical fertilizers, pesticides and wind processing systems; these only add to the twin risks of petroleum peaking and climate change (p. 57).

The ephemerality of fuel supplies, the potential for its combustion, and the deforestation and industrialization that contribute to global warming exposes cities, towns, and villages to unique aspects of vulnerability. These influences have also contributed to fresh water shortage and the retreat of glaciers and snow cover. In the light of current circumstances, "the move away from fuel systems triggers powerful growth in local and regional employment in renewable more labor-intensive energy industries"(p.57).

## THE SEARCH FOR AFRICAN HYDROCARBONS

The decline of the North Atlantic oil resources, the intense and severe global competition for and reliance on the Middle East oil and gas resources, and in the wake of terrorism, the rise of the superpowers such as the E.U., China, Japan, and India, whose high demand for hydrocarbons cannot be satisfied, the African continent has become the new energy magnet upon which exploration, drilling, pipeline construction, transportation of energy, and its consumption is being managed in terms of determination and designation of markets for the products, negotiation of "posted price" royalties (Okogu 2003) ,and signing of business contracts between countries and governments or between countries and individual corporations (NGOs) that practice monopolistic and oligopolistic tendencies. The proximity of Middle Eastern oil wealth region to these powers and their unstoppable demand that drives habits that their development and in the wake of global terrorism and global anti-Americanism, the demand for more new oil and gas sources in Africa and the search for more hydrocarbons on the African continent, has made the quest for oil more mandatory in American, European and Chinese geostrategic and global ambitions. Their foreign policies toward Africa have, after years, decades, or centuries of neglect, been reconfigured in the light of new diplomatic landscapes that rely on democratic politics (governance to facilitate) economic, technological and cultural exchanges between the superpowers and the African governments in the region). In addition, futuristic projections concerning the decline and gradual extinction of desert oil wealth, since nothing is infinite, has influenced the superpowers, particularly the United States, which fears continuous instability in the Middle East, to turn to Africa for its economic salvation. African oil, natural gas, timber, fibers, spices, minerals, and exotic fauna and flora are being exploited for good or for a curse. By the way, poverty is a curse.

In North Africa, Algeria and Libya are major oil producers that also are members of the OPEC cartel. In Africa, South of the Sahara, six African countries – Nigeria, Angola, Sudan, Equatorial Guinea, Gabon, and the Republic of Congo produce oil for the global market. The continent as a region produced ten to twelve percent of the world's energy consumption during the first decade of the third millennium. The ten African countries provided millions of barrels of oil per day. Algeria, Libya, Guinea, and Nigeria provided much of natural gas.

Given the availability of capital for investment in oil drilling and infrastructure, the African continent could lead the world in energy supplies and provision for its security. For instance, newly discovered oil and natural gas resources that have not been exploited have been found in huge quantities in offshore in Ghana, Tanzania, Mauritania, Morocco, Western Namibia, Libya,Kenya,Somalia and Mozambique. Some of these countries have well developed small scale natural gas production industries that specialize in petrochemical fertilizer processing.

Table XV.1. Global Dependency on African Hydrocarbons

| Country | Million Barrels per Day | Government Revenue (%) | Current Reserves | GDP Amount (%) | Markets |
|---|---|---|---|---|---|
| Algeria | | | | | China, France, Italy |
| Nigeria | 2.5 | 80 | 180 trillion cubic ft | | E.U., US, China |
| Angola | 2.0 | 90 | | 40 | US, China |
| Sudan | 500,000 | 50 | 5 billion barrels | | Canada, India, China, France, US |
| Equatorial Guinea | 400,000 | | 1.28 billion barrels | | US, E.U., China |
| Gabon | 230,000 | 60 | 2.5 billion barrels | 40 | US, E.U., China |
| Republic of Congo | 235,000 | 80 | 1.5 billion barrels | 90 | US, E.U., China |

*Source*: *Council on Foreign Relations: A Resource for Nonpartisan Information and Analysis*, January 26. 2007. Also, evidence shows that 10 more African countries have oil.

## CHINESE ECONOMIC AND FOREIGN POLICY TOWARD AFRICA

Since 1999, more than 800 Chinese companies have invested in the African oil, gas, and raw material industries that continentally contributes to more than $55 billion annually. China has also promised to double its aid toward Africa within a short time. It has given two billion in export credits to African nations and established a five billion fund resource for promoting investment companies. China has planned to train thousands of African professionals to transfer agricultural technology. These investments have in the last five years, contributed to Africa's five to six percent growth rate. Though Chinese labor and materials rather than African labor and materials are largely used for investment, and despite the use of international restrictions on corruption and transparency issues including China's inability to pressure Sudan to solve the Darfur question, such controversial issues have not yet negatively impacted on China's performance in Africa. Even though, China, India, Turkey, and Brazil, all of which have developed interest in doing business with Africa, should be regulated by international business and environmental standards that should be enforced by the AU.

China's growth rate is 10.7 percent. Such phenomenal performance has created a high demand for oil and gas consumption. Such high growth, which has been maintained for over three decades, requires plenty of hydrocarbons for driving the engines of productivity and business culture. China has managed to negotiate good deals with African governments because it employs "diplomacy, trade deals, debt forgiveness and aid packages" (Pan 2007, 1). The 'aid for oil strategy has resulted in increasing supplies of oil from African countries" (p. 3). As the first largest world consumer of oil (before the U.S. and Japan), China's great energy demand has contributed to a 700% growth of Sino-African trade volume. Rumors suggest that China now leads the world in energy consumption. This has made China the third largest trade partner of the continent after the U.S. and France. Challenging the U.S. and E.U. quarter, Chinese are investing heavily in textile industries all over the continent. For instance, in Angola, China exports 25% of its oil production to China. Beijing has secured a major stake in future oil production with $2 billion package of loans and aid that includes funds for Chinese companies to build railroads, schools, roads, hospitals, bridges, and offices; lay a fiber optic network, and train Angolans telecommunications workers (p. 4). This comprehensive and exploitative model of development has been used by the U.S., Japan, and Europe in the past.

To cement industrial and military cooperation with the African oil producing states, which need security, Chinese military experts train people for African oil producing states which need security, Chinese military experts train Africans militarily particularly in Sudan, Equatorial Guinea, Ethiopia, Bemendi, Tanzania, and Zambia. It has "cancelled $10 billion in bilateral debt from African countries, it sends doctors to treat Africans continentally, it hosts thousands of African workers and students in Chinese universities and training centers" (p. 6). China is a new actor on the African scene on which the results of its experiment (model of development) will determine the quality, suitability and sustainability of its missionized trajectory of the superpower's triangular struggle for global dominion and Sinification of its geoeconomic and geostrategic rationality.

## THE DARFUR CRISIS AND THE CONSPIRACY OF SILENCE

The Sudanese political regime and its paramount elites are Sunni Muslims who dominate the political, economic, and cultural spheres of the Sudanese society. Of the six or seven foreign countries that extract oil from the country,

China takes the largest share (64 percent). Chinese policy makers believe that in a global world that is characterized by anarchy and instability, it is necessary to chart new directions in foreign policy only by separating politics from economics. That is why, in spite of its sale of arms to Sudan for oil extraction, it does not interfere in the host country's internal affairs. Although this position is rationalizable at least, it is based on the sound ethics of international relations and its moral obligations, an untenable form of hypocrisy and the abuse of double standards for national self-aggrandizement. Gerard Prunier (2005) has analyzed the situation better. He has contextualized the Darfur crisis within the realm of colonial and contemporary globalism. He has also, to a smaller extent, reflected on the regional geopolitical dynamics of Sudananese political culture including that of the crisis-ridden Darfur, and the more than 30 years of civil war between the North-Muslim and the South-Christian, has cost more than 2 million lives.

Historically, Darfur has existed as an independent country (size of California) for centuries. During the colonial time, it was annexed to Sudan in 1916. Its size is one-fifth of the Sudanese territory. The current crisis exploded when two nationalist movements (the Justice and Equality Movement (JEM) and the Sudan People's Liberation Army (SPLA) joined forces against the government of Sudan (GOS). Under the capable leadership of Dr. John Garang, the two movements put pressure on the Sudanese government for power sharing endeavors as Sudan people's Liberation Movement (SPLM and SPLA). The GOS under which Darfur had existed for over 80 years, and in which a large number of its people serve in the military, Sudan economically, and politically marginalized the Darfurians for many decades. With the death of President Garang of Southern Sudan, the political leadership vacuum derailed the momentum of the two nationalist movements. The central government in Khatum "opted to outsource the quelling of the rebellion to the Arab militia known as Janjaweed" (Prunier 2005, 323). For the last six years, Janjaweed has committed crimes against humanity by abduction, raping, massively looting, and killing of more than 300,000 people, and internally and externally displacing more than 2 million Darfurians. This has been called genocide by Colin Powell (former U.S. Secretary of State), the E.U., and the AU. This has happened and is happening while the whole world, including China believes in the separation of economic and political issues and noninterference in other nation's affairs. It is happening while the superpowers are practicing the model of the "cacass and the fultures". This is ironic and enigmatic. Where has humanity taken its decency? Who is extracting the gold in Darfur?

Seven interpretations have been offered as meaningful and explanatory rationalizations of the existing situation. First, the crisis is viewed as explosive forms of tribal conflicts that were and are exacerbated by climatic conditions of which drought and famine are periodic occurrences. The second interpretation which the West buys is one which views the conflict as "a counterinsurgency campaign gone awry" because the government employed excessive pressure in its attempt to control the nationalistic rebellion. Third, it can be seen as a form of ethnic cleansing. Fourth, ethnic cleansing is a form genocide employed by the GOS in order to displace or eliminate the entire African ethnic groups by replacing them with more Arab tribes. Fifth, a national sympathetic and international conspiracy to forcefully remove Darfurians from their ancestral patrimony, by using any means necessary in order to excavate oil and gold from Darfurland, technologically and economically speaking, will be obtained cheaply and cost effectively by the global competitors of which China, France, U.S., India, Britain, and Canada are the beneficiaries. This indeed is the "Casass and the fultures" model of development practiced during the twentieth century by European countries. The sixth interpretation might be advanced by arguing that Northern Muslims who are dominant in the central government tend to use organs of state power to supplant the peripheral majority Christian Southerners in order to silence their nationalistic ambitions, which, left unchecked, could dismember the nation, control its oil wealth which lies in their territory and use the newly acquired oil wealth as power to delegitimize the GOS and create a separate nation recognized by the U.S., the West and the UN. Seventh, left unchecked, the unification of SPLM and SPLA could marginalize, dismember, or destabilize GOS – hence violence against the two.

## RECOMMENDATIONS

In the wake of Americanism and its attendant antiglobalization rhetoric, the E.U. and the U.S. should reconstruct a positive rather than negative foreign policy toward Africa that will enhance the evolution of a new form of tripartite economic and geopolitical engagement that benefits all the three regions rather than benefiting just one or two at the expense of the other(s). Such a new policy of engagement should be constructed in the light of careful and detailed analysis of the nature and character of resources needed in terms of capital, personnel, technology, physical and technological infrastructure and locational and geological structure, texture and viability for investment in hydrocarbons. A comprehensive analysis of the internal and external environments of the comparative consumption and distribution practices of the regions should be used as a base for potential futuristic trajectory in the field of energy security. A holistic rational analysis of the problem will not underscore issues related to emergency energy preparedness for the regions, diversification and consolidation of supply routes, and synergistic harmonization of policies that concern the abundant availability of hydrocarbons.

Second, Western countries, particularly the U.S., should not overly rely on the realist and neoconservative school of thought in international relations if that school largely leads to social engineering that has provoked a vigorously challenging antiglobalization regime. Instead, the U.S. should diversify its foreign policy making theories in order to enhance effective aspects of paxa Americana. For instance, the U.S. should constructively engage Russia in a dialogue for the purpose of respecting international treaties, agreements and energy protocols that ensure the healthy functioning of energy supply lines, protection of energy markets with confidence assured measures.

Third, establish energy security alliances that constantly study and revise their consumption, distribution, and geostrategic manuals in order to ascertain the needs of their consumers. By so doing, the freedom, prosperity, and security of consumers will be enhanced. In addition, technologically advanced countries should doubly diversify their search for alternative energy sources that are more environmentally friendly. Such sources may include biofuels, wind, solar power, clean coal and nuclear power.

Finally, in the era of terrorism, it is necessary to employ a multinational surveillance and interdiction operations in order to ensure viable energy supplies that enhance the promotion of regional and international security. Also, the West, should empower AFRICOM with resources (technological, scientific, military and economic) in order to strengthen democracy, alleviate HIV/AIDS, malaria and all modern forms of terrorism that make the African continent, endowed with natural resources that have not been exploited for its own development and the development of the global community. They also need to lessen total ecological disruption of the global system by making the use of energy to be globally efficient. States should provide capability to use military force to ensure reliable supplies. They should provide aid or assistance within short notice in order to protect people and their economic systems from disaster. All institutions of international cooperation should promote aid and trade rather than war, confrontation or conflict which may exacerbate elements of ecological disruptions. In case of NEPAD, it should foster the adoption of policies, standards and "best" practices that can lead to political stability, high economic growth, sustainable development and accelerated sub-regional and continental economic integration" (Stults 2007, 250). Such measures will attract foreign investment measures that will also attract foreign investment capital that is essential for continental economic revolution and industrialization.

## CONCLUSION: DEGLOBALIZATION FOR A NEW PARADIGM

> While Africa's problems—poverty, corruption, disease, and instability—are well known, we must refocus on the bright promise offered by many countries on that continent. We must strongly engage on a political, economic and security level with friendly governments across Africa, but insist on improvements in transparency and rule of law. Many African nations will not reach their true potential without external assistance to combat entrenched problems, such as HIV/AIDS, that afflict Africans disproportionately. It should establish the goal of eradicating malaria from the continent – the number one killer of African children under the age five. In addition to saving millions of lives in the world's poorest regions, such a campaign would do much to add luster to America's image in the world (Anonymous).

The U.S., China, and E.U. should:

- Take technology and science to Africa
- Help Africans to become democratic and transparent in policy making
- Educate oil companies to develop infrastructure and education systems in order to improve their interdependent economic, political and cultural tools and exchanges.
- Eliminate common illnesses and diseases such as malaria and HIV/AIDS
- Introduce new forms of energy consumption and distribution in Africa
- Minimize the role of conditionalities from theAfrican development problematique.

## REFERENCES

Adelman, Morris. 1974. Politics, economics and world oil: *American Economic Review* 64: 58-67.

Barnett, Steven, and Rolando Ossowski. 2002. *Operational aspects of fiscal policy in oil producing countries. IMF Working Paper 02/177.* Washington: International Monetary Fund.

BP-Amoco 2002. *Statistical Review of World Energy.*

Brookhyser, Jason. 2007. Message from the Editor. *The Whitehead Journal of Diplomacy* VIII 2:7

Chen, Matthew E., and Amy M. Jaffe. 2007. Energy security: Meeting growing challenging of national oil companies. *The Whitehead Journal of Diplomacy and International Relations* VIII 2:37-55.

Dalby, Simon. 2007. Ecology, security and change in the anthropocene. *The Brown Journal of World Affairs* XIII, II:153-62

Dietz, Simon. 2007. The impacts of climate change: Perspectives from the *Stern Review. The Brown Journal Affairs* XIII, II:173-86.

Eitzen, Stanley D., and Maxine B. Zinn. 2009. *Globalization: The transformation of social worlds.* Wadsworth: Cengage Learning.

Falola, Toyin, and Ann Genova. 2005. *The politics of global oil industry.* Westport, CT: Praegar Publishers

Foss, Michelle M. (2008). Africa: A new frontier in oil and gas exploration. *Geotimes: Earth, Energy and Environment News.* February.

_________. (2008). Africa: A New Frontier in Oil and Gas Exploration. *Geotimes: Earth, Energy and Environment News,* February, http://www.geotimes.org/feb08article.html?id=feature_africa.html.

Gardner, Edward. 2003. Wanted: More jobs. *Finance and Development* March.

Goodwin, P.B. 1992. A review of new demand elasticities with special references to short and long run effects. *Journal of Transport Economics and Policy* 26:155-63

Graham, Daniel J, and Glaister Stephen. 2002. The demand for automobile fuel: A survey of elasticities. *Journal of Transport and Economics and Policy* 36:1-26

Griffin, J.M., and D.J. Teece, eds. 1982. *OPEC behavior and world oil prices.* London: George Allen and Unwin.

Hotelling, Harold. 1931. The economics of exhaustible resources. *Journal of Political Economy* 39:137-75.

International Energy Agency. 2001 and 2002. *World Energy Outlook*. Paris: OECD.

Klare, Michael T. 2007. The futile pursuit of energy security by military force. *The Brown Journal of World Affairs* XIII, 2: 137-52

Legendre, Thierry. 2007. The North Atlantic Treaty Organization's Future Role in Energy Security. *The Whitehead Journal of Diplomacy and International Relations*, Summer/Fall, VIII, 2:23-8.

Lugar, Richard G. 2007. A concert in energy security: Building trans-atlantic cooperation to confront a growing threat. *The Whitehead Journal of Diplomacy and International Relations* VIII.

Maugeri, Leonardo. 2006. *The age of oil: The mythology, history and future of the world's most controversial resources*. @Ebook.

McLean, Iain. 1996. *The concise Oxford dictionary of politics*. Oxford, UK: Oxford University Press.

Mitchell, John V. 2000. Energy and the environment. Paper prepared for conference on the Seventh International Energy Forum, Riyadh, Saudi Arabia, November 17-19.

Okogu, Bright E., (2003). *The Middle East and North Africa in a changing oil market*. International Monetary Fund.

Pan, Esther. 2007. China, Africa, and Oil. *Council on Foreign Relations: A Resource for Nonpartisan Information and Analysis*.

Peter, Droege. 2007. Energy cities and security tackling climate change and fossil fuel risk. *The Whitehead Journal of Diplomacy and International Relations* VIII, 2:55-64.

Pindyck, Robert S. 1978. "Gains to producers from cartelization of exhaustible resources," *Review of Economics and Statistics* 6: 238-51.

Prontera, Andrea. 2009. Energy policy: Concepts, actors, instruments and recent development. *World Political Science Review* 5, 1: 1-30.

Prunier, Gerard. 2005. *Darfur: The ambiguous genocide*. Ithaca NY: Cornell University Press.

Satanovsky, Ye. 2007. Russia and the rapid modernization of the Middle East. *International Affairs: A Russian Journal of World Politics, Diplomacy and International Relations* 52, 4:57-64.

Sterner, Thomas. 1991. Gasoline demand in OECD: Choice of model and data set in poolied estimations. *OPEC Review* 15, 2: 91-101.

Tal, Alon. 2007. Degraded commitments: Reviving international efforts to combat desertification. *The Brown Journal of World Affairs* XIII, II: 187-200.

Verleger, Phillip K. 2003. What goes up … Why oil-producing states must husband their resources. *Finance and Development* March.

__________. 1993. *Adjusting to Volatile Energy Markets*. Washington: Institute for International Economics.

__________. 1982. OPEC as a cartel. In J. M. Griffin and D.J. Teece, eds. *OPEC Behavior and World Oil Prices*. London: George Allen and Unwin.

# Section Four: Conclusion

Section four, which covers chapter sixteen, is a deconstructive critique of contemporary globalization. Thematically, this chapter comprehensively defines the meaning of globalization in its laissez-faire, Schumpeterian, Thucydidian, Nietzscherian and Huntingtonian perspectives that are the antithesis to constructivist , Obamarian engagement, managed and humane governance models articulated by French intellectual and professor Nye and Oppenheimer. Collectively, this variety of views do not only suggest the necessity and evolution of a new paradigm of governance for global regionalism, but it makes it essential for orchestrating positive as opposed to negative globalization. Putative and positive forms of regional globalization should be created and spearheaded through constructivist Obamarian engagement and other multilateral structures. This type of policy related centers articulate liberal multilateralism and responsibly oriented approaches that will enhance constructive multilateralism that deemphasize unilateralism, preemption, and war in the face of the emerging "new but wild center of multipolarity" – Asia.

# Chapter XVI
# Deconstructive Critique: The New Paradigm

## Definition of Globalization

Globalization is the process of interdependent, intensive, and extensive social, political, economic, cultural and technological interconnectedness of the human species on planet earth and in psychological and abstract reality. Through the globalization process, "goods, information, people, money, communication, fashion … move across national boundaries" (Eitzen and Zinn 2009, 1). The cross-border diffusion, which is historically cyclical, involves the transfer of skills, knowledge, scientific techniques, ideas, inventions and a variety of cultural forms from one culture or society or continent to another.

The process of globalization is characterized by speedy happenings, voluminous exchanges and dimensional and interactional selectivity. A large amount of the speedy happenings and their voluminous and dimensional nature is "associated with the factory products of the global assembly line" (p. 3) that are produced by low-wage workers and shipped for sale in developed countries. U.S., Japanese and European corporations have heavily invested in China, India, Mexico, Malaysia, Korea, and Taiwan etc. Between 2001 and 2006, the U. S. lost 3.2 million manufacturing jobs because of globalization through NAFTA. Technologically, the tools upon which globalization depends include but are not limited to "robotics, fiber optics, container ships, computers, communication satellites and the internet." These tools have "transformed information storage, retrieval, communication, production, and transportation" (p. 4). The Usage of these technologies has not only made the world smaller or compressed, but such smallness has raised questions concerning the relevance of geography, culture and linguistic variety.

Corporations have restructured, outsourced and decentralized production in order to concentrate economic power (Harrison 1994). Currently, there are "over 2,000 largest global corporations from 55 countries, employing 68 million... total revenues of $24 trillion, assets of $88 trillion, and profits of $1.7 trillion" (Forbes 2006), of the "total $60 trillion global economy" (Mohammad 2008, 38). Since the end of World War II, when modern globalization became more dominated by the Bretton Woods institutions (IMF the World Bank, GATT (WTO) etc.) its neo imperialistic overtones have continued to increase dependence because "Globalization has taken from poor countries control of their own economic policies and concentrated their assets in the hands of first world investors. Although it has enriched some Third World elites, it has subordinated them to foreign corporations, intersectional institutions, and dominant states" (Brecher, et al. 2000, 3-4)

In the global environment, employers have disempowered the employee by downsizing, outsourcing, reducing job security arrangements, work regulations, worker compensation, healthcare, pensions and have subjected them to the whims of the market that simply treats their relationship as that of "buyers and sellers of labor" (Eitzen and Zinn 2009, 5). This market's legal and illegal migrants are largely feminine, marginalized and enslaved as nannies, maids, nurses and sex workers.

Contemporary globalization is animated by neo-liberal ideology called the Washington consensus. The ideology is rooted in John Locke's and Adam Smith's laissez-faire economic theory which argues that "market forces produce prosperity, liberty and democracy if left unhindered by government intervention" (p. 6) or the "removal of barriers to trade and foreign investment, and exchange rate policy that the market, and eventually...privatization of potentially competitive assets" (Victor 2007). Such a climate of neo-liberalism has politically, economically, and culturally disempowered the sovereign nation-state that has lost its power of governance over its territory and citizenry. Supranational organizations and NGOs regulate transnational trade and international law. They also control corporate decisions concerning outsourcing, downsizing and movement of capital regardless of the wishes of the nation-states' citizens (Beynon and Dunkerley 2000).

Globalization has politically and geographically promoted the porosity and permeability of borders, so much so that air, water, foods and the environment have severely become polluted. Incurable diseases such as Mad Cow disease, HIV/AIDS, Saahs etc. have become contagiously globalized. The same permeability of borders has allowed the proliferation of criminal elements that have global and strategic networks of which illegal migration, drug trafficking, prostitution, slavery and sweatshops are rampant. Worst of all, though ecotourism has become economically beneficial to some countries, its unsupervised or unrestricted components may promote destructive and socially undesirable aspects of transnational terrorism.

Contrary to the past, relatively static and traditionally established national cultures in terms of places, time and ethos, ideas, symbols, stories, idioms and shared national consciousness and identity, contemporary globalization has homogenously tried to enculture and assimilate many people who have been culturally detribalized, de-ethnicized and deterritorialized. The people are or have acquired a global culture that is "sustained by the media, corporate advertising and the entertainment industry" (Eitzen and Zinn 2009, 6). The bye product of this kind of "mixing of everything with everything" is a world culture "centered on consumerism, mass media, Americana, and the English language" (p. 6). This form of social and cultural homogenization entails either progressive cosmopolitanism or oppressive imperialism (Scholte 2003, 23). The contemporary and western consumer lifestyle is epitomized in products such as Nike, fashion, pop music, Disney products, movies, Coca-Cola, McDonald's, ESPN, CNN, and other brand names (Beynon and Dunkery 2000). The global culture is neither uniform nor universal. Local cultures clash with global ones in areas where cultural diversity and multiculturalism have not been institutionalized. Wherever, whenever and however global communications and markets have adapted to function in local environments, this is a form of "glocalization" (Eitzen and Zinn 2009, 7.) or "glonalization". In essence, globalization then is the "transformation of world society in terms of flows of people, goods, capital, and ideas across national boundaries, linkages, institutions, culture and consciousness (p. 7; Lechner and Boli 2000, 2). Without questions and inadvertently so, viewed from the globalized's rather than the globalizers' perspective, globalization is a complex economic, political, cultural and psychological system whose inherent ideological tenets empower winners and disempowers losers on the global plane of inequality, social stratification, institutional exploitation and massification and intensification of social, economic and political problems which serve as a filter for the protection of the privileged few at the center's core and their agents at the periphery. Above all, the dimensions of globalization's scope and variety are epitomized in transnational migration, transnational trade, transnational finance, cultural globalization and globalization of disease, terrorism and war. It is instructive to compare contemporary globalization with nineteenth and twentieth century forms of colonization.

## COLONIALISM: COMPARISON WITH GLOBALIZATION

Globalization is a form of neocolonialism. Clearly, Professor Ochieng is disappointed and frustrated because just nationalist revolutionaries and reformers' work is still incomplete. Neocolonialism is another monster, more deadly than masqueraders. Yet there is a general feeling

> among people that colonialism benefited Third World peoples and Africans. Capitalism, after all, is a political system in which an external nation takes complete control of a territory in other areas of the world. That's the definition of colonialism. Moreover, the colonized people do not invite the colonial power, nor do they have any say in how they are governed. Colonialism is by definition and practice undemocratic, exploitative, racist, and oppressive, etc. That is, no matter what form colonial rule took, all colonial systems were undemocratic. Colonial governments did not allow popular participation of native peoples. There were no mechanisms for the people to officially express their feelings, wishes & opinions. Also, colonial rule was most often imposed from above without consent from the African people. People were not happy for being governed without any representation, and colonial governments faced the potential of civil disobedience or outright resistance and revolutionary change. Therefore, since colonial regimes risked failure due to disobedience and outright resistance, to their rule and law, functionalism was a top priority of colonial governments. In most African colonies, more money was spent on developing and maintaining a police force and an army than was spent on education, housing, and health-care combined. Colonialism also placed emphasis on exploitation of raw materials for export. Colonial regimes searched and exploited the most profitable

natural resources in each colony. In mineral- rich colonies, the emphasis was placed on mining, in other territories; the colonial power identified agricultural products suitable for export to Europe. In either case, the emphasis was on developing the resources for export, not for local use or consumption; not for the benefits of Africans but for the benefit of Europeans. Profits from the export of mineral and agricultural goods were sent to Europe. Profits that could have been used to promote social and economic development in the colonies were not available. Colonial regimes were biased, ethonocentric and exclusionary. The social distance between them and the natives was maintained and institutionalized (http://w'ebmail.onenet.net/lunet.edu/frame.litml?rtfPossible-true &lang=en).

In other words, globalization is more modern, more complex, more concentrated, more politically, economically, technologically and culturally entrenched than colonialism. The former imported raw materials and exported technical personnel in the form of colonial administrators, doctors, settlers, missionaries, and high school and college teachers. Nowadays globalization whose "younger sister" is regionalization, imports new and exotic cultures, immigrants, finance, raw materials, Third World experts, nannies, nurses, women, refugees, terrorists, criminals while exporting technology, NGOs, Western popular culture, eco-tourists, investors, democracy and Bretton Woods institutions. Globalization is a concentrated, massive, and destructive form of direct as opposed to indirect form of neocolonialism. Compared to pre-industrial modes of life, feudalism, capitalism, and Chinese communism, globalization is the highest stage of advanced capitalist development. Its profound and entrenched evolutionary roots and its late twentieth century nature, expansionary, dynamic, and synergistic heritage has contributed to the destruction of historical structuralism of the ideological Marxist order and a variety of traditional cultures.

In his book, *A theory of global capitalism: Production, class, and state in a transitional world* (2004), William I. Robinson used a Marxist approach to profoundly argue that globalization represents a qualitatively and quantitatively new form of political economic order of global capitalism that is characterized by: (1) an accelerated expansion of international trade (2) the extraordinary internationalization and growth of financial markets and services; (3) the segmentation and internationalization of production processes; and (4) the reintegration of these components of the value chain in ever-widening transnational corporations, investment and ownership connections, and business alliances. Therefore, the contemporary form of globalization is comparatively different from its earlier eighteenth, nineteenth and early twentieth centuries explained by Professor Ochieng in the previous paragraph. An objective and subjective climate of globalization provides conditions that are conducive to the formation of an increasingly self conscious 'transnational capitalist class (TCC) that has the capability for agency and that deliberately pursues its class interests in a Marxian style. The economic organization defines class identities and interests. The organization processes produce a class structure whose power relations are derivatively political. Changes in the economic organization tended to undermine the political and economic foundation of "(Post- World War II Fordism, Keynesianism, labor-capital compromises, and developmentalist policies that enabled the growth of organized labor and the welfare state" (Robinson 2004). These policies have influenced economic and political elites to view their interest within the global, rather than national, frame of reference. The elites who benefited from such policies are comprised of senior management officials of the industrial and financial firms, state actors at the highest level of government, and an expanding cadre of well known professionals who support the development of the 'transnational state' (TNS) that is evolving from the existing system of nation states. International organizations-such as the IMF, WTO, the U.N.O. and the World Bank are among the multilateral institutions whose trade agreements are part and parcel of the infrastructure of the emergent (TNS) (Sagini 2001).

As indicated earlier, the TNS evolves within the historically defined international system; the nation state is anarchically resituated within the TNS. Within the context of international relations theories of neo-realism, neo-liberalism, constructivism, historical structuralism and imperial, unipolar and hegemonic stability theories, existing states do not wither away as Lenin and Marx believed; they are transformed into constructive menu for the advancement of global capitalist formation. In other words, domestic neo-liberalism is a mere reflection of the wishes of the TNS. Contrary to the views of the 'weak state' expressed by some scholars, the national state, though subordinate, is "still potent" source of global hegemonic class. Indeed ... the United States is constrained to act in the interests of the TCC and on behalf of the TNS" (Robinson 2004).

## Comparative Regionalism

The globalization of the world is largely propelled forward and creatively animated by regional economic rivalry of the U.S. led North America, Franco-German led E.U. and Chinese- Japanese led Asian regionalism. In terms of their Gross Domestic product — (nominal) per capita reported by Wikipedia in 2007 and amplified by IMF in April 2008, the following statistics produced by IMF, World Bank and Central Intelligence Agency are instructive.

Though statistics vary from year to year, they help to predict the standards of living for each country or region and its purchasing power in terms of the value of economic output in domestic and international global climate. In a way, purchasing power is a form of economic, political and military power that determines and influences national, regional and global influence.

### Theories of Regionalism in East Asia

There are several economic and political theories which explain the competitive essence of global regionalism. Economically, economists argue that regionalism may increase or decrease material welfare while affecting the terms of dealing with global trade. Although regional integration produces and distorts trade, such cooperation is beneficial to developing nations because such regionalism promotes peace and stability, enhances sound macroeconomic policies, facilitates greater technology transfers, increases economic policies and leads to larger involvement in multilateral economic integration. In the light of these theoretical assertions, *APEC* and rationalists are Ernst Haas, Philippe Schmitter, Leon Lindberg, Joseph S. Nye, Robert O. Keohone and Lawrence Scheineman. Professor Joseph Nye of Harvard University has listed a seven point criteria for the creation of functional regionalization and regionalism: (1) functionalist linkage of tasks or spillover, (2) rising transactions (3) deliberate linkages and coalition formation, (4) elite socialization, regional group formation, (5) ideological, identities appeal, (6) rising transactions, and (7) involvement of external actors" (p. 368). Professor Nye concluded that the politically and economically essential conditions for regional integration are: symmetry of unity, elite value complementarity, existence of pluralism, and capacity to adapt and respond" (Nye 1971; Wan 2008, 368).The international regime theory explains regionalism in the following way:

> regimes refer to the principles, norms, rules, and decision-making procedures. International regimes can be both formal and informal.. .overcome collective action problems by reducing transaction cost and encouraging reciprocity because of repeated interactions...international regime theorists see regionalism as resulting from the incentives institutions may provide countries in the region to cooperate for a common good (p. 368).

Table XVI.1. GDP (Nominal) per Capita for Selected Countries (US Dollars)

| **Country** | **IMF** | **WB** | **CIA** |
|---|---|---|---|
| E.U. | 32,842 | --- | 33,379 |
| UK | 45,575 | 39,257 | 45,347 |
| France | 41,511 | 36,699 | 42,313 |
| Russia | 9,075 | 6,926 | 9,096 |
| Germany | 40,415 | 35,168 | 39,550 |
| China | 4,800 | 2,016 | 2,458 |
| Japan | 34,312 | 34,194 | 34,104 |
| India | 978 | 822 | 965 |
| United States | 45,845 | 43,968 | 45,793 |
| Canada | 43,485 | 38,947 | 42,108 |
| Mexico | 8,479 | 8,052 | 8,154 |

*Sources:* Wikipedia.com. 2007; IMF April 2008; CIA Analysis 2008.

East Asian regionalism that consists of Japan, China, South Korea, Taiwan, Singapore, Hong Kong, Indonesia, Malaysia, Philippines, Thailand and Vietnam was formed for functionalist/ institutionalism purposes after the 1990's Asian financial crisis associated with dollarization. It was created to address perceived needs in the region. In particular, attempts were made to increase intraregional trade by creating stability of the region's FTA, will benefit member states while ASEAN and FTA will not. Optimal currency area (OCA) theory and other regional integration tools are lacking because they do not maximize welfare — a fact which has contributed to the absence of institutionalism of integrative efforts in Asian regionalism and, therefore has weakened its evolutionary development.

Politico-economically, and based on the analysis of (Mansfield and Milner 1997), their textbook, *The political economy of regionalism*, shows that "functional/ institutionalist, realist and constructivist" theoretical paradigms are collectively and independently essential to the development of the political economy of regionalism (p. 367; Sagini 2001). In this case, regionalism refers to geographic closeness or matters, or deliberate comparative advances. According to Andrew Hurrel, the five major components of regionalism include but are not limited to "regionalism, regional awareness and identity, regional interstate cooperation, state promoted regional integration, and regional" (Wan 2008, 358). To regionalize (regionalization) is to concentrate economic activities to a region that is largely influenced by market forces and political involvement. On the other hand, regionalism is the political coordination of government policies for the purpose of greater regional economic development of a regional political community. David Mitrany's (*A working peace system*) in which he advances the functionalist/ neo-functionalism of regionalism, argues that during the last century, countries needed to cooperate in order to deal with 'functional problems a cross national borders' (p. 368), victories experienced in "one functional area" – hence "ramification" (p. 368).

Western geo-strategic interests of realism and neo-realist notions of regionalism and international politics are anarchically important. Individual sovereign states tend to fend for their survival. Because regionalism requires the presence of hegemony, the East Asian region which lacks hegemony for obvious reasons experiences difficulties in regional economic and political cooperation. In addition, the region, both through APEC and FTA does not embrace U.S. hegemonic influences although its hegemony tries to be filtered through "Japanese looking glasses." Also, tensions between Japan and China, which originate from myopic conceptions of nationalism, tend to frustrate the evolution of institutionalized and well balanced regional integration although the existence of the two more established forms of Western regionalism provokes Asiatics to do something for themselves as well by having and expressing a collective voice in regional and global affairs. Hostility toward Asia has relatively strengthened its East Asian relations which have proved to be strong, commercial and monetary systems. In comparison to European and North American regionalisms, Asian regionalism is not integrated because Asian nations have not learned to shift their loyalties to supranational (regional) institutions comparable to these in the E.U. and NAFTA or those within the United States' formal empire. As a result of collective Asian weakness in regionalization efforts, achieving regional cooperation is very difficult given the fact that both Japan and South Korea are economically and geo-strategically anchored in the West rather than in South East Asia from which India has been coopted by the same forces.

## Western Geo-Strategic Interests

Realism and neo-realist notions of regionalism and international politics are anarchically important. Individual sovereign states tend to fend for their survival. Because regionalism requires the presence of hegemony, the East Asian region, which lacks hegemony for obvious reasons, experiences difficulties in regional economic and political cooperation. In addition, the region, both through APEC and FTA does not embrace U.S.

hegemonic influences although its hegemony tries to be filtered through "Japanese looking glasses." Also, tensions between Japan and China, which originate from myopic conceptions of nationalism, tend to frustrate the evolution of institutionalized and well balanced regional integration. This happens although the existence of the two more established forms of Western regionalism provokes Asiatics to do something for themselves as well by having and expressing a collective voice in regional and global affairs. Hostility toward Asia has relatively strengthened its East Asian relations which have proved to be strong commercial and trading alliances. As far as constructivist explanations are concerned, people make the world not only for material interests, but also for other reasons such as ideas, norms, identity and the comparative aspects of other regions. Some of the obstacles of building East Asian regionalism include the fact that rules and democracy are not universally shared in the region. Comparatively, China, the potential hegemony, has no democratic institutions largely due to the fact that throughout its history, the evolution of its intellectual culture advanced the development of a political culture as opposed to a political philosophy. For centuries, Chinese intellectuals have communally, familiarly and culturally used collectivistic notions to rationalize power. That is why collectively, culturally and socially approved values produce autocratic rather than democratic leaders and institutions (McLean 1996). However, the young and competitive who use modern telecommunications, and who understood the character of Western global regionalism, could make a difference in the region. Also, U.S.'s dominance in global affairs and China's fear of Japan's motives may have made countries in the region to be more cautious concerning the nature and character of emerging Asian regionalism.

Strategically, East Asian strategy has not helped the region to institutionalize itself because of open regionalism (APEC) in which the U.S. dominates. Both ASEAN= Association of South East Asian Nations and AFTA=ASEAN formed in the 1960s. Free trade areas are smaller regional organizations that were viewed to be ineffective for assisting member nations to effectively compete in the global arena. Their perceived ineffectiveness was reinforced when the Asian financial crisis of the 1990's struck. Further still, there is division in ASEAN because Indonesia has weak internal problems associated with terrorism while Singapore is searching for its own bilateral FTAS (Wan 2008). Moreover, Japan, which has close and expansive trading and commercial deals with Europe and North America, originally, saw the benefits of synergistic regional involvement with a region that was less economically suitable for its post-war global economic imperialism and, a region that was dominated by fundamentally powerful elements of Marxist oriented historical structuralism. Japan, therefore, through the influence of Makoto Kermode, asserted that Asia should integrate naturally and gradually because if it starts to "build its own economic bloc to counter the creation of other parts of the world. ... Asia would lose more by confronting the other groups" (p. 371). Instead, Asia "should promote a global free trade regime" (p. 371). However, during the 1990's and partly due to the Asian financial crisis, Japan favored the idea of regionalism as opposed to globalization because "a stronger regional financial structure" is complementary to a strong global financial structure" (p. 272), was essential. However, because Japan is fearful of potential Chinese dominance in Asia, she is interested in an East Asian regionalism that includes Australia, New Zealand and India. In addition, Japan would like to continue its current relationship with the U.S.

South Korea's regional interests correspond to those of Japan and go beyond it to include Chile. Although Chinese interest in regional integration is a more recent phenomenon (since November 2000), she wants ASEAN plus three (China, Japan and Korea). In such a region, China would like tariffs to be lowered while the U.S. will not favor an agreement which works against the 50-60 year old Bretton Woods' arrangement of which GATT and WTO are components.

The two competitive and comparatively interesting Western global regions have defensively created pressure on the East Asians to do something for themselves. That is why China, the emerging World giant, has taken the initiative to construct FTA with ASEAN, Japan and South Korea, ASEAN plus 3. South East Asia accounts for 20% of global output, nearly 20% of global trade, and hold well over 50% of the World's international monetary reserves. Moreover, the region is ripe for growth, it accounted for 31.4% of the World's population in 2005 that is more than NAFTA and E.U. combined ... the IMF's 2008-2011 outlook figure clocked growth at 7.9 percent for Asia, dwarfing the 2.5 percent for major developed countries (Martin 2007, 73) and the two major global regions.

Also, "trade volumes between ASEAN + 3 countries expanded to $317 billion in 2005, continuing the average annual 16% increase that has persisted since 1975. Including Hong Kong and Taiwan, the share of interregional trade stood at 52% in 2005, higher than that of even NAFTA countries" (p. 77). Above all, the U.S. should not try to frustrate the evolving East Asian regionalism because it will be costly, U.S. is the looser rather than the beneficiary in this terrorist global atmosphere. However U. S. should, if anything, diplomatically encourage such a form of regionalism in order to protect its economic interests in the region in spite of the fact that domestic political conditions in the countries involved, tend to frustrate evolutionary forms of Asiatic regionalism.

Though the evolving East Asian region is favored by most Asian nations, and though some nations are uneasy because of what regionalism means in terms of their strategic, or national or regional interests, the formation of a stronger, reformatory and more open regionalism would be a better force for human civilization than a smaller and inward looking and exclusive form of regionalism.

After the end of European colonization of the Third World (1940s-1970s), the market oriented global economy was more international than regional. Most developing nations pursued "inward-looking development strategies called import substitution industrialization" (Oakley 2005, 43). Import substitution economic strategies were largely static mechanisms to economic development because the state, as opposed to market forces, took the initiative to create manufacturing industries in order to enhance trade and economic development. This unrestricted regulatory approach created trade barriers that kept foreign manufactured goods out of the local domestic market. Also, "by subsidizing credit for industries targeted for development, and by sometimes creating and owning manufacturing enterprises themselves, policymakers used the power of the state to transform largely agricultural societies into 'modern' industrialized economies. Governments tightly controlled imports to minimize foreign competition with domestic producers" (p. 43). Through this approach, states used resources from the sale of agricultural products to buy manufactured goods from abroad. The negative aspect of import substitutions was the accumulation of large debts by developing countries and their inability to service the debt factor. With the rising deterioration of the international economy that was also impacted by the collapse of the USSR's political, economic and ideological structure, these countries were forced to turn for their help to IMF and the World Bank during the 1980's. This was the era of structural adjustment (p. 43) in which state governments of Third World nations "were encouraged to scale back the state's role in the domestic economy" (p. 43) in order to reinforce the role of the market. Governments were required "to deregulate their domestic economies, devalue their currencies, reduce trade barriers, make it easier for multinational corporations to invest in the domestic economy, privatize state-owned enterprises, and establish and maintain a stable macroeconomic environment" (pp. 43-44). This anti-import substitution strategy of economic liberalism and political neo-liberalism of the "Washington consensus" emphasizes trade openness, economic growth, and democratic peace. Though this approach has benefited Asian and East European nations, African and Latin American countries have not benefited from the structural adjustment strategy that benefit's the wealthy center as opposed to the periphery as Stieglitz and Danni Rodrik have shown. The declining influence of structural adjustment has been reinforced by globalization.

## NAFTA

NAFTA means North American Free Trade Agreement. For almost 20 years, regional trading agreements (RTAs) which are called preferential trading arrangements (PTAs) are trade agreements that use tariffs to discriminate against nonmembers. In a free trade area (FTA) such as North America, E.U., and the evolving one in East Asia, "governments eliminate tariffs on goods entering their markets from other FTA member areas, but each member government retains independent tariffs on goods entering their market from nonmembers. In a customs union, like the E.U., member governments eliminate all tariffs on intra-union trade and create a common tariff for goods entering the union from nonmembers" (Oakley 2005, 147). Throughout the last 60 years, RTAs have grown from 0 to 300.

Although there is controversy concerning the effective usefulness of RTAs, Scholars such as Robert B. Zoellick, U.S. trade representative, assert that the RTA system "liberalizes trade through multilateral, regional, and bilateral agreements. This strategy of 'competitive liberalization'... will create "a web of mutually reinforcing trade agreements to meet diverse commercial, economic, developmental and political challenges. The U.S. combines this building block approach to free trade with a clear commitment to reducing global barriers to trade through the WTO" (p. 149). In a sense, RTAs are stepping stones to a global free trade system. On the contrary, professor Bernard K. Gordon of the University of New Hampshire "argues that regional trading agreements are inconsistent with American economic interests and are already generating opposing regional blocs that will make it harder for American producers to capture foreign markets" (p. 149). Gordon believes that RTAs are a stumbling block to global free trade because of regionalism. A third school of thought thinks that these two positions are, in the long-run, neither here not there. It advocates a synergistic approach that constantly charts new directions to adapt workable arrangements that ensure fair global competition, durability and equitable development in the periphery. This approach will minimize interblock trade wars, maintain low tariffs, and enhance more gradual interblock and intrablock cooperation rather than rapid competition particularly in developing regions such as CAFTA and AU. Notwithstanding the loss of 3.2 million manufacturing jobs in the U.S. largely due to outsourcing, American NGOs overall contributed greatly to the growth of the global economy.

## EUROPEAN UNION

The Economic, political and cultural evolution of the E.U., which has been gradual in its development, and that is characterized by weak inherent regional institutions that are heavily dependent on state (national) domestic considerations. Also, the E.U. has left many questions unanswered concerning the validity of its neocolonial mission and the longevity of its geopolitical and geostrategic Europeanism. It thereby jeopardizes the Europeanization of its new values at the expense of the nonexistent and pre-contemporary institutional values. Such a situation, which potentially leaves the entire region ready for "unbundling", casts doubt on the viability, stability and historic potentiality of the multi-cephalous empire whose regionalism has no solid center nor firm constitutional and cultural foundation (Sissenich 2008). Therefore, lacking in constitutional authenticity, linguistic monocentricism, and cultural uniformity during its formative period could problematize and contradict the vision of its genius.

Though European regionalism is a product of positivist and constructivist socio-scientific divisions of European and Western Intellectual culture and elite dynamism, its diversity in terms of "insiders" and "outsiders" (Eastern Europeans, Turkey, and the Epistemics) have different policy agendas whose goals maybe inconsistent with the region's (union's) raison detre—principles of economic, political and ideationally grounded democratic liberalism. Though the outsiders may through persuasion, monetary rewards, "twinning" (Sissenich 2008, 150) and elite and mass socialization, be influenced to accept NATOs enlargement of Europe, this form of "coercive assimulation" may be too illiberal and colonial to attract opposition from within (E.U.) and from Without (Russia and the Middle East). Since the E.U. is economically dependent of both Russia and the Middle East for oil and gas, its attempt the economically and socially marginalize the epistemic and Russian neocolonial, political and economic autarchy could backfire and destabilize the region whose post "Roman Empire's" history is characterized by political instability, the worst of which was evidenced by twentieth century socialist and fascist experiments in Central, Eastern, and Southern Europe.

The E.U. is not only a work or project in progress, but, it is also an element of informal conditionality (p. 147) in which democratic considerations are at odds with technocratic concerns and different directorates-general have competing ideas on how to proceed. Often, it appears, the Commission encouraged formalism at the expense of substance" (p. 147). As a result, the E.U.'s accession conditionality makes it to operate "inconsistently, imprecisely, and sluggishly as it exists between "regional reforms in central and Eastern Europe and E.U. accession conditionality" (p. 137). E.U. integration "does not produce institutional and policy convergence, as judged by the evidence on regional reforms in the candidate countries" (Sissenich 2008, 148). The reforms, which are derivatively the products of path dependence, are characterized by institutional obstacles that radiate from home country member states rather that the E.U.'s or NATO's policy agenda. Evidence based on the *World Values Survey (*1999-2002) showed that "both in the old member states and the 2004 entrants," into E.U., "citizens identify first and foremost with their region, next with their country and last with Europe as a whole" (p. 148). Such differences make the E.U. region to experience governance problems because global, European, national and local agenda can not easily be monitored and enforced, compliance due to regulatory conflicts that are by nature rooted in the multinational, multilevel, multidimensional and multicultural diversity make integration far from reality if not contradictory in terms. Though reform may be externalized by using pressure and guidance associated with the UN, and for the purpose of enhancing integration that's potential for producing change, status-quo or disaster can only be explained in historical terms.

Morgan (2005) has argued that the main purpose or logic for European integration is not welfare-centered democratic institutions, but realist centered logic of security that challenges U.S.'s unipolarity because the latter enhances hegemonic, pre-emptive and unilateral behavior which provokes disorder, chaos, insecurity and instability as opposed to security. For instance, interest to pursue superpower status for itself, rather than cede this ground to competitors, NATO has never been an alliance of equals. Europe's dependence on the United States places the very definition of sovereignty in the hands of one superpower, with risks already evident in the Bush era's unilateral handling of this concept. As a superpower, the U.S. espouses multilateralism only when this suits its interests. American unilateralism places Europe at risk....Hence, the E.U., like the United States earlier, will have to centralize foreign and security policy" (Sissinich 2008, 1).

For now, the E.U.'s foreign and security policies are culturally centered in nation-states—hence the autocephalous nature of the E.U.'s concept of regionalism that is not, and that will hardly be integrated for absolute integration will, as history has shown, cause disaster. The issues of national sovereignty, internal and external security, military alliance, and federalism will require political and military coercion of Western European States which post-World War II European reasoning explains why neo-realism is intellectually and pragmatically challenged by European liberalism and social constructivism. Worst of all, such a challenge is even potentially more psychologically paralyzing with Putin's declaration that the dissolution of the Soviet Union was "the greatest geopolitical disaster of the twentieth century" (Brzezinski 208, 27) and the nationalistic symbolism of attacking Georgia in preparation for reclaiming its global post-Soviet empire the West currently controls. In fact, a new Cold-War has emerged between the East and the West and globalization's days may be numbered in a faulty post-imperial and hegemonic Americana.

## NEGATIVE AND DESTRUCTIVE GLOBALIZATION — US CULTURAL DECAY

Aspects of destructive globalization are caused by boundaryless liberalization, economic speculation, and paternalistic neo-colonialism that are pursued through institutions such as the IMF, World Bank and NGOs whose agents are arrogant in making demands such as "Do what we tell you and you will prosper" (Eitzen and Zinn 2009, 121). In this arena, "capital markets are just such a fickle task-master; even ardent advocates talk about their bouts of irrational exuberance followed by equally irrational pessimism" (p. 121). America's inability to exercise self-restraint, dissociate itself from contemporary and competitive economic mercantilism, the decline of its hegemony that makes it to realistically struggle for its survival in the uncontainable proliferation of multipolartity, its economic and ethnic polarization that uses religion to soothe the problems, the Washington Consensus which places emphases on rapid trade, financial markets, deregulation and diminished government spending, conditionality and regime change (Oppenheimer 2007/08), have contributed to the global questioning of America's model of development that is viewed as unfriendly, exploitative and greedy. Trade agreements which were designed by post war order to develop the world economy have become discriminatory to

and impenetrable by some nations. U.S. agricultural policy uses subsidies for protectionism that makes Third World agricultural competitors to "perish". America's Post-War financial architecture has become untenable. Its conditionality is wanting. The U.S. has failed to stabilize global financial markets that are essential for liberalization. The failure of Bretton Woods institutions to service Third World nation-state loans and its unattractive conditionality has caused these nations, particularly those in Africa, to be serviced by Chinese and Indian governments and financial institutions. In addition, such inability has resulted in regional arrangements that stabilize currency and assist member countries to be financially secure. For instance, in 2000, the Asian Monetary Fund was established by ASEAN+3, while Brazil and Venezuela established the Bank of the South in 2007. In the light of these scenarios,

> Any major U.S. effort to strengthen the IMF, by reallocating voting shares towards emerging market countries, enlarging mandates or reinvigorating the policy agenda … will suffer from diminished leverage. The American economy represents a declining share of global output, and, at recent growth rates, will be surpassed by China sometime around 2020. The U.S. portion of global trade is also diminishing. The dollar continues to fall against other currencies, while the pace at which foreign control of banks are diversifying their reserve assets away from dollars has quickened. Emerging markets and oil exporters, owning huge pools of saving, will demand greater influence over financial governance structure, even as they demand less borrowers in terms of liberal conditionality (p. 5).

Such a situation has eroded the validity of American social, cultural and intellectual institutions whose vibrant coherence served as a glue for its imperial architecture. The loss of vital institutions has produced a dependent culture that may find it difficult if not impossible to compete with Europeans and Asiatics. "This dependence of culture" has been weakened by the loss of its "soul" because of materialism, individualism, godlessness, loss of the protestant ethic and use of lies to capitalize on "quick fixes", its people suffer from obesity, mental illness, depression, confusion and never ending lawsuits. Scientific humanism and secularization have reinforced national cultural atheism which sees religion as a form of "universal obsession neurosis" (Krauss 2002:40).

Michael Saler (2006) has also argued that Western modernity's elite has bought the attributes of cultural mass enchantment of which irrationalism, magic, fiction, mesmerization, and delight are classic examples. Unlike its seventeenth-nineteenth centuries elitist counterparts which relied on reason, logic, and science that produced the Enlightenment, modernity's enchantment with inferior mass and popular culture has contributed to the decline of society whose elites' inability to employ the interpretive disciplines (humanities and social sciences) for societal edification has been corrupted by the influence of scientific materialism. These weaknesses have evolved with the development of capitalism whose globalization is the highest stage of development. Such capitalism has immensely contributed to global market failure and inimical aspects of wealth transfer from traditional capitalist enclaves to oil producing countries that redistribute it in interesting and paradoxical ways- thereby undermining the development of ascendant and reformatory capitalism. The paradoxical ways include cronyism, terrorism and war (Garson 2008).

According to Joseph Stiglitz, Professor of economics at Columbia and recipient of 2001 Nobel Prize in economics, new liberalism is fundamentally based on the notion that "markets are self-correcting because they tend to allocate resources efficiently and thereby serve the public interest." In the past, such market fundamentals were not only reminiscent of Thatcherism, Reaganomics or the current Washington Consensus, but these nation-prone economic philosophies that place emphases on privatization tend to be recession prone or depression prone largely because they are not supported by economic theory. Amaertya Sen, who believes in democracy, thinks and views development to be a form of freedom. Globalization is characterized by regression in most countries and shows "increase of criminal activities, childhood in danger, flow of asylum seekers etc). Globalization is practically and theoretically malaise-prone.

Globalization, which is *Washington Consensus* intends to "extend freedom, human rights and democracy" to the whole world. Globalization ignores the moral and religious values of Third World Cultures. It underestimates the power of dictators and their political regimes that exacerbate terrorism and chaos. War has undercut globalization benefits, such as trade, education and development by embracing conflict and cultural relativism rather than a more comprehensive and solvent globalization.

Both world growth and global growth have expanded in the core areas at the detriment of the periphery. This contributes to uneven global economic development especially in Africa, South America, the Middle East and the former U.S.S.R. states. These countries are unable to be integrated into the World economy. Based on the 2005 UNICEF Survey, *The states of the world's children: Childhood under threat*, more than half of all children in the world suffer from extreme deprivations of such problems as poverty, war and HIV/AIDS. In totality, more than one billion children lack adequate shelter, proper sanitation, safe water, information, health care services, education and food. About half of the 3.6 million people who have been killed in war since 1990 are children. Some of the children-orphans are sexually abused or are enslaved by their owners for economic gain. Evidence has shown that psymmetric *free trade theory*, through which the processes of globalization are expected to equalize incomes and reduce the need or necessity for migration, does not work. The theory asserts that rich countries, which specialize in high-tech need to be capital intensive while poorer countries which provide cheap labor should specialize in labor-intensive techniques of production. This theory of economic globalization promotes international migration to developed countries whose populations, influenced by cultural, technological and family values, continue to decline drastically. Such declines are replaced by immigrants particularly those who have the skills the markets demands? This is an "inside-out rather than outside in" eighteenth century mercantilist approach to global and colonial trade. The migratory trajectories are encouraged by Northern industrialists and political regimes because immigrants come for economic, family and asylum reasons. Globally, there are cultural challenges that have become barriers for the spread of democracy and freedom. Democracy and freedom mean and need different means for their orchestrated articulation before their ends are met if at all. Authoritarian civilizations have a different interpretation of democracy than Western civilizations.

Economically, the West's creation of the WTO is viewed as a form of 'savage liberalism' whose dialectical import of market exchanges produces buyers versus sellers, employers versus employees, and lenders versus borrowers to coordinate supply and demand. In this climate, the wage earner who sells his/her skills and has no control over capital, is in the long run, marginalized in and by the mercantile system. Most of the time, he/she experiences the "confessions of an economic hit man."

Globalization has created conditions for the evolution and diffusion of "transnational crime, worker exploitation, environmental degradation" global warming and new forms of "slavery that has more than 27 million slaves worldwide" (Eitzen and Zinn 2009, 240).

Through regionalism, we are or we will be witnessing the transnationalization and supra-nationalization of political institutions whose legalization, juridification and constitutionalization has contributed and to the processes of transforming and reinternationalizing international relations. For instance, in the area of migrant labor, a force that is uniquely and fundamentally transnational, this force has become a creative sector of state re-territorialization of migrant export sector that is purposively involved in generating external finance through remittances. On the other hand, the same sectored force happens to increasingly possess the demand for political representation and participation from those who work or want to be elected to office (Bach and Solomon 2008). In the light of this argument, the transnational migrant worker tends to influence unique forms of political articulation for political membership. An attempt by this force to politically and institutionally formalize their transnationalism requires the creation and centralization of institutional mechanisms for nation-states with large migrant populations to be well managed, have their grievances effectively channeled, and enable them to forge relations for political action and objective subjectivity.

## NEGATIVE ASPECTS OF GLOBALIZATION

Author Steve Sjuggerud has argued that: historically, when government intervenes in markets, things tend to go sour. For instance during the 1990"s, Japan ended with the "lost decade" in economic development. Initially Japan had a huge real estate bubble. Japanese banks overlent at massive scale by offering risky loans that stimulated the stock market and real estate to fall. Though the Japanese central bank tried to save the economy by lowering interest rates, this strategy never worked because the financial crisis was compounded by hoarding of the money by the same banks. Instead of lending the money, the hoarding mechanism paralysed the economy. Asset prices went down, people were confused because they could neither invest in stocks nor in the real estate market. This experience taught the Asiatics the essence of fiscal regionalism, which FTA is developing. During the last 30 years, we have witnessed the greed of Wall Street, with the deindustrialization of the nation (U.S.). The nation should invest in new technologies that will help develop it as opposed to the destructive financial institutions that use policies that create meltdown rather than bubble up conditions. Regulation rather than deregulation is essentially imperative. The Clinton, Reagan, and Bush II eras therefore led to the nurturing of socialization of risk, which was caused by the "parasitic and robbing" existence of Wall Street. The second guilded age has been with us for about 30 years; its millionaire and billionaire champions have been shrewd Wall Street gamblers who believe in trickle down rather than trickle up economics. They rationalize laissez-faire theory of economics.

Specifically, and within these three decades, the US wall street financial industry created an "attractive save haven in investor confidence" that promoted global influx of money into the US financial institutions. The institutions offered low interest rates to Americans and enabled them credit with "irrational exuberance." People massively borrowed money to buy cars and houses and for college tuition and leisure. New entrepreneurs used the loans to start business in order to create jobs. Credit became easy to warrant not only massive, excessive and inappropriate lending practices, but many mortgage companies issued loans to their clients without assessing their ability to pay. The borrowers who bought unaffordable homes in anticipation of refinancing or selling them at a profit, were unable to do so, overproduction of homes created an imbalance between supply and demand. The prices of houses fell drastically while the subprime lending through the adjustable rather than fixed interest rate loans became too burdensome to motivate the repayment process. Because investors were discouraged by the global "mortgage-backed securities," more than ten million investors stopped making payments.

The mortgage companies were chartered by congress. This condition made them to borrow and lend to investors extravagantly. They "flooded" the deregulated market with questionable investments and put the financial system at risk. The same market, for example during the 1990's and after, a CEO used to earn $556 million. This was 400 times more than what an employee earned. Such behavior makes the share of corporate tax base to dwindle. As the CEO's money is further invested in stocks, the returns to the total portfolio drastically increases the economic disparity and inequality between them and the lower classes of society.

In periods of economic and financial meltdown associated with inflationary, deflationary, stagflationary and recessionary manifestations, and given the fact that excellent managerial and intellectual talent has moved to the corporate sector, the public which used to view economic inequality to originate with social circumstances now reads otherwise. The publics's perceptions that lack of talent in political leadership may have exacerbated the rapaciousness of market robber'barons and venial politicos' (John 2008, 2) to misappropriate the stock market industry, is viewed as the villains by the larger public which may experience either a populist political backlash reflective of the economic and cultural issues of the day, or a revolutionary and a "disaffected realignment to the left." On the other hand, if the larger society understands fully how the economic crisis was caused, it might become the harbinger for the emergence of a new political order that is "less rooted in culture and geography than in economics and class"(p. 2). That new political order may be globally suffering from aspects of lack of fastness or slowness associated with our endemically drugged cultural lifestyle. (Tofler 1996; Ksir, et al. 2006).

## Positive Aspects of Globalization

Though the U.S.'s hegemonic globalization of the last 60 years is gradually declining, its positive contributions in terms of benefits cannot be underestimated. Through globalization, transnational interactions in trade, finance, technology, and ideas, have widened the range of global players from diplomatic representatives and firms and individuals, civil society groups, mid-level government officials, and terrorist organizations. These actors have hard a deepening influence on the conditions of life in communities around the world, and on the policies and structures of states … more open political and economic systems increased prosperity and mitigation of conflict. While it acknowledges negative effects -income inequality, financial volatility, economic and physical insecurity, these are considered surmountable with improved national and global governance, and the continued spread of markets" (Oppenheimer 2007/08, 1).

American political decision making and diplomatic negotiations and compromises produced a liberal global structure for creating "market demand, financial liquidity and stability, and physical security" (p. 2) even by using the tactics of the *"Confessions of an economic hit man"* (Perkins 2004), which are predatory and destructive. The Post-War generation of American leaders successfully employed hard and soft power that was instrumental to the demise of the U.S.S.R., the emergence of China and India as global powers and for its survival, the economic and military entrapment of Japan in the Western Comp. With the use of the Marshall Plan, Americans motivated Europe to become economically integrated, used multilateral bodies to liberalize trade, make payments, used the dollar to facilitate global transactions including the provision of solid reserves for the central banks. This process created a huge and relatively open market that provided economies of scale and investment opportunities to European firms. Evidently, all these happened in a U.S.

created geo-strategic environment that reintegrated German into the Western umbrella and exclusively controlled Soviet-Western dialectical dynamics. Such a form of "embedded liberalism" (p. 2) acknowledged that globalization was an interpenetratably dependent and interdependent phenomenon. In order to *Trade* effectively, Washington influenced the reduction of tariffs, elimination of quotas and replacement of GATT with WTO. China, Russia and its satellite states and other growing markets were allowed to join WTO. Poverty, autarchy, and political and economic insecurity were eliminated from certain quarters of trade and commerce, while art, painting, music, technology, literature, movies, dancing and entertainment menu were allowed to spread across national boundaries.

How did all these things happen during the cold-War? Several forces were at play: bipolar conflict with a powerful and dangerous Soviet adversary produced strong incentives for compromise among the United States and its allies, and a strong common interest in conferring legitimacy on U.S. power. American economic and military preeminence within its coalition delayed competitive threats (until the transitory Japanese technological challenge of the 1980's), and facilitated U.S. political acceptance of economic and strategic free riding by allies; the compelling and recent experience of interwar economic and political collapse, attributed to weak global institutions, U.S. detachment, and European appeasement, provided powerful lessons to a "new generation of decision makers, bipartisanship in foreign policy, and East Coast intellectual primacy maintained policy primacy continuity, reassured others of the reliability of security commitments, and provided lobbying opportunities for governments whose future was primarily dependent on influencing American political leadership" (Oppenheimer 2007/08, 3)

Though both Senators Clinton and Obama feel that NAFTA should be renegotiated to prevent the loss of manufacturing and high-tech jobs, lower oil, energy and food prices whose inflationary condition has contributed to an "economic slowdown overall, living standards in the U.S. are higher by $1 trillion a year or $10,000 per household than they would have been without economic openness and trade" (Fischer 2008, B15). Robert Z. Lawrence, a professor of International trade and investment at Harvard's JFK School of Government, also, argues that greater openness to trade has not been a drag on the American economy. Exports have done well though globalization has losers particularly in Africa and Latin America and the less educated in the United States. In the U.S., a social insurance health policy for every American who is not insured would, if backed by both divisions of the federal system, bridge the gap between the haves and the have-nots of the American global project. In this case, either of them may have to cut taxes and decrease spending in order to provide socialized universal health care coverage or raise taxes on the wealthy to stimulate demand in the health care industry. The latter was Barack Obama's choice that cost his party in midterm elections in 2010 for getting AHCA ratified.

Contemporary Republicans practice economic liberalism, fiscal conservatism and social conservatism. Democrats are economically, fiscally, and to some extent, socially liberal. Regardless of the party's ideological differences, both parties are largely united in foreign policy agenda of the U.S. The United States of America needs to end the overstretched war in the Middle East and save money for domestic reformatory innovations. It should establish a new team, new policies, and new credibility for managing domestic and global affairs.

Its foreign policy realists must reinforce Wilsonian realism, demilitarize U.S. foreign health care industry, policy agenda, and replace it with instruments that enhance diplomacy rather than war. The United States should determine how national security strategy is to be used (criteriawise) and it should lower the rhetoric of terrorism for in the long run, this will be a European problem rather than a U.S. one. It should focus on good governance, political accountability, democracy and the strengthening of vibrant institutions (Fukuyama 2006). Forcing and desiring the creation of democratic institutions in the Middle East where the U.S. has no credibility and moral authority is self deception that will prolong war that might bring down the empire.

The U.S. should use soft power and indirect rule rather than hard power and direct forms of governance. Power is most effective when it is not arrogantly displayed, latent rather than manifest, that will enable it to, as Bismark did, prevent the formation of hostile coalitions. Bismark created the 1884/5 Berlin conference, a reinsurance Treaty that reassured rather than intimidated neighboring countries of the coalition. Less brilliant German rulers scared the peace of Europe which created the Franco-Russian and British Entente that became the base for the First World War. Whenever and wherever a policy lacks international legitimacy, it will be faced by defeat as the Iraq War has demonstrated.

## THE NEW PARADIGM FOR GLOBALIZATION

Given the conditions and challenges facing the U.S. failure to lead and manage the global community, more humanely during the Bush II administration, and with a more soft rather than "hard ball," it is imperative for the American leadership to chart its globalization trajectory in the context of futuristic multipolarity as opposed to hegemonic unipolarity whose recent situation particularly in Iraq was new, wanting, and in disarray. In other words, the U.S. should accept rather than reject the plausibility of heterogeneous globalization. Heterogeneous globalization will portray the breath in the distribution of wealth and power that can still benefit the liberal democratic agenda of the United States and its allies. The U.S. should negotiate the regulations concerning "trade and investment, the power structure within global and regional institutions, the direction and size of global flows" (p. 7). In other words, the more powerful states and their civil societies should negotiate and employ soft power regardless of their divergent interests, global agenda and domestic policies. In this arena, Washington should take the lead to "support reform of global institutions to increase emerging country representation; openness and confidence in the dollar . . . and apply hard power, with the collaboration of others, to secure this highly vulnerable system from a symmetric threats" (p. 7) without the exercise of "neoconservative social engineering and the application of structural theories of democratic peace" (Piki ish-Shalom 2007/08, 535). Structural theories are associated with the end of the Cold-War, Zionism vs. the neo-Palestinian Islamic dialectic, the neoconservative agenda of overthrowing Iraq Baathism, the 9/11/2001 terrorist attack, and the controversial and conservative works of Fukuyama's *The end of history* and Huntington's *The clash of civilizations*. The former is optimistic while the latter is pessimistic. Both of these two theories could be deceptive misinterpretations of history largely because they encourage the possibility of social engineering.

If the United States invests more in a multipolar rather than in its obsession with univocal and hegemonic stability theses, it should "remain open, non-discriminatory,... less modeled on the American experience, less organized around U.S. commercial and financial interests, reflects a country both chastened by recent experience with its strategy of primacy, and aware that its prosperity requires a renewed commitment to the project" (Oppenheimer 2007/08, 7).

In other words, this policy of self restraint as opposed to the one characterized by "new conservative paternalism, illegal warmongering, destabilizing crusades and cynical demagogry" (Piki ish-Shalom 2007/08, 550) of the Bush regime and the one associated with Clinton's regime change will enable the U.S. not to drift towards political and economic isolationism. The U.S. should reconstruct the values of its domestic empire in order to effectively parallel them with its foreign policy elite who influence global governance. This is imperative because Cold- War simplicities which united America with its allies for more assertive and putative globalization have been vaporized by the new and challenging pressures of multiplicity and its tide of rising expectations. In this arena, "Issues such as income inequality, race and gender, the death penalty and the size of American prison population, energy consumption and environmental degradation, the electoral system, and the balancing of executive power will greatly influence the consent others grant to America "(p. 8) - the legitimacy and primacy for them. Obviously, the evolving heterogeneous globalization will, due to state rivalry for power, influence and architecturally establish multiple governance structures to coexist with each region's persistent insecurity and doubt. In such an atmosphere, the U.S., despite the pains of its potential dethronement from the pinnacle of global power and splendor, should accept a new security architecture that enhances the values of multiple globalization in spite of its inherent and logically illogical global dialectics.

Because China, India and the E.U. have competitively started to undermine what they perceive to be the U.S.'s illiberal forms of globalization that are associated with its conditionalities, mercantilism and preemptive unilateralism in a multilateral global system, its globalization project has lost its legitimacy. If America insists on the perpetuation of its illiberal globalization, regionalism will be a paramount alternative to globalization because the former is already, what animates the latter in charting new directions for climbing the "cascade of progress." Through the regional historical experience rather than the global one, we can analytically understand the cyclical, linear, dialectical, evolutionary and heroic purposes that animate the progress and processes of human history and biographically prepare to propel them for dynamic or catastrophic change. That form of regional or heterogeneous globalization should improve political, bureaucratic, and corporate governance both in its centralized and decentralized forms. Each region should construct just Laws for regulating regional economy and lay a strong foundation for minimizing or eliminating corruption at all levels of regionalism.

The mere existence of regionalism will not benefit anybody unless it is analyzed in all its facets in order to shade light on its totality and use it for comparative analysis, interpretation, and reflection on each region's advancement in positive governance, human freedom, democratic peace, use of technology to advance human progress and cross-cultural interaction in terms of trade and exchange of cultural, scientific and technological wisdom. They should also understand the causes of the evolution, expansion, decline, collapse, and disintegration of each regional or global civilization in order to reconstruct a new trajectory for propelling global regionalism onto the world stage in terms of materialism, statecraft, cultural refinement and moral rearmament for societal renewal. Each region should regulate political debate on trade policy and digest the dynamics that threaten the region(s) or nation(s) competitiveness in the area of productivity whose efficiency is measured in terms of inputs and outputs, and their effects on American workers, firms and corporations. U.S. companies should reform their health-care costs, by eliminating shortcomings in the broadband and other similar infrastructure. Economists and policy makers, such as Deborah L. Wince-Smith, president of the Council on Competitiveness, a non-profit group of corporate executives, university presidents and labor leaders, have asserted that the U.S. regulatory situation, in respect to U.S. product-liability law is a huge drag that drains innovation. The council has challenged Obama and McCain to "lay out a national strategy for securing access to energy supplies and increasing the country's energy productivity and each company's energy efficiency" *(The Chronicle Reviews* April 25, 2008, B16). The rise in energy costs has made it more difficult for U.S. corporations to compete with their counterparts that exist in low cost energy parts of the world. Clyde B. Prestowitz Jr., the author of *Three billion new capitalists: The shift of wealth and power to the east*, argues that in order to stimulate innovation in energy sector, it "requires A Manhattan Project for energy" supplies (p. B16).

The Organization for Economic Cooperation and Development (OECD) has advised that in order to compete effectively in the global arena, the U.S. needs to convince college entrants to major in mathematics, science and engineering. More minority, women and international students should be encouraged to study these critical subjects in order to enhance U.S. global competitiveness. Parenthetically, the U.S. public-school system should be strengthened by investing in schools, mentoring students, providing schools with teachers who are excellent in mathematics and science subjects and by providing the teachers with ample resources in terms of paycheck and facilities for better teaching. Such innovations should be carried out in all U.S. schools and at all levels of K-12 systems. Charles M. Vest, President of the National Academy of Engineering has constructively proposed that "investment in education has to extend beyond the classroom and into the workplace" (p. BI6). His proposal views GI Bill theory for the twenty-first century to be a better solution. In addition, globalization scholars argue, very persuasively too, that the U.S. needs to "change its immigration policies in order to retain a larger share of the talented international students drawn to American colleges" (p. B16). Due to the fact that immigration law has not been clear concerning the graduates (international students) from American Colleges, it is difficult to automatically and collectively give them green cards for their talents. However, if the U.S. desires, as it does to remain competitive in the era of comparative and evolutionary regionalism in terms of heterogeneous multiplicity, it is imperative to be a magnet for talent rather than a rhetorical and an inconsequential educator for other countries. By 2004, the U.S. was the 17$^{th}$ among industrialized countries in the budget allocated for research. According to Atkinson, good research is that done by universities and national labs as opposed to in-house systems. He suggested that "an expansion of the flat research-and-experimentation tax credit for collaborative research" (p. B16) is essential. Also, a federal agency for the promotion of technology and innovation, comparable to the National Science Foundation which supports basic research, should be established. Some countries such as Ireland, Japan and South Korea have that kind of institution which enhances each country's technological edge and competitiveness. Should the U.S. be engaged in training for India and China alone? No. The U.S. should train for its needs and the needs of its less fortunate allies. However, in the twenty-first century, China's peaceful rise is attributed to the theories of "accommodations, hedging and balancing" (*Political Science Quarterly: The Journal of Public and International Affairs* 2008, 325). Other less competitive Asian states want to have a relationship with China that is accomodationist and hedged for their security while keeping the relationship remaining balanced with the United States (Kang 2007). Why is China ready to use its power to prevent Taiwanese independence and how is that Chinese political behavior likely to provoke a major power conflict? Largely because globalization has caused income inequality in international division of labor, global warming in the Industrialized and industrializing countries, endless debates for and against globalization particularly in respect to the rearrangement of political and economic trends will make it difficult for nations to own "national products ... national technologies ... national corporations...national industries" (Oatley 2008, 361). In addition, globalization has not only exacerbated terrorism, drug trafficking, the rapid and destructive diffusion of diseases such as HIV/AIDS virus, but it has also massively contributed to the reintroduction of slavery and child labor which take place in sweatshops (extreme exploitation, including the absence of a living wage or benefits, poor working conditions, and arbitrary discipline (p. 367) associated with "Scale effects and structural effects" (p. 373). Above all, the globalization outcome, process and debate has generated fear concerning the elimination of jobs, lowering of wages, expansion of income inequality and destruction of the environment. All in all, the basic challenge for each country or region including the United States is to balance its power against existing risks and vulnerabilities. Brands Alan M. Watchman (2007) who is an expert in the history and modern international affairs and Taiwan argues that irrespective of Taiwan's respect for its nationalism, culture and domestic politics, all of which are not irrational fixations, China's dream to have

> control over Taiwan is crucial to the geostrategic security of China. Located 'at the fringe of competing realms' of Chinese and non-Chinese power. ... Taiwan is fated to serve as 'buffer or bridgehead'... either to protect or to threaten the Chinese mainland. In the hands of others – historically, the Dutch, British, Japanese, and Americans – Taiwan has served as a base from which to threaten China. In the hands of China, Taiwan could open the way for the Navy of the People's Liberation Army to contest domination over the waters within the 'first island ring' (the Sea of Japan, Yellow Sea, East China Sea, and South China Sea), and in due course, even to claim presence in the vast reaches of the Pacific (*Political Science Quarterly: The Journal of Public and International Affairs* Summer, 2008, 319).

In such a climate, political actors should not be driven by geostrategic fears, innovation and ambitions rather than logical scientific analysis of facts whose ideological underpinnings will be exposed to provide pragmatic solutions to potential conflict. Largely due to the fact that China has strengthened its nationalism to "buttress" its domestic viability, it can not afford to permanently lose Taiwan through its declared independence from the "motherland." The renegade Province must, no matter what happens, be annexed to the Chinese mainland (Shirk 2007). In the light of these circumstances, the U.S. and Japan should not overreact as China peacefully rises to vindicate its classical and ancient glory.

The Chinese regime is growing fast at home and abroad. Though its power appears to be limited, goodwill it has gained from distant and close allies and neighbors has provided it with a sense of stability that enables it to manage the challenges of change with a mixture of repressive and reformatory measures. For instance:

> Whatever the mix of strategy and political motives, no one doubts that China is preparing for possible war in the Taiwan Strait. Most analysts agree that the Chinese strategy for this potential conflict involves nuclear deterrence against anticipated U.S. intervention, the use of medium-range missiles across the Strait, establishment of air dominance in the Strait, and submarine, electronic, and space warfare to disable Taiwanese and U.S. capabilities. ….John Lewis and Xue Litai describe the historical evolution of this strategy, the organization and command-and-control of the strategic missile forces, the modernization of the Air Force, and – a unique congeries of party and military operations. Although at times overwhelmed by their own reach to everyone's interests – Taiwan's, China's and those of the United States – by the ongoing risk of war in the Taiwan Strait (*Political Science Quarterly: The Journal of Public and International Affairs*, Summer 2008, .320).

In this endeavor, "Beijing's investments in cyberwarfare, antisatellite warfare, antiaircraft and antiship weaponry, submarines, and ballistic missiles could threaten the United States'primary means to project its power and help its allies in the Pacific: bases, air and sea assets, and the networks that support them" (Gates 2009, 33).

The U.S. in the light of Wilsonian, FDR and Truman models, should create a new agenda for the fundamental transformation of the international system. The U.S. should learn to unlearn its traditional prejudices and start to appreciate the accomplishments of others as it deals with the financial crisis, a severe recession, the War in the Middle East, nuclear weapons proliferation, terrorism, energy dependence, climate change and global poverty. The U.S. should renew its policies in trade, investment, immigration, and intellectual property in the realms of drugs, health and education and corruption and foreign aid. It should establish global networks for generating new ideas and recording the most efficient engines of productivity, creativity and reform. It should establish a team-based management structure for managing global competition and conflict by replacing them with cooperation, openness and diplomatic discourse in order to enhance freedom, prosperity and security.

The Globalization movement is a super paradigm of the cognitive age whose skills revolution places emphasis in technology, psychology, culture and pedagogy. Because it is Schumpeterian and Nietzscherian in its evolutionary roots in terms of creative destructiveness, states which place too much emphasis on it will be the first in not only using its power to change and destroy, but they will also be ended fast by the same movement.

## ACADEMIA IN CRISIS (U.S.)

In this economic crisis, the U.S. Education system has considerably been challenged by other world education systems. In particular, China, E.U., and India have more competitive graduate students in science, technology, engineering and mathematics (STEM) programs. The same countries (regions) have rivaled the U.S. in the recruitment and training of international students who do research in the same disciplines and the social sciences. In the economics departments of major U.S. universities, most professors are rationally conservative, elderly and prolaissez-faire as well as anti-regulation in their theoretical orientation. The same departments do not like to hire young scholars whose specialties include a strong bias for market regulation and anti-trickle down economic rationality. In other words, they tend to hire the popular in Samwelson economic conservatism and by so doing, contribute to intellectual inbreeding, paradigm disinnovation and lack of creativity: coupled with the current, global and cultural zeal for "vibrant opium" consumption, they believe that markets are cybernetic (self-correcting) and there is no need for regulation. The result is not only speculation but the crash-related economic crisis. Foreign investment in U.S. securities, the deficit, national debt; and lack of savings by Americans tend to escalate the crisis. Innovations in education can help contain the crisis.

Stimulated by historical, comparative, and competitive ideas of world- class education, the U.S. needs to create an academic climate for articulating domestic and global change geoeconomically, geostrategically, and sociocutechnologically. Higher education Boards of Regents , Trustees, and internal educational engineers and policy makers need to create new policy choices for colleges and universities to strategically reconstruct, thematically redesign, synergistically reengineer, and innovatively reinvent new models for higher education management. In dealing with these issues, the challenges to institutional leaders would be in their attempt to deal with issues related to imperatives of changing international, economic, and political power. The same challenges are viewed in terms of student demands for creative learning, internalizing real world and global problems in the context of economic instability, demographic change and material and technological inequality.

In the new global university, integrating the sciences with the arts and humanities, institutions will educate learners to learn by teaching them to write across the curriculum. They will be challenged to provide resources for high quality education that will help students to thrive in order to change the world and find their place in it. The third challenge is to globally position higher education in such a way that it can relevantly address contemporary and future issues and needs of society. In the light of such scenerio, the following questions are instructive: How does higher education design educational menu for dynamic and essential global learning? What types of knowledge and skills are necessary for meeting the challenges and opportunities prevalent in the twenty-first century? How will students learn to develop and adapt to the future contexts with new demands? How do ideas about demographic change, diversity, civic engagement, ethics and social responsibility translate to the new global conditioning and frameworks? How liberal will liberal education be? How will educational success be measured? Judged by the global yardsticks of learning, of which U.S. educational liberalism, the Bologna Process and a variety of creative and competitive Third World variants, serious, goal oriented, multifaceted, and broad thinking students will successfully correlate and compete in an interdependent and global economy by using civic, ethical and diverse worlds as spring boards for finding their place in the world in order to change it.

The questions that were raised in this complex and deconstructive conclusive critique can also be answered on the basis of empirical evidence in terms of creating opportunities for students to find their own global identities and "niches" by intensively focusing on aims of education, learning outcomes and assessments, curriculum designs, and promotion and enhancement of students' global capabilities. The same students should be exposed to "big-picture" thinking, creative problem-solving skills, and innovative and purposeful approaches for designing, financing, and delivering general education.

In the era of retrenchment, globalization and technological competition, legislators, trustees, and the public at large have voiced reductions in college and university expenditure and tuition increases while improving graduation rates. Such demands have provoked debate concerning shortening student learning options. Some institutions and communities have responded by giving suggestions that will be employed to merge high school and general education offerings in order to shorten the time for graduation with degrees.

Employers want higher education to produce graduates who excel in innovative, creative, and technological knowhow. On the other hand, public officials want higher education to produce graduates who can actively participate in a demographically changing and diverse democracy. Similarly, many other countries want the same values instilled in their learners. In essence, society wants colleges and universities to graduate candidates who are ethically astute, morally sound, collaborative problem-solvers that are open to new trends, opportunities and paradigms. By addressing concerns about cost and completion, the concerns should be handled carefully and in a balanced way without sacrificing the broader and deeper learning in specialized majors that form the synergistic dynamic for robust and integrative liberal education for which all Boards and Trustees, administrators, faculty, staff and students are accountable.

Higher education particularly the Historically Black Colleges and Universities (HBCUs) should institutionalize undergraduate research and writing across the curriculum. The institutions should have strong institutional, departmental, and programmatic mechanisms for providing resourses for research learning and writing in order to prepare students for contemporary and future careers and citizenship. The students in HBCUs should prepare for meeting challenges and demands from society. These multicultural students should use research and writing to develop competencies in the realms of creativity, innovation, problem solving, systems thinking, civic, social, technological, and personal responsibility. The research should articulate student learning goals, integrate research preparation and practice into departmental curricula, course offerings, and capstone requirements. Departmental faculty should assess student undergraduate research to determine if they have achieved major learning outcomes. To institutionalize undergraduate research effectively, the offices of undergraduate research should be strengthened with motivation, expertise, and resources for broader participation.

Colleges and Universities should create multistage, multilevel, and multicampus strategies for providing STEM disciplines on each campus. The campuses should adapt, scale up, and sustain effective practices in STEM teaching and learning. These institutions should develop faculty and institutional leadership in STEM reform, broaden student participation and success in STEM disciplines and fields, better assess engaged STEM learning in majors, general education, and preparatory education. They should connect the reengineering of STEM learning with on going institutional work in Liberal Education and America's Promise (LEAP). These institutions should use research in cognitive psychology and cognitive science to understand and promote learning assessment, engaged learning practices, and instructional models such as problem–solving tasks and just-in-time teaching. Complicating this issue is the concern about student interest, participation, and achiement in STEM related subjects especially for underrepresented students. For their preparation, all students should be treated either as critical consumers or innovative creators of STEM knowledge that is essential for global interconnectedness. In a nutshell, higher education should support efforts of STEM faculty, deans, department chairs, and their colleagues as they institutionalize and pervasively mainstream STEM in all levels and facets of the academy.

Finally, colleges and universities should redesign their organizational cultures in order to accomodate diversity learning and use it as a pathway to inclusive and synergistic educational excellence. Students should be aware that global, national, local, institutional, and classroom learning climates are structurally characterized by deep political, economic, religious, social and cultural divides that weaken excellence in diversity learning in organizationa management. Such divides tend to hinder our aspirations for democratic governance, justice and inclusion. Such inequalities may inadvertently and societally become the genesis for economic instability, lack of citizenship and legal rights, inadequate healthcare, violence, corruption, and environmental degradation. In other words, excellent universities are effective schools because they create pathways for multicultural and synergistic integration and learning.

## References


Armstrong, Charles K., Gilbert Rozman, Samuel S. Kim, and Stephen Kotkin, eds. 2006. *Korea at the center: Dynamics of regionalism in northeast Asia.* Armonk, N.Y.: M.E. Sharpe.

Back, Jonathan, and Schott M. Solomon, 2008. Labors of globalization: Emergent state responses. *New Global Studies* 2, 2.

Baldwin, Richard E. 1999. A domino theory of regionalism, In Jagdish Bhagwati, Pravin Krishna, and Arvind Panagariya, eds. *Trading blocs: Alternative approaches to analyzing preferential trade agreements.* Cambridge: MT Press: 479-502.

Bartels, Larry M. 2008.*Unequal democracy: The political economy of the new gilded age.* Princeton, NJ: Princeton University Press.

Baynon, John, and David Dunkerley. 2000. *Globalization: Reader.* New York: Routledge.

Bhagwati, Jagdish. 2007. The race to the center and other lessons of globalization. *The Brown Journal of World Affairs* XIII: 271-6.

Bergsten, C. Fred, ed. 1999. *Whither OPEC? The progress to date and agenda for the future.* Washington, D.C.: Institute for International Economics.

Bieling, Hans-Jorgen. 2007. The other side of the coin: Conceptualizing the relationship between business and the state in the age of globalization. *Business and Politics: Business Power and Global Governance* 9, 3, 5:1-20.

Bowles, Paul. 2002. Asia's post-crisis regionalism: Bringing the state back in, keeping the (United) States out. *Review of International Political Economy* 9, 2: 244-70.

Brands, H.W., et al. 2009. *American stories: A history of the United States.* New York: Pearson Longman.

Broadman, Harry. 2008. China and India go to Africa. *Foreign Affairs* March/April: 95-109.

Brzezinski. 2008. Staring down the Russians. *Time* August 26-7.

Carruthers, Susan. 1995. *Wining hears and minds: British governments the media and colonial counter-insurgency 1994-1960.* Leicester, UK: Leicester University Press.

Césaire, Aimé. [1955] (1992). *Discourse on colonialism.* New York: Presence Africaine.

Cohn, Theodore H. 2008. *Global political economy: Theory and practice.* New York: Pearson Longman.

Dieter, Heribert, and Richard Higgott. Exploring alternative theories of economic regionalism: From trade to finance in Asian co-operation? *Review of international Political Economy* 10, 3: 430-54.

Drezner, Daniel W. 2007. The power of the state in the global economy. *The Chronicle of Higher Education* June: B16.

Eitzen, D. Stanley, and Maxine B. Zinn. 2009. *Globalization: The transformation of social worlds.* Wadsworth: Cengage Learning.

Falkner, Gerda, et al. 2005. *Complying with Europe: E.U. harmonization and soft law in the member states.* Cambridge, U.K. Cambridge University Press.

Farr, Thomas F. 2008. Diplomacy in the age of faith: Religious freedom and national security. *Foreign Affairs* March/April: 110-2.

Fischer, Karin. 2008. Economic competitiveness a campaign primer. *The Chronicle Review: The Chronicle of Higher Education* April 25: B15.

Forbes. 2006. *The global 2000.* April 17: 158-61.

Friedman, Edward, and Sung Chull Kim, eds. 2006. *Regional cooperation and its enemies in northeast Asia: The impact of domestic forces.* London: Routlege.

Fukuyama, Francis. 2006. *America at the crossroads: Democracy, power and the neoconservative legacy.* New Haven, CT: Yale University Press.

Garson, Michael. 2008. *The Oklahoman* June 25: 11 A.

Gheciu, Alexandra I. 2005. *NATO in the "New Europe": The politics of international socialization after the cold war.* Stanford: Stanford University Press.

Gibbon, Edward. 1952. *The decline and fall of the Roman empire.* Penguin Books. The Viking Press, Inc.

Haas, Ernst B. 1958. *The uniting of Europe: Political, social, and economic forces 1950-1957.* Stanford: Stanford University Press.

Harrison, Bennett. 1994. *Lean and mean: The changing landscape of corporate power in the age of flexibility.* New York: Basic Books.

Higgott, Richard, and Richard Stubbs. 1995. Competing conceptions of economic regionalism: APEC versus EAEC in the Asia Pacific. *Review of International Political Economy* 2, 3: 516-35.

http://Abcnew.go.com/section.living.healthology.psychologicaleffects.html

Hughes, James, et al. 2005. *Europeanization and regionalization in the E.U.'s enlargement to central and eastern Europe: The myth of conditionality.* New York: Palgrave Macmillan.

Huntington, Samuel P. 1996. *The clash of civilizations and the remaking of world order.* New York: Simon Schuster.

Kahlet, Miles. 2001. Legalization as strategy: The Asian-Pacific case. In Judith L. Goldstein, Miles Kahler, Robert O. Keohane, and Anne-Marie Slaughter, eds. *Legalization and World Politics.* Cambridge: MIT Press: 165-87.

Kamien, David G. 2006. *The McGraw-Hill homeland security handbook: The definitive guide for law enforcement, EMT, and all other security professionals.* New York: McGraw-Hill.

Kang, David C. 2007. *China rising: Peace, power, and order in the east Asia.* New York: Columbia University Press.

Katzenstein, Peter J. 2005. *A world of regions: Asia and Europe in the American imperium.* Ithaca, N.Y.: Cornell University Press.

Katzenstein, Peter J., and Takashi Shiraishi, eds. 2006. *Beyond Japan: The dynamics of the east Asian regionalism.* Ithaca, N.Y.: Cornell University Press.

Kim, Samuel S. 2004. Regionalization and regionalism in east Asian. *Journal of East Asian Studies* 4, 1: 39-67.

Krauss, Steeven. 2002. A plumber's wisdom: The weakening of America. *The Fountain: A Magazine of Critical, Scientific and Spiritual Thought* 38: 39-41.

Krieger, Joel. 2006. *Globalization and state power: A reader.* New York: Pearson Longman.

Krueger, Anne O. 1999. Are preferential trading arrangements trade liberalizing or protectionist? *Journal of Economic Perspectives* 13, 4: 105-24.

Ksir, Charles et al. 2006. *Drugs, society and human behaviour.* Boston: McGraw Hill.

Lechener Frank J., and Hohn Boli, eds. 2000. *The globalization reader.* Oxford, UK: Blackwell Publishers.

Legro, Jeffrey W. 2005. *Rethinking the world: Great power strategies and international order.* Ithaca, NY: Cornell University Press.

Levy, Philip I. 1997. A political-economic analysis of free trade agreements. *American Economic Review* 87, 4: 506-19.

Lewis, John W., and Lital, Xue. 2006. *Imagined enemies: China prepares for uncertain war.*

Lincoln, Edward J. 2004. *East Asian economic regionalism.* Brookings Institution Press.

Lindasy, D. Michael. 2008. Evangelicalism rebounds in academe. *The Chronicle Review. The Chronicle of Higher Education* May 9:B12-B14.

Lindsay, James M. 2003. *American politics after September 11.* Cincinnati, OH: Atomicdog Publishing.

Manning, Patrick. 1996. The problem of interactions in world history. *American Historical Review. AHE Forum*: 771-82

Mansfield, Edward D., and Helen V. Milner, eds. 1997. *The political economy of regionalism.* New York: Columbia University Press.

Martin, Christopher . 2007. Grafting a U.S. response to the emerging east Asia free trade area. *The Whitehead Journal of Diplomacy and International Relation* VIII, 2:73-84.

Mclean, lain. 1996. *The concise Oxford dictionary of politics.* Oxford and New York: Oxford University Press.

Meyer, Karl E., ed. 2007/2008. *World Policy Journal* XXIV, 4: 1-12.

Milner, Helen. Industries, governments, and regional trade blocks," In *The political economy of regionalism:* 77-106.

Mitrany, David. 1996. *A working peace system.* Chicago: Quadrangle Books.

Mohammad, Ahmed. 2008. *Time.* March 24: 38-9

Morgan, Glyn. 2005. *The idea of European super state: Public justification and European integration.* Princeton University Press.

Muller, Jerry. 2008. US and them: The enduring power of ethnic nationalism. *Foreign Affairs* March/April: 18-35.

Munakata, Naoko. 2006. *Transforming east Asia: The evolution of regional economic integration* . Washington, DC: Brookings Institutional Press and Tokyo: Research Institute of Economy, Trade and Industry.

Nexon, Daniel H., and Thomas Wright. 2007. What's at stake in the American empire debate? *American Political Science Review* 101, 2: 253- 270.

Nolke, Andreas, and James Perry. 2007. The power of transnational private governance financialization and the IASB. *Business and Politics: Business Power and Global Governance* 9, 3, 4:1-25.

Nye, Joseph. 1971. *Peace in parts: Integration and conflict in regional organization.* Boston: Little, Brown, Brown.

Oatley, Thomas. 2008. *International political economy: Interests and institutions in the global economy.* New York: Pearson Longman.

Owen, J. Judd. 2007. The struggle between "religion and nonreligion": Jefferson, Backus, and dissonance of Americas founding principles. *American Political Science Review* 101, 3: 413-504.

Pangariya, Arvind. 2000. Preferential trade liberalization: The traditional theory and new developments. *Journal of Economic Literature* 38, 2: 287-331

Paulsen, Han. 2007. Beyond stereotypes. *Adventist Review.*

Pempel, T.J., ed. 2005. *Remapping east Asia: The construction of a region.* Ithaca, N.Y.: Cornell University Press.

Phillips, David L. 2005. *Losing Iraq: Inside the postwar reconstruction fiasco.* New York: Basic Books.

Philpott, Daniel. 2007. Explaining the political ambivalence of religion. *American Political Science Review* 101, 3: 505-26.

Piki ish- Shalom. 2007-08. The civilization of clashes: Misapplying the democratic peace in the Middle East. *Political Science Quarterly: The Journal of Public and International Affairs* 122, 4 533-54.

Ravenhill, John. 2000. APEC adrift: Implication for economic regionalism in Asia and the Pacific. *Pacific Review* 13, 2: 319-33.

Reinert, Erik S. 2007. *How rich countries got rich and why poor countries stay poor.* New York: Public Affairs (Constable).

Robinson, I. William. 2004. *A theory of global capitalism. Production, class, and state in a transnational world.* Baltimore, MD: John Hopkins University Press.

Rozman, Gilbert. 2004. *Northeast Asia's stunted regionalism: Bilateral distrust in the shadow of globalization* . Cambridge: Cambridge University Press.

Rozman, *Northeast Asia's Stunted Regionalism.*

Rubenstein, Richard E. 2004. Muslims and civilization: New families, old theories, *The Chronicle of Higher Education* January: B4.

Sagini, Meshack M. 2001. *Organizational behavior: The challenges of the new millennium.* Lanham, MD: University Press of America, Inc.

Sartori, Anne E. 2005. *Deterrence by diplomacy.* Princeton NJ: Princeton University Press.

Shambaugh, David, ed. 2006. *Power shift: China and Asia's new dynamic.* Berkeley: University of California Press.

Sheppard, Eugene R. 2006. *Leo Strauss and the politics of exile: The making of a political philosopher.* Waltham, MA: Brandeis University Press.

Shirk, Susan La. 2007. *China: Fragile superpower.* New York: Oxford University Press.Scheve, Kenneth F., and Slaughter Matthew Jr. 2008). A new deal for globalization. *Foreign Affairs* July/Aug: 34-47.

Schulte, Jan A. 2000. *Globalization: A critical introduction.* New York: Palgrave.

Sicanqndan, A. 1996. *Race and Class: A Journal for Black and Third World Liberation* October/December, 38-2:1-81.

Sissenich, Beate. 2008. Postnational rulemaking, compliance, and justification: The new Europe. *American Political Science Association* 6, 1: 143-57.

Snow, Donald M. 2008. *Cases in international relations: Portraits of the future*. New York: Pearson Longman.

Strozier, Charles B. 2007/08. Dissecting the forever war on terror. *World Policy Journal* XXIV, 4: 90-8.

*The 9/11 Commission Report: Final Report of the National Commission on Terrorist Attacks Upon the United States.* (2003) New York: W.W. Norton and Company.

Tofler, Alvin. 1996. *Power shift*. New York: Bantum Books.

Vachudova, Milada A. 2005. *Europe undivided: Democracy, leverage, and integration after communism.* New York: Oxford University Press.

Vandiver, Frank E. 2005. *How America goes to war*. Westport, Ct: Praeger Publishers.

Vietor, Richard H. 2007. *How countries compete: Strategy, structure, and government in the global economy*. Boston, MA: Harvard Business School.

Wachman, Alan M. 2007. *Why Taiwan?Geostrategic rationales for China's terrorial integrity*. Stanford, CA: Stanford University Press.

Wan, Ming. 2008. *The political economy of East Asia: Striving for wealth and power*. Washington, D.C: CQ Press.

Westem, Hon. 2005. *Selling intervention and war: The presidency, the media, and the American public*. Baltimore, MD: John Hopkins University.

www.money.cnn.com/2003/04/02/news/economy/factoryorders.reut/index.htm

www.Money.cnn.com/2003/01/27/news/economy/consumer/index.htm

www.money.cnn.com/2001/11/09/companies/afters:.ockinsurance/index.html

www.tgorski.com/Terrorism/talkingpointbulletion01psycheffectsofgerrorism.htm

Yoshimatsu, Hietaka. 2005. Japan's keidanren and free trade agreements: Societal interests and trade policy. *Asian Survey* 45, 2: 258-78.

Zurn, Michael, and Christian Joerge, eds. 2005. *Law and governance in post national Europe: Compliance beyond the nation state*. Cambridge: Cambridge University Press.

# Index

# About the Author

Dr. Meshack M. Sagini distinctively passed the Cambridge Ordinary and Advanced level (diploma) examinations in 1966 and 1968, respectively. He also studied at the University of East Africa Dar-es-Salaam for two years, Middle East College in Beirut, Lebanon, for two years, Newbold College, England, for one year, and University of the West Indies for another year and received a B.Ed. (Honors) in History and a minor in Education in 1979. In 1982, he received a Masters degree in higher education management from Andrews University in Michigan. In 1987, he was awarded a Ph.D. in college and university administration from Michigan State University after submitting his doctoral dissertation on strategic planning and management. In 1997, Dr. Sagini completed a postdoctorate course in management and public policy from Oklahoma State University.

Professionally, Dr. Sagini is an educator with thirty years' experience in the teaching profession. Initially he worked as a teacher in elementary and high schools in Kenya during the late nineteen-sixties and early nineteen-seventies. He also served as a deputy high school principal for three years at Nyanchwa High School in Kisii, Kenya. In 1979/80 academic year, Dr. Sagini became a lecturer in Northern Caribbean University in the West Indies, Jamaica. At the same time, he intermittently worked as a sales manager for a Norwegian corporation (Norskbokforlaget) for eight summers (1976-83). Before the completion of his doctorate from Michigan State University, Dr. Sagini worked in the University as a Swahili language tutor for three years and as Graduate Administrative Assistant for one year. Between 1989 and 1991, he served as an assistant professor of Social Science and Organizational Psychology at Lansing Community College in Michigan. Since 1991, he has worked at Langston University as an Assistant and Associate Professor of History, Political Science, and Management Studies.

Since 1999, Dr. Sagini has actively participated in public policy research and analysis. He has published several articles in professional journals and five books. His first book, *The African and the African-American university: A historical and sociological analysis,* was published in 1996. This book was written while Dr. Sagini was an adjunct associate professor at the University of Oklahoma (1994 and 1995). The second book, *Organizational behavior: The chal-*

*lenges of the new millennium,* was published in 2001. His third book is *Strategic planning and management in public organizations* (2007).

UMI published his *Comparative perceptions of planners in four Michigan community colleges* in 2009. His fifth and current book is *Globalization: The paradox of organizational behavior— terrorism, foreign policy, and governance.* In 2006, the U.S. Congress awarded Dr. Sagini the *Congressional Order of Merit* for service to the country. In 2009, he was awarded the Outstanding Political Scientist of the Year by OPSA. President Barack Obama awarded him honorary membership of his "Kitchen Cabinet" in 2009.

Dr. Sagini has traveled extensively by visiting four continents (he has not visited Australasia and Oceania). He has been awarded a variety of honors, the best of which was given in the summer of 1997 by the American Political Science Association (APSA) for excellence in teaching. Second, Professor Sagini was selected for inclusion in the 8th edition of *Who Is Who Among America's 5% Outstanding Professors* in the country in 2004. He is a member of several professional organizations including the American Political Science Association, Oklahoma Political Science Association, Oklahoma League of Political Scientists, Mid-America Alliance for African Studies (MAAAS), Association for International Development, African Professionals Association, and Langston University National Alumni Association. Currently, Professor Sagini was President of MAAAS (2002-2003) and Vice President of AAA (2001-2004). Above all, Professor Sagini is an interdisciplinary scholar who writes proposals for funding, presents scholarly papers in professional organizations and teaches with power, interest, and excitement. For instance, in August 2011, Dr. Sagini was awarded the Langston University Outstanding Scholar Award for exemplary performance in teaching, research, and service. In addition, between 2002 and 2008, he founded the Langston University International, Scholarly, and Scientific Organization (LUISSO), which published two volumes in *The Journal of Scholarly & Scintific Perspectives.* At the same time, he was instrumental in founding KESSA, an international organization that publishes a journal and books.